Nick Cameron spent twenty-four years in the military, sixteen of them in the SAS. He was awarded the Military Cross for bravery under fire in Bosnia. Since leaving the army in 1999, he has worked as a security consultant in many of the world's most dangerous spots – most recently, Kandahar in Afghanistan, and Ramallah in Palestine.

D1536450

THE COMPLETE
SAS GUIDE TO
SAFE TRAVEL

NICK CAMERON

PIATKUS

Copyright © 2002 by Nick Cameron

First published in 2002 by
Judy Piatkus (Publishers) Limited
5 Windmill Street
London W1T 2JA
e-mail: info@piatkus.co.uk

The moral right of the author has been asserted

A catalogue record for this book is available from the British Library

ISBN 0–7499–2286–9

This book has been printed on paper manufactured with respect for the environment using wood from managed sustainable resources

Text design by Paul Saunders
Edited by Barbara Kiser

Typeset by Palimpsest Book Production Limited,
Polmont, Stirlingshire
Printed and bound in Great Britain by
Mackays of Chatham Ltd, Chatham, Kent

Contents

3. Rail and Underground Safety · page 75

4. Vehicle Safety · page 89

5. Martitime and Water Safety · page 116

6. Safe Business Travel · page 138

7. Personal Security · page 153

14. Dangerous Animals · page 316

15. Dangerous Places · page 333

16. Safety in Cities · page 357

17. Medical Safety · page 380

18. Basic Navigation Techniques · page 395

References · page 414

Acknowledgements

I would like to express my gratitude to my companions on my extensive travels, Sonya, Morgan and Cameron, especially my wife Sonya for holding the fort whilst I have been off to more dangerous destinations, and without whose patience and support this book would not have been possible.

In addition I would like to mention my colleagues at AKE Ltd, one of the most successful training and security companies in the UK. In particular the managing director Mr Andrew Kain whose drive and determination was an inspiration (without knowing), and Mr Paul Brown, whose medical knowledge is extensive; there are many people alive today who would not be had it not been for his advice.

I would also like to thank my agent Barbara Levy for her infectious enthusiasm and encouragement on this book.

And I would also like to mention the publishing team without whose advice and hard work this book would never have got off the ground. Alan Brooke at Piatkus Books for his encouragement and advice and Barbara Kiser for her hard work in making sense of this ambitious project.

Introduction: Who Dares Travels

THE MORNING OF 11 SEPTEMBER 2001 was the start to a beautiful autumn day in New York City. Then, out of a crystal-clear blue sky emerged the new face of international terrorism. The fanatics who caused the devastation that day aimed to kill as many people as possible. My initial sentiments were like those of many others: I wondered whether this was the opening salvo in a monumental, violent global struggle.

In the aftermath of this shattering event the travel industry braced itself for the inevitable reverberations. Multinationals refused to send their business executives overseas; thousands cancelled holidays, parents stopped their children from travelling abroad. But by Christmas, four months later, the travel industry was pleasantly surprised by the fact that while there had been a downturn in business, it had not been anything like as bad as predicted. After the Gulf War in the early 1990s there had been a similar lack of enthusiasm for travel, but this was also shortlived.

Round this time I found myself on a flight to what was then probably the most dangerous place on earth. I was on my way to the centre of the storm – Kandahar, Afghanistan – as a safety advisor. I immediately began to wonder whether I should go, or if it was too dangerous, and how I would get out if something went wrong. I was hardly a novice: I've travelled to Kosovo, Macedonia, Pakistan and the Middle East, among other hotspots of violence. Finally, although this trip seemed an altogether more daunting prospect, I decided to keep faith with the elements of travel security I've always adhered to. I felt sure that a bit of common sense and essential preparation would prepare me for any problem Afghanistan could sling at me.

The fact is that we need to travel. In today's global economy, the wheels of commerce that generate our wealth are turned by our ability to travel. Most people crave the chance to escape from their normal routines to travel and see the world. Ask anyone what they would do if they won the lottery, and at the top of the list you will see 'travel and see the world'. This urge to travel will not be tempered by events like the destruction of the World Trade Center. The drive to escape, explore and experience is within most of us and isn't easily extinguished. Within weeks of that tragic event in New York, those still eager to travel were snapping up flights and cut-price holidays.

In fact today, travel is almost a rite of passage for many people. For most of us it arouses a passion and desire for adventure, a throwback perhaps to our nomadic past. But now we think nothing of travelling to the other side of the planet for a business meeting. A journey that a short time ago was fraught with life-threatening dangers is a mere jaunt today. The slow, exhausting, romantic journeys of the golden age of travel have been replaced by efficient, unbelievably swift journeys organised by the computer-age travel industry. Superfast jumbo jets and flying at 35,000 feet are just the way it is now.

And more and more of us go abroad. Honeymooners, gap-year students, office workers – all of us are eager for the otherness of foreign places. Travelling abroad is a chance to meet the rest of the world, for good or ill. Some of us return home reinvigorated. Others have been shocked by what they saw and feel life will never be the same again. And there are those who do not come back at all.

For the UK alone, the statistics are stark. Forty-four Britons were murdered on holiday abroad in 2000, compared to 35 in 1999. The Foreign Office reported that 8000 holidaymakers were relieved of £1.25 million by pickpockets alone. That could represent 8000 ruined holidays. Seventy-nine British women were raped and 22 people abducted during the same period.

Then there's the bigger picture. At the start of 2001, there were more than 22 wars and serious terrorist insurgencies going on around the world. There are many other, less widely publicised conflicts. While most are in well-known trouble spots, some can come as a surprise. It can be quite a shock to arrive in a foreign country and find armed security forces or armed militia groups on the streets. And the danger is not confined to remote conflict zones. Sporadic terrorist attacks have occurred in London, Oklahoma, Madrid, Paris, Athens and Tokyo.

Terrorist campaigns reach across international borders, and disrupt travel without warning. The circumstances within conflict zones can change quickly. Front lines can move, people in positions of power can change, journeys which at one time had been possible can quickly become deadly affairs. Tour operators were taking bookings for holidays in Croatia just days before the war broke out, stranding some holiday-makers in potentially life-threatening situations. However, the mere fact that conflict exists within a country does not always mean that one should not go there. You just need to take the necessary precautions to reduce the risks involved.

Taking precautions means having the necessary information. In March 1999, Rwandan Hutu rebels abducted a group of tourists from a rainforest game park in Uganda. The tourists were on what might have been seen as an idyllic holiday – to see one of the last populations of mountain gorillas in their natural habitat. After their abduction, five of the tourists were murdered. The unfortunate travellers believed that the Ugandan authorities would not have let them enter such a dangerous area. However, there had been similar incidents in the area some months before. Had they known the reality, it is doubtful that any of them would have been willing to accept the risks.

This book is about learning to take the right kind of precautions. Not the kind that prevent us from enjoying travel or indeed risk, but the kind that make travel safe, while keeping that edge of adventure intact.

After spending almost a quarter of a century in the army, serving mainly with the Special Air Service regiment, I have been fortunate enough to travel widely. Much of it has been in hostile environments, and I don't mean just war zones. Such conditions may be encountered anywhere – in modern, sophisticated cities, in the desperate conditions of a sub-Saharan African refugee camp, in a Middle Eastern conflict zone and on a freezing Scottish hillside. All present their own unique challenges. The trick is adopting simple risk reduction strategies that can be applied to any climate and any situation in any location.

In June 1999 I decided that it was time to call it a day, leave the regiment and venture out into the big bad world. Were my globe-trotting days over? Through operations and exercises I had encountered not only hellholes, but also some of the most stunningly beautiful of locations. And in essence, I loved it all. My passion is the exotic. Whether I've been holed up for months at a time in South East Asia's lush tropical rainforests, or living in a tent in the desert, a Kraal in southern Africa or a hut in the Arctic, travel for me has been a wonderful experience. Could I readjust to a sedentary lifestyle? Any thoughts of settling down to a quiet family life in the country were bound to perish, as my wanderlust soon re-emerged.

I also needed a job. Like the majority of ex-SAS members I found myself headed for the potentially lucrative 'security circuit'. This is a world unlike any other, a murky underworld inhabited by sinister individuals operating on the extreme edge of legality. Here the most bizarre of plans are hatched and one can be sent on the most hare-brained schemes to distant parts of the planet. One of these ill-advised journeys took me to northern Somalia, where I was surrounded by hostile locals, many of who would have liked nothing better than stringing me up – a fact they broadcast to me at every opportunity.

Even before I left the regiment, word was out. One morning I received a call on my mobile phone. A gravelly voice intoned, 'I've 'eard you've just left the reg. I might 'ave a bit of work for you – are you interested?' With nothing planned I said I might be. 'Well, I'll pay a thousand pounds for a few hours' work.' I tried to imagine it. Was I to help this fruitcake dispose of a body, or waddle through an airport security checkpoint with a bellyful of condoms filled with some deadly narcotic substance? How else did one earn that type of money? The thought made me shudder and I told Fruitcake that unfortunately I already had a job.

And some days later I embarked on one – to the Ivory Coast, where I was part of a small team looking after an American diamond dealer. He had been offered an enormous amount of money, diamonds and gold to relocate two scallywags who claimed to be members of the Sierra Leonean 'royal family'. They had supposedly escaped from the country with this vast wealth and wanted to relocate to the US or Europe. It looked like a scam and indeed it turned out to be one, where the 'client', after being repeatedly warned, was fleeced for $50,000. After being ourselves fleeced for money by the customs officials, the army and the police, and after almost being caught with firearms which we had acquired for our personal protection, we made a quick exit.

I spent the best part of the next year working and travelling to some of the world's less attractive places – Kosovo and Nigeria among them. But dangerous as they were, I was able to live and work in them by adopting the same simple strategies which I have used over the last quarter of a century. It became clear to me that if you are travelling for work or pleasure in potentially hostile territory, or even just as a tourist to a holiday resort, you can significantly reduce the risks by applying these principles.

I travel even more now than I did when I was in the army. I spend much of my time advising journalists how to keep out of trouble in war zones. Sometimes I accompany them and offer advice on matters related to their security. In Kosovo, only days after the war had finished, I found myself in Pristina looking after security for the BBC. At that time Pristina was still a very dangerous place, but it was an interesting time. And I still relish challenging locations.

One thing I've noted, however, is that while the majority of travellers return safely, terrorist attacks on the tourism industry, crime, and injury through accidents or other reasons have shown a significant and disturbing increase. The traveller taking necessary precautions could have avoided many of these incidents. The disparity between the wealth of the traveller and those living on the periphery of the tourist meccas is very real. The ticket price to some locations is more than those waiting outside the airport terminal could hope to earn in a year. Relatively affluent foreigners are tempting targets. No matter that you had saved hard for this trip, may even have taken out a loan to get there; compared with the reality in some regions, you will appear filthy rich.

Personal security while travelling is an issue bound closely with safety, security and health. There are many travellers with tales of woe, ruined holidays, disrupted business trips. Some have got caught up in catastropic, brutal events. They've been victims of road accidents, terrorism, physical assaults; they've contracted malaria, amoebic dysentery or typhoid. The exciting, pleasurable experience of travelling can turn into a nightmare scenario.

In today's high-tech, globalised community, of course, we face all sorts of risks at home. We accept them as part of modern life, and within our daily routine have developed strategies for reducing or even eliminating them completely. But abroad, the risks are different. There, things that in our home environment might be considered innocuous can lead to anything from interruption and inconvenience to outright disaster.

Behaviour or dress that would be nothing at home can provoke offence or even hostility in other countries. Your nationality, race, religion, language, gender, cultural emblems and social class can arouse passions that place you at risk. Local tensions might be temporarily high because of economic, political or religious crises over which you have little or no control. When travelling in a potentially hostile environment, you have to become familiar with the local status quo and turn on your cultural radar.

There are even areas where tourists *per se* may not be welcome – where there are disputes over environmental issues or social conditions near hotel complexes, for instance. Some extremists have targeted parts of Egypt, Spain, Turkey, Indonesia and Malaysia to make a political point. Travellers need to be aware of local sensitivities.

Then there's air and maritime safety – piracy, hijacking and kidnapping may be rare, but they do exist. We need to know how to cope with emergencies in a time of increased international tensions.

The last thing most people about to embark on a journey want to do is think about reducing the risk of accidents or crime. But whether you are an experienced world traveller or merely venturing out on your annual family holiday, your safety and that of your family is vital. No matter how experienced or streetwise we think we are, the fact is that visiting foreign countries means exposure to the unfamiliar. We need to practise discretion and common sense, gather as much knowledge about our destination as we can, and be aware of the potential hazards and how to deal with them.

And that's where this simple, user-friendly guide to planning a safe journey abroad comes in. It's a distillation of experience abroad that will help you learn the range of risks, and prepare for them. Once you've mastered this, you'll have the peace of mind to delight in the pleasures of 21st-century travel.

1

Planning Your Journey

W HEN IT COMES TO TRAVEL, most of us worry about the same
things – having our house burgled, becoming ill, encountering
bad accommodation. And of course, in the wake of September 2001,
we worry about terrorism. It's clear that there are a range of risks
you need to prepare for, and it is up to you to take responsibility for
your own security.

Preparation, including thorough research, is the key to a successful holiday or business trip. At home, the mechanisms are in place to
help you deal with most problems. The police, emergency services or

legal assistance are only a phone call away. Once on unfamiliar territory, however, there may be few such services to fall back on, and you may have to rely on your own resources. By doing your homework before you go, you can identify the dangers and work out contingency plans in case something goes wrong. So here's the first step in protecting yourself – and preventing the journey of a lifetime from becoming an expensive nightmare.

Travellers' Threat Assessment

A basic threat analysis is a security 'snapshot' of the situation in the country you're heading for. It will show you where you need to be vigilant. The security professionals of major multinational companies frequently carry out this kind of assessment for business travellers. Tour companies also keep an eye on security situations at holiday destinations and advise their tour reps about any dangers. But huge numbers of people still leave the UK and other countries every year without knowing much about what is really going on at their destinations. Many travellers work on the assumption that as nothing has happened there in the past, nothing will happen this time. The problem is that we live in a fast-changing world.

In 2001 and 2002, tourists in Nepal have been stunned to find out that the country is in the midst of a violent and increasingly bloody Maoist terror campaign that has claimed the lives of thousands. Many tourists faced life or death decisions when confronted by a terrorist attack in Bandranaike airport in Sri Lanka. Putting together a simple threat assessment before you go could save heartache later.

What kind of potential threats will you be looking at? A petty thief stealing your passport can spoil your holiday as thoroughly as a terrorist attacking the city you're staying in. After you have identified the threats, you can prepare your security plan accordingly. Different places demand different safety strategies: a holiday at a tourist resort in the US isn't really comparable with a backpacking expedition in Kenya.

Tourism is the economic lifeblood of certain regions, so it is understandable that some countries try to avoid adverse publicity about incidents involving tourists. Many incidents go unreported, in fact. When you research your trip, try to obtain up-to-date information. Your local library will probably only provide last year's. Remember: things change fast. (See References, page 414 for the best research sources.)

When analysing risks in particular countries, here are the points you'll need to cover:

- Assess the relations between your home country and the one you'll be visiting. A favourable political link between them generally means you'll have a warmer reception. This was graphically illustrated for me in July 2001, when I was visiting Macedonia and citizens of the UK were welcome. When the international community forced the Macedonian government to accept an ominous peace settlement, this changed, and several British and other Western citizens were attacked in the capital, Skopje. This was a classic example of how events in the international political arena can have potentially disastrous consequences for innocent people.

- The political, social and economic situation in the country and regions are crucial. Are there any major internal conflicts, which may affect your travel plans? When I travelled to the Ivory Coast in 1999 I was not surprised to see heavily armed soldiers at every corner – I had conducted a brief analysis and identified that there were major economic and social problems there. They erupted into violence some months later. Also identify whether there are any disputes with neighbouring countries, which may influence your plans. In some volatile regions it may not be possible to move between quarrelsome neighbours.

- Ethnic or racial tensions frequently precipitate civil disorder. Social polarisation brought about by high unemployment and the unequal distribution of wealth also triggers civil tensions. Attacks on the tourist industry throughout Spain during 2001 resulted in tour companies issuing warnings to tourists to remain alert and be suspicious, but how many people actually knew what they were looking for?

- If there is tension between tribal groupings in a country – say, like that in Rwanda recently – try to familiarise yourself with what is happening between them now. Cultivate a basic understanding of the conflict and the different cultures. Try to work out where the various ethnic groups live so that if you pass through different areas you can gain an understanding of the conflict from each perspective.

- Are there a lot of active pressure groups within the country? Environmentalists and social pressure groups have targeted some tourist areas in order to focus attention on local social conditions.

- Are there any health concerns you should be looking at? Malaria is a growing problem in many countries, for instance, and prevention is not straightforward. (See also Chapter 17.) Animal health can be an issue, too. In 2001, huge areas of the British countryside were out of bounds to everyone due to the foot and mouth crisis, resulting in serious consequences for many tourists.

- Religious tensions may be plaguing the country. The worst incident in recent years was the massacre of tourists in Luxor, Egypt. Religious zealots rounded up foreign visitors to the famous temples and coldbloodedly executed more than 50 of them.

- What are the social norms in the country? Alcohol use, dress and conduct, behaviour between the sexes – you need to think about the implications of all this before you go.

- Look at law enforcement in the country. Is the army in charge? Military law enforcement is more forceful than a civilian police force. On that visit to the Ivory Coast I found the low-ranking military personnel manning checkpoints corrupt and sometimes aggressive. When you arrive in any foreign country, try to assess the local reaction to the police or military. This will indicate how you yourself should react.

- Look at patterns of criminal activity. In very poor areas, petty crime is endemic. Is there a history of crime against foreigners? If so, ask what kind. In some countries, taking hostages has become an industry. Armed robberies, vehicle theft, physical assaults and kidnapping have affected many British travellers, for instance.

- Have there been any industrial disputes in the country? In 2001, pressure groups in the UK launched a series of actions aiming to force the government to reduce fuel taxes. The entire country was brought to a standstill. I flew into the UK at the height of this dispute and was stranded at the airport. Such actions can ruin a holiday and disrupt business trips: find out what you are getting into.

- Assess the country's infrastructure. Airports, shipping ports, railway systems and roads are essential to your mobility as a traveller. A cursory check should provide you with sufficient information on their reliability and security.

- How's the weather there? If you jet off to the tropics expecting glorious sun-drenched beaches, you need to avoid the monsoon season. Tropical storms, hurricanes, typhoons and torrential rain can ruin a visit. If you'll be going to a high elevation it can get very cold, even in tropical regions.

Cultural Sensitivities

One of the main reasons we travel is to experience different cultures. Yet visitors to regions with strong cultural traditions may fail to understand the sensitivities of local people – and get into trouble. Visitors from the West may be shocked by what they see abroad: the way women are treated in some strict Islamic countries, the restrictive caste system in India, the treatment of animals in the markets of China, children begging on the streets of Eastern European capitals. But however appalled we may be, we need to know that there are risks in protesting.

In the West we have relatively high standards of living, freedom of speech and human rights. When we travel we assume that if we show people respect we will be treated in a favourable way. However, in many parts of the world, basic human rights do not exist, and by speaking out against the authorities you may be placing yourself in real danger. British citizens have found themselves enduring long prison sentences for protesting about the restrictive policies of the military administration in Myanmar. We have to accept that when we travel we will experience things we may not like.

As part of your threat assessment and to boost your cultural awareness, think about the following points:

- Does the country you're visiting have cultural affiliations with your own? If so, chances are you won't experience an enormous culture clash.

- How do local people view foreigners? There are some areas where tourists are resented.

- As we've discussed, one of the most emotive aspects of a culture is the prevailing religion. Emotions can quickly become inflamed over perceived offence. Be aware of the religious groupings in countries and regions you'll be visiting. In some regions it is normal for communities to be built around religious beliefs. Within countries there may be areas dominated by certain religious groups. It is vital to understand how to behave so you do not cause offence.

- Pinpoint topics likely to be sensitive. It is great to converse with local people while you are travelling, but if you become involved in discussions of a sensitive nature you can quickly find yourself getting into trouble. When I was travelling in the Balkans, the best advice I received was not to become involved in discussions about history. Very wise! Talking about politics, religion and sex may best be avoided.

- In times of international crisis, or if you are visiting a particularly volatile country, remove cultural emblems from your luggage. British flags or offensive slogans may get you into trouble.

- Avoid wearing any openly religious symbols in certain regions. Christian, Islamic or Jewish religious symbols may attract the wrong type of attention.

- Identify the acceptable dress code. When I was in Somalia we were required to conduct some physical fitness training. After running through the town of Bossasso, I was surprised to be told that I had offended a lot of people because I had worn shorts. Provocative clothing such as short skirts, or T-shirts with explicit motifs, may not be tolerated in certain countries. You will have to research what is acceptable.

- Be aware that open displays of affection are not tolerated everywhere. A man and woman kissing may end having a brush with the law. Women engaging in this behaviour may also be sending out the wrong signals, which could attract unwanted attention.

- In some developing countries where poverty is endemic, affluent travellers will be seen as making a statement. Designer-labelled clothing, expensive-looking watches and jewellery, pricey sunglasses, cameras and computers – displaying all this can attract resentment. Many luxurious hotel complexes are within striking distance of shantytowns where people live in abject squalor. Avoid flamboyant displays of wealth.

- If you end up needing medical attention, be aware that in some areas it is unacceptable for women and men to attend the same medical facility.

- Traditions can be a flashpoint. In certain regions it is considered a serious insult to refuse hospitality. In some countries there are rather obscure traditions, which if you get them wrong can cause enormous offence. In Somalia it is considered a great insult to show someone the soles of your feet.

- Identify anniversaries, religious or cultural holidays that could invite risk, particularly if you're to visit areas of unrest. During the Muslim holy month of Ramadan, for instance, Muslims fast during the daylight hours, and believers must adopt a rigid routine.

- Photography can create difficulties. In some cultures, if you want to take a photo the subject will expect to be paid. Many won't want to be photographed. And there is a security aspect: if you are caught taking photographs of airports, military establishments, government buildings or any other sensitive sites, you can be arrested. If in doubt, ask.

- Be aware of any laws concerning alcohol. In some moderate Islamic states it is legal for non-Muslims to consume alcohol. But if you were to be caught sharing a drink with a Muslim, you could end up in prison. If alcohol is permitted, ensure that you don't exceed your legal allowance when entering the country.

- Stay clear of drugs. In most countries having or taking them is a serious crime. In some regions travellers caught peddling even small amounts of drugs will spend a long time in prison. Some have been executed.

Information Sources

These days, finding the information you need to ensure that you are fully prepared for your trip is easy. The following are some of the best sources.

- Travel guides – the Rough Guides, Lonely Planet books, Footprint Handbooks and Eyewitness Travel Guides among others – are valuable. They cover almost every country on the planet, and give overviews as well as detailed information. These books will give you cultural information, where to stay, cost of living, what to do and much more. However, you do need to buy the most recent edition to stay abreast of developments, and sometimes you'll need more specialised information. Information can also be obtained from www.ake.co.uk. AKE will provide up to date and detailed country risk information detailing the culture, commerce, crime patterns, medical intelligence and other specialised information for travellers to any region. Alternatively, you can write to AKE, Mortimer House, Holmer Road, Hereford HR4 9TA; there is a £5 fee for this information.

- Maps are a huge source of information and a travel plan essential. It makes good sense to purchase maps covering all the countries and cities you intend to visit. When studying your map identify all the vital locations – embassies, security force locations, hospitals and major hotels. Even in a developed, sophisticated city it is important to identify these locations and work out a route to get to them. (See Chapter 18, page 395.)

- The Internet is a boon. There is a huge variety of sites giving detailed information on almost every country in the world. The UK Foreign Office site (http://www.fco.gov.uk/travel/countryadvice.asp) is a reliable source of information, regularly updated. In addition to travel alerts and the like, it gives the telephone number of the UK consulate or embassy in other countries. (See References, page 414.)

- If you're not online, get direct travel advice by contacting Britain's Foreign and Commonwealth Office at the Travel Advice Unit, Consular Division, Foreign and Commonwealth Office, Old Admiralty Building, Whitehall, London SW1A 2AF. Or call 020 7008 0232/0233.

- Travel agents and tour operators will assist in providing accurate information about various countries and regions. However, situations do change fast and travel agents may not be able to help if you are caught in an unpredictable situation. Many agents were concerned by the outbreak of violence that raged through Kingston, Jamaica, in July 2001. Twenty-five people were gunned down, and many were injured in the city streets as armed gangs and police battled it out over the control of illegally held firearms. Order was only restored after the army was deployed. In this situation, all the agents could do was advise people to stay away from the affected areas.

- Travel journals such as *Wanderlust* can be very useful for timely information (see References, page 414, for a longer list of journals and websites).

- Newspapers, such as British broadsheets, provide a limited overview of what is happening in certain countries. Most Sunday newspapers have a travel section. Newspapers from the country you're visiting, which can be purchased from specialist newsagents or accessed in online versions, will help flesh out your understanding of the current situation. Crime, national emergencies and conflict are the lifeblood of many newspapers. By reading them you will keep up to date with current events.

- TV can be a useful source of information. If you are aware that the country you are visiting is being featured on TV, you may want to video the programme and study it in greater detail. Be aware that most travel shows will concentrate on the attractive features of a country and rarely mention the realities of life outside tourist locations. You'll find travel information on BBC2, CEEFAX, page 470 onwards. TV documentary channels such as the Discovery Channel regularly feature travel guides.

- Shortwave band radios are an invaluable source of information once you're on the road. Obtain a list of frequencies for the BBC's World Service; these should enable you to tune in during your travels. The frequencies change from region to region and throughout the day, so identify the right ones for your destination. There are radio broadcasts, which will keep you informed about the situation in certain regions. One evening, on my recent trip to Macedonia, I was listening to the World Service. The BBC transmitted a warning to all British citizens in Macedonia to leave immediately. I then heard about the trouble engulfing the north of the country on the radio.

- Ask friends, relatives or business colleagues who have just returned from the area what's happening there. Or ask your travel agent to put you in touch with someone who has just returned. Draw up a list of your main concerns before you question them.

- For health advice from the British government, call the Department of Health on 0800 555 777. They will supply you with a leaflet on staying healthy while travelling.

- The Medical Advisory Services for Travellers Abroad (MASTA) will provide you with assistance on immunisation details, malarial prophylaxis and news on the latest health issues. To obtain a printout from MASTA, phone 0906 8224 100. It will provide assistance 24 hours a day, 7 days a week, and will dispatch information by first-class post. MASTA will also provide information on passports, visa applications, costing, many travel destinations, and British consulates and embassies abroad. Just call 0906 5501 100 or write to MASTA, the London School of Hygiene and Tropical Medicine, Keppel Street, London wc1e 7ht.

Prisoners Abroad is a charitable organisation providing information, advice and support to British citizens imprisoned abroad, as well as their families and friends. At the time of writing, Prisoners Abroad was assisting more than 1400 people in over 80 countries. The charity can help in finding lawyers and negotiating with prison authorities, advise on prison transfers, provide essentials such as medicine, food and clothing, link prisoners with pen pals, send magazines and books to clients, and offer after-care services. Prisoners Abroad can be reached by phone at 020 7561 6820; fax at 020 7561 6821; and email on <info@prisonersabroad.org.uk. Alternatively, you can write to Prisoners Abroad, 89-93 Fonthill Road, Finsbury Park, London n4 3jh.

British Consulate Services

The British Consulate's service mission is to promote British interest and relations within foreign countries. It will also provide assistance to British travellers who for whatever reason find themselves in difficulty. In countries where there is no British consular representation, you should try any other European Union member country that has a diplomatic mission in that country. Of course, if you're of another nationality, you'll need to seek the consulate or embassy representing your own country.

Many travellers who find themselves in trouble assume that the British Embassy will provide assistance free of charge. This is not the case. For many services the consulate will charge a fee. These fees are reviewed annually, so the prices may vary. It is pointless confronting the consulate officials about this payment, as the consuls are obliged by British law to implement charges. You will generally be expected to settle charges in the country where you receive assistance, and it is normal to pay in advance. However, in extreme circumstances, the consular officials can make alternative arrangements.

The British consular services will:

- Issue emergency temporary passports or travel documents if yours is lost or stolen.

- Contact nominated representatives to arrange for money transfers.

- Provide information on safe money transfers.

- In certain cases, cash cheques up to the value of £100 if you present a valid banker's card.

- In extreme cases, facilitate a loan, which must be repaid when you get home. However, this only applies if there are no alternatives.

- Provide information on in-country legal representation.

- Provide information on in-country medical services, such as doctors.

- In the event of an accident, inform relatives at home.

- In certain circumstances and if there is no alternative, pass information on to relatives and friends in the UK.

- Provide information on organisations that deal with missing persons abroad.

- In certain circumstances, communicate on your behalf with the local authorities.

- Visit British citizens who have been arrested in that country.

The British consular services will *not*:

- Provide assistance in the event of a local court case.

- Obtain your release from local prisons.

- Provide you with legal representation if you end up in court.

- Investigate crimes committed by you or against you.

- Negotiate for favourable treatment in local hospitals or prisons.

- Provide accommodation.

- Make travel arrangements for you, such as booking flights.

- Provide employment or work permits in the visiting country.

- Put up bail to allow people arrested to be released from prison.

- Conduct services such as recovering your car.

Before Departure

As I've said, terrorism is the big fear now for a lot of holiday-makers. But that doesn't mean they're not worried about having their house burgled, too. It seems that we have become accustomed to the expectation that sooner or later we will become a victim of some sort of crime. However, there are some basic security measures that you can adopt which will help protect your property while you're sunning yourself – or working – abroad.

By following these simple guidelines you will significantly reduce the chances of returning home to a disaster.

- Tell details of your travel plans only to the necessary minimum of trusted relatives and friends. The fewer people who know that your house is empty, the better.

- Inform the local police that your house will be empty. They may alter their patrol patterns to show a presence at vulnerable times around the area of your house.

- Ensure that all your valuables are discreetly hidden and out of sight, safely under lock and key. Better still, if you live in a high-crime area, take your valuable possessions to a friend or relative before you depart.

- Ensure that there are no large postal deliveries to your home while you are away, or arrange to redirect them to your neighbour, or ask your neighbour to collect them.

- Get a relative or trusted friend to live in your house while you are away. House sitting is becoming very popular and is a very effective measure to combat house crime.

■ Arrange to divert telephone calls to your mobile, first ensuring that you have mobile phone coverage at your destination.

■ Cancel newspaper and milk deliveries.

■ If possible, leave your car parked outside your house to create the illusion that your house is occupied. Criminals are much less likely to burgle occupied houses.

■ Time-delay light switches are a cheap and effective way of deterring inquisitive callers at night. Preset the devices to switch on an hour before the onset of darkness. If you cannot obtain these switches then leave at least one light on, preferably one that is visible from outside your garden.

■ If you have a trusted neighbour, ask them to keep an eye on your house and help keep it looking occupied. They could open and close curtains before dark and in the morning, or switch on your TV or radio during the night and turn it off during the day. The noise may be enough to deter criminals.

■ If you have a dog, ask your neighbour if they'll look after it – walking it, feeding it, letting it into the garden during the day and back into the house at night. Dogs are a big deterrent to burglars. You can return the favour when your neighbours go on holiday.

■ Right before you leave, ensure all doors and windows are securely locked and that any alarms are programmed.

For additional security measures, see Chapter 16.

Preparation

Since September 2001, the travel industry – which was on a roll through the 1990s – has been thrown into chaos. Airlines have gone into liquidation and there have been mergers and a distinct downturn in business. But the slump hasn't been as big as predicted, and security, of course, has never been better. There is much hope that the pace of air travel will pick up again: the Airbus consortium would not have invested in its super jumbo jet, which will carry in excess of 500 people, if it did not expect a rapid growth in long-haul journeys. (See also Chapter 2, 'Safe Air Travel'.)

So even in these uncertain times, there is still a lot of pressure on the traveller to prepare for their journeys well in advance. Here's how.

■ Book your ticket well in advance to avoid disappointment. It is also essential that you reconfirm your seat a few days before you travel. Airlines frequently overbook in order to ensure that the maximum seats are occupied. If you have any individual requirements (if you're vegetarian or eat Kosher, or if you have a particular medical condition, for example), it is essential to mention them to booking staff. If you need to ask what you are permitted to carry onto the aircraft, see 'Dangerous Air Cargo', page 26. Be sure to get an up-to-date list, as the rules have changed since the September 2001 incident in New York.

■ Make sure you have sufficient time left on your passport to cover you for your entire journey (see 'Passport Security', page 27).

■ Check to see if you'll need a visa. When you fill in your visa application, check to ensure the information is correct. If you are on a business trip you may be required to apply for a business visa (see 'Passport Security').

■ Identify any inoculations or malarial prophylaxis you'll need. It can take some time to arrange for certain inoculations, which have to be administered over a period of some days (see Chapter 17).

■ It is sometimes a good idea to reserve a room in a number of different hotels. If you arrive and for whatever reason the hotel cannot offer you a room, you have an alternative. If you get a room at your first attempt, you can call up and cancel the alternative.

■ When you arrive at a foreign airport, you may have arranged to be met by a tour guide or a driver from your hotel. The normal procedure is that they hold up a placard with your name on it.

From the security perspective, this isn't the best option: what he is doing is actually telling everyone else who you are. Instead, obtain the driver's name before you go, and have him display it so you can identify him.

- It is a good idea to have all your personal paperwork in order before you depart – all your insurance details, a will and a nominated individual to look after your affairs in the event that something goes wrong.

- Check with your mobile phone provider to ensure that you have mobile phone coverage at your destination.

- Identify any import restrictions at your destination. This may be done at your travel agent's or by contacting that country's embassy in your home country. Be aware of any import or export restrictions relating to currencies.

Luggage Security

One of the greatest risks to the traveller is that their luggage will be stolen or lost in the overloaded systems of airports. Even when your luggage arrives at an airport, there is no real certainty that it will remain secure. We place our trust in baggage handlers, yet in many regions of the world they are paid very little, and easy access to all that luggage must be a huge temptation for some. When I travelled to Croatia some time ago, I found that my luggage had been rifled and some items were missing.

You can make your luggage more secure by following the points below.

- Never pack valuable or sensitive material into your checked luggage. If you have to carry important business documents, say, put them in an envelope addressed to you and forward it to the hotel at your destination. Call the hotel and tell them you are expecting a delivery. You can collect it when you arrive.

- If there's no alternative, and you have something valuable that must go into your checked luggage, place a carton of cigarettes or something similarly attractive in the same suitcase. If your luggage is rifled, the cigarettes alone may just quench the looter's thirst. I have used this ploy many times.

- The safest luggage to use is the rigid plastic type. It's robust and can take a knock, and can't be cut through like a leather suitcase.

- Ensure that there are locking mechanisms on your suitcases. If the lock is the combination type, ensure that you reset the combination from the factory setting (000). These locks are, however, very simple to defeat. If your case has two locks, as most of them do, set each lock to a different combination.

- If you are travelling with a number of suitcases, ensure that they are set with different combinations. Also, number the cases and count them after each leg of your journey. Frequently travellers forget articles of luggage, leaving them at airports, in taxis or coaches.

- Avoid writing your name on the suitcase. It is more secure to use a closed nametag with your business address and contact details. Or pack a sheet of A4 paper containing your name and address into the case. This will prove it's yours if someone else accidentally picks it up. Avoid flag stickers or other cultural emblems and company logos, especially when travelling to areas of unrest.

- Avoid using military-style luggage. Army rucksacks, kit bags or aviation bags may send out the wrong signals.

- Use security straps to ensure that your luggage does not accidentally open when being thrown around by baggage handlers.

- If travelling with a rucksack, ensure that you are able to lock it. Buy a sturdy padlock and luggage strap to secure it. Avoid placing valuable items in the side pouches or the top pouch.

- When you've arrived, avoid making unnecessary journeys across town if you are burdened with luggage. Don't walk hundreds of metres to a taxi rank with heavy baggage. This presents an opportunistic thief with a golden opportunity: if he were to snatch one of your bags you will be unable to give chase without the risk of losing the rest of your baggage.

- Ensure that your luggage is adequately insured. Many airlines will limit the value of any lost baggage unless you have declared that you desire a higher value, in which case you will be required to pay a premium. Most airlines will pay around £7 per pound for checked luggage, and £280 per passenger for unchecked baggage. Some airlines will refuse to assume liability for fragile or perishable items. You should contact your airline for details of insurance claims. If you intend to complain to your airline for damaged possessions or luggage you must do so within 7 days. If your luggage has been delayed and is damaged, you must file your complaint within 21 days from its delivery.

- Particularly in the wake of the September 2001 events, airlines are carrying out even more thorough searches in all luggage. When airport security staff are unable to determine what something is in the X-ray, they will open your case to look at it. To facilitate these searches, leave presents unwrapped until you arrive at your destination.

Storing Your Luggage

There may be times you want to leave your luggage in a safe place while you visit or explore. If you go on an excursion, you may only want to take a day sack with you, and leave your cases behind. Ask your travel agent in advance about the policy on left luggage. Your hotel, hostel, airport or railway station may provide a reliable facility to leave your baggage. However, don't leave valuables in your baggage: remember, your luggage will not be completely safe, even in a left luggage facility. Some left luggage facilities consist of leaving perhaps dozens of cases, rucksacks and bags piled high in a storeroom. There is little or no coordination and many articles of luggage go missing.

There is an element of trust involved in leaving your property in the hands of strangers. Ensure that you are comfortable with the security arrangements before leaving anything. It is always helpful to strike up a good relationship with hotel staff, porters, bellboys and clean-ers. If they think that you are a good person they will be less likely to steal from you. You may decide to tip the left luggage reception-ist. They will look after your baggage and make it less likely that your bag will be given to someone else by mistake. Ensure that you obtain a receipt for your luggage stating the date, time and person on duty when you handed over your baggage.

Make sure that the zips are completely done up and locks are secured to avoid prying hands. Ensure, too, that your luggage is clearly identifiable and your personal details containing your name, address and tour company are inside. Remember to check opening times; the last thing you need is to return from a gruelling trek only to find you cannot get access to your luggage.

Dangerous Air Cargo

For obvious safety reasons, some items cannot be carried on an aircraft. You may use a number of them at home, but changes in temperature and pressure mean they constitute a hazard on an aero-plane. If you rely on certain medical devices, check at the airport to ensure you are able to travel with them. Getting caught carrying any prohibited item will make you liable to prosecution.

The following items are classified as dangerous air cargo, but you should check with your travel agent if there are any doubts.

- Explosive material and firearms: matches, sparklers and other fireworks, flares, gunpowder, ammunition or other ordnance, blasting caps, commercial explosives, firearms, knives and swords. Check with the airline about replica weapons and children's toy guns.

- Gases and pressurised containers: flammable aerosols like hair spray, spray paint, or insect repellent; carbon dioxide cartridges, oxygen tanks (scuba or medical), Mace, teargas, pepper spray, self-inflating rafts and deeply refrigerated gases such as liquid nitro-gen.

- Flammable liquids and solids: gasoline, propane, butane and other fuels; lights with flammable fuels, matches, flammable paints, paint thinners, some cleaning solvents, some adhesives, cigarette lighters and lighter fluid.

- Oxidizers and organic peroxides: bleach, nitric acid, fertilisers, swimming pool or spa chemicals and fibreglass repair kits.

- Poisonous material: weed-killers, pesticides, insecticides, rodent poisons, arsenic and cyanide.

- Infectious materials: laboratory specimens, viral organisms and bacterial cultures.

- Corrosives: drain cleaners, car batteries, wet cell batteries, acids, alkalis and mercury.

- Organics: fibreglass resins, peroxides.

- Radioactive materials: smoke detectors, radioactive chemicals, and other radioactive materials.

- Magnetic materials: strong magnets such as those in some loud-speakers and laboratory equipment.

- Security cases with installed intrusion detection systems that generate smoke or gas.

- Any material that could get you arrested at your destination.

Passport Security

Your passport is the most valuable document that you'll carry while travelling. You should keep control of it at all times; lost or stolen passports will ruin your trip and mean endless hours of running around trying to obtain a temporary passport so you can get home.

There is an extremely lucrative market in stolen passports, so you must make every effort to protect yours. Britons of ethnic descent are particularly vulnerable to passport fraud. It is easier for criminal gangs to pass off passports to people from a similar ethnic background. Stolen passports have been used in order to gain illegal entry to the UK, or even to provide criminals operating abroad with fake identities. This has led to people being wrongly associated with the criminal activities of others.

While waiting for a flight at Zurich airport in July 2001, I watched a woman leave four American passports and flight tickets unattended on a table in the lounge. There were many shady characters lurking around, some paying unhealthy attention to the potential goldmine lying on the table. I pointed this out and her reaction was one of complete shock – surely no one here would steal them!

Follow the points below and your passport – and trip – will stay safe.

- Never give your passport to anyone as a guarantee for a loan or service. Once, travelling in Nigeria with some business people, I tried to get through the crowds at Lagos airport. We were confronted by what appeared to be an airport official. He was dressed similarly and was displaying an identification badge. Without our knowledge, one of the businessmen in our charge handed over his passport and ticket to this individual, who promised that he would fast-track us through the check-in. I managed to retrieve the travel documents before this impostor was able to get out of the airport. Our business colleague was totally unaware that he had just handed over a small pot of gold to this crook.

- When travelling to volatile areas, put a plain cover on your passport to conceal your nationality. In Britain you can buy these at your nearest Post Office, or in travel shops.

- If you are a regular business traveller, apply for a second passport. Keep one for business and the other for leisure travel.

- In most hotel chains it's the norm to leave your passport at reception, so you don't run off without paying. There have been cases, however, of passports being stolen from hotel reception desks. If you leave your passport at reception, do not leave it there indefinitely: 24 hours is usually enough. In most modern hotel chains, they have secure safety deposit boxes at reception. You must accept, however, that if you give your passport to someone else you have lost control of it. The only real way of ensuring that it is secure is that you carry it at all times.

- You may be required to carry your passport in order to identify yourself to the authorities or to cash your travellers' cheques. In this case it is inadvisable to carry everything in one wallet or a pocket. A money or document belt or holster that can be worn next to your skin will give a greater degree of security.

- During long trips you may decide to place your passport and other essential documents at a local bank or similarly safe establishment.

- Do not leave your passport or travel documents in your luggage or in the outside pockets of day sacks, rucksacks or bags. You should fill these outside pockets with your dirty socks and underwear. Any thieves will very succinctly get the message.

- Do not be tempted to leave your passport in your hotel room. Remember that a stolen passport can fetch in excess of £5000 on the black market. Would you leave £5000 lying around your hotel room unprotected?

- Photocopy the back page of your passport and carry two spare passport photos. Ensure that you also have two photocopies of your visas or letters of invitation. Pack the copied documents in separate envelopes and put them in different items of luggage. If something goes wrong these will speed the process of obtaining new travel documents. Alternatively, leave copies of your travel documentation at home, which can be faxed to you if the need arises.

- Most countries require passports for children, even babies. Find out the requirements at your destination before you go, allowing enough time to get a passport for your child if they need one.

- Ensure that your own passport is not outdated and that it will remain valid for the entire trip. To be safe, you should have at least six months remaining on your passport.

- If you lose your passport or it is stolen, the British Consulate can issue temporary travel documentation. You have to pay for it, however, and it can take some time to process if the consulate is busy.

■ Inquire about visa requirements at the earliest possible moment in the planning stage of your trip. Some visas take weeks to issue and can be fairly expensive (see page 421 in 'References').

Pre-departure Checklist

Some days before you depart, you'll need to check to see whether you've got all the documents you need. If you are travelling with a group (with other gap year students or with your family, for instance), one completely reliable person needs to be designated as responsible for checking everyone's documents.

These documents, cards and tickets will include the following.

■ *Passport with appropriate visas or letters of invitation.* It is useful to have photocopies of these documents in a separate envelope packed in your luggage (see 'Passport Security', above).

■ *Flight tickets and reservation slips.* It is routine to confirm a flight 48 hours before you travel. Don't forget to do so.

■ *International Vaccination Certificate* with the relevant and up-to-date information.

■ *Contact details for your country's embassy or consulate* at your destination, including address and telephone numbers (both business hours and out of office hours).

■ *Contact details and reservations slips for your hotels*, and contact details for travel firms and holiday reps.

■ *If you're eligible, student cards.* These enable you to acquire sizeable discounts and deals in many countries and will make a huge difference to your budget. Mature students can apply for them, too.

■ *Car hire details and driving documentation.* International driving licences are available in Britain from the Post Office, at a price of around £5. You need a valid British (or other) driving permit to buy one.

- *Details of any medical conditions or ailments you suffer from.* If possible, have this information translated into the language of your destination country. If you suffer from a serious condition, translate the procedures you require. Obtain medical authorisation for any medication you are carrying with you. If you have to carry medication, ensure that it is in its original packaging to avoid suspicion during customs checks.

- *A list showing your blood type and any allergies you suffer from.*

- *Insurance documents.* These will detail your insurance company, in-country representative and what you are covered for (see page 32 below).

- *Credit cards.* Carry only the ones you'll be using for your trip. Photocopy the details of your credit card and carry the phone number of the credit card company so that you can cancel the card if it is lost or stolen.

- *Travellers' cheques.* Carry separate details of the cheque numbers, as well as the contact details of the issuing agents so that you can cancel them if they are lost or stolen.

- *Local currency.* It is useful to have some small-denomination local banknotes, enough to last you until you are able to change your cheques at a bank or exchange bureau. Avoid changing large amounts in cheques or cash at the destination airport as this will attract attention. Small-denomination notes also allow you to drip-feed corrupt officials, if need be, without showing them large bills.

- *Emergency contact list and contingency plans.* These should contain details of family members, your office at work and anyone else who will need to be contacted in an emergency, and the plans you will follow if you're involved in an incident or accident (see below).

Emergency Contact List

If there's an emergency or tensions suddenly flare up in the country you're visiting, people at home – family, friends and your business colleagues – will want to know that you are safe. Prepare a list of appropriate contact details to give to close associates and relatives before you begin your travels. This will ensure that you can always be contacted and you can always touch base with home.

Telephone and fax numbers and email addresses for the following should be on your list.

- Your home embassies or consulates at your destination – both day and night numbers.

- Your country's foreign office.

- The embassy or consulate of the country you are visiting in your own city.

- International operator number.

- Airline helpline and booking office (available from travel agents and on flight tickets).

- Hotel numbers and room extensions (available from travel agents).

- Tour or excursion company (available from travel agents).

- Adventure activities companies and reps (available from booking agents).

- Car hire details (available through the booking agent).

- Your mobile phone number (check mobile phone coverage).

- Insurance company contact details.

- In-country legal representative.

- Local police station.

- Contact numbers of next of kin or those to be informed in the event of an accident.

Also be sure to leave an itinerary of your travel plans detailing where you will be at every stage of your journey.

Basic Communications Planning

Your contacts list is only the start. You'll also need to work out who your key contact person will be, and the optimal ways of staying in touch. In an emergency, you may need help from those at home, and of course they themselves will need to know how you are. Relatives may not be the best people to rely on in this type of situation, however. They will almost certainly become distressed if they think that something has happened to you. They could even become a liability if they become angry with embassy or consulate staff. Your primary contact at home should be someone level-headed enough to handle a dicey situation in a capable manner.

- If there is no mobile phone coverage at your destination, buy an international or local calling card before you go.

- Remember the international dialling codes of both your home country and the country you're visiting.

- If there is political or social unrest in the country you're visiting, ensure that people know where you are at every stage of your journey. A useful procedure is to arrange to call home twice a day – one call in the morning and a further call in the afternoon/evening, both at the same time every day. This way, if you miss one of your calls people will become aware that something may have gone wrong, and if you miss two consecutive calls people will be alerted to the fact that all is not quite right. After a further day they can start a search for you, for example by telephoning your country's embassy or consulate in your destination country.

- If you intend to stay in a volatile area for two weeks or longer, register with your country's embassy or consulate when you arrive at your destination.

- Leave details of your flight, including stopovers, flight numbers, and times of arrival and departures, with friends or relatives so they can check your movements if they need to.

Equipment

In your rush to get ready for your trip it is all too easy to forget the essentials. The following list is by no means exhaustive, but it's a good start.

- What type of clothing will you need? Is the climate hot or cold, wet or dry? Even in the tropics there are some cold locations. If you work on the layer principle, you will be able to regulate your body temperature. Layering a number of lighter garments provides better insulation than wearing two pieces of thick, heavy clothing.

- If you are visiting a culturally conservative area, you must stick to the dress code. Avoid flamboyant clothing. Women may have to dress more conservatively when visiting certain Middle Eastern countries, for instance. Short dresses will inevitably invite trouble.

- Avoid any clothes, such as T-shirts, with sexually explicit motifs or political slogans.

- Try to travel light. You can move more quickly and free up your hands, which is safer and more convenient. You will also be less tired from lugging big cases around, and less likely to set them down where they might be stolen.

- Buy appropriate shoes, particularly if you'll be walking a lot. Blisters spoil your day as surely as more serious injuries. Ensure that any footwear is 'broken in'.

- If you're travelling to remote areas or to less developed countries, buy enough shampoo, soap and the like to last the trip. Toiletries may be difficult to obtain in some regions and can be prohibitively expensive.

- In some regions, sunscreen is also very expensive. If you are travelling with kids, take a sunscreen strong enough to give them adequate protection. You may not find one with the right sun protection factor (SPF) abroad.

- Pack a power point adapter if you need to recharge mobile phones, video cameras or laptops. It may prove difficult to obtain the right connection in some regions.

- You'll need to pack a first-aid kit from a chemists' or good travel shop, or make up your own. It should contain plasters, bandages, tweezers, alcohol wipes, mild pain killers (in their original wrapping) including children's paracetamol if you're travelling with kids, needles for injections, suture sets, scalpel blades, antiseptic cream, insect bite cream, rubber gloves, anti-diarrhoeal tablets such as Imodium and rehydration salts. This last is especially important if you're travelling with children, who can quickly become dangerously dehydrated if they have diarrhoea.

- Disinfectant hand wipes are a boon. In many regions of the world, hygiene is very different from what you expect at home and the surfaces you touch, particularly in toilets, might be very dirty.

- If you are going to an area where malaria is a real risk, it's essential to invest in the right kind of insect repellent. Ask at your nearest travel shop or chemists' for the best kind. A good repellent will also protect against other biting insects.

- Apropos of malaria, it's equally essential to get preventative treatment from your doctor or a traveller's advisory service such as MASTA in the UK (see page 17), and your own new, hole-free mosquito netting. Buy enough malarial prophylaxis to last for at least a month after your trip has finished. That way, if you are delayed at least you'll have enough to get you back home.

- Bring enough of any other essential medical treatments to last the trip.

- Lay in a small supply of high-energy food such as bars or drinks, which are sealed so that they will last the duration of your trip. These are available from any sports or health shop or chemists'. Put it in your day pack and keep it for emergencies only.

■ For travel in remote areas or some developing countries, water sterilising tablets are essential. Chlorine tablets make water quite difficult to drink, but they work. You can try iodine tablets or even hand-held water pumps, which will purify the most brackish water.

■ A shortwave radio will keep you in touch with the BBC World Service – invaluable in emergencies. Camera equipment, and a camcorder with power cables and/or spare batteries, are vital too.

■ If you're embarking on an adventure holiday, pack your qualifications: a dive logbook with the requisite authorisation, climbing qualifications with your club membership, ski lift passes, maps and compass/Global Positioning System (GPS) (see Chapter 13).

■ For purchasing useful security and travel accessories, you can contact the website www.ake.co.uk and follow the leads to shops.

What to put in your hand luggage

■ Passport.

■ Visas.

■ Tickets.

■ Reservation slips.

■ International Driving Licence.

■ Car hire details.

■ Travellers' cheques and cash.

■ Moist wipes.

■ Sunglasses, spectacles or contact lenses.

■ Leisure material, books, tapes, CDs and players, and spare batteries.

■ Maps and guidebooks.

What not to take

Only take with you what you can afford to lose.

- Leave all unnecessary credit cards, permits, letters, or anything with your home address on it.

- Avoid any hoax cards, saying 'Secret Agent' or 'Secret Service'. When you're abroad with one of these, you might find yourself with some explaining to do.

- Leave valuable jewellery at the bank or hidden at home. Even fake jewellery can attract unwanted attention.

- Military equipment – even military books, notebooks or torches – could get you into trouble.

- Offensive literature, be it politically sensitive or pornographic, should never be carried.

- Any defamatory literature about the country you're travelling to, or its political or religious establishment, should not be taken.

- Do not carry suspicious material, surveillance equipment or anything that might make customs officials suspicious. Be aware that in some regions customs officials are not as user-friendly as they are at home.

- Excessive amounts of cash or travellers' cheques are unnecessary.

- Avoid taking drugs or any narcotic substances. The penalties are harsh and young travellers can expect increased scrutiny when passing through foreign customs.

Travel Insurance

Risk is, of course, part of travel, and one of the best ways of dealing with it is to take out travel insurance. Today, businesses take out extensive insurance cover to provide some measure of protection for their employees when they go abroad. Many travellers, however, set off on holiday without giving a thought to the possibility that something will go wrong. This is misguided: travel insurance is an essential part of the cost of your trip.

Insurance can protect you against being stranded abroad when your tour companies or airlines go bust, missed flights, accidents or illness, natural risks such as extreme weather or earthquakes, and of course terrorism. Any of these can disrupt your holiday, but if you have to pay for the consequences or treatment too, they can disrupt your life long afterwards. Having no insurance cover could mean enormous financial burdens: hospital and repatriation costs, additional accommodation and travel charges, the loss of valuable possessions. It really isn't worth the risk.

There is a huge variety of insurance policies to choose from, and you might want to talk with an insurance broker before you decide which one suits you. If you travel frequently it may be wiser (and cheaper) to buy an annual insurance policy. Under this, you can make as many trips as you want and still be covered, as long as you don't travel to areas excluded by the policy. Look around and compare different companies: some will be cheaper than others. Remember that many people take out extra policies only to find that they were already covered. Check your home insurance policy, which might provide basic cover for losses while abroad. If you have homeowner insurance, car insurance or private medical cover, it is worth calling your agents to identify exactly what you are covered for. Check the small print, though, to see whether travel overseas is included. If you have two policies, do not expect two claims; insurance companies will negotiate with each other to ensure that they do not pay out twice for the same incident.

Many of us buy travel insurance from our travel agent. They are not insurance brokers, however, and they may not have a detailed understanding of insurance policies. It is essential that you go prepared when you're buying insurance. Work out your questions beforehand, then go over them with your travel agent. If you aren't happy with the response, call your insurance agent. They can tailor policies to meet your specific needs.

If you're about to embark on buying travel insurance, note the following.

- Consider buying travel insurance even before you book your holiday. You can request cancellation cover; this will provide protection in case you have to cancel your travel plans due to ill health, if you lose your job or for many other reasons. However, you need to check closely to see what you would be covered for.

- Insurance companies and travel agents may offer policies for those leaving their home country for longer periods, such as people who leave Britain in the winter for warmer climates. These can provide protection against your home being burgled while you are away. However, some insurers will stipulate (in the small print) that the cover is only applicable to homes left unoccupied for less than one month, unless prearranged with your insurer. If you're planning a long journey, read the small print and ask your insurance agent for the details.

- Medical and auto insurance policies may also provide some coverage. Some credit card issuers offer life insurance on flights. Remember that double coverage doesn't bring double protection. Insurers usually have a provision in their policies to prevent duplication of payment for the same coverage and communicate with each other to pinpoint the extent of their individual obligation to you.

- Medical cover is vital. Even a minor medical procedure overseas can be a major problem: there may be poor medical facilities, the treatment itself may be inadequate, and it can be horrendously expensive. A short-term stay at a hospital overseas may leave you with a bill for many thousands. When you take out emergency medical cover you will have to declare any pre-existing medical condition. If you do not, your policy may not pay out. And if you are considering travelling abroad to receive medical treatment, it is unlikely that you will get insurance cover. Some insurers require you to obtain a doctor's certificate authorising you to travel before issuing a policy. If you have to pay for any treatment or medication you must ensure that you retain the receipt as proof when you make a claim. Some insurance companies will waive the medical excess if you are carrying an E111 form (see page 43). If you obtain an insurance policy before travelling you must ensure that you take it or a copy of it with you, in addition to the contact details and instructions.

■ You can buy insurance that covers you in case you have a medical emergency that requires you to be evacuated. However you must look at the small print; see if the policy means an evacuation only to the nearest medical facility or all the way home. In an emergency, you would probably prefer to be closer to home.

■ If you are involved in an accident that demands medical attention while abroad, inform your insurers immediately. The extent of your injuries will dictate the sum paid out. In addition to the policy and contact details, make sure the insurers or their agents have a 24-hour help line. This is essential when trying to deal with local issues relating to insurance and claims. Some companies will issue an accident notice printed in different languages to you. This allows you to communicate with others without admitting liability, for example in the case of a road traffic accident.

■ If someone else is injured or killed as a consequence of your actions, or you have damaged the property of someone while overseas (say in a road traffic accident), you will have to inform your insurance company immediately. If you have taken out personal liability cover, you will be protected if the other party tries to sue you.

■ If you are involved in an incident and find yourself needing a lawyer while abroad, you could be in for a hefty bill. You can obtain policies that will cover you for any legal expenses you may incur as a result of an accident.

■ With the recent dramatic expansion in the travel industry, delays and cancellations are now commonplace. It is possible to obtain cover for travel disruption. For example, if your flight is delayed or cancelled, you may have to pay for additional accommodation and transport. If you have obtained cover for this you will be able to claim. However, you must check on the specific details; some policies stipulate that your flight must be delayed for a specified time before you are covered. If you miss a flight that departs on time you may be compensated, but you will need a convincing explanation.

- Most policies provide cover against the loss of personal possessions, but you are expected to show the same diligence in protecting them that you do at home. If you leave your camera or other valuable items lying around and they are stolen, you can hardly expect the insurers to compensate you. If you are travelling with particularly valuable items you can obtain insurance against them being damaged. However, you will be expected to name the expensive items before travelling. If you lose a valuable possession you must inform your insurance company within 24 hours. You may need a local police report to support your claim.

- You may be able to claim against your policy if your passport is lost or stolen. Getting a new passport or travel document may be a time-consuming process, and you may find yourself staying on at your destination during it, which adds on accommodation and possibly further travel costs. Ensure your policy covers you for this.

- Luggage does sometimes go missing. Most of it turns up, hopefully on the next flight, but if it's lost you may go some time without your luggage. You can obtain cover enabling you to buy replacement items of clothing to last until your luggage catches up with you. Keep the receipts for everything that you buy in order to support your claims.

- If you lose your luggage permanently or damage your equipment or clothing, you will be covered by your policy as long as you have followed the instructions. Usually a maximum sum is stipulated, and this may actually be less than the cost of replacing them. Check this. If you are carrying valuable items, you must inform your insurers. They increase the premium for items that are more expensive to replace.

- If you lose cash and or travellers' cheques you may be covered, but only for a certain amount. Find out from your insurers what the limit is for cash and travellers' cheques. Inform your insurers immediately; a police report may also be required to support your claim.

- If you are intending to participate in any adventurous activities, tell your insurers. Bungee jumping, rock climbing or abseiling, parachuting or scuba diving are popular, but kill or injure tourists every year, many without insurance. Many activity operators will have liability insurance so that you will be able to sue them if you are injured. However, participants usually sign a disclaimer before they are allowed to partake.

- Winter skiing in Europe demands a specific insurance policy. The high chances of injury make these policies rather expensive, as medical costs can be very high and just getting you from the point of the incident to a local medical facility can be very pricey. Someone injured high on a ski slope may require airlifting to the nearest hospital, for instance. If you cause an accident on a ski slope, you may be sued by the others involved. With policies designed for winter sports you will be asked your level of expertise, and if you are injured in an area you should not be in, you may not be covered. If you are new to it all, stick to areas designated for novice skiers.

- Motoring insurance is widely available. There are many organisations such as the RAC and the AA, which can advise on policies. While your normal vehicle insurance will be sufficient for driving at home and in other specified countries, generally it will not provide sufficient protection if you are involved in an accident. You will have to enquire whether you are covered for incidents such as theft abroad, fire and vehicle damage and third party insurance. Many vehicle insurance policies will not cover driving abroad.

- For almost all travel insurance claims you will be required to pay an excess – the first £50 to £100 of any claim you make. If you are insuring particularly expensive items, the excess may be much more. Check the small print to identify the excess amount.

- There are other areas where you should be vigilant when arranging your policy. If you sustain an injury and have been found to be drinking or using drugs, your insurers will in all probability not pay out.

- If you are heading to an area where there is instability or conflict, you may not be covered for injuries related to this. In some areas, the risk of terrorism is high. Many policies will exclude acts of terrorism in specific countries. You must look at the small print. In today's climate of heightened security, when you head off to high-risk destinations you will be expected to declare which countries and regions you will be travelling in, and you may have to pay a higher premium.

- Insurance cover for specialised risks such as kidnapping is available. This is not automatically included in your normal travel policy, and you may have to purchase a specific policy for that risk. In countries such as Colombia, Mexico or the Philippines, the premium for this type of cover may be high. There may even be regions of the world where the situation is such that insurers will refuse to cover those travelling to that region.

- Women who are pregnant must ensure that they have adequate insurance cover while overseas. If a woman has difficulties during pregnancy which demand hospitalisation or even repatriation, they may find that they are not covered by the policy.

- If you claim for an article that is lost or damaged while you are overseas, insurers may link this with your household insurance policy, resulting in you losing your no claims bonus. Look at the small print and weigh up the advantages or disadvantages of making a claim against your insurance company. If you are able to absorb the cost of the loss without too much discomfort, you may consider doing this. By losing your no claims bonus you may incur a much greater loss.

The E111

If you are a citizen of a European Union country and will be travelling within it or the European Economic Area, fill out an E111 form and take it with you. The E111 entitles you to free medical treatment while you are in an EU country. The forms are available free from post offices in Britain, are easy to complete and all you need bring with you is a proof of identity (such as your passport) and your national insurance number. You may not be eligible to use this service if you are resident in an EU country but are not an EU national.

It is a good idea to check before you set off to ensure that the country you are visiting has signed up to the protocol ensuring that all EU citizens are entitled to free medical treatment regardless of which EU country they are in. Unfortunately, this ruling is interpreted differently in different areas of the EU. In some countries you will be required to pay for the treatment, while in others you will be offered treatment at a reduced cost or completely free of charge. If you're visiting France or Germany you can expect a good response when you present an E111, but visitors to Spain have found themselves paying for a service which is legally free.

You may be asked to submit proof of residence and if you're British, be required to show your NHS medical card – so you must take these documents with you, in addition to your E111.

Consider the following points about the E111.

▪ Many travellers rely totally on the E111 when they travel to Europe instead of buying an insurance policy. The E111 will cover you for urgent medical assistance for illness or accident, and pregnant women should also be provided with treatment. You should also be given access to medication and hospitalisation if required. You will be provided with free dental treatment, but only to relieve pain. For medical treatment judged not to be urgent, and which can be delayed until you return to your country of origin, you will not be covered by the E111.

▪ You are not allowed to travel to other parts of the EU specifically for medical treatment. To do this you must have an E112 form, which has to be authorised by your local medical authority.

▪ Failure to produce an E111 or proof of identity will result in your having to pay the full cost of medical treatment. You will be able to recoup your expenses when you return home, but you will need to produce all of your receipts in order to support your claim.

■ The E111 form will only cover you for the actual medical treatment. If you incur additional expenses for, say, accommodation or travel, missing your flight or losing your luggage, you will need a travel insurance policy – or you'll end up paying out of your own pocket.

■ If you have an E111, are injured while travelling in the EU, and have to pay for the treatment, you may face reams of red tape trying to recoup your money. It is essential to get receipts for everything that you pay for while you are abroad to support your claim.

■ Some countries not in the EU have an agreement to treat EU nationals. These include Australia, Barbados, Malta and Russia. EU applicant states such as Poland and the Czech Republic also have this agreement. Take an E111 with you when you travel to these countries.

■ Photocopy your E111 and take both this and the original document, carrying them in separate places. Some countries require this, and in some your photocopy may be retained by the hospital authorities. E111s are supposed to be permanent, that is to say once you have one you should not need a new one. However in some countries doctors have demanded E111 forms issued in the year of travel.

■ Children under 16 will be expected to be included on their parents' E111. It is essential that children are provided with one of these forms if they are going on an organised trip, say for example a school or club field trip overseas.

Medical Repatriation

When you come down with a serious illness or suffer a bad injury, travel insurance comes into its own. But there are some policies that only cover your treatment and medication. If you're abroad and suffer the kind of injury that will prevent your travelling in a commercial aircraft, you may be in for a long stay. If you become injured in a remote area, the likelihood of your receiving adequate medical attention is not good. In cases like these, the only solution may be an emergency medical repatriation.

If you are not covered for this, you or your family may have some stark choices to make. Trying to charter an aircraft to facilitate the evacuation is prohibitively expensive for most people. There are organisations, however, which will arrange this service for a relatively acceptable fee. Many companies provide this service. International SOS, one of the most notable, has call centres located all over the world. It's a good idea to check on the Web for an emergency repatriation service near your home.

If you want to get this kind of cover, consider the following points.

- A dedicated air ambulance may not be needed if your injuries allow. In that case, commercial airlines will be used and an emergency medical team will be dispatched to escort you home.

- There are many emergency repatriation services, and you must ensure that the one you choose has a global reach, and that they are able to get to your destination with the minimum of delay. Enquire what their reaction time is and how long it will take them to bring a casualty back home. Ensure that you receive a card detailing the emergency telephone response number and the instructions on how to activate the emergency recovery operation.

- Whether you travel in groups or alone, you will be able to obtain this service. Most companies will accept clients whether they're taking a short break or are long-term visitors to a country. If you are travelling with someone who has a recurring health problem or if you are visiting a particularly high-risk environment, consider this service.

- Some people who require specialist medical treatment may need the services of an emergency evacuation team. These teams are highly trained and have a detailed knowledge of how travelling in a pressurised aircraft flying at 30,000 feet will affect a casualty. This combination of factors can present problems for most medical staff, as conditions can change quickly.

- Some emergency repatriation services will also liaise with the local medical staff at your destination and ascertain the best possible treatment for you, and any preparations needed before you are moved.

- Many emergency repatriation organisations will ensure that you receive the best possible treatment at the best available hospital. They will conduct surveys of the local medical facilities to discover their conditions and capacities.

- Most evacuation services will have the necessary experience in dealing with the bureaucratic procedures involved. These procedures can cause interminable delays if you do not know what you are doing. There will be paperwork to fill in and there may be rigorous guidelines for removing a person from hospital.

- Many evacuation services will provide replacement medication if your supplies are lost or stolen, and will also coordinate your treatment at the local hospital and act as a liaison between you and your family or employers.

- They may also provide for money to be transferred from your home to your destination, and arrange for the services of an interpreter. If you have lost your possessions or your travel documents (say, in a fire), many of these organisations will help you get new documentation. Many will also arrange for the provision of legal assistance if, for example, you were involved in a road accident.

- Many also arrange for those travelling with you to be repatriated, either along with you or, if you have to remain in hospital, on their own.

- If you do sign up with one of these organisations, always carry the emergency instruction card with you. If you are travelling with children ensure that they are familiar with the procedures for activating the emergency evacuation procedures.

- In an emergency, inform your emergency evacuation provider if possible, or have someone else inform them. Then go to the nearest medical facility. A medical professional will be available by telephone to assist you, arrange treatment and inform your family, and if you are unable to receive adequate treatment, they will evacuate you back to your home country.

- There are some organisations that will only recover you from the nearest safe airport. This means that you will have to get yourself from the area where you were injured to the airport. This may be achievable in most holiday destinations, but in volatile regions this may pose more of a problem. You must look into this before you sign up.

2

Safe Air Travel

Commercial Air Travel

It's not an exaggeration to say that since the outrage of 11 September 2001, air travel has never been safer. Airlines have rushed to tighten up security and introduced many new regulations. Yet inevitably, the incident has left many feeling that flying is an even riskier proposition than ever.

Commercial air travel is a phenomenon that won't go away, however. Our collective wanderlust and the globalisation of business mean we need to get to places fast, and a plane is the way to do it. Three million people take to the skies every day, and in 1998 an estimated 1.3 billion people flew on almost 20 million commercial flights – with only 10 fatal accidents. It has been estimated, in fact, that there are more people killed and injured on British roads in any four-month period than have been killed by commercial aviation accidents during the last 60 years.

If you fly from a European or North American airport, chances are the aircraft and airline will be subject to the most stringent of safety standards. The country you're travelling to may, however, have less stringent checks and regulations, particularly if it's in an unstable region. In areas like these, normal standards of maintenance and control may be difficult to implement. The Flight Safety Foundation has found, for instance, that China accounts for 16 per cent of all flights, but 70 per cent of all accidents – and that Africa has 21 fatal accidents for every 100,000 flights, whereas North America has only two.

Yet when one considers the actual volume of people in the sky on any day, the chances of dying on a commercial flight are shrinking each year. Air travel is getting safer. The key for travellers is gauging how safe an airline, or indeed an aircraft, is. An amazing array of factors is involved in aviation safety – aircraft maintenance, weather conditions, operating conditions such as mountainous terrain, pilot training and experience, and of course airport security. It's very hard to generalise given all these variables, but you will be safer flying on an aircraft operated by a major international airline company than, say, a smaller company in a developing country. In some regions, smaller aircraft have to fly lower because of their shorter range, and are not subject to the stringent safety procedures of the main aviation companies. One American study estimated that the accident rate for smaller aircraft was around 11 accidents per 100,000 hours flying, as opposed to 0.8 for commercial jet aircraft.

The one major glitch lies in the sheer numbers of people who want and need to fly. The dramatic surge in air travel has subjected the aviation industry to almost intolerable stresses, and delays in overcrowded and uncomfortable airport departure terminals are getting more common. In 2001, some 200 million people flew from airports in Britain alone, and that's slated to grow to around 237 million within the next five years. The organisation involved in getting all these people to their destinations on time is mind-blowing. The intricate choreography taking place at 30,000 feet, as air traffic controllers guide aircraft safely to their destinations, is becoming increasingly difficult to orchestrate as volume increases. So when selecting your airline, choose one with a good punctuality record. If they can manage to fly on time among all the other chaos, they must be doing something right.

The next section will look at how countries measure up in the air safety stakes.

Airline Safety

As I've said, there are so many factors involved in aviation safety that it's very hard to determine which airlines to avoid. The statistics in the tables below do, however, provide a good overview of safety by country, and can help you choose.

Number of air accidents by country, 2000 and 2001

Country Where Accident Happened	2000	2001
Angola	3	1
Bahamas	0	1
Bahrain	1	0
Canada	2	1
China	1	0
Colombia	1	2
Congo	1	2
Costa Rica	1	0
Estonia	0	1
France	3	1
Gabon	1	0
Ghana	1	0
Guatemala	1	1
India	1	0
Indonesia	0	2
Iran	1	0
Italy	0	1
Ivory Coast	1	0
Laos	1	0

table continues ▶

Country Where Accident Happened	2000	2001	
Libya	1	0	
Mexico	1	1	
Nepal	1	0	
Nigeria	1	1	
Panama	1	0	
Papua New Guinea	1	0	
Philippines	1	0	
Russia	1	4	
Sri Lanka	0	1	
Surinam	0	1	
Switzerland	1	1	
Taiwan	0	1	
Thailand	1	0	
UK	1	0	
US	7	7	(including 11/9/01 events)
Venezuela	2	0	

Fatal air accidents, by airline

Europe

Airline	Year of last fatal event	Total number of accidents to date
Aer Lingus/Commuter	No events to date	0
Air France/Air France Europe	2000	7
Airlines of former USSR	2001	19
Alitalia	1990	3
Austrian Airlines	No events to date	0
Braathens	1972	1
British Airways	1985	2
British Midland Airways	1989	1
Finnair	No events to date	0
Iberia	1985	4
Icelandair	No events to date	0

Airline	Year of last fatal event	Total number of accidents to date
Lufthansa/Condor	1993	3
KLM/City Hopper	1994	3
Olympic Airways	1989	3
Sabena	No events to date	0
SAS	No events to date	0
Swissair/Crossair	2000	4
TAP Air Portugal	1977	1
Turk Hava Yollari	1994	8
Virgin Atlantic	No events to date	0

United States and Canada

Airline	Year of Last Fatal Event	Total Number of Accidents to Date
Air Canada	1983	3
AirTran/Value Jet	1996	1
Alaska Airlines/Horizon Air	2000	3
Aloha Airlines/Aloha Islandair	1989	1
American West Airlines	No events to date	0
American Airlines/Eagle	1999, then 2001	13 (2 in 11/9/01 attacks)
American Transair	No events to date	0
Canadian Airlines	No events to date	0
Continental Airlines/Express	1997	5
Delta Airlines/Connection	1997	6
Hawaiian Airlines	No events to date	0
Jetblue Airlines	No events to date	0
Midway Airlines	No events to date	0
Midwest Express	1985	1
Northwest Airlines/Airline	1993	4
Southwest Airlines	No events to date	0
Tower Air	No events to date	0
TWA (Trans World Airlines)	1996	6
United Airlines/ Express	1997, then 2001	11 (2 in 11/9/01 attacks)
US Airways/USAir Express	1994	8

Latin America and the Caribbean

Airline	Year of Last Fatal Event	Total Number of Accidents to Date
Aerolineas Argentinas	1992	2
Aeromexico	1986	4
Aeroperu	1996	2
Air Jamaica	No events to date	0
Allegro Airlines	No events to date	0
Austral Lineas Aereas	1997	4
Avianca	1990	4
BWIA West Indian Airways	No events to date	0
Cubana	1992 (2 accidents)	8
LAN Chile	1991	2
Mexicana	1986	1
TACA	No events to date	0
TAESA	1999	1
Transbrazil	1980	2
TAM	1997	5
VASP	1986	6
Varig	1989	3

Africa and the Middle East

Airline	Year of Last Fatal Event	Total Number of Accidents to Date
Air Afrique	1987	1
Air Zimbabwe	1979	2
Egypt Air/Air Sinai	1999	6
El Al	No events to date	0
Emirates	No events to date	0
Ethiopian Airlines	1996	2
Gulf Air	2000	2
Iran Air	1988	2
Kenya Airways	2000	1
Kuwait Airways	No events to date	0
Nigeria Airways	1995	3

Airline	Year of Last Fatal Event	Total Number of Accidents to Date
Royal Air Maroc	1994	2
Royal Jordanian	1979	3
Saudi Arabian Airlines	1996	3
South African Airways	1987	1
Tunis Air	1987	1

Asia and Australasia

Airline	Year of Last Fatal Event	Total Number of Accidents to Date
Air China	No events to date	0
Other PRC airlines	1999	14
Air India	1985	3
Air New Zealand	1979	1
All Nippon Airways	1971	1
Ansett Australia	No events to date	0
Ansett New Zealand	1995	1
Asiana Airlines	1993	1
Cathay Pacific	1972	1
China Airlines (Taiwan)	1999	9
EVA Air	No events to date	0
Garuda Indonesian Airlines	1997	8
Indian Airlines	1999	12
Japan Airlines	1985	5
Japan Air System	No events to date	0
Korean Air	1997	7
Malaysian Airlines	1995	2
Pakistan International	1992	7
Philippines Airlines	1994	8
Qantas	No events to date	0
Singapore/Silk Air	2000	2
Thai Airways Company	1987	3
Thai Airways International	1998	2

Aviation Terrorism

For the terrorist, aeroplanes are an irresistible temptation: the high profile of air travel, and the media frenzy that follows every major incident, means planes will remain a favourite target. The extraordinary events of 11 September 2001 underline this with a vengeance. Airlines have, as I've said, rushed to bring in measures designed to foil similar attacks, and this has made air travel a very safe option.

That said, absolute security is impossible. Just as airlines analyse terrorist incidents and learn from them, terrorists themselves study attacks and try to think of new ways to exploit the weaknesses of the aviation industry. One thing is certain – this isn't the last terrorist attempt on an airliner.

Studies of air terrorism between the 1940s and the 1990s have found that there had been an astounding 1420 attacks against aircraft, 250 against airports and 500 against airline offices. So it was hardly a new problem. The only difference was that up until September 2001, the methods of attack remained constant. Hijacking was overwhelmingly the most common, accounting for 90 per cent of the incidents and causing a fifth of total fatalities. Most of those people killed died in crashes triggered by the attack, others by the hijackers, or in gun battles between the terrorists and security forces. Between the 1960s and the 1990s, some 2700 people died in such attacks.

Most hijackings before 2001 aimed at gaining some direct advantage over the authorities of a country. But since the World Trade Center atrocity, every air terrorist incident is now treated as a potential suicide bombing. As a result, governments all over the world will be more willing to order the destruction of hijacked aircraft in order to prevent an even bigger calamity. So crew and passengers now face an extra risk in the event of terrorist attack.

Hijacking is only part of the story, however. In the same 50-year study it was found that there have been about 90 bomb attacks against airports, and 20 armed attacks. And we could see more: with security focusing on the planes, terrorists may switch their attention to the airports themselves. Airport security is key, in fact, in preventing terrorism, a fact that came to the fore after 11 September.

All this leaves airlines big players in the war against terror. And they face an enormous challenge. Even with highly visible security measures such as fences, armed security guards, explosive detection devices and luggage X-ray machines, terrorists can slip through the net because essential problems remain. One is that airports are a hive of activity and it is difficult to monitor everyone in them. Then, too, many of the world's most desirable tourist destinations are places where security is a luxury, and their airports are the Achilles' heel of the international air network. In fact, in many locations there is no airport as we know it. On arrival at the grandiosely named Bossasso International Airport in northern Somalia, we landed on a clear patch of desert, and entered a passport office that was little more than an infested tin hut. What kind of obstacle would that present to a determined terrorist?

Airports in other unstable regions can be very heavily patrolled, but still be highly vulnerable because of the ferocity of the attacks they're subjected to. Bandranaika Airport in Colombo, Sri Lanka, is a case in point. In July 2001, around 50 British travellers were terrorised as they were caught up in the Tamil Tiger suicide assault. It was down to luck that many were not killed or injured during the attack. Families, some with small children, had to run for their lives in a hail of mortar bombs and machine-gun fire. Thirteen aircraft were destroyed. Many people later complained that no one came to their assistance and they had to get themselves out of trouble.

So what can be done? One of the most effective security measures may be the vetting of anyone applying at flight schools to acquire the skills needed to fly a large wide-bodied aircraft. Many airlines have fitted impenetrable doors to the cockpits of aircraft to prevent anyone other than crew from entering. Security professionals have been recruited by some airlines as sky marshals. And some airlines encourage passengers to take a proactive role in the event of a hijack. A heartening example of this happened in Christmas 2001, when passengers and crew on a US-bound flight overpowered a British terrorist belonging to the Al Qaida network as he tried to light an explosive charge built into his shoe. To configure a high explosive charge that would activate without a detonator – which would surely have been picked up at airport security screening – shows that these people know what they are doing. It's a problem that is unlikely to go away any time soon, so we need to be prepared. Find out how in the next section. Pointers on what to do in case of hijacking are on page 69.

Airport Security

It is essential that you consider the following points to reduce any chance of becoming involved in an incident at an airport.

▪ Allow enough time for check-in procedures when you're leaving for the airport you're departing from. Most airlines specify that you arrive two hours prior to departure. However, during peak travel times you'll have to allow for delays. And if you are travelling in a group, allow more time. Trying to usher a family group or even a group of gap-year students through an airport check-in generally takes more time than travelling alone.

▪ Because of the events of September 2001, check-in can be extremely slow. Before a recent visit to Pakistan I was searched five times and had my hand luggage checked four times. These are necessary precautions, but you need to be aware of growing tension if the flight is delayed. At such times airports can become pressure cookers full of irate travellers. Avoid any altercations, especially during hot weather. Steer well clear of people who have had too much alcohol. The combination of excess drink and flight delays is particularly dangerous.

▪ Arrange for a flight early in the day. The earlier you fly, the less chance of encountering delays. Any delay early in the day has a knock-on effect for the entire day's schedule.

▪ Before travelling to the airport, remember to take the necessary documentation (see Chapter 1, page 30). If travelling in a group, it is better to have a nominated leader who keeps all the documents. I saw a group of students trying to check in on to a flight from Vienna to London. One of the group had forgotten her passport and had to be turned away. Not only did she spoil her own holiday, her best friend elected not to go without her.

- After check-in, go directly to your departure gate. The secure area is between immigration and the departure gate. In times of heightened tension, it may be better to avoid all shops and cafés outside of this area.

- Maintain a close watch on your baggage while you're in the airport (see Chapter 1, page 23). Putting illegal articles such as narcotic substances in the baggage of some unsuspecting individual is a common crime. The criminals' intention is for their victim to transport the stuff and unwittingly smuggle it through customs at the other side, after which it will be retrieved. If you are caught, you will be held accountable. Never carry luggage for anyone else, even your best friend. If something comes up and you have no alternative but to do so, say you are carrying items for someone else when you reach the check-in desk.

- If you see unattended luggage or packages, stay well away from them – they could contain explosive material. By the same token, if you leave your own baggage unattended, you should expect that it will be removed, forced open, or even destroyed in a controlled explosion. Stay away from dustbins; explosive devices can be easily concealed in them. You cannot find dustbins in any British train stations or airports for this very reason.

- As we've seen, airlines are the frontline in the war against terrorism, and airport security is a serious business. When you're at the airport do not be tempted to start joking that you've got bombs or firearms in your luggage. You will be taken seriously and arrested, and then cause massive disruption to other travellers, as officials will have to unload your baggage. If you co-operate with airport staff, there will be a minimum of disruption.

- If you are travelling with children, do not allow them to wander around. Some international airports are magnets to criminals.

- Do not assume that everyone dressed as an airport porter actually works there. It is easy to acquire fake identification. Bogus porters can make off with your luggage, given the opportunity. Be especially wary when outside the airport; there can be many skulking opportunists waiting to prey on the unwary traveller.

- Due to bomb threats, some airport security procedures may mean that suspect vehicles will be destroyed by a controlled explosion. Ensure that you do not illegally park your vehicle. At the least your car may be towed away or clamped. Also ensure that on returning from your journey you have sufficient funds to pay for the parking fees. If not, they may impound your vehicle.

- Many cars are stolen from airport car parks, so ensure that you have locked yours and fully done up your windows. It has been suggested that approximately 50 per cent of all stolen vehicles were left unlocked. Take your keys with you: it has been estimated that nearly 20 per cent of all vehicles stolen had been left with the keys still in them. Never conceal a spare set of keys in or near your car – extra keys can easily be found. If there is a space near the attendant, park there. This will deter any inquisitive would-be thieves.

- Try to avoid flights with stopovers in unstable areas. Such flights may be cheaper, but you will also be more vulnerable to terrorists and criminal gangs. Passengers from the British Airways flight that stopped at Kuwait airport while Iraqi forces were attacking that country were detained and held as human shields for many months before release.

- Listen to security announcements at airports. If you are required to evacuate, the message will be broadcast over the airport's public address system. Ensure that you know where you are in the airport, and identify the emergency exit route. If you are travelling with a group, keep the group together.

- Treat immigration and customs officials with respect. Sometimes this is hard work, but remember that in today's climate it is all too easy to get yourself in trouble. There are countless examples of officious airport employees making travellers' lives a misery. The idea is to be courteous and patient.

- In some regions it is routine to pay bribes to customs and immigration officials. There have been cases of Britons being arrested and spending long periods in prison after being set up with bogus drug offences – and all because they have failed to pay a small bribe. In this situation you have to ask yourself if it is worth all the trouble. It is not right that you should have to pay up, but the consequences may be worse.

■ Be aware of what you are allowed to import/export from different countries. If in doubt, ask customs officials.

■ When your baggage is checked through an X-ray conveyor belt, always keep an eye on it. There is an increasingly popular scam whereby a team of thieves gets in front of and behind you. As your luggage emerges from the other side of the machine, a criminal picks it up and at the same time places a metal object in the machine. Everything is stopped until the security staff check it out, by which time the crook has made off with your bag.

Seat Selection

Many travellers try to identify which seats, if any, are the safest on an aircraft. But aircraft accidents are unpredictable, and it is difficult to assess which seats give you the greatest chance of survival during an accident. There is no evidence to suggest that any one part of the aircraft is safer during an air accident. By far the greatest danger is that of luggage falling from overhead storage bins.

When reserving your seat, consider the following factors:

■ It's possible that flying on a wide-bodied aircraft could reduce the chances of being involved in a terrorist incident. The Boeing 747 and other big planes can only land at specific airports, and this reduces terrorists' options because they are less likely to hijack a 747. The large number of passengers carried on a wide-bodied craft is also a hindrance to gangs of terrorists because they would have to have a lot of people on board to control everyone. A partially filled 747, however, would present much less of a challenge to determined terrorists; so be very wary if you're ever in that situation.

■ When selecting your seat, avoid the aisle seat. Many people opt for these in the belief that they will be able to move around at will. However, in this position you become a target for any incident while in flight. Any terrorist incident – or even air-rage incident – is more likely to involve people sitting next to the aisle.

- When you are travelling with a partner, it makes sense to book a window and aisle seat. This will leave the centre seat of a row of three empty. It is normal practice to allocate the centre seats last of all. The chances are that if the flight is not full you might have a bit more room.

- When you reserve your tickets, ask the booking agent for a look at the diagram of the aircraft's layout. You may even search the Internet and check for diagrams of seating in the plane on the airline's website. This will allow you to identify seats next to the emergency exit. These seats normally have extra leg-room that will let you stretch out. However, you will have to book them well in advance.

- If you are seated next to an emergency exit ensure that you fully understand the instructions showing how to open the aircraft door. If you cannot understand the door mechanism in an emergency, not only will you put your own safety in jeopardy, you will also endanger those behind you. Exit doors are heavy and you have to be physically capable of opening them. Be sure you are confident enough to operate the door handle. If you aren't, it may be better to change seats with someone more able to operate the door.

- Regardless of where your seat is located, it is essential that you identify the nearest emergency exit. Note the direction and count the number of rows to the exit so that you will be able to get there in thick smoke or in the dark. If you are travelling with children ensure that they are aware of what action they should take in the event of an emergency.

- Ensure that you check under your seat to confirm that you do have a life preserver. There is no need to get it out; these are routinely checked by most airline companies. If you identify where they are, it will be easier to find in the chaos of an emergency. Although the incidence is very rare, it is also a good idea to check under your seat for a bomb.

■ Most airline companies provide illustrated safety cards to inform travellers how they should use the emergency equipment and how to leave the aircraft in an emergency. Make sure that you read them and understand the instructions. Surveys have suggested that passengers are always too occupied in an emergency to read safety instructions, but you should make the effort to read them. Chances are you will be on your own and will have to know what to do. The cabin crew will be as scared as everyone else.

■ When boarding has been completed and if the aircraft is not full, you may decide to move to a more comfortable seat. However, you have to be quick: most other travellers are thinking the same. I have noticed on many a long-haul flight those lucky individuals stretched out over the centre row of seats, sound asleep. While you disembark at your destination exhausted, they skip off fully refreshed. You have to be bold when making your move; if you hold back, someone else will get there first. It is helpful to be polite and friendly with the cabin crew – they may take a shine to you and help you get a better seat.

Overhead Luggage

Recent studies show that injuries from objects falling from the overhead storage bins in aeroplanes have increased. The Flight Safety Foundation has estimated that some 10,000 injuries result from it each year, often because the bins are too full. If it's a turbulent flight, the bins can suddenly open and release heavy bags onto the heads of passengers sitting below, causing cuts and bruising. Once I watched as a bottle in someone's hand baggage smashed and covered a passenger in foul-smelling liquid.

To reduce your chances of being injured by falling baggage, consider the following points.

- Avoid sitting under the overhead bin. Identify the designated number of the aisle seat and ask for another seat.

- Ensure that you check in all of your heavy objects at luggage check-in. It is wise to carry only light hand luggage.

- If you see anyone else placing excessively heavy articles in the bin above your seat, tell the cabin crew and have them moved.

Air Travel Safety

It might seem astonishing, but an estimated 70 per cent of aircraft accidents are survivable. One American survey showed that 71 per cent of the people who die in a survivable air accident do so after the airliner has completely stopped. Many people waste precious seconds because they are unprepared. Some people are gripped by what is known as behavioural inaction – they freeze in the face of a life-threatening emergency and are unable even to undo their seatbelts. Some panic.

In practice runs of aircraft evacuation procedures, it has been shown that airliners can be evacuated within 90 seconds at night. However, the reality may be very different. If you become trapped behind older travellers or those with disabilities during a real emergency evacuation, they may slow down the entire procedure. The cabin may be filled with smoke, passengers may attempt to leave the aircraft with hand baggage – all sorts of factors can add to the chaos. Many passengers fail to understand the emergency instructions because they did not listen to the pre-flight safety briefings and do not understand the emergency instruction cards.

There has been a rise in 'air rage', incidents where passengers themselves place the aircraft in danger. In December 2000, a British Airways overnight flight from London to Nairobi was in danger of plunging from 35,000 feet when a deranged passenger broke into the cockpit and tried to grab the aircraft controls. The pilot and co-pilot spent many tense minutes wrestling with this lunatic, and it was down to their courage that the flight landed with nothing more than a scare. Many of the people who start these incidents are drunk, but there are other triggers: frustration over long-haul flights, the no-smoking policy of most airlines and overcrowding. Passengers can now be convicted for air rage offences, and the penalties are steep.

To minimise the risks when using commercial airline travel, consider the following.

■ Fly from a major international airport. Smaller regional airports in some countries may have few or no safety standards. If you have decided to fly in a small aircraft, avoid flying in bad weather (check the local forecast) or at night.

■ Avoid airlines that are not permitted to fly into major international airports; this can mean they have a poor safety record. Ask your travel agent before booking to find out where else the proposed company operates.

■ Some countries allow passengers to travel on military flights. Be cautious, especially in areas of active conflict or where there is a terrorist threat.

■ Pay attention to the pre-flight briefings by cabin crew, and remember to familiarise yourself with the locations of all the emergency exits.

■ In the unlikely event that you have to evacuate the aircraft, leave your hand baggage behind. Carry all your absolute essentials in a money-belt or holster carrier, and wear it at all times.

■ Wear your seatbelt when you're sitting down. This will provide you with protection if your aircraft hits a patch of clear air turbulence. This can happen suddenly, and has been responsible for serious injuries and even fatalities during routine flights.

■ In the unlikely event of a terrorist incident or even a fellow passenger making trouble, it's a good idea to stay out of it. If there are terrorists on board, remove any sensitive material you are carrying, such as military, police or civil service identity cards. Terrorist groups will be more interested in government employees.

■ Avoid drinking too much alcohol during your flight. Aircraft cabins are pressurised, and the effects will be felt much more intensely than at sea level. Remember, too, that you're probably dehydrated after the effort of getting to the airport and passing through arduous check-in procedures. The combination of dehydration, altitude and alcohol can have serious consequences. Don't overeat, either, as you can easily become ill in the unnatural conditions of the cabin.

■ If you have been diving on holiday, ensure that you do not fly for at least 24 hours. You will still be in danger from decompression sickness, and need to allow time for any build-up of toxic gases to naturally dissipate. If you are in any doubt, ask at your diving school for more details.

■ Try to wear natural fabrics when flying. Synthetic fabrics are more dangerous in a fire as they tend to melt when exposed to flame. Loose natural fabrics that will allow free circulation of air will also prevent overheating. Long sleeves and long trousers are ideal, as it's best to have your skin covered in the event of a fire. Wear appropriate footwear made from natural materials. High-heeled shoes can damage escape chutes and should be avoided.

■ Aircraft fires are mercifully rare, but smoke from a fire can quickly fill the cabin. And whether you're airborne or grounded, smoke can be fatal as toxic fumes are emitted. Be aware of the safety procedures. Following the route to the nearest exit using the floor markers as guides, and moving very quickly, can improve your chances of getting out. The commercial availability of disposable smoke hoods that keep out toxic fumes via a series of filters will increase your chances during a fire. There is a debate over these, as it takes time to put them on and this will delay getting out of the plane. However, I do know people who carry them on every flight.

■ Decompression can suddenly hit an aircraft, and the effects can come on in as little as a few seconds. In this case, you must put on your oxygen mask as quickly as possible, and activate the flow of oxygen. You'll need to put on your own mask first, then help others. This is where the pre-flight briefing by the cabin crew comes into its own. The cabin crew themselves will be unable to help as they will be putting on their own masks.

■ Aircraft have ended up in the sea, for instance when the pilot over or underestimated the distances to the runway. In this situation it is essential to know where your lifejacket is and how and when you should use it. Identify where the life-rafts are and how they are inflated. Other buoyancy aids, such as seat flotation cushions or empty, capped water bottles, may be of value.

Small Aircraft Safety

In some regions, travel by small aircraft is the only way of getting around – for example, when on an aerial safari or if you are travelling to remote wilderness areas. Small aircraft normally operate out of very basic airfields, and themselves carry specific risks.

The following guidelines show how to avoid them.

- Keep out of the areas in the airfield set aside for taxiing, and never approach aircraft on foot or in a vehicle without first checking with the airfield authorities. You should avoid running in the vicinity of a moving aircraft.

- When you are in the airfield, stay away from aircraft, propellers, rotor blades and jet engines. The minimum safety distance from propellers is around 5 metres; from the front of jet engines, around 25 metres; and from the rear of jet engines, around 50 metres. Airfield noise can confuse your judgement, especially when more than one aircraft is moving. Pilots of taxiing aircraft cannot always see the ground around the plane, and the presence of other aircraft and general commotion may mean that the pilot is not aware of your presence.

- Be aware that the noise taxiing aircraft make can actually damage your hearing. It may be advisable to obtain some ear protection from a travel shop.

- Make sure that all loose objects such as baggage, and particularly hand luggage, are secure in the vicinity of aircraft.

- Comply with the airfield's no-smoking policy, especially around aircraft and fuelling equipment, aircraft themselves, and aircraft hangars.

Helicopter Safety

Helicopters are an increasingly popular method of transport. Organised aerial sightseeing tour companies regularly use commercial helicopters to ferry tourists around. Business executives are routinely shuttled to and from business meetings by helicopter. However, helicopters present a great danger if you do not treat them with respect – particularly the rotor area. The high-pitched engine noise can conceal the noise from the tail rotor.

The following are guidelines for staying safe near helicopter landing pads.

■ Never enter the landing pad area without first obtaining permission from the appropriate authorities.

■ Never approach a helicopter from the rear. The pilot is unable to see you and the tail rotor is very dangerous. When moving around a helicopter, always move to the front where the pilot can see you. On no account duck under the tail boom.

■ Avoid moving towards a helicopter down a slope or exiting a helicopter and walking up a slope. You could walk into a rotor blade.

■ Ensure that when you are approaching a helicopter you maintain eye contact with the pilot, and if the pilot signals, that you obey his instructions.

■ If the rotors are turning, only approach the helicopter when signalled to do so by the pilot. As you approach, ensure that you duck your head down as the rotor blades can sag. If the helicopter is on uneven ground there is a greater danger of being hit by a rotor, and you must ensure that you have enough headroom before you move closer. If in doubt, don't move.

■ Do not get on or off the helicopter until told to do so by the captain. Ensure that all your luggage and equipment taken on board a helicopter are properly secure.

■ Helicopter rotor wash will blow ground debris such as dirt, sand and vegetation all over the place. The landing area should be kept clear of debris. However, on a holiday excursion you may have to land on unprepared landing points. Shield your eyes as the helicopter comes in to land, and make sure all your baggage is secure and that you've taken off all loose items such as hats.

- Ensure that you keep any long items of luggage such as tripods parallel to the ground to keep them out of the rotors.

- Your seatbelt should be fastened throughout your journey, as helicopters are particularly vulnerable in any bad weather conditions. Check beforehand that the weather is actually suitable for helicopter travel. If you are crossing a body of water, wear a life preserver.

- Ensure that you are able to communicate with the pilot throughout the flight. Pay attention to the pilot's safety brief, and be aware of how to open the doors in case of an emergency.

Aircraft Hijacking and Survival Strategies

Hijacking aircraft is extremely rare, but as we've seen, it's one of the optimal ways for terrorists to make a statement and get noticed. The threat is taken very seriously by the aviation industry. And of course, after the horrors of September 2001, it is probably one of the most feared terrorist actions.

It must be remembered that those events were the only suicide hijackings in history. It is difficult to predict whether these constituted a one-off, or the start of a terrifying trend. In any case, hijacking *per se* is unlikely to go away just yet.

A pattern to hijackings has emerged over the last few decades. After the initial seizure of the aircraft, the terrorists violently subdue passengers and crew, generating fear by making lot of noise and brandishing weapons. Alternatively, the terrorists go to the flight deck and tell the pilot that the aircraft has been hijacked. The pilot will make an announcement telling the passengers this – their first indication that anything is going on. Whatever the case, the terrorists themselves are at risk in this situation and their behaviour will be irrational and volatile, rapidly exploding into violence.

There are a number of steps you can take to avoid becoming a victim.

- Rumours of many hundreds of potential suicide bombers waiting to strike at American or European airlines have thankfully not materialised – so far. However, these people are dangerous and will strike again. If you are in an aircraft that is being hijacked by suicidal fanatics, you face two threats: one from them, and one from governments in whose airspace you're flying who might sanction a military strike against your plane. A good indicator that the terrorists are of this type is if they are yelling religious slogans. If you believe that there is no other course of action than to act, you must act quickly. Try to generate support for your actions from other passengers and crew. Remember that if your flight originated in an American or a European airport, the terrorists may well have no actual weapons like guns (the 11 September hijackers only had box cutter knives). You may decide to confront the terrorists directly. The passengers and crew on the American Airlines flight who fought with and prevented a terrorist from detonating the bomb in his shoe saved their own lives.

- If you suspect that the terrorists intend to carry out a conventional hijacking and redirect the aircraft to a different destination, do not attract attention to yourself and stay calm. Panic at this stage will single you out to the terrorists. Encourage those with you to behave calmly too, and keep in mind that most of these incidents result in passengers and crew being released unharmed.

- In a conventional hijacking, do not confront the hijackers. They will be tense, frightened and dangerous. They know that if they are caught they will at least spend a very long time in prison. They will be desperate. The fact that they have taken this course of action means that they are willing to take an enormous risk.

- If instructed to do something by the hijackers, comply, be polite, retain your dignity and avoid becoming involved in an argument, as you will draw attention to yourself.

- Avoid prolonged eye contact with the terrorists. This will be seen by them as aggression and a challenge to their authority. Look down. Only look at them if you are told to do so by them.

■ Avoid divulging too much information about yourself, and be guarded if you work for an official organisation, which is associated with the state.

■ It is probable that your passports will be collected, so you will attract attention if you try to conceal your passport. You may be split into groups based on your nationality or gender. It is a good idea to comply without complaining. Do not try to hide your money or possessions – once more, you need to avoid attracting attention to yourself.

■ You must try to maintain a positive state of mind and not allow panic or other passengers to influence that. Remember: the chances are that this incident will be resolved without your becoming a casualty.

■ These incidents can take some time to resolve. You must prepare yourself mentally for a prolonged ordeal.

■ Avoid trying to make contact with the terrorists even if you are ill or suffering from some discomfort. It may be better to attract the attention of a crew member. However, as the hijack unfolds, you may feel comfortable in speaking to one of the terrorists.

■ Attempt to conduct a basic psychological profile of the terrorists. After some time you will have an idea of who the leaders are. You may find that some are more amenable than others. If so, wait until the most approachable one is around and speak to him. However, be cautious of trying to solicit more favourable treatment.

■ It is normal for the authorities to demand the release of women and children in exchange for food or fuel. If you are travelling with your family the chances are that women, children and the infirm will be released first.

■ Usually these incidents are resolved when the authorities agree to the demands of terrorists by releasing political prisoners, or allowing them to fly to another airport. A military assault will be launched only in the most extreme cases. The hostage release operation from an aircraft is a notoriously difficult and dangerous operation, but can be successful. It depends on many factors, such as which country you end up in, the experience of their military/police at this type of operation and the capability of the terrorists.

■ During a hostage release operation, the first indication that something is happening may be loud explosions, noise, smoke and shouting. The idea is to distract and confuse the terrorists. You should make yourself as small as possible. If possible, get onto the floor and do not look up until the noise has stopped.

■ If you identify any military movement outside the aircraft, you should expect that something is about to happen. Be prepared.

■ In the event of the aircraft catching fire, head to the nearest exit and get out. Remember: the smoke will be toxic and dangerous.

■ The terrorists will initially be confused and scared, and will focus their attention on the attacking force. However, after the initial shock they may turn their attention to the passengers. This is where being calm and co-operative pays off, as those passengers who have been difficult are the most at risk.

■ If you are instructed to leave the aircraft by a military rescue unit, do so as quickly as possible. Avoid sudden movements – which may be taken as a threat – put your hands in the air, and shout that you are a passenger, to avoid being mistaken for a terrorist. Follow the instructions of the police and military once you have left the aircraft.

■ It is normal procedure to treat everyone exiting an aircraft with suspicion. Hijackers may have concealed themselves among the passengers, so you can expect fairly robust handling until your identity has been confirmed.

Air Travel Health

Dehydration is a real hazard when flying. Aircraft cabins have very low humidity, which exacerbates dehydration, so it's vital that you consume plenty of water. Avoid too much alcohol, tea and coffee, as they will increase dehydration.

■ If you suffer from any respiratory illnesses, consult your doctor before you fly. If in doubt, consult your travel agent, who will put you in touch with the airline's medical representative.

■ Industry experts have noted that some flights are exposed to unusually high levels of radiation. Passengers who take five roundtrips on the recently initiated North Pole route between the US and Hong Kong could be exceeding the annual limit for radiation exposure. Frequent flyers between these two routes may consider different routes to reduce exposure.

■ Jet lag can spoil your trip if you find it difficult to adjust to a new time zone. Your body clock can be thrown into confusion as it tries to readjust to functioning at times when you would otherwise be asleep. If you have to attend an important meeting, make your trip a few days in advance so you can become accustomed to the new time schedule.

■ A few days before you depart, try to adjust both your eating and sleeping patterns to match those in your destination country.

■ If you are flying west, avoiding bright light after 6 pm has been found to alleviate jet lag. If you are flying east, avoid bright light until around 10 am.

■ On a recent trip to Hong Kong I heard about melatonin, a natural hormone that helps regulate sleep. Many people are now using it to recover from jet lag. I have tried it, and it has worked for me; however, I must state that this drug is not yet prescribed, and no safety or quality control standards have been established. Some experts recommend taking small doses of around 0.5 milligrams three days before your flight, when it is about 8 am at your destination country. Once there, repeat the dose until a normal sleeping pattern has been established.

■ Deep vein thrombosis (DVT), also known as 'economy class syndrome', has recently been in the news as causing death and injury. British airlines have now been ordered to hand out health warnings for long-haul journeys. Any form of travelling that forces you to remain seated in a single position for more than four hours – be it by car, aeroplane or train – increases the risk of developing blood clots in the legs, according to some experts. In any case, elderly people or those with heart or circulatory conditions who travel on long-haul flights are already at risk from potentially lethal blood clots. It's essential to keep your circulation going while you're flying. Remove footwear or wear comfortable slippers and move your legs up and down regularly, or take walks in the aisles. Inflatable exercise cushions have also proved to reduce the dangers, as does drinking plenty of water (it improves blood flow).

- When you have arrived after a long-haul flight, keep on exercising. This will prevent swelling of the feet and legs, which can be dangerous for older travellers.

- Flying with a cold can cause ear or sinus problems, as the changes in air pressure can cause discomfort, and you may be unable to equalise the pressure in your inner ear with that outside. You can try holding your nose and blowing if you have discomfort. Try to get rid of this complaint before you fly, or if you can't, ask you doctor whether it's safe. Your doctor may advise a course of antibiotics or decongestants before you fly.

- Women more than 36 weeks pregnant should consult their doctors before flying. Ensure that when you book your ticket that you inform them of your condition. Some airlines will refuse to carry passengers more than 36 weeks pregnant. Pregnant women are at greater risk of thrombosis and should remain active during long-haul flights.

- If you suffer from travel sickness consult your doctor, who may prescribe travel sickness pills.

- Babies and young children may find it difficult to clear their ears as the cabin pressures change. It is wise to have a bottle to hand during landing and take-off so they can suck on it. Older youngsters should be given something to eat, which will assist in equalising the pressure.

3

Rail and Underground Safety

Rail Safety

For many travellers, train travel abroad is still a big draw. For some it may satisfy a nostalgia for that golden age when the train was the most advanced mode of transportation. For others, travelling by land may simply look more attractive in the wake of recent air scares.

And it's true that rail travel is relatively low on risk. Statistically, it has been assessed as the safest form of travel on land. Fewer people have been killed on trains since their introduction more than a century and a half ago than on Britain's roads each year. During the last decade, the chances of being killed or seriously injured while travelling by car have been assessed as 15 times greater than travelling by train. The UK have a favourable safety record, as do Japan and most of Western Europe and North America.

But industrialised countries are not immune, and given the nature of the beast – the train itself – this is not surprising. On average, an electric passenger train can weigh up to 400 tonnes and can travel at speeds in excess of 160 kilometres per hour. If a train is running late, it is common for drivers to try to make up the time by travelling too fast, even on dangerous stretches of track. The fact that most passenger trains come without seatbelts means that when the trains come to an abrupt halt or are involved in a collision, injuries are much more likely.

Recently London suffered two tragic train crashes, at Paddington in 2000 and at Southall in 1997. The year 2000 also saw serious train crashes in Norway and Japan. Vandalism on railway tracks is a serious problem in some Western countries, and has caused collisions. There have been demands in Britain that all trains be fitted with the computerised Automatic Train Protection system (APT), which warns of signals ahead and stops the train automatically in case of the driver's error. But in many regions of the world, rail network safety is not even on the agenda.

And obviously, travelling by train to and in countries whose governments do not regulate rail safety involves big risks. Sometimes the experience can be disastrous. In August 1999, some 275 people were killed and 297 injured when an express train in west Bengal collided with a train bound for Delhi. The two trains were overcrowded, carrying more than 2500 passengers, and were travelling at almost 100 kilometres an hour at the moment of impact.

What's the direct cause of such serious accidents in developing countries? The maintenance of trains and rail networks, and human error, are some of the biggest culprits. In Java, a series of crashes have been blamed on signal failure, with the two latest, in September 2001, killing a total of 340 people. There have even been suggestions that in some poorer countries, railways have been sabotaged by placing obstacles on the tracks to draw attention to local protests.

Railway systems are also extremely vulnerable to terrorist attacks. Their very size works against them here: rails can cover many thousands of kilometres, making them practically impossible to protect from dirty work. In London alone there have been many explosions and countless bombs defused, to say nothing about the hoaxes, which cause incalculable disruption. In 2000, a bomb destroyed a crowded passenger train in the southern Pakistani city of Hyderabad, killing more than 10 people and injuring a further 30.

Crime on the railways is a serious problem, too. In certain volatile regions, travellers have been abducted from trains, and countless others have been robbed in 18th-century-style train hold-ups. In the UK, there are 2109 transport police who watch over the entire 16,000 kilometres of track. It's a big job: in 2000/2001 they recorded 70,000 crimes. And these were just the reported ones. It's an insight into what it's like to travel by train in a relatively safe and well-policed country, but of course patterns of criminal activity vary from country to country.

So no matter where you are in the world, it pays to protect yourself before you get on that train. Here's how.

Railway Stations

- Even before you depart from your home base you should research whether the rail systems you'll be using are safe. In many developing countries, freight trains and passenger trains share the same track, and there may be no communications infrastructure to coordinate these movements accurately. In some countries, such as India, accidents happen with alarming frequency. Get in touch with the country's embassy to discover whether there have been recent collisions, terrorist attacks or criminal activity directed against rail travellers.

- Once in the country, try to book your ticket in advance and arrive at the station well before the train is due to depart. In many countries trains can become dangerously overcrowded. If you are unable to buy a ticket before your journey, at least find out how much the ticket costs. That way you can avoid bringing out bundles of notes when you get to the ticket office. Pay for your ticket with local currency if possible. It is also helpful to know enough of the language to get the job done quickly. This gives the impression that you know your way around and may not be an easy target for criminals.

- Be aware that you may be singled out by the ticket seller for 'special treatment'. In many developed countries, you will be expected to pay more than a local would. The extra, of course, goes into the pocket of the official selling the ticket, who is probably woefully underpaid. In some developing countries this practice is endemic. The chances are that you will have to pay or you won't get a ticket, or at best end up at the back of a queue hundreds of people long.

▪ When in railway terminals don't draw attention to yourself by dressing provocatively or behaving in an offensive manner. Never assume that because you are a 'wealthy Westerner' you will receive preferential treatment. Your attitude towards local people will affect their attitude to you.

▪ Don't forget that some of the people you travel among will be members of the area's criminal community. Railway terminals are magnets for criminal gangs and also provide terrorists with ideal locations for launching 'spectaculars'. Be cautious while in railway terminals and spend the minimum amount of time hanging around. Be aware of suspicious packages and luggage. Even dustbins in stations can hide an improvised explosive device, which is the reason they're banned in the UK's railway stations.

▪ While you're in the station, identify the emergency exits and familiarise yourself with the station layout so you can respond to an emergency quickly. Avoid hanging around outside the station: terrorists and criminals have been known to target these areas if they think there is a possibility that they will be caught inside the station. If you are travelling in a group, stay together and keep a close watch on your children.

▪ Many railway platforms get dangerously overcrowded, and people have fallen or been thrown onto the tracks after being jostled by the crowds. Avoid standing at the edge of a crowded platform as the train comes into the station, particularly when it's been raining and the surface is slippery. Wait until the train has stopped before moving towards it.

▪ Standing close to the edge of the platform is risky for another reason: trains not stopping at the station may be travelling so fast the driver would be unable to stop if someone fell onto the track. Pay attention to the instructions on the public address system.

These generally inform of the status of any approaching trains, and provide safety and security information.

- Unless you are a seasoned traveller, don't go it alone. In many countries there will be no privacy in the compartment, and both there and in the station you will have great curiosity value, particularly in poverty-stricken areas. Stay alert to the dangers of theft. If there are at least two in your group, one person can rest while the other keeps an eye on your possessions. Even if you have a cabin to yourselves, don't leave your luggage unattended. Trains slow down and stop to allow other trains to pass or to allow time to change tracks, and even in remote areas this provides an opportunity for thieves to board.

- In some countries, vendors trying to sell their wares immediately surround trains when they stop at a station. Thieves may be lurking among them, so avoid hanging out of the window with handfuls of cash or holding your wallet or purse, and keep your camera firmly in your grasp.

- When you prepare for your trip you should consider what will happen if the train breaks down hundreds of miles from anywhere – not an unknown occurrence in certain countries. You may be there for some time before a recovery vehicle is sent. You should bring enough extra food and water to cope with delays.

- In some developing countries, there are no platforms as such and travellers are allowed to freely wander on or near the railway tracks. Electric rails and oncoming trains make this a highly dangerous option: stick to designated areas such as platforms and recognised pedestrian crossings. Tracks can also become very slippery when wet.

- In many countries, gangs of pickpockets swarm through the station, quickly grabbing what they can before disappearing into the crowds. Do not make it easy for them. Keep your valuables out of sight and your luggage near to you.

- Be aware of any criminal ploys intended to distract you while someone else removes your luggage. Fights between locals, loud arguments, screaming or any other attention-diverting activity may be a ruse.

Rail Travel

Collisions and fires are the big risks of rail travel. If the train you're travelling on is involved in a crash, has to brake hard or leaves the track, you could suffer impact injuries or burns. Diesel trains are most vulnerable to catching fire because their fuel tanks are liable to rupture on impact.

In an emergency like this, instructions from the crew – assuming that the public address system is working – are vital. However, if you do not understand the local language, chances are you will end up following everyone else. The problem with this is that when people become frightened, some will panic and some will be gripped by 'behavioural inaction' – freezing in the face of danger. You must make your own decisions. Speed and awareness are crucial.

The average statistics for rail accident casualties in the UK are shown in the table below.

Fatalities in UK train accidents, 1986–1995	
Type of incident	**Fatalities**
Train accident	7
Entering or alighting from trains	2
Falling off platform and being struck or run over by train	7
Falling from door while train is running	2
Other falls from carriages during running of trains	1
Leaning out of carriage windows	1
Falling on board a train	1
Ascending or descending steps and escalators	2
Struck by non-railway vehicle	1
Total	24

Before you travel by train you should consider the following points:

- On many trains there is a sizable gap between the platform and the train. Many travellers have been injured when boarding or exiting trains, especially when burdened by heavy luggage.

- If a train suddenly brakes, it's all too easy to be injured by flying bags and other loose objects. If overhead racks are stuffed with a lot of heavy luggage, avoid sitting under or near them. If you are in a sleeping carriage, use the ground-level storage space.

- Identify escape routes on the train before your journey starts. Many trains are fitted with automatic sliding doors or standard manual doors that are centrally locked. Ensure that you are familiar with the operation of the door by reading the instructions. But be aware that after a collision, the train's power may fail, making it impossible to open the door normally. You may have to unlock it by breaking a pane of glass above it and pulling the emergency release handle. If the train's doors are narrow and look as if they'd be a difficult option for a crowd of panicked passengers, consider the windows as an alternative route.

- On trains in some countries, a small hammer is kept above the window to break the glass in an emergency. All you need to do is tap the corner of the window to shatter the glass. However, the hammers are sometimes missing, or are not fitted in the first place.

- If the train leaves the rails, it may come to rest at an angle. Reaching up to break a window could become difficult because of awkward angles, and if you do manage to shatter the glass there can be extra danger – either from falling glass, or having to jump down out of a window edged with jagged glass. You may have to completely remove the glass from a window to exit uninjured. It has been suggested that this is one of the main reasons people fail to get out of trains after a collision.

- In any case, you need to move fast. You won't know whether the fuel tanks have been ruptured, creating the risk of fire. Leave your luggage and get out of the train, first making sure that there are no other trains on adjacent tracks. You should go far enough away from the train to remain uninjured if it catches fire. When you have to escape along the tracks, be careful and avoid stepping on any cables. Overhead power cables of up to 25,000 volts may have collapsed onto the ground or tracks.

■ Don't count on assistance from the crew – the driver may have been injured or worse, and other crew will probably also be fighting to get off the train. You should adopt the attitude that no one is going to help you get out. Look after yourself, and when the situation has stabilised you may decide to help others.

■ On an old or poorly maintained train, don't lean against the doors when it is moving. They may open spontaneously.

■ Wait for the train to come to a complete stop before trying to get off. There have been incidents of people getting caught between the platform and the still-moving train.

■ If you are travelling with babies or small children, you should ensure that they are sitting securely in their seats or carry-cots. Do not hold babies in your arms: if the train has to brake, you will be thrown forward and could fall on top of the child.

■ You should never stick your arms or head out of the window of travelling trains. On many railway systems the trains pass close to each other, and there is usually very little room between the train carriages and tunnel walls. In 1997, two British soldiers who had just finished a rigorous jungle-warfare training course in South East Asia decided to take a rest travelling by rail through Thailand. One night they decided to climb onto the roof of the train to experience the thrill of rough riding. Both were killed instantly when the train went into a tunnel.

■ An American study compiled after a train accident in 1996 in New Jersey killed three passengers indicated that you may 'incur a significantly higher risk of serious injury' when you ride in the first carriage of a train that has its engine to the rear. In some countries, this type of train configuration is common. If you intend to travel on one of these trains, try to get a seat at the rear.

- In some countries, fast-moving trains may have no glass in the windows and doors. You must remain alert when travelling in an open train like this. Be cautious when you are moving between carriages, and stay away from the windows.

- For some adventurous travellers, the chance of a cheap ride on a freight train may prove irresistible. However, you are taking a big risk. There are even fewer safety measures on freight trains than there are on passenger trains. And you are at the mercy of the other 'passengers' who may be riding the rails. At least on a passenger train there are other passengers around who may help in the case of accidents.

- If you are carrying a long item of luggage near the train, you should carry it parallel to the ground to avoid it coming into contact with any overhead cables.

- In many countries there are gaps between railway carriages, where they are connected together. You should avoid going across these gaps, through the door at the end of one carriage into the next. These gaps may be dangerous places, especially on ill-maintained rail networks where the trains move around quite a bit on the track.

- If you are travelling in high-crime areas you should sit near the buffet carriage. There will always be people near these carriages. The buffet will also more than likely be manned by railway staff and, in the case of an incident, you should be able to summon assistance.

- If you are travelling in a high-crime area, don't select an empty carriage. If people get off at stations along the route and gradually empty your carriage, move to one with more people – particularly if you are a lone woman or two women travelling together.

Level Crossings

If you're driving on your holiday, it's highly likely that at some stage you will encounter a level crossing. In the UK there are some 8200 level crossings, and in 2000 there were 32 serious accidents on and near them, resulting in 13 deaths and many injuries. There were also reports of hundreds of near-misses. Yet in the UK we have relatively sophisticated safety measures and automated level crossing barriers, so in countries with no barriers, lights or safety regulations the risks are considerable. It has been suggested that the biggest factor is the behaviour of drivers negotiating the crossings. Consider the following points:

- Look and listen for trains as you approach the tracks. At night and in areas of poor visibility, ensure that there is no distracting noise in your car. Loud music will mask the sound of an approaching train. For safety's sake take one last look before you attempt to cross.

- If you encounter a lowered automated barrier you should never attempt to go around the gates or drive over the tracks. Pay attention to the hazard warning lights and follow the instructions. In some cases automated crossings may operate with painful slowness, but a shortcut could be certain death.

- In areas where there are no barriers, you must make sure that you can get across before you start. In some regions you may cross not one or two tracks but many. If you think there may be a risk, do not try to make a dash: wait until the train has passed.

- While you are crossing, ensure that you travel at a reasonable speed and maintain momentum. Try to avoid changing gears while you're crossing, as you may increase the chances of stalling your vehicle.

- If your vehicle stalls on a level crossing you must get everyone out immediately and move away from the track. If there is an alarm system or an emergency telephone, you should try to contact the rail authorities. If you have mobile phone coverage, call the local emergency number and inform the emergency services from the tracks immediately. If your vehicle becomes stuck on a railway track for some reason and a train is approaching, get everyone out and run away from the tracks as fast as you can. If the train hits your car it may propel it to the sides as well as forward.

- Ensure that if you are stopped at a level crossing, your windows are fully up and your doors are locked. Leave enough room in front so you can see the bottom of the wheels of the car in front or, if you are the first car, enough room so that you can conduct an emergency U turn in the event of a criminal attack. You could be halted at the crossing for some time. Be aware that depending on whether the train is hauling freight or passengers, it could take up to 2 kilometres to come to a stop.

Undergrounds/Subways

Most countries with underground transport systems or subways also have relatively good safety records. When you consider that in the region of 1 billion individual journeys are made on London's underground network every year, you can see that your chances of emerging at your destination unscathed are very good. However, accidents have happened. At King's Cross station in London, for instance, 30 people died and many others were injured in 1987 during a fire in the station.

However, such accidents are exceptions. You're more at risk of becoming a victim of the many criminals operating on or near underground or subway stations. Around 150,000 people enter London's system every hour, and among them there are both opportunist criminals and organised criminal gangs hoping to prey on the unsuspecting. The following statistics can give a basic overview of safety on the London Underground.

Casualties on the London Underground, 1994–2000

Year	Fatality	Minor injury	Major injury
1994–95	6	2047	57
1995–96	4	2000	86
1996–97	7	2344	95
1997–98	4	2409	108
1998–99	1	2468	123
1999–2000	6	2503	106

It's obvious that at underground stations, as at most major transport hubs, criminals gather because the hoards of people travelling through provide easy pickings.

Terrorists may also target underground transport systems. In seemingly stable and prosperous Tokyo, members of an obscure cult, Aum Shinrikyo, committed an atrocity in March 1995. They released the deadly chemical nerve agent sarin in the city's subway system, killing over a dozen people and injuring many more.

If you are considering travelling by underground transport, consider the following points:

■ Escalators are potentially dangerous, particularly in crowded stations. London Underground's 408 escalators are kept very busy transporting those 150,000 travellers per hour, for instance. Stay alert on escalators, especially when carrying heavy luggage.

■ If you are travelling with children, particularly younger ones, keep control of them on the escalators. Hold their hands firmly. Dress them in high-visibility clothing, both in case they stray and to help busy adult commuters avoid knocking into them. Tie loose shoelaces, fasten flapping jackets, and tuck in any hanging straps on backpacks or luggage – all these could get caught on the escalator's moving parts. If you get into trouble, press the emergency button at the top or bottom of the escalator. Take extra care if it's been raining, as escalators can become slippery.

■ People have suffered serious injury when they have been caught between the handrails and the moving components of the escalators. For this reason don't run up and down escalators – walk slowly. You should always face the direction that the escalator is travelling. Hold the handrails while keeping a firm footing on the steps.

■ Be suspicious of unattended baggage, packages and bicycles. In the past, terrorists have been known to disguise improvised explosive devices as innocent-looking objects.

■ As you buy your ticket at the ticket dispenser, keep control of your possessions. While you're putting coins into the machine, it's all too easy for criminals to grab any unprotected item and disappear into the crowd. There have been many laptop computers snatched in this way.

- Once on the train, continue to hold on to your possessions. People get uncomfortably close to each other on underground carriages, and pickpockets take advantage of this. Mobile phones hanging on waist belts are a particular target.

- Try to get a seat rather than hanging on to the handholds provided. In an accident you're safer if seated.

- If the train stops between stations, listen to the instructions of the train crew. Usually it's just a temporary halt and the train will restart in a few minutes. If the train driver instructs passengers to evacuate, you may need to open the doors manually. This should be done using the emergency door-opening device, normally located above the door. It's a good idea to look at these instructions every time you get on a train to familiarise yourself with them, as this will save valuable seconds during an emergency.

- Once you've evacuated the train, if the crew doesn't lead you to safety for whatever reason, you need to manage it yourself. If you can see the light from the nearest station, move in between the tracks ensuring that you do not touch them, and walk towards the light. Stay away from the electrified rail, which is the furthest from the platform. Do not run.

- If you cannot see a light at the end of the tunnel, it's probably better to remain in the train and move to the centre of the carriage. Most underground systems have procedures for recovering stranded trains.

- If someone becomes trapped in the doors, or if any other potentially life-threatening incident occurs, you should consider using the emergency stop device. If you pull this, the train will stop immediately.

- You should avoid travelling on your own at night. However, if you must travel at night try to avoid travelling on your own, particularly if you are a woman. If your carriage begins to empty, move to an occupied one at the next station.

- Avoid dark and isolated stations late at night. Try to arrange your journey so you arrive at the nearest manned and illuminated station – a much less attractive option for criminals.

- In many wealthy cities such as Rome and London, aggressive beggars try to intimidate vulnerable-looking people into handing over money. Women are frequently targeted by these bullies. If you are approached by a menacing character, be firm but polite, and act confident. Walk away if necessary. If they persist, try to attract attention from other travellers. When you see genuine and unfortunate people who have had to resort to begging and wish to give money to them, don't take out your purse or wallet – keep loose change in your pocket for this purpose.

- Before you travel, check to ensure that there are no major events that may disrupt your journey. Football matches are a classic example. Overcrowding at the relevant stations is the least of it: innocent travellers have become caught up in fights between gangs of football thugs. Big, potentially violent political demonstrations could also pose problems. If an event is likely to cause tension, try to avoid stations in that area.

4

Vehicle Safety

Road Traffic Accidents

One of the most common causes of serious injury and death is not violent attacks, diseases, hotel fires or air crashes. It's road traffic accidents. And in some holiday hotspots you're more likely to be involved in one: the incidence of traffic accidents has been assessed as 7 to 13 times higher in developing countries than in Western Europe.

Early on in my military career I was serving with the first battalion of the Argyll and Sutherland Highlanders in Northern Ireland in the early 1980s. It was a very tense time to be in the area, and in the two years we were stationed there we lost one man to terrorist action. After our tour was completed we were posted to sunny Cyprus. Within a few months we had lost five men to driving accidents, most involving alcohol. It dawned on me that we had been conditioned to accept the dangers of the Northern Irish conflict, but were woefully ill prepared to accept the dangers of socialising on holiday in a place with relatively lax road safety.

It's dangerous enough driving at home in the developed West. But in unfamiliar environments, where driving conditions are at best chaotic, it can be nightmarish. If you're British, you'll have to cope with driving on the right side of the road in unfamiliar vehicles while trying to adapt to different regulations and driving systems. In some countries the road signs are difficult to interpret. In many others, road safety simply isn't very high on the agenda.

When I was in Cairo in 1996, a policeman who had been given the task of looking after us was driving us along the main motorway back to the city, after a week in the desert. Things were going fine when there was an accident involving a car and a donkey hauling a fruit cart on the other carriageway. Seeing this, our driver sped up to the next turnaround point a few hundred metres on. We then zoomed back towards the commotion, our community-minded policeman intent on jumping into action and assisting the injured. Or so we thought. When we arrived at the scene, the policeman rolled down his window and, turning to us in the back and without even a hint of sarcasm, asked, 'Do you guys want any fruit?' We then drove off. Different countries, different cultures!

If you decide to visit a country where road safety is a very low priority, it is unwise to drive yourself. When you hire your car, hire a driver too. However, ensure that you stamp your authority on the driver. Offer a bonus for safe driving, and threaten to withhold it if they start to speed or drive erratically. Be bold, be firm and above all maintain control. Your life is in his hands.

If you are in a position to drive, remember that while you may be a brilliant driver, at home you are sharing the motorway with other relatively capable drivers. Abroad, the situation could be very different.

The casualties in the table below are for every billion passenger kilometres travelled, and range from deaths to minor injuries needing hospital treatment. As you can see, in terms of sheer numbers, car driving in Britain is loaded in your favour.

Transport casualties in Britain, 1999

Mode of Transport	Number of casualties per billion passenger kilometres
Air	0.04
Rail	20
Water transport	34
Bus or coach	212
Car	343
Van	108
Two-wheeled motor vehicle	5372
Pedal vehicles	5743
Pedestrians	2415

But as I've indicated, travelling abroad could well bump up the risk. The following statistics indicate the total number of fatalities for all road traffic accidents in certain countries. The table is just an overview, however, as there are many factors involved in such accidents.

Deaths in road accidents by country, 1999

Country	Number of fatalities
Australia	1763
Austria	1079
Belgium	1397
Canada	2972
Czech Republic	1455
Denmark	514
Finland	431
France	8487
Germany	7772
Greece	2116
Hungary	1306
Iceland	21
Ireland	413

table continues ➤

Country	Number of fatalities
Japan	10,372
Luxembourg	58
Netherlands	1090
New Zealand	509
Norway	304
Poland	6730
Portugal	1995
Republic of Korea	10,756
Spain	5738
Sweden	580
Switzerland	583
Turkey	5975
United Kingdom	3564
US	41,611

Many other countries have even worse accident rates than those in the table above, and do not bother to record the statistics.

What can you do about all this? The best course is to choose the safest car, drive it as safely as you can, and be prepared for some very different driving experiences. You can never be entirely sure what's around the next bend.

Vehicle Selection and Preparation

When you need to rent a vehicle abroad, you may find that standards at the rental agencies don't match those at home. The chances of being duped into accepting an unroadworthy vehicle could be correspondingly high. Then, too, the driving tests in Britain and other Western countries ensure that most road users are reasonably proficient. In some regions, however, all you need to start driving is enough money to buy a car.

If you intend to drive in a foreign country, ensure that you have an International Driving Licence and the right level of insurance cover. You will have to inform your insurance agent that you intend to drive abroad; if you do not inform them you may not be covered.

The following are ground rules for renting a car abroad.

- Join the AA, RAC or local recovery service. You need to ensure that if you are involved in a breakdown or other incident, you are able to get assistance. If you are driving in Europe or any developed country, your membership at home can be extended to cover your travel destination. You just need to inform your emergency recovery organisation before you go.

- Use an internationally recognised car hire company. This will have the infrastructure to ensure that their vehicles are well maintained and meet the safety standards of the country in which you intend to drive. They also have the insurance support to ensure that if you do find yourself in any difficulties you will be covered. They should provide you with a vehicle operating manual, which you can use for maintenance and troubleshooting. Your travel agent or hotel can arrange this.

- Do not be tempted to hire from unregistered dealers who offer deals too good to be true. You get what you pay for: cheap deals invariably mean dangerous vehicles.

- If you are a frequent traveller and always hire a car you will be aware that rental cars all look pretty much the same. It is useful to write down the registration number, make, model and colour. If it is stolen or if you forget where you have parked it, at least you can give a description.

- Ensure that your car fits in with the local environment. If there is unrest in the area you're visiting, it is better to have a simple car in a dull colour, which won't attract attention. On a recent trip to Nigeria, we were offered a modern four-wheel-drive vehicle. However, we elected to have a 20-year-old Peugeot, simply because most of the local cars were around that age. Later we were stuck in heavy traffic in the market district of Lagos city centre, with thousands of very poor people streaming past on both sides. No one even bothered to look in our car, but had we been sitting in a new, shiny, four-wheel-drive vehicle, we almost certainly would have been a tempting target to some.

▪ Conduct a check of the vehicle, starting with the outside. Look at the tyres and ensure that there is sufficient tread for the expected road conditions. Also check to see that there is enough air in them: tyre pressure (or the lack of it) is a major factor in car accidents. Cars are weight-bearing vehicles and every time the car moves, the weight is shifting throughout the vehicle, which ultimately means pressure on the tyres. And for every 10°F change in temperature, the tyre pressure will have to be adjusted by 1 psi from the manufacturer's recommendations. If you will be in the country for some time, it is worthwhile checking the tyre pressure monthly to ensure that it is set to the manufacturer's recommendation. Remember: heavily laden vehicles and deflated tyres will dramatically increase your chances of being involved in an accident.

▪ Check the vehicle lights – four-way flashers, indicators, and the brake, parking and reversing lights. It's essential that they are all in good working order, day and night.

▪ Before you drive it, check the body of the vehicle for signs of damage and point out any to the agency rep. You want to avoid paying for someone else's accidents. If the vehicle has been recently painted this may be an attempt to conceal recent damage.

▪ Check that the doors, windows, boot and bonnet lock properly. Select a car with universal door locks and power windows, which will give you better control of access to the car. An air-conditioned vehicle is preferable in hot climates, as this will enable you to drive with windows closed. Keeping the doors locked is a good idea too: even in the UK there has been an increase in attacks on stationary vehicles.

▪ Make sure the windscreen wipers are in good working order, and that there is sufficient oil in the engine and water in the radiator and windscreen-washer container. Check that there is enough life left in the vehicle battery.

▪ Enquire about the vehicle's fuel consumption and ensure that you have enough fuel for the journey you intend to take. As a general guide, most medium-sized cars will have a range of around 28 kilometres per gallon in cities, compared with a range for smaller vehicles of around 37 kilometres per gallon. A medium-sized car will travel in the region of 270 kilometres on half a tank of fuel; a small vehicle, around 176 kilometres. You should plan your journey with this in mind.

- Check the boot for a spare tyre, ensuring it's the right size, and has enough tread and air. Make sure you have the appropriate toolkit, containing a complete vehicle jack, wrenches and spanners that fit your vehicle, and an accident warning triangle. You may consider bringing a small handheld fire extinguisher.

- Check inside the vehicle to ensure that the car is fitted with seatbelts and has enough seatbelt anchor points. Also check that the inside lights are working and that you are happy with the operation of the vehicle. If it has an alarm system fitted, make sure you test it and are familiar with its operation.

Safe Driving Techniques

When I was in Egypt in 1996, I was amazed at the frenzied driving I saw on the roads. Drivers took little interest in what anyone else was doing, and I expected to be involved in an accident at any moment. However, in the months we spent in Cairo I saw very few accidents. One of our Egyptian colleagues told us that the government had hired a Japanese company to devise a more controlled traffic system for the city. This company set up their computer-controlled traffic monitoring systems all over Cairo. At the end of the long monitoring period, a confused Japanese traffic control expert conceded to the Egyptian officials that they could not understand how traffic was able to move at all. They suggested leaving the system as it was.

Driving in foreign countries can be nerve-racking at the least, especially in areas where the traffic is disordered and there is a security threat. You should apply the same strategies that you do at home, such as always wearing seatbelts. The following points may also help reduce the chances of becoming a victim while driving abroad.

- As I indicated at the start of this chapter, it's too dangerous to drive in some countries. In this case, hire a vehicle and driver. Ensure that you're the boss here – make it clear that you will offer a bonus for safe driving. In the event of an accident, however, let the driver sort it out. Getting involved can lead to major trouble. I saw this clearly in Somalia in 2000. We were driving into the town of Bossasso. An hour before, two lorries had been involved in a head-on collision. The wife of one of the drivers had been travelling in the cab of his truck, and was killed in the accident. The bereaved husband attacked and killed the driver of the other lorry. He was later arrested and spent a few days in detention before going to court. At the trial a few days later, the verdict was that he was right in doing what he had done, and he was awarded the possessions of the driver he had murdered. In some regions it is clearly unwise to drive.

- In some countries, rental cars have telltale registration plates, and you'll need to be extra careful about preventing the car from being stolen. It's also a good idea to remove any rental company stickers from the car before you drive it. You can reattach them before handing the car back.

- Try to avoid driving immediately after getting off a long-haul flight. You will be tired and possibly jetlagged. For someone in this condition, grappling with an unfamiliar driving environment is a recipe for disaster.

- Driving too fast affects your ability to react to changing road conditions. When you drive at 80 kilometres an hour, you are moving at around 23 metres per second. If you have to look around to see what is going on behind, you will take your eyes off the road for a minimum of two seconds – and you will have covered 46 metres without seeing what is going on in front. It is essential that your car is fitted with rear view and wing mirrors, and that you drive at a sensible speed.

- When you're driving at speed, your peripheral vision is reduced. This is a crucial factor in car accidents. It has been shown that when they're not moving, most people can see roughly 90 degrees to each side of whatever they are looking at. However, when you are driving at around 65 kilometres an hour, you will be able to see only 60 degrees to either side of what you are looking at. If your speed increases to 130 kilometres an hour, your peripheral vision will shrink to 30 degrees on either side. Drive at a sensible speed for local conditions, using your own judgement. And drive defensively. Don't just avoid accidents, but be very aware of who's sharing the road with you – pedestrians, cyclists, scooter riders, even criminal gangs.

- If you are driving in wet, muddy or icy conditions, manoeuvre the vehicle slowly and deliberately. Turn and brake slowly and speed up gradually.

- Leave enough space between you and the vehicle in front, especially in wet or icy conditions. If you are too close and he gets into trouble you will have problems. It is difficult to make and act on split-second decisions in bad weather and on unfamiliar roads.

- If your vehicle starts to skid on a wet or icy road, it is essential that you turn your steering wheel in the same direction as the skid. If your vehicle begins to skid right, turn your wheel right and do not brake. If you do brake, your vehicle will turn into a dead weight and you may be unable to stop it.

- If your vehicle does not have an automatic braking system (ABS), which is designed to prevent your brakes from locking, and you have to apply your brakes, use cadence braking. This means gently applying and removing pressure on the brake pedal, and will be more effective than a constant pressure on the pedal. However, in vehicles with ABS, a constant braking pressure on the pedal is advised.

- When driving down a steep hill use a low gear. Identify a safe speed for the descent and stay under that speed by gently applying pressure to the brake pedal. Don't career down the hill at speed and try to control your vehicle at the bottom.

- If you are driving off road and hit a soft, wet area, there's a risk that your tyres will sink in. If you find yourself in this situation, get your passengers out quickly to lighten the load. You can then try to drive out before your vehicle settles too deeply. Do this by driving forward a few inches, then backward a few inches, using a rocking motion. If you stay in one position spinning your wheels, the chances are that the tyres will heat up and in icy conditions you will melt the ice and create a deeper hole. Articles placed in the tyre ruts can provide traction for the tyres – try using vegetation, wood, clothing or any material lying around. If the ground is covered with snow, you can try reducing the tyre pressure a bit; more of the tyre will be in contact with the surface of the snow, thereby enhancing the traction. Be aware that this should only be tried as a last resort, however.

Driving Security

Criminal gangs and terrorist organisations rarely expose themselves to needless risk and will take great care in selecting their target. They prefer the weak and unsuspecting. By displaying a basic awareness and adopting a confident attitude even while driving, you'll give such people the impression that the risk is too high, and they'll opt for a softer target.

- When driving in dangerous areas, concentrate on what is going on all around you. This way you may get warning of any incidents before they take place, and take avoiding action. Be particularly alert in slow-moving traffic or when waiting for traffic lights to change.

- Ensure that you have more than one set of keys to the vehicle, and carry the spare with you at all times in your moneybelt, document pouch or even your wallet or purse.

- The way you act behind the wheel or even as a passenger will give off signals to other road users and pedestrians. If you appear nervous, vulnerable, or unsure of where you are, others will pick up on this. If you look wealthy, you will increase your chances of attracting the wrong type of attention. Keep valuables out of sight, even when you are driving, and plan your route while maintaining awareness of what is going on around you. Display confidence when you are travelling and you will be less likely to become a victim.

- Ensure that your vehicle is displaying its vehicle registration number plate and tax documentation if that applies. This will prevent unnecessary brushes with the local authorities.

- Ensure that when you are in a vehicle you get into the habit of locking the doors and windows. If you are stuck in traffic, never open your windows to speak with street hawkers or people who wash your windscreens. In volatile areas never open your windows to ask strangers for directions.

- Try to maintain a sense of where you are at all times. Before you venture out identify possible areas of danger and bad parts of town, and avoid them. Have access to a city map, and if you have to read it, keep it below the level of the dashboard – you don't want anyone seeing that you're unfamiliar with the area. If you need to, cover the map in a newspaper; this will conceal it from inquisitive pedestrians on the street and still allow you to read it. If you become lost, drive to the nearest safe area before consulting your map. Avoid leaving the map on the dashboard or seat when you leave the car.

- It is helpful to plan your route beforehand by writing down the road numbers, street names and junctions so you can tick them off as you pass them.

- If you have hired a driver, do not distract him. Avoid engaging in conversations of a sensitive nature – religious or political, for instance. Avoid reading a magazine or newspaper in the front passenger seat, as the driver will also browse through the headlines.

- If you are a staying in the country for a prolonged period, identify the congestion points and times so you can avoid travelling when traffic is bad. Find the local radio network on the car radio so you can get an idea of the traffic in certain areas.

- If at all possible, avoid driving at night and during bad weather. Driving in wet, foggy or icy conditions is doubly dangerous when you're in an unfamiliar place trying to find your way.

- In tourist hotspots, avoid driving after the pubs and clubs have shut. There will be many drivers on the road who are under the influence of drink or drugs. There may be road users from all over the world out there, and a mix of many different standards and driving cultures does not make for good driving conditions.

- Never drink and drive, or take narcotics and drive. Next year's holiday season will be accompanied by next year's casualty statistics, and many of these people will have been the victim of drink, drugs and roads.

- Use visual measures to make your vehicle secure, such as wheel-locking and gearstick-locking devices. If the criminal has to remove these before he can steal your vehicle, he'll be prolonging his exposure to risk, and this may well put him off. He would rather go for a car with no security devices.

- When you park your vehicle, ensure that the wheels are turned towards the curb. This will make it more difficult to tow off. Do not leave attractive items in sight – place them in the boot. Nor should you leave the vehicle registration documents under the sun visor.

- Never leave your vehicle running while you pop into a shop or garage. A minute or two is enough time for an on-the-ball thief to steal it. If this happens, you may find that your insurance company will refuse to pay out; after all, it would be considered your own fault.

- If you have access to a garage, use it and lock the door. If not, park your car in a well-lit area. This may be enough to put off opportunistic crooks.

- Travellers have been targeted at service stations when they stop to fuel up or even rest, so remain alert and be aware of who is paying undue attention to you. Only stop at busy stations, and do not draw attention to yourself. Even if you are tired, never just pull off the road and go to sleep. Keep going to the next station or town. If you suspect you are being followed after you have driven off, try going round roundabouts a few times in order to confirm whether you are being tailed. If you are, don't go back to your accommodation. Head to the nearest police station, big hotel or some other location that will offer assistance.

- Criminals frequently pose as beleaguered drivers or pedestrians to trap the unwary driver. It's a ruse that's been around for centuries. After flagging you down, they'll assault you and rob you of car and/or valuables. Never stop to give assistance to people you see on the road, no matter how serious the incident looks. If you've got your mobile phone with you, assist by calling emergency services, or drive to the next town and inform the police or hospital. Be aware of other tricks. For example, criminals have left tacks or nails on the road that puncture the tyres of unsuspecting travellers, and then offered assistance in changing the tyre.

- Never pick up hitchhikers or strangers in trouble, and be cautious of lone policemen on the road stopping you. There have been many occasions where bogus policemen have stopped unsuspecting drivers, who have then been robbed. If you are in any doubt, drive to the next town or wait until you are in heavy traffic before stopping.

- A classic scam is to crash into the rear of a hire car. The criminals' aim is for you to get out to inspect the damage. Once out, you will be assaulted, robbed and possibly relieved of your car. If your car is bumped from behind do not stop: drive to the nearest police station and seek assistance.

- Ensure that when you stop at traffic lights or road works you remain aware of what is going on. Avoid stopping your vehicle in dark and remote areas. If you feel vulnerable – for example if you are a woman – you may consider an improvised weapon in the door compartment. Deep-heat aerosols used for treating muscle pain are very effective when sprayed at the face of an attacker. However, this must be used as a last resort. If you injure someone, even an attacker, you may be called on to justify your actions.

- If you are attacked while in your car, press on the horn and do not stop. Drive out of the area to the nearest safe location. If you are forced to stop and are unable to drive out, do not resist or argue with your assailants. Ensure that you make no sudden movements, and keep your hands where they can see them. The criminals are themselves at risk and will be on edge.

- In some countries, road rage has become a serious problem. In the US, such incidents have ended in shots fired at people for the most trivial of reasons. If you become involved in such an incident, do not stop. Head to the nearest police station or similar safe establishment.

- If you are travelling for long distances, carry a spare can of fuel from a reliable source. Soon after the Kosovo conflict had finished, I worked with a media company in Pristina. There was very little fuel to be had and local people were selling the stuff from drums at the side of the road. On more than one occasion I saw cars break down a few hundred feet away from one of these improvised refuelling stations. Much of the fuel had been contaminated with water.

- It may helpful to carry basic emergency equipment in case of breakdown. A mobile phone and a list of emergency numbers are invaluable. It is a good idea to have all your emergency contact numbers pre-programmed on your mobile. Also useful are a torch, spare tyres, food and water and, depending on the climate, warm clothing.

- If your car breaks down in a volatile area, get off the road, take out your valuables and keep them with you, hide, and only then attempt to summon assistance. Ensure that you get the name of the firm and the name of the individual who is going to help you. If you have decided to remain inside your car, do not open the door until you have confirmed the identity of the person who is offering assistance.

- If you have a flat tyre in a dangerous area, do not stop. You can still drive on a flat – just drive slowly and head to the nearest safe area before you stop.

- When driving in volatile areas, familiarise yourself with the places you need to avoid. Then identify safe areas along your route. If something happens, you will know where to go to get out of trouble.

- Don't stop outside places of religious worship or in crowds, or outside pubs or clubs near closing time. Emotions can turn violent quickly at these places, so keep the car in gear and stay alert.

- Although it's relatively rare, shots have been fired at tourists driving in particularly troubled regions. If you are unfortunate enough to be caught in a situation like this, you may consider speeding swiftly away from the site. Crouching down inside your vehicle will make you a smaller target. The further away you get from the gunfire, the harder you will be to hit. If you cannot drive through the area, you may decide to get out of the car on the opposite side from the gunfire and move quickly away from the noise. The safest part of the car to hide behind is the engine block, as this part of the vehicle has a significant amount of metal.

- At night after you have completed your day's driving, leave your vehicle headlights on while you are opening your garage door and parking your car inside the garage.

Carjacking

Physically attacking motorists in order to steal their cars, known as carjacking, is becoming more common in certain parts of the world – including some holiday resorts. Carjackers have used violence and weapons when targeting motorists. They may be working on their own, be part of an organised criminal network targeting specific cars, or even be criminals trying to evade police after committing a crime. Be aware of the following points:

- Vehicles are vulnerable to carjacking at traffic lights and at main junctions where you have to stop. Motorway service stations and supermarket car parks are also high-risk areas for carjacking. Never leave your keys in the car, even if you are only leaving it for a moment to pay for petrol.

- When you've left your car and are walking back, maintain the appearance of confidence and stay alert. As you approach your car look around the area, and if you are suspicious leave the car park and obtain assistance before opening the car door. If you do get in and then see, say, a group of men walking towards you, quickly get into the car, lock the doors and drive out of the car park.

- If you have to stop at lights or in traffic you should be aware that street hawkers, people asking for directions and people handing out leaflets are all potential carjackers.

- If carjackers approach with weapons, let them have the car. It is insured, and you can always get another one. Your life is worth more than your car. Note the carjackers' identification, dress, age, hair and eye colour and any distinctive features. Leave the scene as quickly as possible and report the incident to the authorities.

- If you're in a high-risk area and a big demonstration, for example, has just hit the streets, keep your driving to an absolute minimum. A lot of the action will take place on the main roads of the city. The police may be on the streets in large numbers. In some countries, the army will also be on the street. Most armies are trained to fight wars and may have had little experience in policing operations, so you can expect more aggressive and robust handling from the military.

- If you have decided to travel through a dangerous area or plan to travel at night, team up with another driver. Get them to follow you and in the event of a breakdown or an incident that requires you to leave your car, at least you will both have another vehicle at hand.

Roadblocks and Checkpoints

Roadblocks and checkpoints can be a common feature in some troubled areas, and you'll need to know what to do as you approach. Here are the ground rules.

- When travelling by car in an area of unrest, be alert to the possibility of encountering a roadblock. You may be able to anticipate their locations if you have been in the area for some time. However, roadblocks can be set up very quickly, and they may be positioned at a point on the road where they will surprise drivers. It may be difficult to see roadblocks at night, but if you are signalled to stop by military personnel or a police patrol, you should obey their instructions, even if you know that you are going to get fleeced. There have been many occasions where soldiers and police have opened fire on a vehicle purely because it failed to stop at their checkpoint.

- In some countries you will need to learn how to approach a military or police checkpoint. In Northern Ireland, for instance, drivers would have to slow down and switch off their lights as they approached the checkpoint. It was believed that the vehicle headlights would illuminate the soldiers and expose them to sniper fire.

- Regardless of where you are and who has stopped you, it is important that you cooperate and do as they tell you. Failure to comply with their instructions will only invite trouble, and if they are particularly ill disciplined or even inexperienced, they may overreact. Remember that in many regions you will have to pay or you will end up in a local prison on some trumped-up charge. It is just not worth the trouble. A soldier or policeman at a checkpoint will be satisfied with less than his superiors. If you are arrested, you will end up having to pay more than you would have had at the checkpoint.

- When you are stopped at a checkpoint manned by armed soldiers, policemen or even guerrillas, you must avoid any antagonistic behaviour. Make no sudden movements and do not become embroiled in an argument. You should be firm but polite and retain your dignity. Act with confidence and you will reduce the risk of getting into any trouble.

Motorcycle Safety

The statistics in the table on page 91 above show that in Britain at least, motorcycle riding is the most dangerous form of mechanical travel. Some have suggested that the danger is not with the motorcyclist but with other road users who fail to see them. Evidence has suggested that up to 75 per cent of all motorcycle accidents involved crashes with another vehicle, normally a car. The remaining 25 per cent are accidents where the motorcycle went out of control and crashed on the road or into some fixed object near the road. The culprit here is punctured tyres.

And that's only the seasoned motorcyclists. Those of us who can't resist the temptation to hire mopeds and trail bikes when abroad will go haring off pretending that we know what we are doing. Only we usually don't. There are many tourist resorts where you do not need a licence to hire a motorcycle – all you need is cash.

Have a look at the following points, and you may just reduce your chances of mishap while riding a motorcycle abroad.

- If you intend to ride a motorcycle when you go abroad, buy insurance cover. You must inform your insurance agent: a failure to do so can bankrupt you, as you will be expected to meet the costs of any accident. Accident insurance at holiday destinations is available, but be warned – it may be difficult to get them to pay up. It is far safer to arrange this at home.

- Ensure that you use a reputable rental agency.

- Before hiring the motorcycle, conduct a quick safety check to give you an indication of its roadworthiness. Check both tyres to see if they're at the correct pressure; many accidents are due to tyre failure. If you are unsure of what that is, ask for the user's instruction manual. If you intend to carry a passenger on the motorcycle, you may need to adjust the tyre pressure by as much as 10 per cent.

- Start up and check that the front lights, indicators and brake lights are working. Check the brake fluid and engine oil. It is sometimes difficult to get an accurate engine oil reading when a motorcycle is cold, so you may have to run the engine for a while to get an accurate reading.

■ Ensure that the fuel gauge, if there is one, is opened, and look in the tank to ensure you have enough fuel for your journey. Ask about the motorcycle's fuel consumption: how far can it run on a full tank of petrol? Remember that riding at high speed or off road will burn up more fuel.

■ Conduct a cursory check of the motorcycle, looking for damage. Chances are the bikes will have been well used, and a significant proportion involved in accidents. If the machine looks damaged, ask for another.

Motorcycle safety tips

■ There are many factors contributing to motorcycling accidents. As I've indicated, sometimes holidaymakers do not know how to ride them, but insist on doing so anyway.

■ Most injuries do not happen when you come off the motorcycle, but when you hit something or become trapped between it and the road surface or another vehicle. If you are unfortunate enough to come off a motorbike or are about to hit something, try to get away from the bike.

■ Alcohol is a big factor in fatal motorcycle accidents. It impairs your judgement, and if a motorcycle goes out of control there's no protection for the rider.

■ Accidents that happen in towns are attributed mainly to motorists failing to see motorbikes. Wear high-visibility clothing when riding.

■ Speeding is a major cause of motorcycle accidents, especially on secondary roads with two-way traffic. You should constantly think to yourself, 'If something were to go wrong now, can I avoid it?'

■ Leathers or other appropriate clothing will give you an element of protection should you come off the motorcycle, and helmets are essential. In many holiday resorts you can see bikers racing up and down without helmets and wearing shorts and T-shirts – a care-free attitude that is dangerous practice.

■ Statistics have shown that if you are not a regular motorcycle rider, the most dangerous part of your journey is within the first 8 kilometres.

■ In many countries, the road conditions are nowhere near as good as in, say, the UK. Sand, gravel, oil spills and the like will affect road conditions and can be a major cause of accidents.

■ Safe bike handling, such as cornering, has been identified as a major factor in motorcycle safety. It has been suggested that a motorcyclist will have less than 2 seconds to carry out all collision avoidance manoeuvres before they collide. However, if you are carrying a passenger braking is different. You should continue to use your front brake, but the increased weight over your rear wheel means the stopping distances increase. You should apply more pressure to the rear brake as it is less likely to lock up.

■ If confronted by a situation that requires you to brake hard, avoid snatching at the front brake, as this may cause it to lock up. Gradually apply pressure to the front brake initially, then apply more pressure as a way of avoiding the wheels locking.

■ Defensive riding on a motorbike is essential. You must always remain alert and expect danger at every turn.

Travelling on Buses

Travelling on a bus or coach means you are essentially in the hands of the coach operators, and mainly the driver. In some countries there are no seatbelts on coaches, so passengers are in real danger of sustaining serious injury. And this can be nasty. When a vehicle crashes, three collisions are involved. The first is the impact of the vehicle against another object, followed by a rapid deceleration. The second is that of passengers hitting objects inside the coach – seats, other passengers, the inside walls of the coach – or falling out and hitting the ground. The third happens when the internal organs come up against bones or other organs inside the victim's body, which causes a large proportion of the actual injuries, as passengers are propelled forward on impact.

You are still vulnerable to criminal and terrorist activity when you're on a coach. Such marginal groups have been known to target popular tourist coach routes, and in some regions, hold entire coaches up and rob the passengers. In Burundi around Christmas 2000, a bus was stopped and robbed and some 20 people were killed, among them a UN aid worker. The bus route was known to be dangerous.

Perusing the following points could lessen your chances of becoming involved in an incident while travelling by bus or coach:

- Use a reliable, widely known bus operator. If you elect to use a cheap operator you will invariably be travelling in a poorly maintained vehicle. Your travel agent should provide you with the details of good bus operators.

- Check the route the bus will take. If it's dangerous, avoid the bus and try to take a safer route by some other means. In some countries it is inadvisable to move by road and much safer to fly. Ask if there has been a history of previous attacks against coaches or buses and if so, find out when the last incident took place and what the motive was for the attack.

- Avoid travelling by coach during politically tense periods and at night. If you are travelling by bus, ensure that you inform someone when you are going to depart, and when you expect to arrive at your destination.

- Select a bus with seatbelts or some other passenger-restraining device, and ensure that you use them. If the bus does collide or come to a rapid halt, these devices will help reduce the chances of serious injury.

- Identify the location of the emergency exits and familiarise yourself with the working of the emergency door handle. In a collision, the windows may be the quickest routes out of the vehicle. If the windows have not shattered, they may be difficult to break.

The best place to attack the window is in the corners. By banging the corner of a window hard with a metal emergency hammer, the window will shatter.

- If you are carrying soft luggage, place this in front of you and against the seat in front. This will help absorb the force of impact if there's a collision.

- During a collision, passengers are likely to be propelled forward with the momentum of the bus. It may be helpful to adopt a 'crash position' with your knees wedged high up against the seat in front and your head against your knees. If you are wedged tightly in, you may avoid being ejected out of the window of the coach on impact. Approximately half of bus accident fatalities are estimated to happen in this way.

- Avoid storing heavy luggage in the overhead storage racks, and don't block the aisles with large items of luggage.

- Passengers in some countries travel on the roof of buses. Don't. As buses turn corners, disproportionate force may be exerted on the upper part of the vehicle and it may be difficult to hang on. Also avoid putting your head, arms or hands out of the window.

- In some regions, terrorists target buses. If you see unattended bags or packages on your bus, alert the driver and do not touch them.

- Keep control of your luggage. Make sure that you see it placed in the luggage hold and keep your hand luggage with you at all times. In some regions it is unwise to sleep on buses, as this gives the opportunist criminal a chance to pick your pocket.

- Many bus drivers try to engage passengers in conversation. Avoid this to ensure the driver concentrates on his job. Evidence suggests that many coach accidents are caused by drivers' errors.

- Don't carry any flammable, toxic, or otherwise hazardous materials onto the bus. If the bus were in a collision, these substances would increase the chances of a fire.

- If you are travelling alone by bus or coach through a dangerous area, take books or magazines with you. You can avoid being drawn into conversation – and potential conflict – if you are reading. In sensitive areas, avoid eye contact; this is likely to be followed by a question, which may then force you into a conversation.

■ Once you've got off the bus, be careful about crossing the road. In some regions buses travel in special lanes that move against traffic flow.

■ Avoid getting on an overcrowded bus, which means that you have to stand or sit in the aisle. If you're in this position during a collision you are much more likely to be injured.

■ After leaving the bus, ensure you have eye contact with the driver. Wait for a signal from the driver before you cross the road, keeping an eye out for traffic changes. If a parked car or other obstacle blocks your vision, move to where you have good visual contact with the traffic flow. Ensure that you stay clear of the bus's rear wheel as there are blind spots where the driver will be unable to see. If you do have to walk on a road without a pavement you should walk facing the traffic; in this way you can take avoiding action if a car gets too close.

Minibus Security

In many regions of the world the minibus is ubiquitous, and the most popular mode of transport. But there is serious concern over the safety of these vehicles after a spate of accidents throughout the world, including the UK. Some minibuses stand tall but have a relatively small wheelbase, which can make them unstable when they are travelling at speed, especially when cornering.

Take on board the following points before you opt to travel by minibus.

■ Choose a reputable minibus company or the minibus provided by your hotel. These vehicles are supposed to be in a roadworthy condition at all times. Often, however, the driver is responsible for ensuring the vehicle's condition. Monitor the driver's mannerisms, and if you are unsure of him you may also question the condition of the vehicle.

■ Select a minibus with forward-facing seats. Evidence suggests that in a collision, this kind of seat offers greater protection. If they are high-backed with diagonal seatbelts, they are even safer.

■ In some tourist spots heavy baggage is placed at the rear of the vehicle, sometimes piled high on the rear seats. This luggage is normally not secured, and in a collision or even hard braking it may fly out and hit passengers, resulting in further injuries. Insist that all luggage is secured.

■ Identify the emergency exits and become familiar with the operation of the emergency door mechanism. If the minibus has a sliding door, check that its open windows cannot impede operation. Several kinds of minibus have design faults, such as doors that open in such a way that they can trap an arm protruding from an open window. When you're travelling with children, take extra care in minibuses of this design.

■ Do not leave luggage or packages in aisles and passageways, where it is an obstruction. Ensure that no one blocks access to the emergency doors.

■ When travelling by bus through areas of unrest, avoid dressing flamboyantly or wearing expensive-looking (even if fake) watches and jewellery. You may generate unwanted attention, which could escalate and land you in trouble. The idea is to blend in as much as possible.

■ Respect local mores and behave according to them. Be aware of the other passenger. On public transport you are removed from the tourist resorts and hotels and may be expected to behave differently.

■ Try to maintain an idea of where you are, particularly if you are travelling in a volatile area. If the bus is halted for whatever reason, say at a roadblock, knowing where you are means you will at least be able to get to the next safe area by yourself.

Travelling in Taxis

When you arrive at your destination after a long flight, the first thing you usually want to do is get to your hotel and chill out. So you'll race to the taxi rank and grab the first cab that comes along. The problem is, this pattern of behaviour has not gone unnoticed by the criminals lurking around transportation hubs, and many tourists have become victims minutes after they leave the airport terminal.

During the summer of 1999 in Bangkok, an Egyptian was detained over the murder of at least six foreign tourists in the so-called 'taxi murders'. Over an eight-month reign of terror, tourists were fooled into travelling in fake taxis, and were stabbed and robbed. The Thai authorities failed to publicise the killings in case it damaged the lucrative tourist industry.

This is an extreme example, and the worst that might happen is a simple mugging. But beware: when you get into a taxi you are essentially placing your destiny in the hands of someone you don't know. The following points will help you pinpoint what to look out for.

■ When you arrive at the airport, avoid anyone offering to get a taxi for you. You will end up travelling in an unsafe vehicle, and paying the middleman and the taxi driver. Many criminal groups operate in this fashion and vulnerable travellers have been assaulted and robbed. Some of these people can be very convincing, so be wary.

■ If you have any doubts about the taxi service, go to the taxi counter inside the airport and arrange to hire a taxi, even if this means waiting slightly longer. If you go to the taxi rank, you will more than likely take the first taxi which comes along. When the driver sees an apparently wealthy traveller he may try to hike up the price, or introduce additional charges. You can avoid this by sorting everything out at the counter.

■ If you decide to go out once you've settled in at your hotel, think about how you are going to get back before you go, particularly if it's nighttime and you're planning on drinking alcohol. Get the number of a reputable taxi firm from your hotel or travel agent. The call will be recorded and the firm will be able to monitor its drivers. Avoid hailing taxis on the street. If you cannot get a taxi by calling the number you have, try at the nearest major hotel.

- When you do order a cab, do not give your real name, and ensure that you ask for the driver's name. When the cab shows up, ask the driver for his name as confirmation. It is also a good idea to collect and carry the business cards of two reputable taxi companies. At least you will be able to call a cab when you want one. When calling for a taxi, do not let anyone overhear you; if they hear where you want to go or even your name, you may compromise your security.

- Learn the markings used by reputable taxi firms on their cars. This way, if you have no alternative and must hail a taxi from the street, you can at least ensure it's a reputable firm at a glance. Before getting in, ensure the cab has a meter. If it doesn't, you will have to agree a price and just make sure that the driver will take you to where you want to go. If the driver claims his meter is broken and asks for an excessively high price, do not get in the cab.

- Avoid travelling alone in a taxi, and don't permit the driver to stop and pick up anyone else. This is a common criminal ploy. The taxi driver will tell you he has to pick up a relative or another taxi driver. Then they proceed to rob the passenger.

- If the taxi driver tells you that he has engine problems and has to stop, be on your guard. Be forceful and insist that he drives to the next safe place. If the taxi breaks down, insist that the driver calls a replacement. Then stay in the taxi with the windows and doors locked and do not open them until you are absolutely certain you are safe.

- If you cannot speak the local language, write your destination down. Keep a hotel business card or brochure in your pocket.

- It is a good idea to work out key areas along the route you need to take on a map. This can give a taxi driver the impression that you are very familiar with the area, and he will be less likely to deviate from the most direct route.

- If you frequently use a particular taxi company and are happy with the service, tip the drivers. If you have the reputation of being a good tipper you will generally get good service.

- Whenever you travel by taxi it is a good idea to sit in the back seat of the car and call someone at your destination to let them know the name of the taxi company you're using, that you are on your way, and when you expect to arrive at their location.

- In some countries many taxi drivers will offer to take you to a bazaar or market where you will get an especially good deal because his relative owns the shop or stall. The chances are that you will be wasting your time and may even get yourself into trouble. Insist that you are taken directly to your destination.

- The road to or from the airport is a crime hotspot. Be wary when you're leaving or entering the airport by taxi. You may well be a sitting duck, loaded with cash, traveller's cheques and cameras when you arrive, or expensive gifts and souvenirs when you're heading back.

5

Maritime and Water Safety

MANY OF US STILL VIEW TRAVEL at sea as entering the realm of romance and adventure. And, as far as the sensation of voyaging by boat goes, it is. But sometimes the adventure goes haywire. Ships can sink, and are vulnerable to attack by terrorists – and pirates.

This really came home to me in November 1999, when I was flying to war-ravaged Somalia in a dilapidated old Soviet prop-driven aircraft flown by a Russian crew who smelled distinctly of alcohol. Sharing the cabin with a visiting delegation from Afghanistan's then Taliban regime and some farm animals, I sat next to the swilling latrine. In that hot, stinking cabin, I had plenty of time to think about the task ahead: training a maritime counter-piracy and fisheries protection force.

Piracy remains a real threat to shipping in some parts of the developing world. We'll look at the problem in a bit. But first, here's an overview of what can happen when you mess about in boats.

Major Accidents at Sea

In risk to human life, the maritime industry is relatively safe when compared to other forms of transport. Most shipping accidents involve tankers, cargo or fishing vessels with few crew on board. Cruise ships and ferries, however, are 'people carriers' and more vulnerable. They are becoming larger and much more sophisticated and numerous; some luxury liners are able to carry more than 3000 passengers and 1000 crew members. As cruising becomes more affordable, many more ships take to the high seas carrying thousands on the holiday of a lifetime. However, the stakes are high, as these floating hotels are vulnerable to certain types of risks.

Security and crime issues abound, both on board and once passengers go ashore. Even terrorism is no longer confined to terra firma in areas such as Israel, Northern Ireland or Indonesia. This was dramatically exposed when one of the world's most sophisticated warships, the *USS Cole*, was holed in a dramatic suicide bomb attack in the Yemeni port of Aden, killing 17 American sailors and injuring 39 crew members. And since the terrorist seizure of the *Achille Lauro* in 1985, the vulnerability of passenger vessels to acts of terrorism has been a significant concern for the international community.

Most cruise lines will change their itineraries to avoid troublespots, such as parts of the Middle East. Cruise lines don't guarantee that their ships will visit every anticipated port or follow every part of their intended routes during times of increased tension. Passengers expecting to visit certain areas will not automatically receive compensation for parts of the voyage that are cancelled due to security incidents. Check the fine print in your brochure as to the cruise company's liability.

The West has also had its share of disasters. A British consumer magazine warned that if safety measures were not put into place, there could be another disaster like the *Estonia*, when 852 died, or the *Herald of Free Enterprise*, which claimed 193. An accident report into the *Estonia* tragedy, Europe's worst maritime disaster since the Second World War, concluded that the doors of the bow had badly designed locks. It added that if the crew had reacted faster, the chances of survival might have been greater. One of the key recommendations was that crews should have more extensive safety training.

There have been others, equally serious. In 2000, 79 people died when the Greek ferry *Samina Express* sank after the captain left the vessel under the command of the trainee officer, in gale force winds. More worrying were the allegations that crew members had abandoned ship before anyone had been evacuated, leaving the panic-stricken passengers to fend for themselves.

With Greek island hopping so popular, incidents like this are worrying. And in fact, in October of that same year, 65 Greek ferries and cruise ships were forbidden to sail for failing to meet the international safety standards. Safety measures are supposed to be in place by 2002, with some ferry operators in the Mediterranean being given to 2005 to comply. However, sources close to the industry have indicated that even these dates are optimistic. In a recent safety inspection of 26 Mediterranean vessels, all failed the safety equipment check. The condition of lifeboats, life rafts and life buoys were found to be inadequate. The maintenance of life jackets and rope ladders, which are essential for emergency disembarkation, were also defective. And there's more. Some ferries operating on the English Channel had failed to identify emergency muster stations, and had too few handrails and poor public address systems, which would be vital in an emergency situation. And this is only the West – safety standards in some developing countries are non-existent and terrible accidents claiming many hundreds of lives have occurred.

So, while maritime transportation is safe, it is only relatively so. When it goes wrong, it goes very wrong. Is there anything that can be done to enhance your chances of survival in the event of such a tragedy? One of the most vital things is to be prepared, to know what to do. People survive even the most catastrophic of accidents. Those who make it to the top deck, for instance, will stand a better chance of survival than those remaining below.

If you're caught in a maritime incident and must abandon ship, here are the points you need to know.

■ Before you book your ticket, check the shipping company's safety record. In Europe and North America this should not be too difficult. When in poorer regions of the world, however, you may need to ask the locals about the state of the ship and if it is suitable for the journey. Many ships appear as if they're well maintained, but it is easy to paint over the rusted equipment and make it look serviceable.

- On the larger cruise ships and ferries, follow the instructions of the crew – if you feel they know what they are doing. Pay attention to the safety demonstrations and the safety instructions. If you do not speak the language, try to find out this information by asking around.

- Assess weather conditions for the duration of your journey. It can get pretty scary at sea, even in moderate sea conditions, particularly in areas prone to hurricanes and tropical storms. Weather conditions can change very quickly in the tropics.

- Even a cursory check will help to inform you of the condition of the ship and if it is suitable for the anticipated weather conditions. It was reported that on the *Estonia*, mattresses were used to plug up holes in watertight doors, which had been leaking for weeks. How many passengers would have sailed on her if they had known this?

- Avoid overcrowded ships. This has been identified as a major factor in accidents at sea. Remain on the quayside and assess the number of passengers. If the ship looks overcrowded, it may be possible to select another ship. On overcrowded ships, the movement of people can affect the trim of the ship. Vessels will be lower in the water because they are heavier, and if passengers move to one side for whatever reason the ship can tilt and become swamped.

- Identify and familiarise yourself with the quickest routes to the upper deck. When you're below decks you'll have to find your way in bad light conditions. If you become really concerned, a small sketch map of the route out may help. If you are travelling with family or friends, walk the route and identify the key areas.

- Confirm where life preservers or life jackets are stored, and actually look inside the containers to ensure that they are in there. Ensure that they are serviceable and the correct size. Most life jackets will have salt-water lights, which illuminate when they come into contact with salt water. If these are available, ensure that you get one and that the wiring is intact. Many types of life jackets will also come with a whistle, which could prove vital in attracting attention at night. If you are travelling with children, ensure that you find a life preserver that will fit your child. In some vessels smoke hoods are also provided in case of fire on board. Enquire if they are available and once again check that they're serviceable and the right size.

■ Find the emergency muster stations. These should be marked, and the information as to where they are should be pinned onto the door of your cabin or on a corridor wall. There should also be a set of instructions which will tell you what action to take in an emergency. If there are no instructions it will be up to you as to what you should do. Ask the crew members where the emergency muster stations are. Become familiar with the vessel's alarm system and what actions to take if the alarm sounds. If the crew is effi-cient, follow their instructions. Be aware that there may be a language problem, especially in developing countries. It may be advisable to know some basic terms in the local language.

■ It's a good idea to have a grab bag or moneybelt containing essen-tials and valuable items. Your passport, any medication that you are using and money will be necessary.

■ After leaving a distressed vessel, you could expect to be in a lifeboat or life raft or even in the water for some time. However, as soon as it has become clear that something has happened, all neighbour-ing shipping is diverted to the area of the incident. The emergency services will have been aroused. If you end up in the water, try to swim away from the vessel. Sinking ships create a vacuum effect which will pull floating objects with it, including people. After the ship has gone down it will be safe to swim back to the area in order to collect useful floating aids.

■ You can improvise floating aids from clothing. Wet trousers tied at the end of the legs, then filled with air, will support an adult for some time. Any floating debris should be collected. It can be lashed together to provide a substantial platform. Empty plastic bottles or water bottles can be placed beneath clothing. They will keep afloat even those who cannot swim.

- When in salt water, you should be able to stay afloat with the minimum of effort. At all costs avoid panicking: you will thrash around needlessly, becoming exhausted and swallowing water. Try to remain calm and retain control of the situation.

- Try to stay together with others when in the water; if you are in a lifeboat or on a life raft, lash them together. This will make it easier for rescue services to find you. If you are near land, it may be possible to make for it. Be aware of the currents. They may help you, but if they flow in the wrong direction you could end up becoming exhausted.

- The biggest threat, after drowning, is exposure. Hypothermia is the main cause of death: body heat loss is around 25 times greater in water than in air. Even in tropical waters, hypothermia can be a danger. Avoid all movements that increase blood circulation; the quicker your blood circulates the faster your core temperature will cool. Trying to keep warm in cold water will bring on exhaustion quicker.

- In the tropics, the sun can be a problem. Try to cover any exposed parts of your skin. The sun, combined with the salt water, will accelerate dehydration.

- You can tell when you are near land. There may be drifting wood or vegetation, or coastal birds, which fly out to sea in search of food in the morning and return at night. Wind direction may indicate land: generally, wind will blow towards land during the day and away from it at night. Cumulus clouds form over a landmass.

Piracy

The image of the bearded, one-eyed, cutlass-wielding privateer, standing beneath a fluttering skull and cross bones, belongs to history and old tales. But the trade has not died out. The only thing that today's pirates have in common with those of old, however, is the extent of their ruthlessness and brutality. Today's pirates rely on shock effect, speed and violence. On that trip to Somalia in 1999, we were armed with small arms and a rocket launcher, but it was also deemed necessary to have heavy machine guns on the deck of the ship to counter this threat. Typically, latter-day buccaneers operate in small teams of six to 12 men. They usually travel by small high-speed craft and are armed with the ubiquitous AK47 or some other small arms, in addition to the similarly widely available RPG 7 rocket launcher.

Today's pirates tend to be very efficient. Their attacks will not just target ships at sea. Ships at anchor or tied alongside have also been attacked. When they attack a ship at sea, they will most likely approach the stern of the vessel. Coming behind in the wake and throwing a grappling hook will enable them to board. The noise of the ship's engine will normally mask the noise of the smaller engine on the pirate's vessel. Their craft will be low in the water to avoid detection by ship's radar. Once on board, they operate quickly and go for personal valuables and cash. Even ships have disappeared, as pirates have commandeered them and forced them into an unfamiliar port. Here they are stripped, renamed and sold on.

The United Nations Law of the Sea defines piracy as illegal acts of violence and detention, or any act of depredation, committed for private ends against crew or passengers of a private ship, and taking place on the high seas or in a place outside the jurisdiction of any state. Ship owners often downplay the extent of the problem to reduce insurance premiums. In some regions of the world, such as Somalia, where there is no established form of law and order, there are no state agencies to respond to piracy attacks. This means that anyone unfortunate enough to be caught in such an incident will have to rely on his or her own initiative to get out of trouble.

There are specific areas where the risk is greater, as follows.

■ **South East Asia** has the greatest reported number of incidents. The coastal areas offshore from Indonesia, Malaysia and Singapore have become the danger areas. The Malacca Straits, which connect the Indian Ocean and China Sea between Malaysia and Indonesia, are the world's longest. Due to the potentially dangerous currents and the narrowness of the navigation channel and the volume of shipping in the area (more than 600 vessels a day) the Malacca Straits are the world's top hotspot for piracy. Not all the vessels are large cargo ships or tankers; there are also many cruise ships and smaller leisure craft. The proximity to land and the fact that most shipping crews are busy trying to avoid hitting each other in this narrow bottleneck gives the pirates an opportunity to attack the unwary.

■ **Africa** The majority of incidents have taken place off the coast of Somalia, although there have been incidents reported off Nigeria, Sierra Leone and other countries. Many of these attacks were against vessels at anchor. In Somalia, the pirate gangs appear to be well organised and have acted in large groups of up to 50 in several fast launches. They have been armed with small arms, rocket launchers and mortars. Attacks have often been coordinated from shore-based observation posts. There are some vessels in this region armed with ZSU anti-aircraft guns that have a range of some 5 kilometres. Fishing vessels have been intercepted and the crews held to ransom. Small boats such as cruisers and yachts have also been attacked. In May 1999, a small yacht which strayed too close to the shore was intercepted and the two Finnish crew were taken hostage. In similar incidents, people have been held hostage for months.

■ **South America** The area off the Colombian coast is hazardous for small craft, as trafficking in illegal narcotics continues to pose a serious threat. The continuing civil unrest in Colombia poses major security risks for those travelling along the coast. On the inland river routes, the hazards can be higher. In Brazil, the area around the port of Rio de Janeiro is a noted spot for piracy. Many of the attacks here are on vessels at anchor and the primary objective is the theft of valuables and cash. Off the Mexican coast in 1999, armed attackers stormed a ferry carrying around 300 tourists. The attackers were armed with small arms and destroyed the vessel's communications equipment before robbing an armoured truck on board loaded with cash, and many of the tourists.

- **Europe** The area around the Mediterranean has also seen an increase in piracy. In the Aegean Sea around the Greek island of Corfu and the coast of Albania, small boat owners are advised to stay well off shore. This tight channel has seen some particularly violent incidents suspected to have been the work of well-armed Albanian bandits.

So, although piracy is relatively rare, its consequences are serious, and round troubled countries such as Albania, Indonesia and Somalia it may well continue to flourish. In 2001, there were incidents reported in waters off India, Malaysia, Cameroon, Nigeria, Ghana, Ivory Coast, Tanzania, Bangladesh, Sri Lanka, Myanmar, Indonesia, Vietnam and Papua New Guinea.

Avoiding Piracy in a Small Boat

If you are travelling in a small boat, you'll need to think about what to do if a pirate attack is likely in the area. Here are the essential points.

- Before you go, ask if there is any risk from piracy. Try to avoid the piracy hotspots. If you are compelled, for whatever reason, to travel through a risky area, ensure that you post a lookout and have worked out an alarm system.

- Inform someone of your intentions – when you are leaving, what route you are taking and when you expect to arrive. When you do arrive at your destination, tell your contacts.

- At night and in extreme cases it may be advisable to travel through the danger area with your lights off. Most small pirate ships will be without radar, so you will be difficult to detect.

- In dangerous areas, avoid leaving ropes, life rings, cargo nets or anything else which makes it easy for hostile boarders to gain access to your vessel hanging over the side.

- Avoid conducting routine and predictable manoeuvres. If you make regular journeys in small craft, avoid leaving at the same time using the same route.

- Avoid dropping anchor or mooring in areas with previous records of piracy. If you have no choice, enter the area when it's dark. It is vital to have a lookout posted, even at night.

- Illuminating the area immediately around your vessel may act as a deterrent to pirates in some places.

- If a passing vessel hails you, do not heave to until you are certain that they are not a threat. If they are armed and faster, they will most likely board you anyway. If this happens, don't offer resistance. If all they do is rob you and leave, afterwards transmit a distress signal on the emergency frequency passing on your location and the nature of the incident. If they don't have firearms, it may be possible to resist if everyone in your boat is on deck. However, it must be stressed that you should do this only as the very last resort.

Preventing Crime at Sea

Ferries and cruise ships may be carrying a small town's worth of people, so it shouldn't be surprising that like all crowded places, they attract criminals, especially while in port. You need to take the same precautions that you would in any other small town filled with people you are not familiar with. If travelling with your children, tell them they have to follow normal rules of behaviour, not run wild.

Most cruise liners will have an appointed security staff. Some employ ex-Special Forces people as security coordinators. It may be advisable to liaise with the ship's security officer if you have any concerns.

In Your Cabin

You should use the same procedure that you would use in a hotel room (see Chapter 16, page 370). On first entering your cabin, ensure that your valuables are secure. You will still be at the port and many auxiliary staff and contractors will still be aboard. Many people will have access to your cabin. When you leave your cabin, ensure the door is locked. Use all the locks on the door and if there are bolts, use them too. Don't allow your children to open the door to strangers, especially while in port, and ensure that they don't walk around unsupervised. Protect your cabin key and cabin number, and leave your key at the desk when in port. Protect your passport and don't leave valuables lying around in your cabin. Put your wallet and valuables in the cabin's or the purser's safe. These, of course, are all basic reminders, but in the excitement and adventure of sailing it is very easy to forget.

While In Port

Most crimes to do with ships happen when the ship is in port and you are on an excursion. It is while you are ashore that you are particularly vulnerable, because you will be travelling in a clearly indentifiable tourist group. It's the same kind of problem you encounter in most tourist areas: theft of passports, money and credit cards, cameras and any other attractive item. So you should use the same crime-avoidance strategies you would use elsewhere, making it difficult for the opportunist thief to target you.

While ashore, stay with the crowd and do not venture out on your own. Ensure that your group has a pre-arranged, prominent meeting point you can easily identify, so that if you become separated you can make your way there. Once you are missed, people will go to the pre-arranged point to collect you. Take a small sack with all the essentials that you will need for the day. Try to obtain a map of the area. If it is a routine stop, the vessel's shop should supply them. Make sure that you have a list of all the shipping company's emergency telephone numbers and the address of the company representative in the port you are visiting. It is also a useful idea to have the name of the port and the location written in the local language. After leaving a port of call, continue to stay alert with regard to your possessions.

Small Boat Safety

On Rivers

If you are travelling on an inland river by small boat, choose one in good condition that's suitable for the prevailing weather conditions. Then you need to think about the way you'll negotiate the river.

Basically, inland rivers can be placed in one of three categories. (The information below is also useful if you intend to swim in any section of a river.)

- **The upper reaches** are the origins of the river, in the mountain ranges or high ground. Normally, the river here is shallow and you'll be able to wade across, so it is unsuitable for a small boat. If, however, the water is above waist height, the current will be too fast and it will be too difficult to control a boat or keep your footing. As the water continues downhill, some parts become deeper and more suitable for a boat.

- **The middle reaches** appear as the side streams empty into the smaller rivers, which have now descended into the deep valleys. The river here is fast-flowing and there are possible hidden dangers. Forest debris may lie under the surface, which can trap a boat's keel or unwary swimmer. The river continues to descend and becomes deeper and wider and at this stage is prone to flash flooding. Flash flooding occurs when the ground is saturated and can't absorb any more rainfall. This surface water quickly flows downhill and fills up the small rivers and streams. When it gets to the middle reaches this water forms a wave which can overwhelm the unwary. If you suspect that you are in an area susceptible to flash flooding and a heavy rainstorm has begun, it is advisable to get out of your boat, haul it out, climb onto higher ground and wait until the storm has passed.

- **The lower reaches** of the river will be much wider now as it twists and turns in order to find the easiest route through to the sea or ocean. The current may appear slow, but there may be powerful undercurrents, through which it will be difficult to steer the boat, and against which it will be difficult to swim. As the river approaches the coast it will be subject to the influence of the tide which may have a significant impact on the current and the height of the river.

If you are planning to travel in a remote area by boat, and especially if you intend to hire the boat yourself, it is essential that you obtain at least some basic boat-handling experience before you depart. Basic seamanship, navigation techniques and the use of safety equipment and boat/engine maintenance are vital. In the UK, the Royal Yachting Association on 01703 629962 may be able to advise you on what you need and where you can get it.

At Sea

For many people, a holiday is not complete unless they can cruise round the bay or visit outlying islands in a yacht or other small boat. But tragedy can hit, such as when a British family of four drowned after their boat capsized off the coast of Kenya in the summer of 2001. The family were on a fishing trip when a giant wave hit the boat, throwing all the occupants into the water. The crew of three and two Kenyan boys were rescued from the water by local fishermen and divers. Those who survived did so by clinging to the upturned vessel as the family were swept away.

Consider the following points when preparing to go to sea on a small boat.

■ Check the weather forecast by asking locals or listening to the shipping or local weather bulletins. Most countries will have a coastguard. By calling them or, if you have access to a VHF radio, by listening to reports on Channel 67, you will be able to keep abreast of the recent weather developments. They will also be able to inform you of the local tidal conditions and areas of shallow or dangerous water. In the event of an emergency it should be possible to summon assistance by transmitting on the emergency channel. This should alert other vessels in your vicinity that may be able to provide assistance. Carry a portable foghorn or whistle to attract attention if necessary.

- Check the condition of the boat and the engine and ensure that they are well maintained. Make sure that your emergency equipment (see page 131) is adequate for all on board and check that you have a toolkit and essential spares for the engine. Also have an alternative method of propulsion, a spare outboard engine or some oars.

- Ensure that you have obtained the relevant charts and tide tables before you start – and make sure that you can use them. You can then plan your trip. Identify your route and how long you expect your journey to take, and pinpoint safe stopping locations along the route.

- Formulate a plan including departure and arrival times, your route and ultimate destination. Include a description of the boat and the names of those on board.

- Do not overload the boat: it will become unstable and difficult to handle in fast currents.

- If you are preparing the boat yourself, attach a strip of reflective material along the side. This is especially useful in busy shipping lanes, where you need to be easy to see to avoid being run down.

- Everyone on board needs to know the drill in a 'man overboard' situation. If passengers are inexperienced, it is advisable to run through a practice before setting off. In attempting to assist someone who is in the water, first try to reach them by offering your arm or any object which is lying around, clothing, an oar or piece of wood. You might have to throw something which will float, such as a life ring or piece of wood. If they are too far away and you are in a lifeboat or life raft, it should be possible to row to their assistance. As a last resort, go into the water and swim to the aid of the distressed person. Be aware that there are now two people in danger; you should only do this if you are a competent swimmer and have had some life-saving training.

- If you are involved in a group outing or journey, ensure before getting on the water that everyone is aware of what to expect. Ensure everyone knows where the safety equipment is located. If rescue is necessary, it is important for rescuers to act decisively. Someone must take charge of the situation and coordinate the rescue effort. Communication is vital. Consider the following points.

▨ After a person has spent 30 seconds underwater it is obvious they are in difficulty and will require assistance.

▨ If a casualty has been submerged for 2 minutes you will in all probability need to resuscitate them.

▨ After someone has been submerged for approximately 10 minutes, major brain damage will have occurred.

Basic Safety on a Small Boat

Top Ten Hints

1. Ensure that you prepare for the trip by carrying adequate safety equipment.

2. Carry approved and suitable life jackets for each person on board. Ensure that when underway, everyone wears their life jacket, even in calm waters.

3. Inform someone where you are going, what route you have taken, and when you are going to return.

4. Watch the weather and try to anticipate changing weather patterns.

5. Carry sufficient fuel, water and food in case you are delayed.

6. Take adequate precautions to prevent fire. Drain any fuel in the bilges before you set off. Ensure that the fuel lines are serviceable and that you have a functional fire extinguisher. If you smoke, ensure that you do so away from fuel and cooking gas.

7. Don't overload your boat, and spread the weight around evenly. An unevenly loaded boat can become unstable even in relatively calm waters.

8. Avoid excessive alcohol consumption if you are in control of a boat – it will impair your judgement.

9. Ensure that you have a water pump to remove excessive water. A plastic bailer is the least you should have.

10. Use the one-third rule for fuel consumption – one-third for the outward journey and one-third for the return journey. This will leave one-third for emergencies and to be used when the wind and surface current cause drifting or blow you off course.

Emergency Equipment

■ Oars or a small auxiliary outboard.

■ Spare can of fuel.

■ Radio and/or mobile phone.

■ Tow-rope.

■ Torch and spare batteries and bulbs.

■ Day and night distress flares. These are available from any good boat shop. However, they are considered to be dangerous air cargo and you will be unable to take them on commercial aircraft.

   ■ Hi-Visibility Hand Smoke: For day use only, visibility 4 kilometres, normal duration around 60 seconds.
   ■ Red Hand Flare: visibility 10 kilometres at night, normal duration around 60 seconds.
   ■ Parachute Illumination Distress Rocket: visibility approximately 15 kilometres (night), with a normal duration of around 40 seconds.

■ Strobe lights. These are useful and emit a powerful pulse of light which can be visible over a long distance.

■ Mirror. Stainless steel mirrors are ideal for signalling at sea.

■ Whistles are useful for attracting attention.

■ Portable air/foghorn.

■ Watertight container carrying your essentials.

- Map and/or chart and compass.

- Life preservers with lights and whistles.

- Drinking water and food for 48 hours.

- A length of rope.

Swimming Safety

Most people head straight for the water the minute they arrive at the seaside. Basically, this is heading straight into unknown danger. Even in the UK, with the onset of summer and warmer weather there are all-too-frequent reports of accidental drowning. Victims include children who have fallen into swimming pools and those who have tried to cool off in rivers and lakes and got into trouble. Diving into unknown stretches of water, with hidden dangers from unseen rocks and vicious undercurrents, is another common summer tragedy.

It is a sad fact that these accidents do not need to happen, and most could have been prevented. Here's how.

- Whether you are swimming in a pool, river or in the sea, always have a friend or relative near in case you get into trouble. Obey warning signs such as 'Dangerous Current' and 'No Swimming' and look out for flags showing the risk level.

- If you are not sure whether an area is safe for swimming, don't swim there. Dangers such as hidden undercurrents, sunken trees and entangling seaweed may lurk just beneath the waves.

- Avoid swimming if you are under the influence of alcohol or drugs, and do not swim if you are tired. Never swim right after a meal; allow about an hour to digest it.

- Don't swim in the sea at night, especially if you are unfamiliar with the currents. It is very easy to become disorientated and swimmers can easily lose their sense of direction.

- Even if you are a confident swimmer, be aware of the sea condition. The weather can turn stormy very quickly. The tidal effects at sea can be dramatic. Check the local tidal conditions and whether the tide is coming in or going out.

■ If you are an inexperienced swimmer, do not be tempted to follow stronger swimmers out. Stay in shallow water and use flotation aids.

■ Water has an almost magnetic attraction for children and there have been many instances of children being swept out to sea because their parents lost sight of them for just a minute. Never allow toddlers or children, whatever their ability, to swim without adult supervision.

■ Maintain all-round observation and be on the lookout for boats, water skiers and jet skis. When you are swimming at sea you have a low profile and will be difficult to see in the water. Fast-moving vessels will take time to change direction – that is, if they see you at all.

■ Swim parallel to the shore. If you swim too far out to sea you may be too tired to swim back, and if you get into trouble you may be difficult to be seen from the shore.

■ Be aware of going too close to piers or breakwaters. The currents around these can be very strong and can test even the best of swimmers.

■ Cramp can occur at any time. However, when you are swimming, cramp can become a life-threatening condition. Try to float on your back. Sometimes this is enough to ward off a greater attack of cramp. However, if the pain is becoming worse, massage the muscle with both hands. Swim slowly back to shore, use an alternative stroke to the one that brought about the cramp attack.

■ Swimming in cold water after eating can trigger an attack of stomach cramps. This can be a serious condition, with severe pain. Try to keep your head above water, and attract attention. Float on your back, breathe deeply and try to relax your muscles.

■ If you are surprised by a large wave and cannot get away from it, dive underneath it and keep your body as low as possible until the wave has passed over you. Or dive into the base of the wave just before it breaks. In shallow water, do not dive under the wave; crouch and keep a low body profile.

▪ Do not overestimate your own strength when you are swimming. Do not become blasé about this seemingly simple activity, especially in cold water.

Pool Safety

Accidents happen not only in open water. Many holidays have been ruined by accidents occurring at the hotel pool. Never allow infants or young children access to the pool without adult supervision.
Consider the following points.

▪ Don't run around the edge of the pool. This area is wet and slippery and you could fall and get hurt.

▪ It is dangerous to mess around after the pool has been closed, especially if you have been drinking. Never throw or push someone into the pool, as they may hit their head on the side.

▪ Avoid diving or jumping into a pool without first checking whether there is someone or something below.

▪ Don't dive into shallow water. Striking an obstacle in shallow water can lead to head injuries, unconsciousness, spinal injury and even death. Ensure that you test the depth of the water before diving and stretch your arms out above your head as you dive in. Your arms will absorb the shock of any impact.

▪ If you are engaged in any water sport, ensure that you are confident enough in the water. This may mean taking swimming lessons prior to your holiday.

▪ If one or more of your party is a weak swimmer, ensure that you have a flotation aid close at hand, and most importantly keep an eye on them. This applies to children and adults.

Crossing rivers on foot

If you have to cross a large river while hiking, you need to know what you're doing. Many people have been killed attempting it. Unsuspecting holidaymakers become victims while trying to cross dangerous rivers, yet if they had taken the trouble to look they would probably find a suitable crossing point nearby. The mistake is underestimating the power of the river. As described on page 127, an understanding of how rivers flow and what happens to the water will help in the task.

Before you attempt a crossing, try to find an obvious crossing point such as a bridge. Ask locals about this, and whether there is a ferry service. Only when you've exhausted all other options should you attempt to cross.

First, don't wade blindly in. An apparently calm river can have a lot going on under the surface. Assuming that you have to make the crossing unassisted, you need to select the right spot. Water will generally move faster around the outside of a bend and will tend to be deeper here. Water will move slower on the inside of a bend and will be shallower. Very sharp bends may have counter-currents or eddies, and may even have whirlpools. This occurs as the fast water collides into the far riverbank where it rebounds and creates deep pools as it removes sediment and gravel from the riverbed below. Any water which is choppy and broken usually indicates underwater obstacles such as rocks or timber.

If you have decided that the river is shallow enough to wade in, there are some sensible precautions you can take. Ensure your trousers are not tucked into your boots. This would fill your trouser legs with water and make them very heavy. If you are carrying a rucksack, only keep one shoulder strap on: if you get into difficulty you can always let go and not get dragged away, trapped in your pack.

When you enter the river, make sure you face upstream and turn your body at an oblique angle to the current. Do not lift your feet too high and always try to maintain stable footholds. Shuffle across the river, moving one pace at a time and maintaining your balance. If after a heavy storm the river is in spate do not attempt a crossing. Wait until the water level subsides, then attempt to cross.

Shark attack

Throughout the summer of 2001 there were an alarming number of reports of sharks massing near popular tourist locations. At one Florida resort, swimmers were ordered out of the water as sharks gathered offshore. In the same area, a schoolboy and an adult were left fighting for their lives after being attacked by sharks in two different incidents. The adult lost a leg and the boy, an arm. In fact, of the 31 shark attacks worldwide that summer, 16 happened in the Florida area.

Some suggest that the increase in shark-feeding dives, where tourists actually hand-feed sharks, is partially responsible because sharks now associate humans with food and have lost their fear of us. Whatever the reason, this is a development that travellers must be aware of.

In the mid-1990s I was diving off the northern coast of Jamaica. It was approaching dusk and I was with another diver, conducting a sea-bottom search at a depth of around 30 metres. In the fading light we were confronted by a huge shark which was just visible. It swam very close and I suddenly felt very vulnerable. However, we kept control of the situation and slowly made our way to the surface and, with the minimum of movement, attracted our safety boat and left the water. The chances were that if we had panicked we would almost certainly have attracted the animal's attention.

The following points will reduce your chances of becoming the victim of a shark attack.

- Stay out of the water at dawn, dusk and during the night, when some species of shark come close to the shore to feed.

- Swim, surf or dive with other people, and don't move too far away from assistance. In addition do not go swimming in high-risk areas if you have an open wound. Women having their periods should ideally stay out of the water, too. Sharks have the ability to detect blood and body fluids in very small concentrations from tremendous distances.

- Some species of shark lurk in and around harbour entrances, channels and water outlets, so avoid swimming in these areas.

- Avoid splashing around and swimming erratically: the vibrations given off attract sharks. If a shark swims close to you, do not provoke or harass it, even if it's small.

- Stay out of the sea if sharks are known to be in the area.

- If you are in the water and see a shark, compose yourself and leave the water as fast as you can. The more you thrash around, the more chance the shark will be attracted to you.

- If other marine animals bolt for no apparent reason they may have sensed a shark. If there are dead marine animals in the water leave immediately. Sharks are scavengers and can detect dead or wounded animals.

- Even areas with shark defences get the occasional shark sneaking in. Shark nets can safeguard against attacks but they cannot provide 100 per cent protection. In March 2000, a shark attacked a surfer at a popular tourist beach on the Gold Coast of eastern Australia. The shark evaded a system of nets that were supposed to prevent the fish from getting too close to the beach.

6

Safe Business Travel

IN OUR GLOBAL MARKETPLACE, COMMERCE IS conducted by battalions of business people who travel all over the planet grinding the wheels of the international economy. But the terrorist attack on New York City's economic heart has put big business centres, and all who deal in them, on the front line.

The new-style terrorism has adopted the same tactics used by the SAS – blending in behind the lines and operating covertly until the time is ripe. Behind the bustling mask, our streets and cities – the places where money is made – are a battleground.

We live in a time when major business centres such as London, Frankfurt, New York, Toronto, Tokyo and Hong Kong must seriously consider the possibilities of suicide bombers stalking their streets, of biological warfare attacks and further danger from the air. In 1986 at the Tory party conference in the Grand Hotel, Brighton, an IRA bomb attack came close to assassinating the entire government. The IRA issued a chilling warning after the attack, which left five people dead. It is a warning we should never forget. 'Today you were lucky, but remember you have to be lucky all the time, we only have to be lucky once.'

We should never forget this message. Relying on luck is a mistake, and possibly a fatal one. You must take active measures to look after your own security in a time of heightened risk.

It has to be said, though, that business travellers have always faced danger when travelling abroad, including crime and terrorism. In 1998, four telecommunications workers from the British company Granger Telecom were sent to install a mobile communications network in the Chechen capital, Grozny. Chechen gangsters abducted and beheaded the men, leaving their heads in a sack on the main road. This tragic incident exposed the folly of trying to conduct business operations in volatile and violent countries without adequate security precautions.

Most multinational companies will go some way to educate their people about the dangers of overseas business travel. But sadly, many independent and small business travellers still venture out from the UK woefully, and in some cases tragically, ill prepared for what could be a very bumpy ride.

Conducting Business Abroad

Business travellers visiting high-risk areas should pay attention to the points that follow. Although the levels of threat vary between countries, the September 2001 attacks have demonstrated that terrorists and criminal gangs can strike anywhere. And remember, the simple theft of your passport could result in a failed business meeting.

- Set aside a period free from work in order to focus on and prepare for your trip (see Chapter 1).

- Ensure that you have conducted a traveller's threat assessment. Your company must provide you with an up-to-date country report, and not what happened the last time someone visited the country. Things change fast and your brief should be relevant to within the last week (see Chapter 1, page 9). Allow yourself time to get all the jabs you need for the country you're travelling to. You may have to prepare weeks in advance (see Chapter 17, page 381).

- Ensure that you are familiar with your organisation's contingency plans. You will need this information if something happens to you, or if there is an outbreak of trouble in the country you are visiting.

- If you do not have confidence in your employer's ability to assist in an emergency, you need to devise a contingency plan of your own and make your family and company aware of it. Remember to provide your family and friends with your emergency contact details (see Chapter 1, page 32).

- In times of tension, Western governments look at ways of evacuating their nationals from unstable countries. If there is a large Western business or expatriate community in a country, their government may decide to organise an assisted evacuation involving the military. So if you are conducting business in a volatile country, liaise with your embassy or consulate there. They have to know you're in the country to be able to help you. Tell them where you're staying, the reason for your visit, and your arrival and departure dates. Give them an emergency contact number, too. The BBC will also broadcast details of any evacuation on shortwave radio.

- Pinpoint the hospital or health clinic nearest to where you'll be staying, and ensure that you know how to get there. Find out what facilities are available and when it opens.

Emergency Situations

For many, the most apalling images from the terrorist attack in New York were of people jumping to their deaths from the towers. This was a salutary lesson for us all that in the event of a fire, explosion or any other emergency requiring the evacuation of a high-rise building, it is vital to be aware of evacuation procedures. Confusion and panic are inevitable, but if you know what to do you can significantly reduce your chances of becoming stranded.

Terrorism is not the only threat. In the UK in 1999, arson caused 466 of the 663 deaths by fire – and this in a country with stringent fire precautions and well-trained emergency services.

But wherever you go, you need to be prepared for the possibility of fire in buildings you're visiting, so consider the following points.

- Ensure that you are familiar with the building's alarm systems and evacuation procedures, even if you are only attending a business meeting. If you will be staying or meeting in the building for any length of time, it's a good idea to walk the emergency escape route, making it easier to follow in the event of a real emergency. Directions for evacuation are usually posted in stairwells and lobbies of major office blocks.

- If the fire alarm is activated, try to remain calm; don't panic, as this could spread to others and lead to further confusion. If you find the source of the fire, you may decide to tackle putting it out yourself. You should only do so if the fire is small and you know where the building's firefighting equipment is kept.

- Most office blocks have fire safety marshals who are responsible for organising the safe evacuation of the building. Generally, you should obey the instructions of these individuals, but if the safety marshals have been injured or you do not trust their judgement, you should leave the building as soon as possible. The safety marshal may, for instance, attempt to calm everyone down, but this can lead to a false sense of security and mask the fact that there is an urgent need to leave the building. Remember that this may be the first time the fire marshals have had to deal with the real thing, and that they themselves might be frightened.

- When you evacuate, leave the building quickly by the nearest emergency exit, remembering to close the door behind you. Avoid taking heavy baggage with you: this will slow you down and obstruct other evacuees. Don't even think of re-entering the building to collect your possessions. If you are unfamiliar with the building or cannot speak the local language, follow the crowd and do not move against the flow of traffic. Keep to the right in corridors and in staircases: this will allow fire fighters and emergency personnel to pass.

■ Smoke inhalation is a very real danger, and has killed many people. If the fire is on a lower floor, the smoke will rise and engulf the floors above. In some cases it will be impossible to do anything but wait for emergency services, but generally it's paramount to evacuate the building as quickly as possible if there is a big fire on a lower floor.

■ If the room you're in fills with smoke, get down close to the ground on your hands and knees and crawl to the nearest safe exit. Be aware that in the event of a major fire the sprinkler system will be activated. This may make it even harder to see, and will certainly leave smooth surfaces slippery.

■ During major emergencies, you must think before you stop to help others. Remember, smoke inhalation can overcome even the strongest very quickly. It may be advisable to place casualties in the safest place you can find, and then inform emergency services of the location.

■ In the aftermath of the World Trade Center disaster, many people have purchased safety smoke hoods such as the Durum safety hood. This is a vacuum-packed hood that will fit into a pocket. It's pulled over the head and will provide adequate protection from smoke inhalation and even a chemical weapons attack.

■ When you exit the building, ensure that you move to the emergency muster location. If this location is deemed to be dangerous, move away from the area.

■ As soon as you are safe, contact your office and your family at home to let them know that.

Bomb Attacks and Threats

Bomb threats are a routine part of life in some big cities, such as London. People can even get used to the inconvenience they cause. But in many countries terrorist bombs hit their mark. In 1995 the Oklahoma City bombing killed 168 people and injured hundreds, while the 1998 bomb attacks against the US embassies in Kenya and Tanzania killed hundreds and injured over a thousand. There have been others throughout Europe, the Americas, Africa, South and Central Asia and South East Asia, often directly targeting the commercial and business infrastructure of the countries. And suicide bombings markedly increased in 2001.

Hoaxes cause damage too, eroding confidence and creating havoc in the workplace; but they have to be taken seriously. In the summer of 1999 I was in the Kosovan capital of Pristina, escorting an official from the World Bank who was at that time working to get the country back on its feet. One evening the official met colleagues for dinner. While they were eating at the restaurant, panic broke out in the streets, with people running everywhere. There had been a warning that a bomb had been placed outside a local hotel, and was due to explode in three hours. My first inclination was that it was a hoax: three hours would give the authorities enough time to find and defuse the device. Nevertheless we evacuated the area, staying clear of glass-fronted shops and hotels. In fact, this was a hoax, but shortly after we left a bomb detonated in Pristina, killing two people and injuring many more. In short: better safe than sorry.

The following points contain vital advice for dealing with bomb threats and explosions in urban areas.

- Take every threat seriously, even if there has been a history of hoaxes. If you are travelling in a group ensure that everyone in it is informed. In many countries, even in the UK, people have become complacent about bomb warnings. Don't be one of them.

- If you are told of a bomb warning try to discover when it is supposed to explode and where it is. This will tell you how long you have to evacuate the building and which areas are not safe.

- If you find you have time, evacuate the building using designated emergency exits. Do not try to use the elevator: it may fail to function and trap you between floors. If this happens it may take some time to launch an emergency rescue.

- During the evacuation, remain alert to the possibility that other bombs have been laid nearby (see below). Avoid suspicious packages, illegally parked cars, dustbins and anything that arouses your suspicion. Trust your intuition. If it looks suspicious, get away from it.

- If you do not have time to evacuate, move to the side of the building furthest from the device, and try to find an area without windows. In an explosion glass becomes a secondary projectile and can cause severe injury. Moreover, glass will not show up in an X-ray, and can go unnoticed during a medical examination.

- Try to get as many barriers, such as walls and large desks, between you and the bomb. Get under a desk or table and stay there until the device has exploded. Cover your head with your hands, books, a ream of paper or similar material which is to hand. Kneel with your face down and your mouth closed but jaws opened; this will reduce the damage to your ears in a loud explosion. You should remain in this position until debris stops flying around the room.

- It is a common tactic for terrorists to lay more than one device at the same time. One device will explode, causing panic as people evacuate buildings. The second device is intended to catch people as they leave or mill around. It's a technique designed to cause maximum casualties. It is wise to remain where you are unless you are forced from the building by smoke or fire.

- Many bombs are detonated by remote control. The terrorists send a signal in the form of a radio frequency wave, which activates the device. It is important that you do not use your cellphone or portable radio in the event of a bomb threat. Radio transmissions have inadvertently caused explosive devices to detonate prematurely.

- Some countries have seen a dramatic increase in suicide attacks. In Tel Aviv, Israel, a suicide bomber killed 20 and injured over a hundred people in June 2001. There is every possibility that this tactic may be used in other business centres.

- When visiting volatile areas, or global business centres in times of tension, you must use caution during large public gatherings. Political and even social gatherings have been the target of suicide bomb attacks in some countries. Use your hotel brochure to see what events are on, and enquire about safety procedures at the event. If tension is high, only attend if there are adequate security precautions in place.

■ Maximum disorder is the primary goal of terrorists the world over. In major business centres, this invariably means launching an attack during rush hour. Packed train stations or subways, taxi ranks or bus stops have all been targeted in the past. In a volatile region or during times of increased tension anywhere, avoid the rush hour when using public transport.

Hostile Surveillance

Commercial espionage is not just confined to thrillers. Businessmen and women travelling abroad carry vital commercial information, and foreign competitors and even states will go to extreme measures to obtain a commercial advantage. Business travellers have been placed under surveillance by commercial opposition, state security services, terrorist gangs, criminals and even media organisations seeking to expose partnerships between government and business. When you travel abroad on business, assume that you will be placed under surveillance and that your routines, contacts and activities are under scrutiny.

In 1999 I was, as I've mentioned, working in Pristina. It was then still such a violent city I was forced to complete some reports lying on the floor of my hotel room, as bullets were flying around outside the window. The security people at the hotel informed me that every guest who checked in was placed under surveillance for at least 24 hours – a legacy of their Communist past, I am sure, but in some parts of the world still routine practice.

Hostile surveillance does not only mean being followed around the streets by shady characters. Today's high-tech surveillance devices mean that your telephone calls, emails, faxes and private conversations are easy to listen in on or intercept. So it's essential to identify where you are most vulnerable, and then modify your behaviour and take precautions. It's particularly important to separate out the most sensitive information you'll be carrying, as you'll need to protect this most carefully. And of course it's vital to learn the signs of unwarranted interest in your activities. I've listed these below.

■ Beware when people who are not engaged in your business or have no connection to your company repeatedly approach you, particularly if they display an undue interest in what you're doing in their country. A common ploy is to follow this up by asking if you know a certain person connected with your business. Be cautious if a stranger tries to discover your nationality. Always avoid individuals who say they're language students and ask to practise their English on you.

■ Think twice before accepting invitations to social or business-related functions from strangers with no connections to your company. When you do attend parties, dinners or other social events, avoid all inappropriate conversation about your activities. Limit your drinking. In really sensitive situations, order your own drinks and in order not to cause offence when offered drinks by strangers, always have a full glass.

■ Be cautious about social contact with foreign state officials, law enforcement agencies or military organisations. This is particularly important if there is internal conflict in the country, or border tensions. Opponents of the state may identify you as a target if they see you conducting business activities with their 'enemy'.

■ One of the world's oldest tricks is the 'honey trap'. Be wary of approaches from local women trying to strike up a conversation or offering to buy you drinks at the hotel bar.

■ If you see suspicious activities, people or vehicles that lead you to think you are under surveillance, pretend not to notice and continue your normal routine, while being extra discreet about your movements, conversations and activities. If you overreact and try to run, they could assume you really do have something to hide, and intensify their efforts. In extreme cases, or if your business is of a sensitive nature, you should consider wrapping up your business and returning home.

■ Successful surveillance is no easy task: many highly trained operators and a relative level of sophistication are needed to coordinate the pursuit of a fast-moving target. If your work is such that you feel real professionals may be watching you, discreetly watch for vehicles circling the area and drivers paying undue attention to you, your vehicle or your hotel. A badly trained surveillance team will stick out from the crowd and use crude techniques. They may have people staring into shop windows across the street from you to watch the reflection, drive vehicles with blacked-out windows, or simply look suspicious.

■ Be aware that well-trained surveillance operators can be men, women or children. Trust your intuition. Surreptitiously record the registration numbers of cars or descriptions of individuals, and report this to the embassy or consulate and pass it on to your company at home.

■ Do not adopt routines: if you do something at the same time every day, you'll make trailing you easy for the surveillance teams. Be a bit unpredictable. Keep schedules secret, and arrange meetings only through reliable channels.

■ Be cautious when you attend a business meeting arranged at a seminar, exhibition or some other impromptu venue. A casual, hastily arranged meeting may have been set up so someone can eavesdrop on your conversation.

■ If you need to make phone calls, or send faxes or emails from your hotel, be aware that they may be intercepted, and avoid conveying sensitive material. In many countries hotel communications are routinely monitored.

■ If you suspect that your hotel room contains an electronic listening device, leave it. If you find one and destroy it, you will only attract more suspicion. Ensure that you avoid talking about your business activities in your hotel room.

- Don't leave important messages on answerphones or mobile phone voice mail. These machines can be easily accessed by surveillance teams. Dictaphones are a reliable way of storing information when you are travelling, unless, of course, they get into the wrong hands.

- Fax machines use disposable rolls of black film during the printing process, which are in effect copies of all the faxes you have received. Do not throw them away. If you are expecting a fax containing sensitive information from your home office, arrange for it to be sent at a specific time when you'll be in the office (remembering the local time difference). Otherwise the information will be compromised.

- Laptops, which have become business essentials, can also make you vulnerable to surveillance. There have been reports of criminal gangs with high-powered video cameras recording the emails business travellers are typing on their laptops. The videos can then be replayed to decipher the message. Or people sitting next to you can easily pry into what you're typing. Be sure you're unobserved when you deal with sensitive material on a laptop.

- When travelling, ensure that only absolutely essential material is stored on your laptop's hard drive. Back up copies of all your most important files and delete any personal details. Some business travellers actually remove the hard drive and store it in a container in their jacket until they need to reinsert it. Make sure your laptop batteries are charged when you arrive at the airport. There have been incidents in which laptops that fail to turn on have been confiscated on suspicion that they contain an explosive device.

- Don't leave anything behind when you go – place it in your locked suitcase. This is something I learned in the SAS. Be careful of what you put in your dustbin: all sorts of information can be gleaned from what you throw out. Surveilliance teams routinely search dustbins looking for any sensitive material, such as notes about your business trip. A sheet of apparently blank paper from a notepad can carry the impression of a note you wrote on the sheet above. Store receipts will give your credit card number. Used flight tickets will show the airline you're flying with, which makes it easier to check on schedules and get an indication of when you intend to leave. Potential kidnappers can then monitor your route to the airport (see page 113).

General Business Travel Security

As I mentioned above, laptops are now part of nearly every business traveller's luggage. Unfortunately, they are also one of the easiest possessions to steal. If you plan to travel with highly sensitive personal and business information stored on your laptop, be aware that it's relatively easy for technologically minded criminals to access it. According to the estimates of one American insurance company, over 307,000 laptop computers worth over $1 billion were stolen in the US alone in 1997 – and only 3 per cent were ever recovered.

Check out the following points for general information on staying safe when you're travelling, including keeping that laptop secure.

- There are a number of laptop security products on the market – cable locking devices and alarm systems, for instance. Invest in one.

- Laptops are vulnerable because they are mobile and relatively small. They can be targeted anywhere; but statistics show they are more likely to be stolen from offices or conference rooms, and in railway stations, airports and hotels. More than 40 per cent of all laptop thefts have happened in offices or during trips. Don't leave your laptop unattended in these places and situations.

- If your laptop is stolen, report the theft as soon as possible to the manufacturer. If your computer is later taken in for repair or servicing by the thief, the shop is obliged to check the manufacturer's database to see whether it was stolen.

- If you are carrying your laptop around in a flashy designer laptop case, you're just advertising the fact that you're carrying a computer worth up to £3000 in a small bag. It's best to conceal your laptop in a small backpack. Pad it out and handle it gently when your laptop is inside. This has the added bonus of leaving both your hands free in an accident or other emergency.

- Ensure that you have compiled emergency contact details (see Chapter 1) in case you have to contact your office at home or your family.

- Keep your company at home informed of your itinerary and any changes to your plans. You should plan a communications schedule with your office before you go. If you call at, say, 9 am, make this a short call to reassure everyone that communications are open and tell the people in the office that all is okay. You could make your main communications call at about 5 pm. During this you could pass on a report of how your day has gone, including any progress with your business meetings. When you make each call, you should tell your office where you are, how long you intend to stay there and when you will be returning to your hotel. If you miss one of these calls, you'll have been out of touch for 12 hours, which will alert your colleagues that something may be wrong. If you miss two calls, this tells your office something *is* wrong, and their emergency-locating plan needs to spring into action.

- Be cautious about giving out your business card. When I was in Nigeria in 2001, I gave my business card only to those I thought were genuine. However, months after I had returned our office received a suspicious email from Lagos. It was quite clearly a scam, offering a huge amount of cash to move funds from a bank in Nigeria. I did not give anyone in Lagos my business card.

- When you are travelling around an unfamiliar city, always carry a city map. It's a good idea to go over the map before you venture out – with hotel staff, perhaps – to identify any areas you should stay away from. Ensure that the map covers the area where your hotel is located.

- Be cautious about telling people where you are staying. If you are living in a hotel, do not give out your room number or its telephone number. You should keep all your information on a need-to-know basis. The less people who know what you are doing, the more secure you will be.

- If your telephone rings, don't answer it by saying your name – state the telephone number instead, and if it's not anyone you know, politely hang up. Do not pass on any personal details or details about colleagues on hotel telephones. Be cautious of calls from hotel reception: they may be false.

- If you're driving or taking a taxi to an important business meeting in the morning, enquire about local traffic conditions. It is a good idea to book your taxi the day before and inform them of what time you want to be at your destination. They will tell you what time you should leave at.

- Many business travellers carry vital documents as well as substantial amounts of cash. Avoid stashing these in your pockets or laptop case; use a hidden document case instead. Shoulder-holster style cases worn under the clothes are very useful and can hold a surprising amount of money and paper. Try to choose a colour that roughly matches your skin. Bright colours such as blue or red could be seen under a light-coloured shirt. Avoid bum bags and anything else with visible straps – they can be cut very easily.

- Ask around to discover whether there are any demonstrations planned in the city while you're there. If there is one in the offing, stay indoors. Locals will give you a good idea of the nature of the event. You should follow their instructions, and stay clear of what they deem to be dangerous areas.

- Be sure you're well briefed about the social and political situations at your business destination before you go. Once there, if you know the language, read local newspapers and listen to news bulletins to stay informed of any potentially problematic developments. If you see pressure groups handing out leaflets, or even spot graffitti on a wall, take note. They may indicate an ongoing campaign of civil disruption, or at the very least warn you that there is dissent within the country.

- Listen to BBC and CNN news reports. Any military action launched by Western nations inevitably means a backlash against innocent Westerners working abroad. Even political rhetoric from your home country that's directed against the country you're visiting could spark tension. If this happens while you're on a business trip, carefully monitor the local reaction and increase your vigilance.

7

Personal Security

EVERY YEAR AN INCREASING NUMBER OF travellers from the West become victims of aggression and violence abroad. Sadly, many of these situations need not have escalated in this way. Most petty criminals will try to avoid actual violence, but threaten to use it to subdue and intimidate their victims.

In some countries, where the security situation is tense or there is a polarised class system, Western tourists have attracted aggression. But the real culprit is alcohol or drug use. In the UK, for instance, the problem of alcohol-related violence, mainly involving young men, has been blamed for the 19 per cent increase in violent crime in the year 2001. In London alone, one newspaper survey found that muggings increased almost 40 per cent that year. And there are countries with worse records. In many countries, the easy access to weapons often results in tragedies over very minor incidents. In the US, for example, it has been estimated that over the last two decades there have been more than 600,000 fatalities attributed to the easy access to firearms.

Travel itself can be stressful, and many apparently innocuous activities can lead to potentially explosive situations. Let's say you've queued at a ticket office for ages. A local then walks to the front and collects their tickets. This may be infuriating, but it is one of many seemingly unfair cultural traits that the foreigner must learn to accept. If handled properly, many of these situations can be resolved peacefully.

Knowing how to defuse a tense situation will enable you to make quick decisions and possibly head off violent incidents before they develop. You will need to develop a crisis management strategy. When travelling to a potentially volatile area, for instance, a very basic strategy should include the three elements of *awareness*, *space* and *escape*.

Maintaining *awareness* of your surroundings when travelling or staying in a foreign country is vital. This means awareness of both your physical surroundings and the local people. You need to discover what is considered acceptable behaviour there so you can identify potentially threatening situations, and to do this you must of course understand local culture and habits. Pay attention to your instincts too. If you become alarmed by a situation or a person, this is your body's internal mechanism for telling you to back off. And if you're suddenly involved in a potential mugging, being aware of the risk–value ratio will help you make a quick decision. It is not worth risking your life for something that can easily be replaced, and the safe option may well be to hand over your wallet or camera.

If you become involved in a confrontation, you need to create a personal *space*. You have to try to keep the aggressor at arm's length or outside striking distance. If they enter this space, move away to maintain the same distance. You can use your voice in an authoritative manner to intimidate him or attract attention from others. If you adopt a confident posture, look him in the eye, and tell him loudly that you understand what is happening and you will not be bullied, he may well back off. Criminals generally prey on the weak and if they anticipate resistance they will back off and look for another, softer target. If they persist and fail to respect your personal space, you may have to hand over what they want or try to escape. Only as a last resort should you attempt to use force – and you'll have to show the aggressor you mean it (see below).

The last element of your strategy is *escape*. This is closely connected with the first element of awareness. Be aware of the safe areas around you – well-lit cafés, police stations, hospitals. If you end up having to escape a situation, you must have an idea of where you are heading.

Controlling Violent Situations

Many physical assaults are preventable if the victim is able to read the signs of danger, or is aware of how these situations develop. People with a propensity to violence will not target those who are 'in control'. They will look for signs of insecurity and uncertainty. By using common sense, taking some simple precautions and behaving in a confident manner, you may reduce your chances of becoming a victim.

Here are the vital points you need to know to defuse potential conflicts.

- When you are travelling in a volatile country, arrange a local guide through your travel agent or hotel. He or she will know what is going on and how to negotiate any problems. However, you must realise that this person is bound by ties of identity and loyalty to his or her country, neighbourhood, friends and family. They are not completely on your side, so keep some distance: never reveal your entire agenda, but just enough to be polite, and avoid giving away too many personal details.

- Give off the right signals – that you are calm, confident and know where you're going, and that you are able to maintain your composure when confronted by aggression. Always stay alert and tuned into your environment, and develop strategies you can use to control your own anger. Walking away from a tense situation, or staying in a group for mutual support, may reduce the chances of a violent incident developing.

- When involved in a tense situation show the other person that you are listening to what he is saying, don't cut him off in mid-sentence.

Even if you are the innocent party, resist the temptation to forcefully pursue your point of view. Get as much information about the disagreement as possible: this will help in understanding the other person's position and may help resolve the dispute. If you use aggressive body language such as pointing or squaring up to the other party, a furrowed brow or prolonged eye contact, you could make matters worse. This type of body language may be interpreted as a challenge.

- If you become involved in a situation such as a road accident, where you may actually be to blame, or even partially to blame, recognise this and avoid blaming others. However, there are some circumstances where even if you were to blame it would be unwise to accept responsibility until you have taken legal advice. Identify a solution that will meet the other person's position halfway, as this will avoid making them lose face.

- Think about the consequences of your actions. The way you react to a tense situation may be reflected by the way the other person reacts. If you adopt a confrontational position you may invite an aggressive response. Consider walking away or attempting to reach a compromise.

- Avoid making the other person lose face. This is vitally important in some regions of the world. In many male-dominated societies, men consider it a great insult against their honour if you make them appear foolish, and this inevitably results in violence. Even if the person is in the wrong, show respect for their rights and position.

- Avoid making comments about the other person's nationality, ethnicity or religion, or any defamatory personal comments. This will almost certainly invite trouble. If you use personal insults, the other person may be offended so much that they will pursue you from the site of the incident. It is just not worth the trouble, as you will invariably come off worse.

- In some circumstances, humour is a good way to defuse tension. For instance, if you are self-deprecating and play up the idea that you are a 'stupid tourist', this may appease someone you have inadvertently insulted. However, be aware that there are some subjects you must not joke about. Religion, cultural traits, local customs, political systems and national leaders are out of bounds. In some countries, it is accepted for local people – but not foreigners – to joke about certain practices. Educate yourself about such cultural subtleties.

- Just as many Westerners have stereotypical views of foreign nationals, many people in developing countries have stereotypical views of Westerners. The image of the rich, arrogant imperialist of days gone by still lingers in many countries. You must avoid living up to this image by being brash and impolite.

- If you are travelling in a group and you have a naturally aggressive demeanour, try to avoid becoming involved in any confrontation. It is helpful if you have a local guide, as they will be able to defuse any tensions, show you the safe areas and tell you the going rate for any bribes you have to pay – a practice endemic in some developing countries.

- If you are in a group and become involved in a confrontation, asking one of the women in your group to do the talking could help defuse the tension in some countries. Women can be better at making peace than some men. However, be aware that in some regions women will be obliged to conform to local customs, and not become involved.

- As a general rule of thumb, people who stop you in the street are not the type of people you want to meet. In many tourist hotspots they are after one thing – money. Avoid getting into conversation with them; even saying no may be enough to start an argument. Stay focused on your route and speak to no one if you feel threatened.

- There may be occasions, especially during the current tense international situation, where you find yourself – a mere traveller – actually being held to account for your country's actions on the international stage. Be aware of speaking out loudly. Broadcasting your nationality may not be in your best interests in politically sensitive times. If you do become embroiled in a confrontation about your country's activities, try to smile and agree with the other person that your country has got it wrong. Even if you do not believe this you may defuse the situation.

Crime

There is no crime-free country. Crime is a global problem and wherever your destination is you must expect to encounter criminal activity. Reported crime rates for different offences vary from country to country, and these may not be completely accurate: some countries fail to report much of the crime against tourists in order to protect their tourist industries. However, most countries suffer from a higher incidence of crime than they did a decade ago.

The financial and physical resources marshalled against criminal activity over the last decade have been viewed by some as ineffectual. Globally, theft and burglary are the most common criminal activity. Violent crime – murder, assaults and robberies – account for only 10 to 15 per cent of all crime reported. However, violent crime is much more evident in some countries. Those countries and regions with the highest murder and robbery rates are the US, Northern Europe and Latin American cities. Most crimes against tourists happen in cities, but outside the main tourist hubs these decrease.

What's the prime motivation for such crimes? Western tourists are relatively rich. It is estimated that almost 80 per cent of the global GDP is produced by the main industrial countries, which account for only 20 per cent of the world's population. The disparity of wealth between developing and industrial countries has more than tripled in the last three decades. Even some of the world's most popular tourist resorts have ominous social inequality and poverty. For example, in Eastern Europe – a favourite with many Britons – more than 120 million people live on US$4 a day. Russian security sources have estimated that there are 8050 criminal groups operating in Russia with a membership of 35,000 – 10 per cent of whom are international criminals.

Some tourist hotspots in Western Europe, such as Italy, have a major (and infamous) crime problem, with three big criminal organisations sporting a total of over 16,000 members. In Japan, 3000 Yakuza or criminal groups boast a membership of almost 80,000. Crime is a truly global problem, so when you travel abroad, it is essential to know the prevailing conditions at your destination.

What may be a crime in one country will be legal in another, and activities acceptable in a Western country may be illegal abroad. At your home base there may be a vast repertoire of services for dealing with crime, but a country you visit may have none. You can raise your level of security awareness by following a few simple procedures that will make you more confident and give you a head start in dealing with potential crises.

To avoid becoming a victim of crime, note the following general security points.

- Use the same sense of judgement while travelling abroad that you would at home. Be aware of criminal target areas such as crowded public transport terminals or street festivities, tourist traps, open-air markets and city black spots.

- In some countries, it's best to avoid places of worship. Religion involves high emotion, and religious followers can become very animated by even the hint of a slight to their religion. Identify where the places of worship are located and give them a wide berth, especially during holy days.

- Become familiar with your environment. Find out which shops, bars, and restaurants tend to stay open most of the day and night. Note the pattern of street life, including dangerous times – such as rush hours – and areas of congestion. If you know the normal pattern of activity, and it alters for whatever reason, you will be able to pick that up. Take note of change out of the ordinary – people paying you too much attention, seeing the same car several times in an hour, receiving unusual telephone calls. If when you're walking around a sinister individual makes you feel uncomfortable, attract attention and escape the situation. Listen to your instincts.

- Find the local emergency services, and where the nearest casualty hospital is located. Find out when it is open and ensure you can find it at night. Also make sure you can find the local police or law enforcement station.

- Ensure that you have mobile phone coverage at your destination and carry your mobile phone with you. If you do not have a mobile phone and are visiting the country for a long time, consider hiring one there. If none are available, try to identify where the nearest public call phones are, and ensure that you understand how to use them. Buy a local telephone card or make sure you have enough of the right coins to make an emergency telephone call.

- When you are out on foot, be aware of slow-moving vehicles or individuals loitering along your route. Plan it to avoid blind spots and secluded roads. Request a city map from your hotel and avoid wandering into city black spots. Be constantly aware of your surroundings. Tourist areas are usually smart and affluent, but if as you travel you identify a significant deterioration in the area, such as poor housing, graffiti or a lack of lighting, you may have strayed into a rough part of town. You should backtrack before you get in too deep.

- When walking in a high-risk area, observe all round you. Occasionally look behind you and take note of who is there. If you feel that the same person or vehicle is following you, make your way to the nearest safe place – a crowded area or somewhere with lights and noise. It's not a good idea to knock on someone's door asking for assistance. A British tourist on holiday in the US thought that a group was pursuing him after he left a late-night bar. He went up to a nearby house and knocked on the door to ask for assistance. The frightened homeowner came to the door with a gun, thinking the visitor was an attacker, and shot him dead. Be aware of different cultural attitudes.

- If you are a long-term visitor, establish good relations with your neighbours. By fostering friendships with those living in your area, you are actually establishing an alarm network. Local people are better equipped to pick up any subtle nuances with regard to security than you are. They can identify suspicious people and cars, for instance. But they can inform you of any changes in the local security situation only if they know you.

- Keep people informed of your movements, and inform friends and colleagues where you will be when you are going out and when you will be returning. Inform them of the routes you'll use and your chosen mode of transport. If you fail to return, they will know to take action. In a high-risk area, alternate your routes daily and make your movements unpredictable. This will make it difficult for the criminal to track you.

- Tell your travel arrangements only to those who need to know. Don't tell anyone your telephone number, home address and financial details such as what kind of credit card you use. Many travellers have returned home to unidentified demands for payment resulting from financial details falling into the wrong hands.

- In areas known to be volatile, get to know the most dangerous places. Avoid compromising your security by venturing into dark streets with little illumination. Be cautious of taking short cuts to and from shopping centres. Criminals often lurk in these areas to prey on travellers laden with new purchases. Avoid long, narrow streets. Once you are on such a street, there are only two ways out – this is a classic criminal hotspot.

- Other areas where criminals are predictably active are outside banks or foreign exchange bureaux. Do not hang around after using a cashpoint in a foreign city, and try not to use one at night; any observer will notice that you have used your card and will be carrying cash. Criminals often loiter near cashpoints.

- Petty criminals such as pickpockets often work in highly organised gangs that can plague an entire area as they sweep through. Operating mainly in cities, they meet up later at a pre-arranged point to split their 'earnings'. When you are in an unfamiliar city be aware that this type of crime is everywhere, and that you have to be vigilant. Common ploys used by pickpockets include someone engaging you in a conversation by asking for directions or the time, and their accomplice then walking into you and quickly removing your wallet or bag during the ensuing commotion. Be aware of any distracting disturbances such as fighting or loud quarrelling. If you watch a street entertainer, keep your hand on your valuables.

- It is far safer to travel around unfamiliar areas in a group. Safety in numbers is a good rule. If you are a lone traveller, ask in your hotel if anyone would be prepared to accompany you. If you do have to walk in an area which makes you feel unsafe, keep away from doorways and areas with lots of bushes and trees. You never know what may be lurking in there.

- Many British tourists have become victims of women with small children, or groups of friendly children, who operate as pickpocketing teams. Use your instincts to tell you who to trust. There are genuine people out there who need our compassion; but you need to be able to spot the bogus version.

- Travellers should be wary of offers that appear to be too good to be true: they generally are. Work on the cynical principle that nothing is for nothing. If someone approaches you on the street offering services that are way below the asking price, be on your guard. Either you will be paying for a sub-standard service, or you may about to be the victim of a scam.

- Criminals often look for moments of opportunity. One is when you are approaching your vehicle or your home. Be aware of anyone hanging around outside your home or near your car. If you feel intimidated by them, do not proceed. When you are approaching your house or vehicle ensure that you have your keys ready to use. If you have to stop to try and find your keys, you will provide the criminal with an opportunity that he can exploit.

- Similarly, when returning from a shopping trip, avoid overloading yourself with packages. This is a moment of opportunity many criminals are looking for. It is safer to hire a cab to deliver you to the doorway of your accommodation.

- Many hotels offer to provide an assistant who will accompany you on your shopping trip. Not only do they ensure that you get a reasonable price, they will also be able to keep a watchful eye out for any trouble.

- If you do become a victim of crime and your passport or travellers' cheques, or even valuable items such as expensive cameras, are stolen, you will have to inform the local police. You may need to make an official police report if you intend to make a claim against your insurance company. This may not be easy and in some countries, travellers have been asked to pay for such a report. You should check with your insurance company as to the procedures.

- Travellers have been verbally accosted for no apparent reason or for an inadvertent transgression of local laws or customs. In such a situation it is advisable to apologise and try to excuse yourself. However, if the attack is prolonged you may consider a firmer approach. Tell the other person in a loud and confident voice to leave you alone, or you will call the police.

- Using force to counter an attacker intent on robbing you is generally not the answer. If you are the victim of a crime it is generally because the criminal thinks he has a good chance of success. In these cases it's likely that you will be outnumbered, or the criminal will be desperate enough to use excessive violence. If you are used to rough and hostile situations, you may want to counter the attack. But for most people, possessions are not worth risking your life for.

- Some people decide to carry a weapon to protect themselves. They may then take more risks than they otherwise would, believing that they are prepared for trouble. However, what happens if you need to use it and bring it out? It may make an explosive situation even more dangerous. What are the legal implications of actually using a weapon in that country? You may actually find yourself in deep trouble. It is probably safer to stay unarmed.

Corruption

In many countries, bribery is a way of life and the international traveller will be expected to pay. Police, the military, and officials in customs, immigration, public transport and government supplement their meagre incomes via the unfortunate Western traveller; and if you don't pay up, the service will simply be withheld and you will find yourself in an endless bureaucratic nightmare. Bribes may come in many guises, but they are rarely obvious, and it pays to understand the local protocol.

A bribe may emerge as additional expenses or on-the-spot fines for some imaginary transgression of the law. Failure to pay can often mean arrest on some trumped-up charge, and a ruined business trip or holiday. Corruption is widespread and not limited to socially deprived areas.

But while tourists may be targeted, locals have to pay too. Petty corruption is the rule in many regions of the world, and local people are conned by public officials on a daily basis. When it's this deeply ingrained it doesn't pay to be moralistic. If you try to tell a low-paid customs official that what he is doing is illegal, you will most probably wish you had paid the $20 after being held for a few hours in a small room.

Usually there are three rates for bribes. The first is the going rate for a local, and here it is useful to find out how much they should expect to pay for a minor traffic violation. You can then judge how much the traveller could be expected to pay for a similar offence. The second is what you will pay to the higher authority if you are arrested, which will be higher than the rate for the policeman on the street. The third is the rate for the foreigner, which is usually much higher than a local's. It can be excessively high, pumped up by local ideas about the wealth of Westerners, which may have been gleaned from Hollywood movies.

Once, during a trip to West Africa, I was stopped and asked for my international vaccination certificate. I did not have it with me and was asked to pay US$100. I knew, however, that I did not need one in that country and saw I was being scammed. However, the alternative was to go through a charade with officials in a feigned pique, which would entail endless hours of bureaucratic negotiations and finally end up with me paying a fine. I paid the immigration official $20 and was on my way in 10 minutes.

Minor traffic violations are another common way of extorting money from the traveller. Broken wing mirrors or brake lights, even on roads where vehicles drive without lights, are to be avoided if you want to escape the trap.

It's equally vital to know, however, that not all people are corrupt. If you offer a bribe to the wrong person, you may end up serving a lengthy spell in the local prison. You need to learn to read the signs properly.

The following points will help, both in finding out whether a situation demands a bribe, or in dealing with corrupt officials.

- Do not automatically offer a bribe to an official as soon as you are stopped. Take the lead from him. If the official tries to drag the issue out and enter into negotiations without actually trying to arrest you, he is looking for cash.

- In my experience, this is the way the scenario unfolds. He will get close to you and speak in a quiet but authoritative voice – obviously he knows that what he is doing is illegal, and he won't want everyone to know. He may then indicate that he does not know how to resolve the issue. What he really means is, Are you willing to pay me? At this point it is helpful if you signal your remorse and apologise for causing any trouble. Even though you are about to be ripped off, you must be diplomatic. If you are brash or insulting, you will almost certainly find yourself being detained and losing all your money.

- It's usual to pay the 'fine' on the spot. However, you may save yourself some cash if you know what the going rate is. In some cases they will take all you have. It is helpful to carry only small amounts of cash, or hide your cash somewhere in your car. Occasionally they will present you with a worthless piece of paper as a receipt for your cash. Be aware that in this situation, humour is definitely off the agenda.

- In an area with predictable patterns of corruption it helps to carry only small amounts of cash in your wallet. If you are presented with an excessive demand you can show them all you have. They will normally take the lot and let you go.

■ A widespread scam is for officials to discover a problem, say with your travel documents, which cannot be easily solved. The official may inform you that he knows of a way round this problem, but it will take time and be expensive. This is your cue to ask how long it will take to solve this 'problem' and how much it will cost. You may then confide in your new-found 'friend' and ask whether he can personally fix the problem. Pay what they ask, unless it's outrageously high.

■ There is no set rate as to how much you should pay corrupt officials – it is a matter of trial and error. They will be out to get as much as possible and you are out to lose as little as possible. The best approach is to find out from those who live there, perhaps a British expatriate or fellow traveller. Remember, in some places it's a way of life: you'll have to add the cost in to your overall travel budget.

■ Serious incidents will require substantial amounts of cash. The higher up the food chain you go, the more you will be expected to pay. If you get to the stage where you find yourself in prison, you may be expected to pay serious money.

■ Arriving in some airports with a computer or any unusual equipment such as a laptop may also be a motive for bribery. Articles not easily recognised by the customs officials may warrant unexpected scrutiny. It is not unusual for customs officials to inform you that you are not allowed to bring this article into the country, even if they do not know what it is. Once more you must be careful here. Some are genuinely trying to do their jobs, but if they are corrupt they will let you know soon enough.

■ Expatriates or those who have been in the country for some time sometimes have powerful local allies and they will know how to treat the police and military. However, tourists are more vulnerable and easier to scare, especially if you are trying to make it to the airport for your flight. It may work if you try to bluff the policeman or soldier into thinking that you live in the country. If you are in a hurry, dropping the name of a local politician or power broker may be enough to intimidate the would-be briber.

- Demands for bribes may be excessive, especially from young soldiers or policemen trying their luck. Here's the moment when carrying small amounts of cash comes into its own. Demonstrating that you do not have that much money by showing them your wallet will work. However, they may take the lot, so keep your credit cards and personal details out of your wallet.

- In some countries, particularly those in the grip of civil unrest or war, you may want to carry a few supplies that will help you get out of trouble. Depending on the country, you may decide to carry a box of cigarettes. The going rate in a war zone is the standard packet of Marlboros. In some countries, a bottle of booze may work, but don't hang around while they drink it. Tinned food, toiletries, acceptable reading material, cheap sunglasses or other 'gifts' may help you to get through corrupt police or military checkpoints.

Drugs

Drugs are a worldwide industry involving millions of users and dealers, it's big business and the stakes are extraordinarily high – so inevitably there are lot of people out there eager to get you involved in it.

When someone tells you about a sweet get-rich-quick scheme, you should know that there is always a catch. If the scheme involves dealing in or transporting drugs, the catch is that you are liable to spend some of the best years of your life in a prison far worse than anything you could imagine. You will be told that the risks are almost non-existent. Sometimes the scheme is even planned so that you do get caught and must pay plenty of money to avoid prison.

If you think that the promise of a few thousand dollars is worth these kinds of risks, you are too stupid or desperate to be travelling.

And the best cure for this state of mind? When you get to your destination, go to the local embassy and find out where some of your countrymen and women are doing time in local prisons on drug-related charges. If you can get permission, go and visit them. They will be extremely grateful for your company and any amenities that you can bring them. In India, there is a mandatory ten-year prison sentence if you are caught with ten grams of cannabis; in Thailand, twenty grams of heroin will get you a ten-year stretch and a heavy fine, and the death sentence for trafficking – twenty grams of ecstasy will get you seven years. In Spain, there is a minimum three years for possession of cannabis, between nine and fourteen for possession of cocaine.

In many countries you'll find hash and marijuana being offered to you and used regularly, although there are now very few countries where it is legal. Even though 'everyone is doing it', the local police may single out foreigners as a source of revenue, at least. In many places, the penalties for possessing drugs are almost as severe as for dealing. In any case, if you are caught, you will have to deal with the local police in situations that will be far from pleasant, and will at the very least involve the payment of sizeable bribes to get you out.

So, if you do drugs at home, don't take them when you're abroad. It isn't worth it.

- You have to be wary of planted drugs in your hotel room, too, particularly if you are staying in a hostel or low cost accommodation. Check your hotel room for any drugs. Look under the mattress, behind drawers, in the cistern and in any other likely hiding places. If you find any, get rid of it immediately by flushing it down the toilet, and look for a new hotel. If you are caught in a room which contains drugs, even if you do not know of their existence, you may end up in prison.

- In some countries police will randomly stop travellers to interdict the flow of illegal drugs. Be aware of whom you are with and what they are carrying in the car; it will not be enough to say that you did not know about the stash in the back of the car.

- Busy airport terminals are also a risk for the unsuspecting traveller. One ploy is to distract you from your luggage, and while you are distracted to slip a small package into your bag. The plan here is to follow you until you clear customs and collect your baggage at your home airport. Keep an eye on your baggage at all times.

■ If you suffer from a condition that requires you to take medication, you must remember to keep the medication in its original container and try to obtain certification from your doctor authorising you to carry the drugs. Some customs officials are very twitchy even about prescribed drugs, and you could find yourself facing detention and delays.

■ If you have a condition such as diabetes that requires you to carry a syringe, you should obtain certification from your doctor that authorises you to carry them. Syringes will attract scrutiny for obvious reasons.

Photography

Carrying photography and video equipment can create problems when you're abroad. In some places, people may feel very different about the security of their country, particularly when there is unrest. If you are caught taking photographs or videos of certain locations, you can be detained, fined and have your camera equipment and film confiscated – or even imprisoned, as were a group of British plane-spotters in Greece in 2001.

Some countries have very strict prohibitions about what you can photograph. Travellers have run into trouble taking photos or videos of border areas, public demonstrations or riots, police or military personnel or installations, and harbour, rail or airport facilities.

The taboos generally include military installations and equipment, even soldiers. It may also extend to bridges, public and government buildings (such as the president's mansion), airports, dams, power stations and just about anything that could be imagined as a target of future attack. Some countries also take a dim view of your taking unflattering photographs of poor people or slum areas.

If there are strict rules, they will usually be posted at borders and airports when you enter, and only occasionally around the specific places that are prohibited. In general, though, avoid taking photos of anything that is very official, and especially military. If a place is guarded, you should probably ask a guard if photography is permitted.

In a few places, the rules are occasionally misused as an excuse for some overzealous soldier to harass tourists. If you do get caught, be friendly and apologise, saying you were unaware of the dangers of photographing a beautiful railway station. If they get serious, give them the film without making a scene; otherwise they may smash your camera.

In areas of the world where there is religious conflict, it may be unwise to take photographs of places of worship..

There are other points to consider if you'll be taking a camera or camcorder.

- When transporting equipment, you need to decide how you'll protect your camera and equipment.

- You may want to register your equipment with your own customs before leaving the country. You will receive a receipt verifying that you owned the equipment before departure.

- Don't forget batteries, a power converter for your battery charger if you need it, and the right kind of electrical plug.

- Do you have plenty of film and videotape? Do you need a lead-lined bag to transport it?

- Have you learned the words in the language of the country you're visiting that refer to photography and shooting videos?

Foreign Legal Systems

When you leave your own country, you're subject to the laws of the country you're visiting. So before you go, learn as much as you can about local law. Good resources are your library, travel agent, and the embassies, consulates or tourist bureaux of the countries you will visit. Also keep track of what is being reported in the media about recent developments in those countries.

You can be arrested overseas for actions that may be either legal or considered minor infractions at home. Be aware of what is considered criminal in the country where you are travelling. This is particularly true if you are travelling in some Islamic countries where there is little differentiation between religion and the law; there are, for example, severe penalties for the consumption of alcohol in Saudi Arabia. Consult your country's foreign office before you go, or your embassy at your destination.

- People buying antiques in certain countries, notably Turkey, Egypt and Mexico, can also be in danger of arrest. Local customs authorities may deem the objects national treasures. In the countries where antiques are important, document any reproductions you buy at the shop. If the objects are authentic, secure the necessary export permit (usually from the national museum).

- When entering a country suffering from internal dissent, be aware of the literature you are carrying, which may be considered seditious. Travellers have been jailed in Myanmar for importing forbidden religious material.

- In many countries, there are restrictions surrounding the amount of cash you can leave the country with. Check the currency laws at your destination country.

- Travellers are now subject to close scrutiny to ensure they do not import illegal meat or dairy products, with severe penalties for those caught. Check with the local consulate of the country you are travelling to.

8

Safe Travel for Women

Specific Threats

If you're a woman and you're thinking of travelling solo, the best course of action is to know the risks and mentally prepare for them. But this doesn't mean they will happen: in most countries, the dangers are more or less the same you'd experience in, say, Britain.

But be aware that along with all the risks we've been examining – from terrorism to targeting by criminals – a few more need to be added to the list if you're planning on travelling alone. First, there is sexual harassment by local men, perhaps even by male fellow travellers. This can range from being harried and pestered to becoming a victim of violence. The British media has accused some tour operators of failing to warn female travellers about the dangers of sexual attack at some popular tourist destinations. The problem is that neither these operators, nor the countries concerned, want to reveal statistics that may damage their tourist industry.

A more devious crime has emerged, however – and the rate has increased dramatically in recent years. Known as drug rape, it involves spiking a female victim's drink with a strong sedative. One travel magazine identified Greece, Spain and Turkey as the countries with the greatest such risk to women travelling there. Statistics from the UK-based Roofie Foundation, which provides information on drug and date rape, found that a total of 307 British women were victims of drug rape in 2000 – 87 in Spain, 78 in the US, 57 in Greece, 27 in Australia, 21 in Turkey, 9 in Thailand, 8 in the Canary Islands and also in Hong Kong, 5 in Saudi Arabia, 4 in Germany, and 1 in Czechoslovakia, Burundi and Brazil. And these are only the crimes which have been reported. And unfortunately, in 2001 there was an increase in drug rape of almost 17 per cent worldwide.

Alcohol is implicated in many rapes. In fact, an American study found that in 97 per cent of all rapes, one or both of the people involved were under the influence of alcohol. The effects are, of course, conducive to the act: women can fail to pick up on the normal danger signs, while some men can get overemotional or violent. So unsurprisingly, rape has been shown to be more likely to happen in pubs and clubs, and (in descending order) business premises, private houses, wine bars, private parties, and on board ships and aircraft. Women between the ages of 18 and 35 are most at risk, but statistics – and news reports – show that rape can happen to women of all ages.

While it's relatively easy for women to take the necessary precautions against rape on their home turf, travelling abroad means you encounter a different set of rules. Cultural traditions may dictate different codes of social interaction between the sexes, and what you might see as perfectly normal behaviour at home could be seriously misinterpreted abroad. Or worse: recently, there have been a number of tragic reports of violence against female travellers. So it's vital to stay alert when you're travelling in foreign countries. You need to look as if you know where you're going, and perhaps most importantly, you need to know how to handle your fear if something goes wrong.

You may be a fairly seasoned traveller, but when you're in a strange environment surrounded by people you neither know nor trust, even minor situations can cause alarm and even fear. If this happens, use it. Fear will trigger your survival instinct and help you extricate yourself from the danger. In 'fight or flight' mode, your heart rate speeds up and muscles contract, and you experience a surge of adrenaline that sharpens your reactions. You can harness that energy to identify the dangers and act, and not give in to panic. During my years in the SAS I was constantly reminded before we went into action that it's not important that you are frightened; everyone is frightened. It is what you do and how you behave while you are frightened that matters.

Gender Awareness

As I've said, cultural differences play a huge role in crimes against women travelling abroad. In many countries, all Western women are believed to be sexually promiscuous. This impression no doubt comes from Hollywood movies – pirated copies are available even in areas of extreme poverty. For many people in the developing world, these movies are the only image available of female behaviour in the West.

In some countries, your mere presence is enough to stimulate interest. You may unintentionally offend local sensibilities without even becoming aware of them. The way you dress and behave may not only generate interest from local men, it can also bring you into conflict with the local women. Remember, in some societies women are forbidden from going out alone or eating alone at a restaurant.

Getting a nasty look in the street is one thing. At the other end of the spectrum is rape – one of the fastest rising violent crimes. But be aware that you can do a lot to reduce the risks. Start before you travel. Research your destination and try to identify if there is a recent history of rape in the area. Some holiday resorts have particularly bad reputations for this type of crime. Once there, identify the vulnerable areas: hotel staff or local employees will inform you of places you should steer clear of. And take on board the following pointers for safe travel.

- Most of us are aware of our drinking capacity. If you're in a bar abroad and suddenly find yourself affected by a surprisingly small amount of alcohol, this probably indicates that your drink has been tampered with. Tell a female friend or someone you can trust if possible, and go to your hotel. If you know that this type of crime has occurred in the area, avoid alcohol altogether.

- If you are at all suspicious, never accept a drink from a stranger, and control what you drink by buying the drinks yourself. Keep your glass in your hand, and if you are with a group of friends or colleagues, look out for each other.

- If a drunk accosts you, it may be very hard to fob him off, as drunks generally won't listen. However, you can pretend to go along with his plan to buy yourself time and decide what to do. If he's very befuddled it should be relatively easy to make your escape.

- If you find yourself in a dangerous situation and confronted by an attacker, retain your dignity and try to remain in control. Be forceful and speak with confidence. Do not show emotion, as this may make the situation worse. If you are in control, he may think twice.

- Fighting off an attacker is never a simple option. He may have weapons or you may have underestimated his strength. It's vital to know that you are not attempting to fight him; you are trying to shock him by your reaction so that he gives you space to get away. In a fight with an enraged criminal, most men *and* women would have terrible difficulties overcoming him. But if you have no choice or decide that you can fight, you must take action quickly before he controls the situation. In some situations, if you act fast while still physically in 'fight or flight' mode, you will have a better chance of deterring the attacker.

- If you do decide to struggle with your attacker you must be committed – a half-hearted effort will achieve nothing. If you are forceful enough you may give yourself a little time to raise the alarm; however, in isolated areas most attackers will retaliate with violence. If you decide to struggle, you must be aggressive and aim for vulnerable areas. (See page 176 below, for techniques and ideas.)

- The minute you get away or the attacker falls back while you're fighting, head to the nearest safe place. If you do not know the area you should run to the nearest place that is well-lit and noisy.

Try to remember what the attacker looks like so that you can inform the police. Even if you only had a glimpse you can still provide an adequate description by using the following easy-to-remember guide.

A = Age
B = Build – is the attacker tall, short, heavyset or thin?
C = Clothing – what colour, motif, label, etc?
D = Distinguishing marks – scars, tattoos, etc
E = Elevation – how tall was he?
F = Face – how would you describe his hair, nose, eyes and eyebrows?
G = Gait – how did he carry himself? Did he have a limp?

- Abductors have tried to force lone females into cars. If a car approaches, you should back off, especially if the door is opened. During an abduction, the only time abductors are exposing themselves to danger is when they are trying to get their victim into the vehicle. Some have suggested lying face down in a spread-eagle position, which will make it extremely difficult for an abductor to get you into a car. This also protects your face and vital organs. Scream and make as much noise as you can. By resisting in this way you are making him stay in the area, where he is exposed to danger for a longer period than he would like. He may not be willing to accept the higher risk. Obviously, if he has a weapon, this option may not be open.

Fighting Back

No matter how safety-minded you are, there may be occasions when you will find yourself with no alternative other than fighting back. A woman may be smaller and physically weaker than her attackers, but if you at least have an idea of what to do and, more importantly, how you can hurt your attacker, this may provide you with the opportunity to escape. The idea is to be proactive, to avoid getting yourself into a position where you have to fight.

Attackers will try to intimidate and subdue their victims, and most do not expect you to fight back. An attacker will use force or the threat of force at the beginning of the attack, and once they have gained a psychological advantage they will generally ease off. If you are attacked, you must identify the most opportune moment for responding. And if you see the chance to fight back, you must do so with absolute commitment, speed and aggression. Fear and apprehension are probably inevitable, as they are natural responses to stressful situations. The trick is to exploit these feelings and use them to your advantage.

Here's what to do if a physical struggle with a man is imminent.

- Your aim is not to beat the man, but to be forceful enough to make a space allowing you to escape. Use your voice: scream and shout as loudly as you can. If the attacker tries to stop you from shouting and uses violence to stop you, you can use this to your advantage. This is the moment when the attacker himself is at risk, as if he is caught he knows that he will probably go to prison. The more you can scream and keep the attacker in the same position, the more at risk he will be. Assess the situation as it develops, however – if he is very desperate, screaming may cause him to resort to excessive violence.

- If you decide to fight back you have to do it fast. You will only have one opportunity, and if you get it wrong things could turn out worse. You must use every natural attribute that you possess to gain advantage.

- If your attacker is drunk, his responses will be impaired. This carries both advantages and disadvantages. He will be unable to move or think quickly, which is good, as you might be able to trick him into going to a place of your choosing. Once there, you may be able to escape. His pain reflexes, however, will be dulled, so you would have to be very forceful if you chose to fight.

- If a drunken man looks as if he is about to approach you, rush him. Move quickly towards him; he will probably not expect this and will be caught off balance. Very forcefully push or punch him in the centre of the chest. He should lose balance and may topple over. This will give you an opportunity to get away.

- Many women have considered the possibility of arming themselves. There are, however, problems with carrying what may be considered a weapon. In the UK everything considered to be an offensive weapon is illegal, and anyone caught carrying one will be liable to prosecution. Even small penknives are enough to get you into trouble. The other problem is whether you have the skill or will to use it. And if you are seen to use disproportionate force you will find yourself in court. In the UK you may receive a sympathetic hearing, but in many other countries you will be treated worse than the attacker.

- You may consider improvising a weapon. A bunch of keys held in your clenched fist, with a small Yale-type key protruding from between your fingers at the front of your fist, is very effective. If you feel threatened, place your hand in your pocket or bag, and arrange the keys as described. Only take them out if you need to use them. If you do have to use them, do so fast and accurately. By bringing your fist down across the face of the attacker you will inflict a relatively serious wound, and could stun him for a few seconds. Use this time wisely and make sure that you get away. The chances are that if he catches you he will be more likely to use excessive violence.

- In many countries, small aerosols containing either tear gas or pepper spray are sold across the counter. These can be effective sprayed in the attacker's face, and will give you time to at least get away. You need to be fast, and if your aim is good, he will be completely incapacitated and less likely to want to continue his assault. If you cannot obtain these sprays, improvise with aerosol oven cleaner. He will suffer irritation to the face, eyes, mouth and respiratory tract and will be unlikely to want to pursue you. Deep heat muscle treatment spray will also irritate an attacker's eyes, mouth and respiratory tract.

- No matter how big and strong a man is, he has vulnerable areas – the groin, for one. If you are confronted by an attacker and decide to fight back, do not kick him between the legs. The chances are you will miss, or he will grab your foot and throw you to the ground. Get close, bring your knee up in a forceful motion, and at the same time push him backwards. It's all about timing. If your timing is good, he will let go immediately and your push will send him down. (See Figure A.)

Figure A

- The windpipe is an even better place to attack. For this use the side of your hand. Using a swinging motion and the outer part of your hand as the leading edge, forcefully swipe your hand across the centre of the exposed part of the attacker's neck. Be quick and aim carefully. Keep your eyes on the target area and strike from a firm position, with your weight evenly balanced on both feet. It helps if you are at an oblique angle to your attacker with the striking arm nearest to him. Be aware that if you don't hit the windpipe, you won't incapacitate your attacker.

- Another vulnerable place is the nose, if struck from underneath. Use the heel of your hand and strike firmly and forcefully in an upward motion, connecting under the nose, to stun the attacker. You need to get close in and try to get your full weight under your strike. If your aim is true, you will certainly push your attacker off and backwards. Then you should run. (See Figure B.)

Figure B

- If your attacker grabs you from behind, the chances are that you will be completely taken by surprise, and will have less opportunity to plan a response. However, if the attacker's face is directly behind you, forcefully bring your head back and try to strike his nose with the back of your head. Your head is much harder than his nose and the chances are he will be stunned for a while. The nose will bleed if struck in the right place, too, and if he sees he has been injured, he will be less likely to continue with his attack. Then run for it. (See Figure C.)

Figure C

- The shin is vulnerable, too. The bone is near the surface, unprotected by muscle or cartilage, and by kicking as hard as you can on this exposed area you will incapacitate your attacker. You should grab him and use him as a leverage point so that you can stay in balance while you kick. Back off as soon as you've kicked him. If you've aimed correctly, he will be unable to pursue. (See Figure D.)

Figure D

Hotel Security

Your choice of hotel can be crucial to your safety while travelling. Read on for some useful pointers.

- If possible, select a reputable hotel or hostel in a busy part of town. If there are restaurants, cafés, bars, late-night shops and so on, chances are there will be lots of people around most of the time. This in itself provides some security. Financial and business districts, however, will be empty out of office hours. If the area you choose looks clean and respectable, there will be less risk of encountering aggressive street hawkers and beggars.

- Ask your travel agent to put you in touch with other women who have travelled to that country; then ask the women where the safe hotels are. If this is not possible, you should go to a major city hotel for your first night and enquire from other women who are travelling, or female staff, where it would be safe for you to stay.

- If you are concerned about your safety when travelling alone, ask for a double room when you book and give your partner's or friend's name. When you check in you can always say that your partner was delayed and will be joining you soon.

- There are hotels that specifically cater for women travelling alone. All the amenities that the female traveller needs are available. Ironically, the very fact that these hotels advertise their women-only facilities in glossy brochures does little for security. The local criminal community will be aware that there are a lot of lone women staying at the hotel.

- In some countries, it's better to see the room before you agree to check in. You should look at the room with a critical eye. Does the door lock properly, do the windows have locks and are there any holes in the walls? If you do not feel safe in the room, ask to see another – or go to another hotel.

- Ensure that you select a hotel or hostel that has some visible security. A hotel with a bellboy or a reception desk near the entrance is more likely to prevent unauthorised access. While you are checking in, try to do so with a female receptionist, and ensure that no one is able to overhear your name, room number or that you are checking in alone.

- Request a room above ground level. This will prevent criminals from getting access to your room through the window. Also ask for a room as far away from the fire and emergency exits as possible. These exits can be forced open to gain unlawful access to the hotel. Avoid taking a room that shares a door with another room;

you never know who is on the other side of the door. It is a good idea to check the door locks before you settle in for the night. If you are not happy with the locks, you should ask for another room (see Chapter 16, page 370). Your hotel room door should, if possible, have a double lock and a peephole.

- Avoid leaving out any 'Please Make Up My Room' signs, as you are only letting everyone know that your room is empty. If you want your room cleaned you should arrange it through the reception at a time of your choosing. By leaving the 'Do Not Disturb' sign on your room even when it is empty, you give the impression that the room is always occupied.

- Avoid getting into a lift or elevator on your own if it already contains a man whose appearance makes you feel uncomfortable. If you are getting unwanted attention from a man in a lift, make a call on your cellphone so it appears you are being met at the ground floor. You may want to avoid using the lift after the hotel bar closes. You may consider asking reception for an escort to your room.

- Even in a secure hotel room you will be unable to rest properly if you constantly have to worry that an intruder may get in. For added protection, you can purchase door wedges or locking devices which will prevent unwanted access. Emergency alarms that look like travel clocks are also available. These devices can be pointed at the hotel room door; if they detect movement outside, they emit a high-pitched alarm tone.

- If you are travelling with other women, ensure that you get their room and telephone numbers. If possible, ask for adjoining rooms.

- If you are staying in a dormitory block or a hotel with communal showering facilities, buy a bag in which you can carry your passport, flight tickets and money. Ensure that the bag is waterproof enough to take into the shower with you.

- Do not open your room door unless you can confirm the identity of the person on the other side. Remember, not all criminals and potential attackers are the rough and aggressive type. Demand identification from hotel officials or law enforcement personnel, asking them to slide it under the door, and do not open your door until you are convinced. Tell any visitor to go to reception and you will meet them there. Then phone reception and ask for an escort to attend the meeting.

■ When you return to your hotel, if the door is unlocked or looks as if it has been tampered with, don't go in. Go to the reception desk and ask for assistance. If you have friends at the hotel ask them to go with you to your room before you enter. You should consider asking the receptionist to allocate you a different room, or even consider moving to another hotel. If your room security is breached, it can happen again.

■ If you feel that your room has been entered while you were out, have a look around. Check in the wardrobes, toilets and shower cubicle, and of course under your bed. This all sounds extreme, but these areas have been used in the past as hiding places.

■ Avoid secluded areas of the hotel during times when there is no one else around. If you use the gymnasium or swimming pool, do so only when there are attendants on duty. These facilities are normally open to non-guest residents and anyone can use them.

■ Be wary when you answer the telephone at your hotel room. In some countries, it's routine for criminals to telephone hotel rooms in order to find out who is staying there. It may be unwise to let people know that a solo women traveller is staying in the hotel room. When you answer the telephone, let the caller do the talking.

■ If you are receiving unwanted attention from a man at your hotel, inform them that your husband or boyfriend is coming back. If you are really concerned try calling out a man's name loudly – the attacker may think that there is another man close by. This may be enough to scare him off.

■ When you return to your hotel room for the night you should fill a small bag with your passport, money, flight tickets, room key, a torch, mobile phone and essentials like medication, and keep it near your bed. If you have to evacuate quickly you have all you need to get you home.

■ If possible, leave the television in your hotel room switched on while you are out. This may deter intruders; at hotels in which the power is switched off after you remove your key from the recess at the door, you might consider a small portable radio which you can leave on while you are out.

General Safety

Some of the riskiest situations for women travelling alone are walking on their own, behaving in a way that offends local sensibilities, and being somewhere, such as a bar or café, where they are duped into doing something that turns out to be dangerous. Take extra care when abroad – the following points could be crucial.

■ It is a good idea to book a flight that doesn't arrive late at night or in the early hours. If you were to arrive at that time, you'd probably face a taxi ride or bus journey through a strange city at night. City nightlife in many countries is the natural environment of the criminal. If you have no alternative, try to book a hotel near the airport for your first night.

■ Be aware of what is going on round about you, including the behaviour of others. An attacker will rarely conceal himself behind a substantial obstacle – it would be too difficult for him to get over the obstacle and he would scare you off. It's more likely he would stand behind something from which he can step out into your path. From a position such as this, the criminal can watch and select his target. Large, dense bushes or houses that abut a road or path can be used in this way, for instance. If you see anyone loitering in such an area, avoid it.

■ Before you go, research the local dress code and patterns of behaviour. While you're there, watch how local women behave by watching them and seeing how they interact with male friends and relatives. This will be a rough guide to how you should act yourself.

You must, however, be aware that some foreign men sometimes treat foreign women differently. If you're in a country where Western women are perceived, however erroneously, as sexually promiscuous, you may get unwanted attention from local men.

- It's a good idea to be particularly careful in conservative societies with strict social and religious cultures, where your mere presence, not to mention dress and behaviour, can draw unwarranted attention from men and women alike. You should do your homework and find out how you are expected to behave under local codes of behaviour. Is drinking or smoking in public frowned on? When you're still at home, ask other women who've been to the country you're going to visit about acceptable standards of behaviour and pitfalls you might encounter.

- Some women wear a wedding ring when travelling solo, even if they are not married. It may deflect unwanted attention. If asked, you can always say that you are waiting for your husband, and display the ring. If you are approached by a man in the street, you should never admit to being alone. In many countries, marriage is more highly honoured than it is in the West, and you will be treated with respect.

- If you encounter other travellers, particularly from your own country, strike up a friendly relationship. The more people you get to know, the safer you will be; potential attackers will be reluctant to attack two or more women together.

- If you are travelling on your own you can observe how women in other countries protect themselves from male harassment. In some countries women will walk everywhere in couples or packs, some holding hands, some walking arm in arm, and will ignore any comments from passing males.

- In some countries, you won't attract much attention if you have a male companion. You may ask a man with whom you feel comfortable – a fellow traveller, perhaps – to escort you when you are out. However, you should be aware of the signal you are sending out if you occasionally appear with a different man.

- Girls who dress the way they normally would in more liberal Western countries may unintentionally end up looking like the stereotypical promiscuous woman of Hollywood movies. Provocative clothing or logos may trigger unwanted attention.

- In some countries, blonde hair is a rarity and oftens provokes all kind of attention. In South and South East Asia, Africa and the Middle East, if you're blonde and want to see the sights rather than be one, it might be an idea to wear a hat or tie your hair up – so suggests my wife.

- If a man makes a pass at a woman in, say, France, the woman may well laugh and possibly engage in conversation. This reaction may be misunderstood in foreign countries. It may be better not to comment if you do not want further contact.

- On home ground many women – my wife included – walk around with their heads up, being friendly to everyone. When travelling in some countries with conservative cultures, you may attract unwanted attention from both local men and women by acting in this way.

- In the West, it's acceptable behaviour to touch a stranger on the arm when you are talking to them to assure them of your friendly intentions. In some countries, however, this is unacceptable in public. If a man you do not know touches you on the arm, you should let him know that he has gone too far. Failure to do so in many countries will encourage further attention.

- Even in Western countries such as the UK, I would advise women travelling alone on public transport to avoid eye contact with strangers. By holding someone's gaze you are demonstrating an interest in that individual, so it would not be unusual if the person returns that interest. When travelling abroad, avoid eye contact, don't be drawn into conversation and don't even smile at someone if you feel at all threatened by them or the situation.

- Ask other women travelling or hotel staff when it gets dark, so you can avoid travelling then. It is also a good idea to know when the sun comes up: if you plan on an early morning excursion, you can avoid hanging around in the pre-dawn dark.

- When you are out and need to get directions, don't rely on information from just one person. Ask at least two. A criminal or someone else wanting to take advantage of you could direct you to a secluded spot and attack or rob you. Avoid approaching men altogether for directions, unless they are accompanied by women.

- If aggressive street hawkers accost you, do not stop. Even persistent hawkers will eventually give up when you fail to stop. Avoid stopping, even to say that you don't want to buy anything. You should fix your gaze in the direction you are heading in, and don't look at the hawkers. If they can delay you for even a moment they will redouble their efforts to sell you something.

- Avoid standing alone at bus stops or taxi ranks, and try not to go into unmanned subway or underground stations late at night. Ensure that you are not stranded after you have been out for the night. Book your taxi before you go out, and ensure you know the driver's name and the cab number. Arrange to meet the cab at a crowded location, which is illuminated, and travel with a friend if possible.

- Be aware and careful in shopping-centre car parks. Lone females have been attacked and robbed while laden with shopping. If you do not feel safe you should ask someone to escort you to your vehicle.

- If you're driving, don't be taken in if a man drives up next to you and points at your wheel, or generally tries to alarm you by indicating that something has gone wrong with your car. Do not stop. Even if you do have a flat tyre, you should continue driving to the nearest safe area.

- If you usually jog or exercise, you should do so only if it is culturally acceptable at your destination. If it is acceptable you should find out how you should dress; you may get unwanted attention if you go jogging in shorts. It may be safer to go as part of a group, or, if you are travelling with a male companion, take him along. When you are jogging try to stick to the main routes, and avoid lonely, secluded roads and park paths.

- While you are on the street, no one need approach you directly unless they have a reason. It is normal to maintain a gap of around four or five feet between you and a stranger. If someone comes too close, back off and try to maintain that gap.

- If you suspect that you are being followed, do not go straight to your hotel or house. If you do, you are letting them know where you are staying. You should consider going to the nearest safe area – a hotel, shop or police station – and inform them of your concerns.

- When travelling and your car breaks down, undo the bonnet of your car and activate your four-way flashers. Then stay in your car and keep the doors locked and the windows up. If someone offers assistance, lower the window just a touch to communicate. If you have stopped on a busy motorway you should get out of the vehicle and move away from it to an area where you feel safe. Call for assistance from there.

- Avoid placing stickers or ornaments that mark you out as a single female. This will attract the wrong type of attention. When you return to your car, always check the rear seats before getting in.

- If you are walking on the street at night and find yourself sharing the pavement with someone who makes you feel uncomfortable, walk to the other side of the street. Trust your sixth sense – the danger is in thinking it can never happen to you. If he follows, you should retreat and if he persists, begin shouting and banging on the nearest doors or windows.

- Try to identify what is permissible behaviour. For example, it may be possible to indulge in topless sunbathing in one area of the country. However, even in the same country on a different beach it may be deemed unlawful.

- When travelling, avoid carrying too much luggage or shopping. This may end up making you an easy target. Wear a small rucksack for all your valuables, and leave your hands free.

- In troubled countries or regions, avoid letting a person you've just met know where you are staying until they win your confidence. If they ask, you can give a false hotel address. Hide room keys, tour brochures or hotel city maps which may link you with a particular hotel. If you want to put someone off the scent you could use matches or business cards from a hotel you're not staying in.

■ While travelling on public transport, you can end up a magnet for locals desperate to try and impress you. You can try sitting on the aisle seat of buses and trains, and leave your luggage on the window seat. Unless the bus or train fills up, you will be left in peace.

■ Travelling at night can pose many difficulties for women travelling solo. One less obvious one is the possibility of driving into a police or military check point in some countries. It is generally safer to stay off the roads after dark.

9

Safe Travel for Families

Travelling with Children

For children, going abroad is not just great fun – it's one of the best forms of education. And while travelling to the remote areas of the world may be tougher with children along, you should be able to take even small children to places you might not have thought possible, as long as you prepare and plan. But protecting your children gains a new dimension when you're on holiday. Children becoming ill or even lost on a trip abroad is every parent's nightmare. And having travelled widely with my own family, I am fully aware of the difficulties.

One problem is that the risks may not be as apparent abroad. Then, with the excitement of the journey and everything else going on, even the most basic of dangers may be overlooked. Children are naturally inquisitive and excited by the prospect of new and different environments, and trying to keep them out of trouble can turn into a full-time job. And you have to be extra vigilant about thieves and criminals. Harassed parents with youngsters, bags and valuables hanging off them in crowded stations provide golden opportunities for the unscrupulous.

But families who have planned and thought about the difficulties in travelling with kids, even babies, can arrive at their destinations safely and in a condition to enjoy their holiday. If you are travelling with small children, let them know some time in advance that you are going on a trip. Depending on your destination, try to arrange your travel schedule to fit in with your children's normal patterns. For some destinations it may be a good idea to arrange for a night flight so that youngsters can get some sleep. When my family flew to South East Asia, a 12-hour flight, with our one-year-old son, we consulted our doctor beforehand. He prescribed a mild sedative which enabled him to sleep for a large part of the trip. This gave my wife and I the opportunity to sleep and then take turns at keeping him occupied when he was not sleeping. Some families who travel on long-haul journeys plan a stop-off in the middle. After a break, the second part of your journey will be less daunting.

If you're planning a family holiday, consider these points.

- Don't forget that your children need passports if you're going abroad. Check with your home country's passport office for specific requirements. In Britain since 1998, even babies must have their own. Many holidaymakers are turned away from airports each year because they do not have passports for their babies. If your child was included on a parental passport before then and is under 16, they will be allowed to travel. However if your child was born post-1998 or if that passport expires, you will need to get them their own passport.

- The British passport office will require evidence of the child's citizenship before they issue a passport. You must take the following documentation to the passport office: birth certificate, parent's birth certificates and marriage certificate. If your child is under 11 they will not be required to provide a specimen signature on their passport. Even newly born infants' passport applications must be accompanied by two passport photographs.

- Ask your travel agent whether the destination is suitable for children. Get references from other parents who have travelled there. Note down your concerns, then call them and ask them the conditions and the facilities at the destination country. Is there anything they did not take which they wished they had – anything provided by hotels that they did not need?

- When you make a reservation at a hotel, ensure that you book a family room, or adjoining rooms. If you are travelling with teenagers ensure that their rooms are next door to yours.

- Some families elect to travel as groups so that they can support each other when they get to their destinations. Parents can take turns at babysitting, giving couples a break and a chance to enjoy the holiday. Try to identify whether there have been any crimes or suspicious activities involving children before you go. Ask tour organisations and other parents who have been there.

- A few days before your departure, it's a good idea to call or email the hotel and confirm that you have a reservation and arrange for collection from your flight. If you were travelling without kids and you were to arrive and find out that you did not have a room, it would be very irritating. However, if you arrive with kids after an exhausting journey to find out that you did not have a room, it would be a disaster.

- Enquire about kids' clubs, babysitters and amenities when you are booking your holiday. Ensure that the club leaders are suitably qualified and not just summer holiday teenagers, and that any child-care organisations abide by strict and appropriate rules. Take the same precautions you would at home.

- When organising holidays, think of how old your kids are. There are medical, climatic and security issues you need to think about. If your child is very young, consult your doctor before you travel. Children will suffer more in extreme climates than adults, and even in some of the European holiday destinations the temperatures can become oppressive. If the health risks are unacceptable, go somewhere else. Find out whether there are vaccination requirements for travelling to specific regions: your children may turn out to be too young, or you may not want then to have the injections. Your doctor will advise you about any side effects.

- Buy a family insurance policy before you go. Children are more at risk from health problems than most adults, and even simple medical assistance for a sick infant can be expensive. In addition if you are a pregnant mother, you will not be covered if you travel in the later stages of pregnancy. Check with your policy.

- When you are booking your flight, tell tour operators or airline staff that you will be travelling with children. It is a good idea to carry enough supplies and spare clothing for the youngster for a few days in your hand luggage. If your baggage goes missing you will at least have some supplies to tide you over until you can buy more. If your child suffers from a health condition you should inform the airline staff, and pack enough medication for the whole trip in your hand luggage. Also, if your child has any special needs, such as a disability, you should make the airline staff aware of them.

- If you are travelling with an infant, ask at the airline office or travel agent if you can take a kids' car seat onto the aircraft. This will make the child's journey more comfortable.

- Don't let your children get dehydrated during the flight. Infants in particular need to be given enough to drink. In Western countries it is acceptable for mothers to breast-feed their children in public places, but in some other regions this is most definitely not tolerated. Find out if there is a designated area where mothers can feed their children.

- Never leave your children unattended, even for a moment, at airports, rail terminals or bus depots. You must have visual contact at least with them at all times.

- When you book your flight request an aisle seat, with your child on the inside. If you do fall asleep your child will wake you up if they try to get past you to the aisle. Ensure that when your child is seated, their seatbelts are securely fastened. When an aircraft meets unexpected turbulence adults have been injured after being tossed around the aircraft; it would take a lot less turbulence to injure a small child.

- You should pay particular attention to airline safety briefs, particularly when you are travelling with a small child. Identify where the nearest emergency exits are and the location of your child's life preserver. Ensure that you know how to attach your child's lifebelt and any other emergency equipment such as oxygen masks.

- If you're travelling to a region with a malaria risk, take enough insect repellent. Take one which will not affect your child's skin; some may be mildly irritating for an adult, and may be more so for a small child. In addition if you are heading off to a hot climate, you will need very high SPF sunscreen for your kids. Take it with you. In some regions you may not be able to find cream with the right factor.

- When you arrive at your hotel it is a good idea to check the room to ensure that it is adequate and suitable for young children. Remember that the room has in all probability just been vacated some hours before and you do not know who used it. Ensure that it's clean and that there is nothing in the room which could harm a small child.

- Check that the windows have locking mechanisms, outside the reach of your children. Check balcony doors and ensure that they also have a lock. If you are not happy with the locks ask for a balcony gate or you may have to move to another room. This is important if you are in the upper floors of a tower block hotel. Keep the keys to the doors out of reach of youngsters. And of course, never leave your children alone on a balcony. If no keys are available, you may consider repositioning the room furniture in order to keep your children from getting at the balcony door. Ensure that you can close the bathroom door. Most hotels will have hot water, and some will have extremely hot water, which can scald little ones.

- If you are travelling with infants or crawling babies, check the floor of your hotel room, bathroom and balcony before you accept the room. Is the carpet clean, is there anything lying around? People have moved into supposedly clean hotel rooms, only to find pills, sharp items or discarded coins, which may be harmful to an infant lying on the floor.

- If the hotel has provided any items such as cots or pushchairs, check them out first before allowing your child to use them. If they are dirty or damaged, ask for them to be replaced.

- In most hotel rooms, there will be a box of matches on a coffee table within the reach of a child, and most minibars are at a height where children can get to them. There may be other potentially dangerous areas – drawcords for curtains, plastic bags in bins and precariously balanced furniture which children could pull from position and hurt themselves. Check to ensure that the electrical cables are secure and there is no danger from power sources.

- If you are on the ground floor of a hotel or in a house, ensure that children's beds are away from the windows. Also make sure that the doors can't be opened while you are sleeping without your being aware of it.

- Ensure that you use only recommended babysitting services, either the hotel service or a known and trusted individual. Keep your plans to yourself and do not let those who do not need to know that you are leaving a babysitter in your hotel room with your kids. Place a 'Do Not Disturb' sign outside your door when you go out. You may also provide a list of contact details so the babysitter can contact you if something does go wrong. It is a good idea to call every few hours, depending on the age of your child.

- You must be vigilant about food and water hygiene. Never allow them to drink untreated water or have ice in their drinks in high-risk areas, and ensure that they use only bottled water for brushing teeth. (See also Chapter 17.)

- When visiting a high-risk area educate your children, without frightening them, about what they should do in the event of an emergency when you are not with them – say, if they are at the kids' club. When you first take your children to a club, introduce them to the staff and then tell your children that they are not permitted to leave the building with anyone other than these people. At the club, leave a list with the staff telling them where you will be each day, and how they can contact you.

■ During excursions, particularly to places like markets and other crowded tourist hotspots, parents need to be on their guard. Instruct your kids that you must all stay close together and if anything happens they must tell you immediately. It may be a good idea to provide your kids with hotel cards. Write down your child's name and your contact details and in the event that they become lost or separated someone may put you in touch with them.

■ When travelling with youngsters it is a good idea to visit all of the tourist hotspots or amusement parks early in the morning. You will avoid much of the crowds, including thieves and criminals.

■ When you're staying in the hotel room during the day with infants who need to sleep then, leave your 'Do Not Disturb' sign on your door. This will prevent hotel employees from entering the room and waking them up.

■ In high-risk environments terrorist groups have targeted mothers, children and husbands, and criminal gangs have kidnapped children for ransom. Families should not attract attention while overseas. Conceal your valuables and move around quietly, without drawing attention to yourselves. You may have to tell the children why all this is so important. Ensure that you and your children (teenagers especially) know which parts of town are high-risk.

■ Tell teenagers to stay aware, and keep to safe, well-lit areas. Warn them off drinking and in particular drugs of any kind – the penalties can be horrendous. It is safer for teenagers to travel in groups with friends.

■ Prepare a first-aid kit that includes items for your child. Ask your doctor for a list. Infant paracetamol for fever, and rehydrating sachets in case of diarrhoea, are useful and may be difficult to obtain overseas. Remember to pack any medication your child takes regularly, in its original packaging.

Children travelling on their own are very vulnerable and it is essential that parents do the planning. Ensure that your child is properly equipped and has the correct travel documentation. Tell the airline that the child will be travelling on their own and whether they need any special assistance. If your child has to change flights, arrange with the airline to have them met at the airport and escorted to the next flight. Identify who will be meeting your child and inform your child of the details of the escort and what they should do if they are not met. They should be given a list of numbers and contact details and instructed to go to the airport help desk in case of any trouble.

Fairground Safety

For children of all ages, amusement parks are pretty much the height of adventure. And it's generally a safe one: most of the rides are subject to rigorous safety procedures. However, they are only as safe as those who use them. Each year there are accidents and fatalities attributed to mechanical failure, but the misbehaviour of children using them is more often the cause.

Many of the more advanced rides will propel riders in open-top cars at ferocious speeds reaching G-forces, which are normally used in training fighter pilots. Exciting? Well, yes, but most of the ride designers calculate risk relying on the people in them staying seated, and injuries can happen even on the kiddie rides if children don't take care. In the US between 1997 and 2000, children under 12 accounted for almost half the injuries sustained on fairground rides. Care must be taken: in 2000 at Disneyland in California, three infants were killed after falling from children's rides.

If your children are drawn by the lure of the fairground, be aware of the following points.

- Your child may become frightened even if the ride is sedate. If your child has never been on a ride before, take them on one with you, tell them what to do, and reinforce the point that they should never stand up or try to get off while the ride is in motion.

- If your child does not want to get on a ride, never force them. Get them used to the idea that you can only get on a ride when it's stopped completely, so if they're on one and want to get off after it has started, they don't get too upset. Tell them beforehand that they must wait to get out until you or the ride attendant releases them from their seat.

■ Tell your child that they must hold on and keep their hands and legs inside the car. If the car comes equipped with a safety strap or restraining bar, tell them they must keep them closed and not undo or wriggle out of them. Metal security bars are generally fitted to the adult passenger and can be loose on a child. So when you are riding with them, tell them to remain firmly seated.

■ Obey height restrictions at fairgrounds. Do not attempt to get an undersized child onto a ride to which they are not suited. If your child is young but tall, don't let them ride alone – you may need to help them behave. Most regulations are designed for children's mental development, not their physical size.

■ If you're not riding with your child, stand where you can keep your eyes on them while the ride is in motion and make sure that they can see you. This may deter them from misbehaving in the car.

■ Never let your child ride alone if you feel they won't do what you say. Children have been killed after trying to get off mid-ride.

■ Never allow children to travel on fairground rides under the control of other children. If one child tries to get off there will be little that a child two or three years older can do to stop them.

■ When teenagers go to fairgrounds with their friends they may do something foolish while under the influence of peer pressure. Firmly explain how you expect them to behave and to avoid messing around on rides. Boys are particularly at risk – they become boisterous and are more likely to fool around.

■ When visiting fairgrounds with children, adults should never ride under the influence of alcohol, alone or with their child.

■ Look at the fairground itself. In some countries, fairground operators are not subject to the same rigorous scrutiny that operators are at home. If you arrive at the fairground and are not happy with the state of the equipment, don't go on the rides.

- Do not allow young children to travel on rides with elderly people who may themselves be too frail to withstand the shocks of the ride, and may not be able to control the situation if things go wrong.

- Do not get on a ride or let someone who is travelling with you do so if you or they have a medical condition which may be affected by the motion. Many rides can be disorientating and will make you feel dizzy. They can also put tremendous strain on your neck and back.

10

Remote Areas

FOR MANY PEOPLE, THE VERY ESSENCE of travel is journeying to the remote regions of the planet. Experiencing a place unspoiled by conflict, consumerism and the human propensity for destructive development is, for many, an energising and uplifting experience. The mad hustle and bustle of our accelerating, globally interconnected, 'twenty-four-seven' lives just underlines how precious natural wilderness is.

Different kinds of wilderness draw different people. The lush tropical rainforests of South East Asia, the desolate wide-open expanses of desert sand, the pristine beauty of the snow-covered poles – all these environments are now only a flight away in our shrinking world. Most of the tourist operations organising these trips are run by environmentally aware organisations that recognise overexploitation will only lead to the collapse of the precious environments that provide their livelihood. They are just part of the worldwide efforts to conserve the wild places of the earth. But while we're on Mother Nature's side, she doesn't always reciprocate.

Roughing it in the wild carries the same distinct dangers it always has. It's just that we may be less equipped than our ancient forebears to deal with them. When we travel to remote areas we leave behind the familiar risks of our cities and enter a realm that runs to very different rules. If we don't know how to cope, it can all turn into the wrong kind of adventure, and we can end up seriously injured or dead.

There's a vast literature on outdoor activities. What follows is by no means exhaustive. It's information I've personally found useful while travelling in remote and hostile regions, and that has so far kept me in the clear.

Tropical Regions

Many people who travel to tropical-belt countries have preconceived notions of how it's going to be, usually featuring impenetrable tropical rain forests inhabited by fierce, dangerous animals. In some places they won't be disappointed. But it's a little more complicated than that.

In the jungles of the tropical belt, the climate and ecosystem ensure that everything from bacteria and parasites to tropical vegetation proliferate, thriving in the hot, humid conditions. High temperatures, which vary only around 10 degrees between day and night, combined with heavy rainfall, produce the intense and characteristic humidity. However, at high altitudes, such as on Kota Kinabalu in northern Borneo, it can get so cold that ice can form.

The onset of the monsoon season, during which rainfall can last for days on end, can be preceded by extreme tropical storms, and there are frequent hurricanes and typhoons. Night descends like a curtain, as it gets dark much more quickly than in northern regions, and sunrise is just as sudden. It is, without doubt, a daunting environment. However, if you know the ropes, the non-stop cycle of life in the jungle becomes its essential attraction. Remember that people have lived in this environment for thousands of years.

Jungle trekking has become a popular activity in the tropics. If you're thinking of going on one, be aware that there are several different types of jungle, depending on the region to which you are travelling.

Primary Jungle

In primary jungle – more or less untouched by humans – there is a constant temperature of between 32 degrees Celsius during the day, and around 21 degrees at night, and heavy rainfall of up to 3.5 metres a year. Huge tropical hardwoods tower up to 60 metres above the jungle floor, their foliage so thick that very little sunlight penetrates. This prohibits the growth of vegetation on the forest floor, which is covered by a thick layer of dead leaves. Moss and fungi grow in this dank environment. Vines twine themselves around the trees, climbing upwards to the sunlight, and the tree can become so densely covered that visibility is restricted to between 10 and 20 metres. Many of the exotic tropical wildlife species live in this kind of jungle. Because of the lack of ground cover, movement is relatively easy, and many of the tourist trekking areas are located in these jungles. You can find primary rainforest in most of the tropical belt that has not been exploited by man.

Secondary Jungle

Secondary jungle, found in the same part of the world as primary, springs up after primary jungle – with its huge and valuable tropical hardwoods – is logged. Logging creates gaps in the jungle canopy, which allows the light to penetrate to the jungle floor and triggers the growth of seeds and dormant vegetation. The thick, tangled vegetation that grows up makes movement very difficult. Secondary jungle is also found along riverbanks and in areas cleared by humans for cultivation and left for the jungle to reclaim.

Tropical Scrublands

Seasonal weather patterns, including a definite dry season, characterise tropical scrubland. In the rainy season the vegetation, which is thick and thorny, is lush and green, but in the dry season the trees lose their leaves. The scrub forests are not as densely packed as primary jungle and there can be relatively large spaces between the trees. The forest floor is mostly free of tangled vegetation, so it's relatively easy to move through it. During the dry season, outbreaks of fire are common, as the thin thorns are subject to the powerful effects of the tropical sun. Tropical scrublands can be found in Central and South America, central Africa and in the Asian subcontinent.

Savannah

Savannahs are large, open and grassy regions typically found in tropical Africa and South America. The trees in this environment are tiny compared to jungle hardwoods, and widely spaced. The thriving grasslands are lush, and support many of the wildlife species of Africa. Movement in this type of environment is easy, although the earth can become boggy after heavy rainfall.

Swamps

Both freshwater and mangrove swamps are common in tropical regions. In mangrove swamps, the trees are densely packed and may be higher than 10 metres, which limits visibility to no more than a few metres. The roots of the mangrove trees are tangled and form a formidable barrier to movement. Mangrove swamps are subject to tides, and the ground is frequently submerged in water. When the tide is out, deep, foul-smelling mud is exposed, and this is slippery and very difficult to negotiate. In mangrove swamps, channels can form between the trees. Freshwater swamps form inland, generally in low, flat areas. They are full of dense, tall elephant grass, reeds and thorny bushes. There are occasional hillocks in these swamps which are dry, but it is generally difficult to see them due to the size and density of the reeds and grass. Much of a freshwater swamp is on unstable ground – deep, peaty mud. Movement on this ground is difficult and unless you know the area can be treacherous. In addition, there is a huge variety of wildlife. Some of these animals are dangerous if disturbed by the unwary traveller.

Jungle Safety

If you're contemplating a jungle trek, first choose a well-established, reputable company. Many of these are efficiently run and highly organised. They may, however, never have actually tested their contingency plans for emergencies, and so don't know whether they would actually work. Then there are the unregistered companies who have no contingency plans, which you should obviously avoid.

Even the best-organised trips can end in tragedy in what is, after all, a hostile environment to most Westerners. In 2001, a British schoolgirl was killed when she fell from a cliff path in the mountains of Vietnam. The trip was well prepared and well organised and led by a former British military officer. However, there had been very heavy rainfall, which caused the girl to slip. The Vietnamese police reported that they were concerned that the area may have been dangerous because of the rain-drenched conditions.

Much of my time in the military was spent in jungles, and I know the dangers only too well. These can be mitigated by knowing how you should behave and being made aware of the potential risks in this most unfamiliar of environments.

The following points are intended to help those involved in jungle trekking expeditions make the right decisions and maintain the ability to get themselves out of trouble in the event that things go wrong.

■ Only use a reputable company when booking your expedition. You should be able to contact suitable companies through your travel agent or hotel activity representative. Avoid offers of cheap trekking guides from those who approach you on the street. You can expect well-established companies to have reasonable procedures in case things go wrong, but touts on the street will have no back-up and if disaster strikes you will be on your own. Enquire about the safety record of the company and ensure that they have adequate medical support. If the travel agent cannot provide you with information, ask for the contact details from another person who has arranged a similar expedition.

■ Ask the trekking company the route you will be taking and the ultimate destination. Cross-check this information with another source, to ensure that it is a safe place to visit. Not only wild animals inhabit jungles. A country in the grip of major conflict could have jungles teeming with militia or rebels, and you won't be equipped to deal with that.

- Be aware of weather conditions at the time of your trek. It will be difficult during the monsoon season – rain can make the going very tough. Identify the best time of year for visiting the jungle. This can vary from region to region. Remember, too, that global warming has had an impact on the weather system in the tropical zone. Weather patterns in South East Asia, for example, have become increasingly unpredictable.

- Ensure that you are medically prepared before going to a tropical region. The hot, humid tropical air and many sources of infection will soon leave any open wounds festering. Ensure that you have the appropriate malarial prophylaxis and inoculations for that region (see Chapter 17, page 381). If you are going on a physically demanding expedition, make sure that you are really up to it. Life in the jungle can be extremely taxing.

- Take the right equipment. Your travel agent or tour operator will provide you with an essential equipment list. Many operators provide that most basic of essentials, the mosquito net. However, many come with holes in them, so I always take my own, dipped in the mosquito repellent permethrin.

- Whenever in a jungle area I wear long sleeves and long trousers. I tuck my trousers inside my boots and apply a liberal coating of mosquito repellent to my boots and trousers. This stops leeches from attaching themselves to my lower leg.

- The jungle is humid, but it's vital to keep both your equipment and some of your clothes dry. You will need these to sleep in. If you have no dry clothes, you may end up unable to sleep and will quickly become exhausted. Totally waterproof bags are available through many outward bound shops.

- One of the most common complaints when walking long distances in a jungle is the sweat rash that develops at the groin and on the inside of your legs. This is caused when your trousers become soaked with sweat and rub the inside of your legs. This rash can become infected very quickly in the jungle air, and can be terribly painful if not treated. A simple way round the problem is to buy a non-padded pair of Lycra cycle shorts. Wear them next to your skin, but turn them inside out as this will prevent the seam from rubbing against your skin and causing a rash.

- If you've hired a local guide, pay attention to what they tell you. This is their patch and they will know the area intimately. Obviously, if your tour group is headed by someone from the West you'll also need to listen to them, but they never know as much about the area as the people who grew up there.

- Don't eat anything from the jungle without first asking the local guide. There are many things in the jungle that look appetising, but quite a few of them are very toxic to humans.

- When travelling in jungles, one of the key rules is never to wander off on your own. Jungles can be very disorienting and due to the limited visibility it is very easy to become lost. This can happen to even the most experienced of navigators. Stay with your group. And unless an expert guide accompanies you, do not move around at night. Even with the assistance of torches, movement in a jungle can be very dangerous, and if you sustain an injury you will probably have to remain in the jungle until at least the next morning.

- Navigation in thick jungle is notoriously difficult, so I suggest staying with the guides. Bring a compass along, however, to maintain a sense of direction (see Chapter 18). Locals appear to possess an innate sense of direction. I have often been amazed at the ability of some indigenous peoples to navigate by instinct.

- I would not advise entering a swamp without a local guide. When travelling in mangrove swamp, identify the channels that can support your boat, and do not get out of your boat. If you have to get out, try to walk on the roots of the trees and avoid the deep mud.

- Walking through the jungle is hard work, but you can make life a little easier. One difficulty is the limited visibility. People new to this environment tend to look at what is in front of them, but if you do this all you will see are trees a few feet from your face. The trick is to look through the gaps in the vegetation and focus on distant trees. You'll have to practise the technique, but you can increase your visibility greatly this way.

- By looking through the jungle and not at it you will be able to select the safest routes for travelling. The thick jungle foliage can hide many dangers, such as cliffs. When walking through thick jungle, you need to identify your route before you move. If you go crashing through you will almost certainly see nothing, all the animals will disappear and you will only be able to hear the sound of yourself crashing through the trees. If you move slowly you may get close to wildlife, and more importantly you will be able to hear and be prepared for dangers such as rivers or falling trees.

- In jungle areas there are many animals that use the same routes to go about their daily activities, leaving easily identifiable paths. These paths inevitably lead to water and possibly to human habitation, and are relatively easy to walk on. Generally, animal paths meander all over the place, so one should use them if they are going in your direction. But use caution: in many tropical regions forest dwellers frequently set traps to catch the animals, which for them are a valuable source of food. Ensure that your guide goes first as he will be able to identify these traps.

- Maintain an acute awareness of what is around you. If you move slowly you may hear the telltale noise of hornets at work. Once in South East Asia I had the unpleasant experience of being the last man in a line of four when we accidentally disturbed a hornet's nest in the ground. We all took off, but I was the easiest for the hornets to get to. They have receptors which are sensitive to carbon dioxide and help them pursue their quarry. I received 15 stings all around the back of my head and neck as the hornets zeroed in on the carbon dioxide trail which surged out behind me as I ran like hell to escape. I jumped into the nearest river and had to pick aggressive hornets off my head and neck. I was in pain for quite some time and it took me a full two days to recover.

- In the hot, humid conditions of the tropics you will require around 15 pints of water a day, and when trekking through jungle areas water is generally in abundance. However, when you start to climb uphill, water will become scarcer the higher you go. It is essential that before you begin to climb you should drink plenty of water and fill your water containers. There may not be water at the top.

■ When walking through rainforest, move slowly and deliberately. Look where you are going and try to keep your footing. You should avoid having to stretch out and grasp at trees or vines in order to keep your balance. Many of the trees have sharp protective spines, which can easily penetrate a hand. I still have the remnants of such a spine in my hand from a painful encounter three years ago.

■ You should avoid cutting vegetation in the jungle. Not only does it damage the fragile environment; it can also be dangerous. Any cuts are sure to become infected. However, if you have to do it, cut away from your body. By swinging your machete in an outward direction away from you, you won't be hurt even if you miss. It is vital that you do not do any cutting in the afternoon. Night falls quickly in the tropics and it may not be possible to evacuate a casualty when it is dark.

■ In the tropics, the rain is frequently torrential. Near coastal areas, heavy rain will be preceded by a pressure wave and a rush of air is felt even in the jungle. Sometimes the rain can be so heavy that it can cause flash floods. Be aware of your location. Many jungle streams are prone to such flooding and the levels of water can rise extremely fast. If you are on flat ground or near a stream or river and torrential rain hits, think of moving to high ground.

■ During heavy rainfall, trees absorb a great deal of water. This can put a tremendous strain on the tops of older or weakened trees. In the morning when the trees are exposed to the strong tropical sunlight, the wet limbs expand and you can hear them creaking and groaning. The sodden branches and foliage can break, and pieces of wood perhaps weighing hundreds of pounds crash to the ground. After heavy rain, listen out for falling branches.

■ Deadfall or dead wood falling from trees can kill you if it falls on you. It is essential that before you select you camp for the night you check the trees above you for deadfall. Look for old trees or trees which have been damaged. You should pitch your camp among strong healthy trees.

Deserts

When you travel in a desert, preparation is all. You'll need adequate water and you need to know how to navigate. The low rainfall and intense sunlight mean it's very easy to become dehydrated, and some deserts appear featureless to the unpractised eye. Yet many are drawn to these harsh and beautiful regions, and desert safaris are becoming popular, with British travellers flocking to Morocco and Tunisia. Before you go, though, it's best to read up on desert environments.

In some desert regions, such as in northern Somalia, the annual rainfall is no more than a few inches, some times not even that. The intense dry heat, which can reach in excess of 145 degrees Fahrenheit (62 degrees Celsius), is made worse by the glare, which is reflected off the sand. The sand and rock store heat during the day and it can become extremely hot, exceeding the air temperature by up to 30 degrees. Then, at nightfall, the temperatures can plummet and chill even the hardiest of travellers – so you have to bring cold-weather clothing. In some desert areas such as the Sahara, the lack of cloud cover and scarcity of vegetation ensure that the temperature difference between day and night is greater than in any other place on earth.

Most of the companies who run desert treks and safaris are well qualified and have adequate contingency plans in case something goes wrong. However, there have been tragedies. A few years ago a British family on holiday in Tunisia set off on an adventure drive into the desert. Their vehicle became stuck in the sand. The only adult male decided to go off and try to get help, nearly dying in the attempt. Eventually, after an epic journey, he managed to summon help and returned to find his family had died from dehydration. As I've said, it's vital to know your deserts.

There are many different kinds of desert environment, as I've outlined below.

Sand Deserts

This is everyone's idea of what a desert is – the classic image of harsh desolation, a huge expanse of golden sand without shelter or shade and scarce water. There are vast flat areas which can stretch as far as the eye can see, and areas of sand dunes that can soar up well over 100 metres and stretch for many kilometres. In sand dune deserts there is generally very little if any vegetation, as few species are able to adapt to the harsh conditions. The vegetation is stunted, with roots spreading out over a wide area in order to exploit the sparse rainfall. Some tree species have roots running down many metres to tap into deep underground water sources. Sand dune deserts are found in the Rub al Khali or Empty Quarter in central Arabia, Africa's Kalahari and Sahara deserts, the Sinai desert between Africa and Arabia, and some desert regions in the American Southwest. Movement through sand dune desert is extremely difficult and should be avoided if possible.

Mountain Deserts

These are predominantly mountainous areas – barren mountain ranges interspersed with expanses of dry, flat sand. The mountains can be over 1000 metres high and are devoid of vegetation and water. Due to the lack of vegetation on the highest mountains, the infrequent rain quickly runs off, eroding channels into the mountainside. During periods of rainfall, flash floods can be a hazard in these channels. In areas such as northern Kenya's Rift Valley around Lake Turkana, huge lakes have formed although the water is undrinkable. I once spent a month by this barren, desolate, crocodile-infested lake. We had to have fresh water delivered. Movement on this type of terrain is hazardous, especially on steep ground.

Rock Deserts

Vast expanses of sandy desert interspersed with huge rock formations and broad areas of broken rocky terrain: these are rock deserts. There may be sporadic vegetation around the rocky areas, partly because the deep gaps between some rock formations can collect rainfall to form natural pools that sustain limited plant life. And where there is plant life there will be animal life too – as much as can be supported by the available vegetation. Overhanging rocks will provide shelter from the fierce sun: the temperature in the shade will be many degrees cooler than out in the open. Again, unless you are a part of an organised group, it is unwise to move around at night.

Wadis

Wadis are dried-out water channels that crisscross some desert terrain. In sandy areas the wadis can be wide although not too deep – say, up to 6 metres or so. Generally, there is no vegetation although there may be a seasonal burst of vigorous growth immediately after the rain. This soon fades away and lies dormant until the next rains. You have to be careful in an area of wadis. Their banks can be a sheer drop, and they may not be visible until you are almost on top of them. This makes movement at night extremely hazardous. I have known people to walk right into a wadi because they had not seen them from a couple of metres out. There have been reports of vehicles driving into wadis for the same reason. If you are walking, do not be tempted into following the course of the wadi unless you are sure it is going in your direction. Wadis can meander all over the place with no real discernible direction.

Desert Travel

There are many hazards involved in desert travel: biting insects, of which there are a multitude; snakes; exposure to the intense heat of the sun during the day, which can cause severe sunburn; and, in some locations, extreme cold at night. If you get sand in your eye during a sandstorm it can cause an eye infection. Desert terrain can make travel very difficult especially if you're on foot. As I've mentioned, navigation can be difficult because there may be few obvious landmarks. But it is these very challenges which, combined with the beauty of these unspoiled areas, draw people to the area in the first place.

If you're off to a desert, you'll need to think about the following points.

- Ensure that the people who are responsible for your safety know what they are doing. You need a reputable company with a good track record. If they are using vehicles, ask to see them to ensure they are up to the rigours of desert travel. Make sure that they have desert driving equipment, including the necessary tools to extract the vehicles from deep sand if they get bogged down. The minimum requirements are sand boards, large thin metal tracks which are placed under wheels when there is no traction between the wheels and the sand. In addition, a turfer or a mobile or self-winching device will be needed to pull the vehicle out of deep sand. Many of the travel operators include camel safaris, which seem a romantic way of getting around in a desert; but there can be problems with travelling by animal (see page 231 below).

- Research the area you're going to trek or drive to to discover whether it is safe and secure. Inform your friends and family at home where you are going, when you will depart and when you intend to return. Don't forget to call them after your expedition has finished to let them know that all is well.

- Ensure that you get an appropriate equipment list from your tour company. Most will tell you what to bring and many will supply you with what you need.

- Many desert areas will have corrosive surface soil with a high mineral content, which can erode clothing and footwear. Ask your tour company which type of clothing to bring. In addition much of the water in these areas is not potable due to the high mineral content, so soaking your clothing and then drying it in the sun will leave mineral deposits. As you travel during the heat of the day, your body will rehydrate the minerals on your clothes and in some cases this can cause a skin rash.

- During many desert safaris, the base camps will be in or near abandoned houses or caves. Many desert creatures, such as scorpions and other biting or stinging insects, will be sharing these dwellings with you. Ensure that you check your clothing, boots and rucksack in the morning. Check anything into which one of these creatures could climb. Do not put your hand down any holes or upturn any stones; you never know what is down there.

- Snakes may also inhabit similar areas and some of them are highly dangerous. However, a snake would rather not attack you. After all, you are a lot bigger than a snake, and they generally only attack if a human inadvertently threatens them. Never tease a snake with a stick: this will force them into attacking. Be aware of where you are walking, wear appropriate footwear and look around before you sit down anywhere.

- The sun in desert areas is intense, and even a few minutes of direct exposure may be enough to burn your skin. You should not attempt to sunbathe in this climate. If you fall asleep the consequences could be severe – you can, for instance, end up covered with large plasma blisters. When these break, they may well become infected by the multitude of insects. You can still get badly sunburnt on an overcast day, as solar rays can penetrate cloud cover. Keep as much of your body covered from the sun as you can; this is why native desert dwellers are covered from head to toe. On areas you cannot keep covered, liberally apply high SPF sunscreen. Remember to apply UV lip balm to protect your lips.

- Don't rub your eyes after a sandstorm, as they can become infected, and wear UV protection goggles, which seal the area of your eye from the environment.

- During the evening and into the night it may become quite cold. Bring adequate clothing and a sleeping bag that's warm enough.

- At night, ensure that the camp refuse is either burned, or sealed and buried. Do not place your camp latrine near your sleeping area or biting insects might plague you. Basic hygiene is essential in this environment as insects spread some of the diseases common in this part of the world.

- One of the fundamental principles of desert travel is understanding the connection between physical activity, air temperature and water consumption. Even in a cold climate your body requires a certain amount of water, but when exposed to the intense stresses of the desert heat, water is a matter of life and death. It has been calculated that an individual undergoing physical work in a temperature of around 37 degrees Celsius will require around 23 litres of water a day. Failure to replace fluids in this circumstance would mean that within a day or so you would be dead. The harder you work, the more you sweat and the more water you have to replace. Sweating is the body's principle mechanism for reducing heat. If you are dehydrated and can't sweat you will develop heat stroke, a potentially fatal condition. You must ensure that you have an adequate water supply. If you can't carry enough water, find out where you can obtain water on the way.

- Many waterholes in the desert may have been contaminated by animals or waterborne microbes that may be harmful to humans. An adequate supply of water purification tablets is essential. I have used chlorine tablets many times in the past. They make the water taste terrible but if you follow the instructions they work well. There are a multitude of water purification devices and tablets commercially available.

- It is helpful to avoid moving around during the heat of the day unless you are with a local guide who knows what he is doing. He will know where the local water supply is and how to get there. It is safer to take shelter from the sun ensuring that you have protection from above, and also from below. Do not sit directly on the sand – remember, it will be hotter that the air temperature.

- If there is a shortage of water, avoid eating high-protein foods. Your body will require more water to digest these. Do not wait until you are thirsty before you drink water. You should make a habit of drinking periodically, as otherwise you will become dehydrated. It has been suggested that if you wait until you feel thirsty before drinking you will dehydrate 30 per cent faster, so you should force yourself to drink at least half a litre of water an hour, even if you are resting at temperatures of 32 degrees Celsius; at temperatures above this you should try to drink about a litre an hour.

One way to ensure that you are getting enough water is to check your urine. It should be clear. If it is discoloured you need to drink more. The darker it is, the more water you need.

■ In a desert, strong winds are frequent and sandstorms can quickly form. The sand can gust at high velocities with the wind or it can swirl in a stream of wind as it changes direction. In sandstorms, visibility can be reduced to almost zero and travel will be impossible. It is advisable to find shelter if possible. If no shelter is available, stop and place some sort of cover over your head. Protect your eyes by wearing goggles and ensure that you cover your mouth and nose to avoid sand inhalation.

■ Mirages are caused by the refraction of the light through the hot air rising from the inland desert floor. A mirage has the effect of making things appear to move, and it can also make hills or objects difficult to identify, which could impede navigation. In a mirage, the shimmering light can resemble the surface of a body of water. If you are travelling by vehicle, by standing on the top of the vehicle or on high ground you can 'sidestep' any mirages by looking down through the hot air.

■ Intense heat is the big problem in the desert. Heat is responsible for many injuries and indeed deaths. Excessive sweating can lead to a depletion of salts and minerals in your body, resulting in 'heat cramp'. This is a severe cramp in your legs, arms and abdomen. If you or a fellow traveller start feeling cramp in any of these areas, stop and get under some sort of shade, then rehydrate with water and rehydration salts. If this condition is not treated you may develop a more serious heat injury.

■ Heat exhaustion is another condition resulting from profuse sweating and loss of water and salt. The sufferer will be uncertain, confused, weak and dizzy. They may become irritable, with cold clammy skin and possibly cramp. This is a serious condition and you must act quickly to prevent a more serious one. Move the person into the shade, loosen their clothing and soak it with water. Fan them to ensure a strong flow of air and cool them off. Give them water and rehydration salts.

■ Heat stroke – the most serious of heat-related injuries – can develop if the person has untreated heat exhaustion. This happens when there is a severe loss of water and salts, which leaves the body unable to cool itself. This is a potentially fatal condition and the person is in real danger. They will not be sweating and their skin will be hot and dry. They will have a fast pulse and feel sick and be vomiting, leading to further fluid loss. They will become unconscious if not treated soon. Act fast to cool them down. Get them into the shade and ensure they are elevated above the hot sand. Loosen or remove clothes, pour water on them, and fan vigorously to maintain a strong flow of air over their body. Give them water and rehydration salts. You'll need to evacuate them as soon as possible.

■ As in any other remote area, never go off on your own. Always stay with the group and obey the safety instructions from those who are in charge of your party. Avoid wandering about at night or during a sandstorm. It is very easy to become disorientated and in a sandstorm no one will hear your cries.

■ If you are carrying any sensitive camera or video equipment you should ensure that it is protected both from the sun and the sand. If exposed to direct sunshine your equipment may get damaged. If you are in an area with cellphone coverage, be aware that a sandstorm may interfere with your transmissions.

Cold Climates

If you're planning a winter or polar journey, you'll need to do a threat assessment. The weather conditions can be very dangerous, and you need to find out as much as possible about them. In recent years, global warming has made the weather rather unpredictable in some places.

When you set out on a trip to a cold climate, ensure that you plan for the worst possible conditions. These environments can be just as dangerous and in some cases even more so than deserts or even jungles. And you don't have to go all the way to the Arctic to experience the risks of cold weather travel. On any Welsh or Scottish hillside during the winter, the conditions can be as bad if not worse. Oceanic activity can shape the weather in relatively temperate zones and bring in Arctic conditions.

In the northern hemisphere, just under half of the total landmass may during the winter months be considered a cold climate. High, exposed ground is often subject to much colder and wetter weather than ground at lower altitudes. Britain and parts of Western Europe are subject to cold, wet weather during much of the year, but other cold regions will be subject to cold, dry weather. In either case, you have to be prepared. Each year more deaths occur in cold climates than in any other type of environment. Even the ski slopes of Europe or North America can be perilous, and certainly mountains that may offer easy strolls in the summer can become treacherous icy wastelands in winter. Not just the hills of Scotland and Wales, but also the Swiss Alps and mountains of Nepal frequently appear in news bulletins telling of travellers who have come to grief through lack of preparation for travelling in cold climates. It may be a good idea to prepare yourself before heading off into the cold. There are winter adventure training courses run in Britain's mountainous spots during the winter, for instance. These are professionally run and not prohibitively expensive, and will provide you with the skills to participate safely in many winter activities.

In a temperate climate, it turns cold during late autumn and throughout the winter. Rain is a constant feature during this time of year, making the ground muddy and difficult to move over, particularly in rough country. During the night the temperature will drop and can result in a ground frost. In the midwinter this can result in a deep freeze during which the temperature does not rise sufficiently enough throughout the day to thaw the previous night's ice.

In more northerly latitudes, at higher altitudes and in the extreme south and Antarctic regions, travellers may be exposed to temperatures that are permanently below -10 degrees Celsius. There is little rain and most precipitation falls as snow. The temperature range can be extreme, ranging from above 10 degrees Celsius to as low as -60 degrees in some regions. In a cold dry environment the constant low temperature ensures that everything remains frozen, so reducing the exposure to mud and water. In this type of terrain, you must use an insulation mat when resting on the ground. This will protect you from the effects of ground water and the freezing effects of the snow.

One of the many dangers travellers face is the wind chill factor, which exacerbates already cold temperatures. If exposed to high winds in a low temperature and with inadequate or wet clothing, you place yourself at risk of hypothermia. If you are wearing wet clothes, even if there is no wind you will suffer up to 30 per cent greater heat loss. During wet, windy and cold weather, hypothermia occurs very quickly. An air temperature of -5 degrees Celsius in a wind of 16 kilometres per hour will have the effect of a temperature of -15 degrees. In these conditions, heat loss and energy essentially mean the same, and the more heat you lose the more energy you lose. Around four hours of moderate to hard walking at -17 degrees in a wind 65 kilometres per hour will result in the loss of your entire day's intake of around 4000 calories. And you will be exposed to wind resistance as you run, walk or ski in cold conditions. You'll need to be vigilant about staying dry and regulating your exertions.

If you plan to travel in a cold climate, consider the following points.

- Use the layer principle when choosing clothes to bring. In icy conditions wear lots of layers of thin clothing rather than thick sweaters. By using thin layers you will trap warm air between each, building a barrier of warm layers around your body. You must protect your valuable body heat by wearing a windproof and waterproof outer shell. Any semipermeable waterproof material such as GORE-TEX will be sufficient. Use the modern material designed to do the job. The layer principle will also help you regulate your body temperature. If you work too hard even in cold climates you will sweat, and this will intensify heat loss. By removing some layers you can achieve a comfortable body temperature, and when you stop working you can replace the other layers.

- Most outdoor shops sell suitable cold-weather clothing. Buy the best quality you can afford. Ask at the shop for advice on the equipment you need. They have suitably qualified assistants who will know. If you intend to take a walking holiday, get your boots some time before you leave. Winter walking boots are classified as 'four seasons', provide rigid support for your ankles and permit the attachment of crampons. You should break them in before you go to avoid blisters on holiday. If your boots are made from leather, break them in by placing them in hot water for around 15 minutes. Then wear them for a while until they mould to the shape of your feet. After a while place them in cold water. Let them dry out and repeat the process until you are happy with your boots.

- It may be difficult travelling in soft snow around half a foot (15 centimetres) deep, and you could need snowshoes. It is virtually impossible to move in deep snow without snowshoes or skis. Sinking into thigh-deep snow as you struggle to make progress can leave you exhausted. Ensure that your tour operator is going to provide snowshoes and skis; if not you may have to purchase your own. You may also need to buy or hire crampons – which will enable you to walk on steep, snow-covered hills without slipping – and an ice axe, which is an essential tool for outdoor winter skills.

- To gain maximum protection from your clothing you must dress properly. Wear a hat; there is a lot of blood circulating in your head and you need to keep it warm in order for your body to stay warm. Through the process of heat radiation you lose around 50 to 60 per cent of body heat through your head. Any exposed areas of your body will lose heat, so protect your neck and areas like your ankles and wrists which have little insulating body fat.

- If you're planning on sleeping outdoors at night a good-quality sleeping bag is essential. Again, buy the best you can afford. Natural down provides outstanding insulation, as do many quality synthetic fillers. Get advice from staff at your outdoor shop. You'll also need an insulating mat to keep you off the heat-sapping cold ground. Even with the best sleeping bag, if you do not have an insulating mat you will become dangerously cold and exhausted the next morning.

- Keep your equipment and clothing clean. Mud and dirt will reduce your clothing's insulation capability, which may result in a cold weather injury. After each day's hike set aside a few minutes to brush down your clothing.

- When you are travelling by foot in snow conditions you will be working hard, and can actually overheat. As you warm up you will begin to sweat. Your clothes will absorb the sweat, and as moisture evaporates from them it reduces the insulation qualities and causes your body to cool. When you get out of your sleeping bag in the morning you may be tempted to just keep on all of your clothes. Then you begin to work and sweat, and it is sometimes difficult to stop to remove your clothes. The result is that everything becomes moist. It is safer to remove some clothing before you start working. It may be cold to begin with, but you will warm up soon enough.

- Buy a can of silicon waterproofing spray before you go. I have used this many times and it helps waterproof most materials. Do not use it on semipermeable material, as you will block up the micropores that allow moisture inside your clothes to escape while keeping moisture on the outside out.

- When staying outdoors in a cold environment, ensure you maintain an awareness of the time: temperatures can plummet rapidly with the onset of darkness. You may have to stop in the midafternoon to ensure that you have sufficient time to establish your camp before the temperature drops.

- In cold climates, snow and wind can have a similar effect to a desert sandstorm. Blizzard conditions arise during a heavy snowstorm which is accompanied by high winds. Visibility can drop to a couple of metres or there can be a complete white-out. A white-out is when there is so much snow in the air that it is impossible to tell the difference between the terrain and the snow-laden air. I once had a frightening experience trying to cross over the French Alps in a small helicopter during white-out conditions. The helicopter was buffeted by high winds and it was impossible to tell the ground from the air. As the pilot nudged the helicopter slowly forward we grew alarmed as dark, menacing cliffs suddenly filled the glass windscreen. We could not get over the mountain range and had to turn back and detour round the south coast of France. So check the weather conditions. If a storm is blowing up, you may want to postpone you travel arrangements until it passes.

- In the mountains the threat from avalanche is very real. It's advisable to travel with a local guide in such terrain. Obey his instructions and stick to the safe routes. If there is a definite avalanche threat, you should travel during the early morning. The previous night's low temperatures will help hold the snow together. As the day progresses, the sun – even if not visible through the clouds – will begin to make the snow more unstable and prime it for an avalanche (see also Chapter 11, page 251).

- Be aware of trying to cross over what appear to be frozen rivers or streams. Often these look stable and solidly frozen enough to support your weight. However, the ice and snow can act as an insulating material for the water perhaps just a few inches below, preventing it from freezing. In Britain each winter there are cases where children or adults venture out onto lakes which have frozen over, only for the ice to break – with tragic results. If you have to cross such an obstacle, follow the watercourse up or downstream until you find a suitable crossing place. This may take you some time but at least you will be safe. If you decide that you want to cross, ensure that you lie flat on the ice to distribute your weight across as wide an area as possible. In this way you should be able to crawl across without breaking the ice.

- Even if it's snowy and icy, the difference between day and night temperatures will mean some thawing will happen during the day. As the day temperature rises even slightly, stream and river levels can rise as the water volume is increased by melt water. You must choose where to camp for the night with care. Even a minor flood from such streams is a major disaster. If your clothes and sleeping bags get wet, not only will you have an uncomfortable time, you will in this climate put your life at risk.

- Once more, in these hostile conditions, never wander off on your own. White-outs can happen with great suddenness, and the moving snow will quickly cover your tracks. If someone in your group is lagging behind, you must wait for them. If they fall back even a metre or two in a blizzard, it may mean they lose touch with the group and this can end in tragedy. On some such trips you will be roped together in order to prevent this from happening. You must carry a map and compass with you too, and know the basics of how to use them (see Chapter 18). In many remote regions there are dangers from different types of terrain. Cliffs and rivers combined with winter weather can be a testing environment.

Cold Weather Injuries

A basic understanding of how cold weather affects your body will enable you to protect yourself by helping you recognise the sometimes imprecise symptoms of cold weather injuries.

Your body's core temperature is 98.6 degrees Fahrenheit or 37 degrees Celsius. Your body can lose excess heat more efficiently than it can produce new heat. When exposed to cold temperatures, your body will involuntarily shiver. This is an autonomic mechanism which your body triggers to produce heat when it's cold. However, excessive shivering can lead to exhaustion, which will use up energy and lead to a further loss of body heat. It has been estimated that a naked person in a temperature of 0 degrees Celsius in zero wind conditions will be able to maintain his body heat by shivering very hard. However, eventually the person will stop shivering due to lack of energy. Even in very low temperatures travellers are able to protect themselves by wearing winter clothing, but you still need to stay active or you will feel the effects of the cold. Cold weather injuries are often difficult to detect at the early stages, but early diagnosis is essential to stop the person's condition from deteriorating further.

Look out for the following signs.

■ When your body heat depletes faster than your body can produce heat, hypothermia – a drop in body temperature – results. It can happen in cold weather after immersion in water, a soaking from heavy rain, or sweating so much that your clothes become wet. The initial sign is shivering: your body recognises that you are cold and is trying to generate enough heat to raise your temperature. In more serious cases the shivering may be uncontrollable. The person may develop symptoms such as slow, slurred speech and become lethargic, irrational and quarrelsome, and state that they actually feel warm. Body temperature may drop to between 35 and 32 degrees Celsius. If you observe any of these symptoms while outdoors, stop the person and remove their wet clothing. Try to warm them. If you are outdoors, get inside a shelter or tent, and put them in a sleeping bag with another healthy person in the bag with them. Ideally, both should be naked to ensure the transmission of heat. If the healthy person complains that he is cooling down too much, ask another person to replace them. If you can get them indoors, run a warm – not hot – bath and ensure that you keep the person's legs and arms out of the bath. If you submerge the person's entire body in the bath you may increase the risk of bringing on a heart attack known as rewarming shock. If the person is conscious you can give them a warm sweet drink, but avoid anything with alcohol as this will further increase the loss of heat. As soon as their temperature begins to rise remove them and wrap in warm clothing, put them to bed in a warm room and monitor their condition.

■ Exposed areas of skin can freeze in very cold weather, causing frostbite. Affected areas will look dull and white, but this may only be skin frostbite which has not penetrated too deeply into tissue. If you lose sensation in your hands or feet, this is an early sign that you are in the process of developing frostbite. If you have lost the sensation for a prolonged period the area may have developed deep frostbite, which can freeze inner tissue and may ultimately mean amputation. To reduce the chances of becoming a frostbite casualty, ensure that you cover exposed patches of skin and maintain blood circulation in those areas by moving them and massaging them. Your ears are particularly vulnerable so you must ensure that they are covered.

■ Every day check your own body, and those of your group, to ensure that no one has overlooked a patch of frostbite. If you detect one, you should warm the area. Then you must ensure that this area will not freeze again. At this stage you should consider calling off your plans and seek professional medical assistance. Never follow suggestions like 'rub the affected area with snow' – this will only result in greater damage. If someone has deep frostbite, the area may be black. In this situation, they will need not only medical assistance but also surgical professionals. Do not try to warm an area of deep frostbite.

■ Where there is snow on the ground and the sun is shining, there is a danger that the UV rays from the sun will reflect off the snow and cause the condition known as snow blindness. Many skiers can testify to the effects of snow blindness when they return from their annual winter skiing trip to Europe or North America. For some people it's only a temporary condition; others develop permanent eye damage after prolonged exposure to fierce UV rays, which are more intense at higher altitudes. All you need to do to prevent this condition is buy a decent pair of UV sunglasses. Better still, buy a pair offering complete eye protection, such as sunglasses with sun shields all the way round or snow goggles. If you have a headache with redness around your eyes and feel a gritty sensation, if your eyes weep or you have some pain in the eye area, especially when you move them, chances are that you will have a degree of snow blindness. Simply cover your eyes and block out any light until you do not feel the symptoms. When you get back, visit your optician to ensure there is no permanent damage.

■ In some locations, particularly at high altitude, the sun's rays can reflect off the snow or ice and even in very low temperatures can burn vulnerable areas of uncovered skin. Patches of exposed skin at your wrists or face, eyes and eyelids, lips and nose are all at risk. This kind of sunburn can blister exposed areas and take weeks to heal, in some cases leaving permanent scars. Treat this as a real threat. Cover up exposed areas and use high SPF sunscreen or sunblock, and lip balm with UV protection.

■ When travelling in cold climates you will at times be required to work hard. In these conditions you will lose body fluids by sweating and in the moisture in your breath. When exposed to really cold climates you will urinate more, which leads to further fluid loss. You will require just as much fluid in a really cold environment as you will in a hot environment. Ensure that you have enough fluids in order to ward off dehydration. Follow the instructions of your guide, or at least ensure that you know what you are doing. It is not just a matter of boiling up some snow and having a drink. With some snow, you will waste a lot of heat and get very little water for your efforts. And at high altitudes it can difficult to melt ice or snow.

African Safaris

African safaris are the dream holiday for a lot of Westerners. The opportunity to see at close hand the savage beauty of African wildlife can be an enormous draw. But these days, you're hardly pitting yourself against the wilderness. The animals struggle for survival under the gaze of a new species – the tourist armed with rapid-fire SLR cameras and camcorders, reclining in safari vehicles to watch the wildest show on earth unfold. This activity safely takes us close to the edge, where we view the sometimes-savage struggle for daily existence safe in the knowledge that we are removed from danger, and will be back in the hotel bar a few hours later.

We place our trust in the people who run safari and wildlife adventures. Most of the time they get it right and we return home with nothing more than glorious memories. However, every year some of them get it wrong, although these are less widely publicised. And it can go tragically wrong. In August 1999 a 19-year-old Briton was killed by a pride of lions while visiting Zimbabwe. A lion had poked its head into the doorway of his open tent, and terrified, he rushed outside and was set upon by up to 12 lions. Many other attacks by lions, elephants, hippos and other big animals have been reported. It's vital to educate yourself about the habits of the animals you will be encountering; for a start, see Chapter 14, page 319. But it's equally important to listen to your local guides. In wild places, you need to follow the advice of those in the know.

It's not just big game that present a threat in Africa. It is an unfortunate fact that many safari locations suffer from perennial conflict. The situation will often be unstable, oscillating between safe and not safe. Currently there are many areas where you should at least show caution when visiting. Angola and the countries on its border are rich with African wildlife, but are also in a constant state of conflict. One of Namibia's richest wildlife areas in the Kavango region is thought to be a danger spot because of Angola's ongoing war. Zambia, Burundi, the Democratic Republic of Congo, Rwanda and countries which border these notorious trouble spots are similarly affected. Kenya – a haven of tranquillity once – now suffers from interethnic and intertribal violence. Before you depart you need to do a threat assessment (see Chapter 1, page 9).

If you're thinking of going on safari, focus on the following points.

- Ask your tour operator about the safety record of the company responsible for your safari. Speak to people who have been on safari with them; your tour operator should be able to supply you with names. Ensure that you use only a reputable company with a good track record, and do not be tempted by those touting for business on the street. They will have no backup or insurance.

- In many countries, safaris are organised through state-run agencies. If something were to happen during your trip and you needed to make a claim against the company, you would in effect be making a claim against that country. The country's legal system may be slow and inefficient – that is, if they even have one. One traveller tried to sue a hotel chain after being thrown from an angry camel, which resulted in serious injuries and a hefty medical bill. A better plan is to have enough private insurance cover before you depart. You must tell your insurance agent that you're going on safari when you buy the cover.

- Safari operators will have strict rules which you will be expected to follow for your own safety. Most wild animals must be treated with respect. They are not domesticated pets, and will see you only as another food source. Lions, elephants and hippos are extremely dangerous and unpredictable, and should be treated as such. Keep a healthy distance away from them and stay within your vehicle. On a recent trip to Kenya I went on a small safari on the outskirts of Nairobi. Halfway round, our vehicle became bogged down in the mud. We quickly got out and pushed it clear of the obstacle, but it was a risk. Our vehicle did not have communications and we would have been there for some time. Ensure that your safari operator can summon help if something like this happens.

- Even if it's only for a week or two, camping out among wild animals is very exciting, and you will probably have the time of your life. But it's imperative that you follow all instructions from the tour operators religiously. You need to close your tent doors at night and remain inside until the next morning. Most operators have an alarm system and issue whistles to blow in an emergency.

- Most campsites will have instructions for dealing with waste. On an African safari, when dangerous and hungry animals may surround you, you must follow these instructions to the letter. Do not leave food in you tent – you will attract animals. Do not leave unwanted food outside of your tent, either, and do not throw unwanted food away. Unless you're in a safe compound you should avoid visiting the toilet at night, so go before you retire. Some operators will provide you with the necessary equipment.

- Never wander off on your own. One time I was in northern Kenya near Lake Turkana, a wild, crocodile-infested place. I decided one day to go for a run and headed inland away from the lake. I had only gone a short way when I suddenly noticed something move off in the distance. I suddenly realised how vulnerable I was and sprinted back the mile or so I had come. The whole time I was gripped by fear at the thought of a pride of lions following behind. Only go off in a group, and inform people where you are going, which route you will be taking and when you expect to return. If things go wrong at least they will have a starting point for where to look.

- Most tourists really have no idea of how to act when confronted by wild animals. Leave it to those who know. If you are told by a safari guide to do something, it is generally a good idea to follow this advice. However, ensure that you are happy with your guide before you set off. Try to strike up a relationship with them and ensure that you are confident with them. You can find reliable guides by asking other travellers when you arrive at your destination, then tracking them down. If a guide thinks that he is making a good name among tourists, he will work very hard to ensure you have a safe and enjoyable trip. Always give him a tip at the end of your tour if you are happy with his service. But learn to trust your instincts, too. If a guide invites you to stroke or touch any animal, don't do it. Many wild or even semiwild animals can carry diseases that are harmful to humans.

- Most local guides are very honest, trustworthy and loyal assistants. They also receive very low pay. If you leave valuables or attractive items lying around you may lose them. Secure everything and leave what you don't want to carry in the hotel safe. Get a receipt from the person on duty and ensure that they sign for your valuables.

- When you are watching wildlife it is often easy to forget what is going on around the area. You must maintain a high level of alertness at all times. There may be other animals in the area that will take advantage of the fact that your attention is focused in one direction for a long time.

- Avoid swimming in rivers and streams in areas where there may be wildlife. This is extremely dangerous. As I've mentioned, Lake Turkana in Kenya is brimming with hundreds of crocodiles just waiting for the chance. Hippos can be a huge danger, too. If you intend to cool off in the local river, ask the tour operator if it is safe. Many dangers will not be obvious. Apart from animals there might be soft sand, or branches from trees that have been swept downriver. These can lie a metre or so under the surface of the river and can be deadly if you become snagged by them. Avoid swimming in stagnant pools of water. Normally these will be animal watering holes packed with harmful bacteria.

- Wear long sleeves and long trousers to reduce your exposure to insects, which carry many of the diseases common in Africa. If you are staying outdoors it might be wise to take along your own mosquito net that has been impregnated with permethrin. Even if you trust the tour operator, you may find that the net they issue to you has a small hole; it is safer to take your own. Ensure that you have decent boots for walking – and remember that many poisonous snakes loiter in the African bush.

▪ Check on the weather conditions in the country you're visiting. The rainy season, which varies from country to country, and around two months after the rainy season, are the peak time for malaria and other diseases like cholera.

▪ Ensure that you are medically prepared for the safari. Ask your doctor what malaria prophylaxis is required for that area. There are treatments that are ineffective in some regions, as the malarial strain has built up a resistance to the regular treatments. In addition, check that you are up to date with regards to your inoculations. If you expect to come into close contact with wild animals, you may consider a rabies inoculation. Many tourists have contracted harmful diseases by drinking unclean water, or swimming in contaminated pools and swallowing water. Ensure that you only drink bottled water and swim in designated areas. Check the seal of your bottled water; travellers have become ill after drinking what they believed to be bottled water, which in fact had been filled from the local tap or stream.

▪ One of the main killers in Africa is AIDS. You should think twice about intimate contact with people you meet. If you strike up a relationship, ensure that you take preventative measures. Condoms bought in sub-Saharan Africa are unlikely to be as reliable as those available in Western countries. Be prepared.

▪ Road accidents are one of the major risks in Africa, and many tourists have been killed or injured while driving there. It may be safer to hire a driver, and control the speed at which he travels. Remember when you hire the driver to inform him that if he does what he is told you will reward him after the job is finished. He will be only too eager to comply.

▪ Many diseases in Africa are transmitted through bad hygiene during food preparation. Most local people will have built up a certain resistance to minor local diseases, but tourists can suffer debilitating effects. You should only eat thoroughly cooked food. If the meal is too hot to taste at first, it has been cooked sufficiently. When you order fruits and vegetables, ask that the skin be left on. When they arrive you can peel the skin yourself. Avoid street food, and be scrupulous about keeping flies and other insects off your food.

Travelling By Animal

When we travel abroad we often fling caution to the wind and engage in activities we are totally unprepared for, and which we're not remotely qualified to engage in. Travelling on the back of an animal is one such activity. Hotels in many tourist locations offer horse riding, or camel and elephant safaris. There is no training given and no experience required; in many cases, you pay your money and are then free to take the animals where you want to. In some regions, too, the welfare of the animals is a secondary consideration.

Horses

Horse riding may seem a safe option, but only if you're experienced. The romantic experience of riding a horse along a beach may make travellers overlook the fact that the animals can weigh well over half a tonne, and travel at up to 50 kilometres an hour. When they rear up most horses will stand over 3 metres high and any fall from them may lead to severe injuries or death. Horse riding, in fact, carries an even greater risk of injury than motorcycling.

- Use only organisations recommended by your hotel. If it's run by the hotel, chances are the staff are trained in managing their animals. They will know the temperament of the animals and in some cases will nominate a specific horse to someone they think can handle it. Check with your travel agent to ensure that your hotel has a good track record and ask to speak to others who have been horse riding at your hotel. Before you go, make sure your insurance agent knows you'll be horse riding; this may increase your premium slightly. Be aware that you may not like the way that animals are treated in some countries.

- Ensure that you are supplied with the appropriate equipment; a hard hat will make the difference should you come off the horse.

Most main hotel chains should be able to provide you with this equipment. Check that the saddle and bridle fit properly. If you are unsure ask the hotel staff to check the equipment and if you are unsatisfied with the standard of the equipment, do not get on the horse.

- Parents should avoid letting their children ride a horse alone unless they are experienced riders. Animals in some hotels will be new to riding. If the horse is excitable and frisky, don't choose it for your child.

- For those unused to horse riding, talk in a quiet voice as you approach the horse, both to comfort it and let it know where you are. Never shout or surprise the horse by walking up behind it. The horse may rear up and even kick out.

- When moving around a horse give it a wide berth. Watch where the animal is placing his feet in case he treads on yours. It can cause serious injury.

- Never wrap the lead or rope from the horse around your hand or arms. If the horse were to bolt you would be dragged behind it.

- If you are taking the horse out on a road, ensure that you know the local road signs, and wear high-visibility clothing. When travelling in low light or at night you should carry a light easily seen from the front and another visible from the rear.

- When riding on a road with traffic coming from behind, turn the horses slightly to the left or right so they can see the vehicle coming up behind.

- Position your feet in the stirrup in such a way that you can remove them quickly if you should fall off.

- If you want to prepare yourself, take a course in horse riding before you go. In Britain, contact the British Horse Society at the following website: www.bhs.org.uk

Camels

Camel safaris are a popular draw in Egypt, Tunisia, Morocco and other desert countries. Most are well organised and safe. But compared to a horse, camels are a very different proposition. It takes time to master the skills required to ride a camel, and most tourists will have to rely on an assistant to help in controlling the animal. Many of these will be expert camel men, but they may have little skill in dealing with tourists.

Camels themselves are very delicate creatures and require a great deal of care and maintenance. It is generally the responsibility of the camel handler to ensure the provision of food and water, without which the animal will refuse to work. The camel can go for a relatively long period without water, but it requires a substantial amount of food, and you will be almost totally dependent on the camel handler to ensure that this is done. If, for whatever reason, the camel is not fed and watered regularly you'll find the expedition coming to an abrupt halt. It is generally thought to be a good idea for you, who are paying for the animal, to be there when the animal is being fed and watered. The camel handler will get used to your being around and you can check to make sure the animal is being treated well.

If you're taking the plunge and hiring a camel, check out the following.

■ Camels are the desired mode of transport for travelling in sand desert, and are also good on rocky and mountainous terrain. Camels are agile and can run fast. You can tell the condition of the animal by the size and condition of its hump and the fullness of its quarters and firmness of its neck. If the hump is drooping and the animal's neck is gaunt, it may not be that healthy. If you are not happy with its condition tell the handler that you would like to see another. Even a traveller with little or no experience will be able to make a comparison between an animal with a drooping hump and one with a firm one.

■ Camels are enormously strong and can carry huge loads over great distances. However, like any animal they will fail if driven too hard. A healthy camel can carry a load of around 135 kilograms or 300 pounds. That total has to include not just you, but food, water and equipment.

- A camel is normally steered using the feet, so wear appropriate footwear. Frequently, however, the camel handler will decide to lead the animal – except over great distances, when the camels might be joined together by rope. You may be given a stick, and can steer by tapping the animal on the shoulder while using a single bridle by a line either to a nose ring or a head collar.

- When riding a camel you need to get used to the rhythm of its movement. Use the rhythm to maintain your balance. When the animal sits down it will bend its front legs dipping its body forward quickly. Anticipate this and counter it by moving your centre of gravity backwards. If you don't you could be catapulted forward. I saw a tourist in Egypt almost thrown down a well when his camel decided to sit down in front of it.

- When camels are tired and hungry, or when they are in the rutting season, they can become aggressive. They have been known to bite travellers and these wounds are particularly nasty. If not treated immediately they can become infected. Stay away from the animal's mouth and if it is making a lot of noise, get the camel handler to deal with it. He should know how to calm the creature down.

- Fleas and other biting insects live on camels and could infest you. Before you start the ride you may consider treating your clothing and equipment with an insecticide.

Elephant Riding

Travelling by elephant will be a new and exiting experience for many travellers. Elephants must be treated with respect, however. They are large and very heavy, and an angry bull elephant will destroy almost anything put in its path, including the unfortunate tourist. Many people are shocked to see how these beautiful creatures are treated. In Thailand, for instance, mahouts are armed with a large, thick piece of wood in which there is a very nasty spike. The spike is used to inflict pain to get the elephant to do what the mahout wants.

If you've opted for an elephant safari, consider the following points.

■ Ensure that you follow the instructions of the mahout and the elephant trainers. Do not walk around on your own near these animals. If a bull elephant is in rut, it can be very aggressive.

■ Unless you know what you are doing, do not get on the elephant on your own. It may be acceptable to travel alone if the mahout is guiding the creature.

■ Ensure that you maintain your balance while on the elephant's back. It can take some time to feel comfortable with this. Use the rhythm to get your balance. Elephant rides can be quite bumpy and you may decide to hold on to the safety rope generally provided, or, in northern Thailand, the side of the riding carriage. Some elephants can be 5 metres high or more, so it is vital to hang on.

■ Avoid making any sudden moves or loud noises when moving around elephants. They are easily spooked and can react aggressively. You should move slowly and deliberately and keep noise down to normal conversational level.

■ Most elephant safaris will have embarkation and disembarkation points. These are normally built up to a height that will let you walk on or off the animal's back. Follow the instructions of the mahout during embarkation and disembarkation. Do not try to get off anywhere else – the animal has been trained to stop at the recognised points.

■ If you are travelling with children, ensure that they do not go too close. Don't feed the animals unless instructed to do so by the mahout. Elephants have attacked and killed people in the past. Treat them with the respect they deserve.

■ Be aware of the route. Many tour operators take tourists on a safari through the forest. Branches from trees and the nests of wasps and biting ants are just some of the hazards you need to look out for.

11

Natural Hazards

MOST OF US ARE CONFIDENT WE can deal with dangers at home – busy roads, muggings and the like. But unless we live in places where flooding or severe gales are the norm, many of us are unprepared for natural disasters – and doubly so when we are caught up in one abroad.

Many beautiful and exotic tourist destinations are also prone to natural catastrophes. One of Europe's most popular tourist destinations, Turkey, suffered from a devastating earthquake in August 1999 that killed 18,000 and injured more than 40,000. In Gujarat, India, the massive earthquake of January 2001 killed nearly 20,000 and injured a further 166,000.

In the West we are just becoming accustomed to dealing with unpredictable weather conditions, but in other countries, geographic location or relative poverty have made the consequences of disaster tragic. Global warming is being blamed for much of the recent flooding which has caused chaos and devastation. In 2000 Mozambique saw hundreds of thousands of people displaced and many hundreds perish as unexpected rainfall swamped entire provinces. Unpredictable weather conditions are definitely becoming more frequent.

And it's not just the weather. In August 1991 Mount Pinatubo, an inactive volcano in the Philippines, erupted and laid waste to large areas of that country, leaving 200,000 people displaced. A tsunami or large tidal wave devastated the southern coast of Papua New Guinea in 1998, killing an estimated 5000 people.

Many of these incidents occur without warning. But if you're aware of weather and other conditions in the country you're visiting, and if you know what to do in different natural catastrophes, you will be ahead of the game.

Earthquakes

One of the most frightening and potentially catastrophic of natural phenomena is the earthquake. Earthquakes can be mild and result in nothing more than a mild shudder – or they can be extremely violent and lay waste to entire regions. Although places like California and Italy are earthquake-prone, many people in the West are unaccustomed to them, and need to know what to do if one hits.

To be prepared for a quake, check out the following points.

■ Research the country you are travelling to and identify if it is susceptible to earthquakes. Earthquake zones are known and in areas where there is a danger the local authorities will have devised a contingency plan for dealing with them. In some regions the threat is taken so seriously that countries such as Japan and the US conduct regular earthquake response training exercises. However, most countries in earthquake areas are relatively poor, and do not have the resources for dealing with major disasters.

■ During an earthquake, the main hazard is not from the actual movement of the earth, but from its effect on the environment. Collapsing buildings and other falling objects are responsible for the vast majority of deaths. The displacement of earth or landslides are also dangerous and, if the quake happens under the sea floor, it can trigger the tidal wave known as the tsunami (see page 244).

- Earthquakes are unpredictable. We know roughly where they are going to happen, we just don't know when. Ideally, when you visit an area prone to earthquakes, stay out of tower block hotels. It is safer to be in a single-storey building. If possible, try to avoid built-up areas; it is safer to locate yourself on the periphery of towns and cities. If an earthquake occurs, you should move out of the building and into an open area. Ensure that the furniture is either attached to the walls or placed so that if it does fall it will not cause you injury or impede your exit from the building. All heavy objects should be kept either on the floor or stored near the ground.

- Familiarise yourself and your family with the escape procedures and routes in case you have to evacuate the building. It is essential to identify an emergency assembly area away from other buildings, especially tower blocks, fuel storage depots, garages and power stations. Walk the route to ensure that you are able to find your way around when it is dark.

- Make sure everyone knows the route to the nearest medical facility. However, you should be aware that in the event of a major earthquake the facility itself might be damaged. It is helpful if you have a medical pack in your room with enough supplies to treat all minor injuries. Ensure that you know how to use the pack. For serious injuries, you will most likely have to go to a medical facility. In this case you should go prepared for a long wait, as there may be large numbers of people seeking assistance.

- Read up on the procedures for switching off the power and gas and water supplies and make sure you know how to do it. Downed live power lines and fractured gas pipes are extremely hazardous. Ensure you have a battery-operated torch nearby for emergencies at night.

- Immediately after an earthquake has struck, there may be mass disruption of the transportation and communications systems. After serious quakes, food has become scarce as the authorities cannot get access to certain regions and normal distribution lines are disrupted. There is an increased health risk as water supplies can become contaminated, so stock up on bottled water and water purification pills. In a high-risk area it's also a good idea to stock-pile some tinned, bottled and bagged food to tide you over.

- If an earthquake strikes when you are indoors, the signs may be anything from a mild tremor felt throughout the building to more severe shaking which will cause plaster and masonry to break off and fall. Furniture and other household articles may also be displaced.

- Ensure that everyone with you is familiar with your plan to evacuate the building and knows what the signs of a quake are. If people are made aware of the signs they may be able to retain their composure during one. Avoid panic – it is contagious and it spreads like wildfire. Try to stick to your plan of evacuation. The body's natural response will be to run and escape from the danger. But if you run around blindly, you may actually run into trouble. All your movements must be calculated to ensure that you stay clear of the very many dangers.

- If you decide that you have to leave the building, dress in long sleeves and long trousers if you have the time. This will help prevent injuries from sharp debris and reduce the exposure to flame. Wear hard-soled shoes to prevent injuries from rubble and glass.

- If you feel that it is not possible to leave the building, try to protect yourself by moving away from windows, mirrors and large articles made of glass. Shattering glass can cause severe injuries. Try to get beneath some hard cover such as a sturdy table, desk or even a bed. Many buildings have reinforced doorways. Check out where the strongest parts of the house are located and use them for shelter during an earthquake.

- As soon as it is safe to do so, you should attempt to evacuate the building. Depending on the severity of the incident and the type of building you are staying in, you may consider waiting until the shaking stops before leaving. In countries such as Japan, the construction industry is monitored to ensure that modern buildings conform to strict building regulations. If you are content that the building has been built to withstand earthquakes you may decide to remain inside. If you are in a country with no such regulations, or a very old building, you may decide to try and get out.

- If you are staying in a tower block in a high-risk area, go to the nearest emergency exit if you feel an earthquake hit. Do not get into the lifts as they may fail to function in the event of a power failure. Once at the emergency exit move as swiftly as you can down to the exit and out of the building. Move away from tall buildings as quickly as possible.

- If you are in an open area and an earthquake strikes, do not run into a building to seek shelter. Stay in the open and keep clear of tall buildings, electricity pylons, street lighting, trees and any other tall object, which may fall and cause you injury.

- When in your car and you feel the earth vibrating, stop in an open area. Do not drive into tunnels or over bridges. Stay in place until the danger has passed. Do not then drive into a built-up area – it will be difficult to get through. After the danger has passed, leave your vehicle in a safe place and walk.

- After the earthquake is over, it is essential that all the injured are dealt with immediately. They shouldn't be moved until the immediate danger has passed. However, if someone is so seriously injured they cannot be moved, you should send someone to get medical assistance.

- Before going back into a building you must ensure that it is not so seriously structurally damaged that it may collapse later. If you smell gas, get away from the building immediately. If you see fire, smoke or sparks indicating electrical short circuiting or live, downed power pylons, do not go into the building. Get away to an open area.

- Communications may be difficult especially if the infrastructure has been damaged. You may have to rely on word of mouth, which is susceptible to rumour at such times. It is likely that power generation will be disrupted or switched off in order to prevent fire. In this case it is unlikely that television or mains-run radio will be available. A small battery-operated shortwave band radio is a boon in these circumstances, as you can keep up with events.

- Avoid re-entering damaged areas and particularly damaged buildings, as there is a strong possibility of aftershocks, some of which may be almost as strong as the actual earthquake. This will affect the stability of buildings damaged by the original quake.

Volcanoes

Volcanoes are, of course, simply sitting there, so we at least know where the source of this danger lies. But volcanoes also hide many other dangers. Visiting volcanoes has become a popular tourist activity – getting close to one of nature's most destructive phenomena enthralls many people. Although it's a predominantly safe activity, tourists have been killed and injured during excursions to volcanoes. On Mount Etna in 1979, nine tourists on a trek were killed, and in Japan in September 1997, four tourists were killed after inhaling noxious volcanic gas.

Volcanic eruptions can be ferocious. Hot rocks and ash can be thrown over huge distances. If you intend visiting an area of volcanic activity, you should be aware of the threat and consider the following points.

- Before you go, find out the date of the most recent eruption. This will give you an indication of the state of the volcano, and how well prepared the emergency services of that country were. If you are living near or are climbing up a volcano, develop a contingency plan so you can get out safely if it erupts.

- If you are trekking in a volcanic area, ensure that you have an emergency communications plan. Inform friends or local authorities where you intend to go, and they will update you on the local conditions. Inform them when you intend to leave and to return. Then, stick to your route; if you deviate from it the emergency services will have difficulty in locating you.

- If you are trekking on an active volcano, go prepared. Wear long trousers and long-sleeved shirts. Old volcanic lava flows can produce rough terrain and the rocks can be very sharp. Wear sturdy footwear. During a volcanic eruption, hot ash can be spewed out of the crater and blown by the wind at high speed. Bring a pair of swimming goggles and put them on if this happens. If the volcano emits noxious gases you may require a disposable mask to filter out any harmful particles.

■ Plan an escape route. If you are confronted by a serious volcanic eruption, lava and hot ash may form streams and begin to flow downhill. If you are on the volcano when this happens you must be aware that lava flows can move relatively fast. If you are in danger move to higher ground above the lava flows. Be aware of the danger of becoming cut off on a knoll by several flows. If this looks likely, move swiftly on the route or your alternative route off the volcano. Inform your contacts to let them know that you are safe.

■ If there is already volcanic activity you should avoid going into the area. During a volcanic eruption there may be a shockwave effect from the eruption, which can travel long distances. Do not be tempted to get into a better position to observe the eruption; by doing so you will increase your exposure to the effects of the blast and debris.

■ If you are downwind when a volcano erupts you may be exposed to the hot ash and any noxious fumes which are given off. You should move your position to a location where you are least affected by the wind.

■ If you are in the immediate vicinity of the volcano when an eruption occurs, avoid seeking shelter in any low-lying area or in basements. Gases and fumes may settle in these areas. In addition if there is any water or lava, the low-lying areas could very quickly become raging torrents.

■ In many national parks where there is volcanic activity, fissures in the ground can emit poisonous gases, even when there is no obvious sign of volcanic activity. Stay away from these areas if there is a history of such incidents there. If you do go, ensure that you are provided with a guide. You may also consider buying a disposable gas mask.

■ If you are outdoors when an eruption occurs, cover your mouth to reduce the chances of inhaling ash and gas particles. If you or a fellow traveller already suffer from a respiratory condition such as asthma, monitor reactions to the effects of the eruptions and move out of the area as soon as possible to seek shelter. Ensure the shelter is strong enough to withstand the weight of the heavy volcanic ash, which can accumulate very quickly on the roof. If you are on an exposed area and there is no shelter, lie on the ground and protect your head with your clothing or equipment. Stay in this position if it is safe to do so until the eruption has sufficiently abated and you are able to escape.

- One of the phenomena frequently associated with a volcanic eruption is mudflows. These are torrential rivers of mud, so powerful they will destroy almost anything in their paths. They are caused when heavy rain mixes with heavy ash fall to produce fast-flowing mud rivers. They can originate in crater lakes, which during an eruption can be breeched and so release a mudflow. To anyone stuck on the flank of a volcanic mountain, they are very dangerous. Stay clear of any low-lying areas or places where mud and water would be channelled after an eruption.

- Immediately after a volcanic eruption you must be alert to any dangers. Before crossing a river or stream you must check upstream. You should look for a build-up of water or mud. If you are approaching a bridge below a volcano and you suspect a mudflow, do not get on the bridge. If you are already on the bridge, get off as quickly as possible. Do not hang around for a better look; try immediately to find high ground.

- If you are indoors when an eruption occurs, move to an area of the house where there are no windows. Breaking glass can cause serious injuries. As soon as it is safe to go outside, check the condition of the building. If there is an excessive amount of volcanic ash there is a risk that the weight of accumulated ash may cause the building to collapse. After the eruption ensure that all undamaged windows and doors are closed. Ensure that any air conditioning systems, which have an air intake on the outside, are switched off.

- Broken utility supply lines, fractured water mains, gas pipelines and fallen electricity cables may create hazardous conditions. The hot volcanic ash can cause fires, so the immediate aftermath of the eruption can be as hazardous as the actual eruption. If it is safe to do so, stay in the building until the emergency services arrive. Due to possible interruption to the lines of communication, this may be some time. It is essential that you have sufficient food and water supplies to last at least two or three days.

- After such a calamitous event there is a possibility of a breakdown in law and order. Reports of looting and theft are not uncommon after major natural disasters. Try to protect your valuables by keeping them out of sight and under lock and key if possible. Ensure that you liaise with emergency services and follow their instructions.

- If you are driving when a volcano erupts, pull over at the first safe opportunity and switch off your engine. The ash and debris can clog up your vehicle's systems and result in your becoming stranded. Visibility may also be reduced by the falling ash, and road conditions will become hazardous.

Tsunamis

Tsunami is the Japanese word for harbour wave. These catastrophic events are generally caused by earthquakes on the ocean floor. Submarine quakes can generate vast waves of water which can travel at over 900 kilometres an hour and be over 15 metres high. Common in many regions, these truly awesome natural phenomena can be devastating. In 1992, a strong underwater earthquake triggered a massive tsunami along the coast of Nicaragua, which killed 170 people. And in 1997, a huge tsunami caused by an undersea earthquake devastated areas of the coast of Papua New Guinea directly north of Australia, killing an estimated 4000 people.

Most tsunamis strike with very little warning, so they can cause a large loss of life in coastal regions. However, seismic activity is monitored closely in some regions, and can give early warning of a coming tsunami. This depends, though, on where the quake occurs. If it happens near the shoreline, the wave might develop so suddenly people cannot flee. But if the quake happens a bit further out, people might actually see the wall of water out to sea and have enough time to escape the danger. It has been estimated that two minutes of warning are enough to allow many people to reach an area of safety, which can be just a few hundred metres inland. In Japan in 1993, a powerful tsunami killed 200 people, but over 1200 escaped by heading inland after they had read the warning signs.

If you are visiting an area susceptible to tsunami, consider the following points.

■ Tsunamis can be unpredictable and can occur at any time. Make sure you have a contingency plan of what you must do in the event of receiving a tsunami warning. Identify where the nearest safe place is and ensure that you are familiar with the route both during the day and night. Ensure that those travelling with you are also familiar with your emergency plan.

■ When you travel to an area prone to tsunamis, stay on high ground or on the upper levels of a tower block away from the coastline. Houses and hotels that are situated on or near the coast in low-lying areas will be more badly affected by the tsunami. If you are in a low-lying coastal area and you hear of a tsunami warning, head inland and climb to high ground. If you are based in a built-up area, go to a high building and climb to its upper levels. Most modern hotels belonging to Western hotel chains have been built with reinforced concrete, and will be strong enough to withstand a tsunami and provide adequate shelter. If you do not have enough time to escape to high ground, head for the nearest tower block hotel.

■ In many regions that have had tsunamis in the past, there will be contingency plans to ensure that the emergency services are able to deal with the aftermath of these potentially catastrophic events. You should make yourself familiar with the local emergency planning, but you must be aware that many developing countries will have little or no resources for dealing with emergency situations. It can be expected that in the worst scenarios the emergency services will take some days to access the area. Ensure that you have enough medical supplies to treat minor ailments, as the medical facilities may be inundated with casualties or be submerged in water.

■ Monitor both radio and television transmissions for information about the situation. However, after a tsunami has struck, electricity supplies along the coastal regions will have been disrupted. Emergency information such as evacuation procedures and emergency relief distribution will be broadcast by the authorities on radio. Small battery-operated shortwave radios will be essential for receiving this information.

■ After a tsunami has struck, the normal lines of communications and distribution may have been disrupted. In this case food will be in short supply, and water supplies will become contaminated. As part of your contingency plan have a safe food supply of tinned and bottled food, and water sterilisation pills. Ensure that you have enough supplies to last at least four days, by which time the authorities can be expected to supply you with what you need.

■ If you are in a low-lying coastal area and you feel the effects of an earthquake, quickly move to an area of high ground. Tsunamis have reached as high as 15 metres or as high as a four-storey building, so moving to 17 or so metres up should be your minimum.

■ Tsunamis that strike long flat coastal regions can be relatively ineffectual, as the waves dissipate over such a wide area. But if you are located in a narrow river valley leading out to sea, the effects can be devastating. The waves are then driven up the narrow valleys where the sheer volume of water is so great that it deluges the entire valley.

■ Tsunamis are often accompanied by a loud rolling noise, which has been likened to the sound of a low-flying aircraft. The tsunami can move fast, however, and the noise from the wave will provide only a few minutes' warning. If you hear it, try to evacuate to a high point.

■ As tsunamis approach a shore, harbours and shorelines can suddenly empty of water that is being drawn into the massive wave.

This is a classic sign of an oncoming tsunami. Immediately move away from the shore and try to gain height.

- If a tsunami is about to strike somewhere else, heed this warning. It may be negligible in one region, but only a few miles away it could be devastating. Do not be tempted to seek a position near the shore from which to observe the tsunami. Immediately move to high ground. If you wait until you can actually see the wave you may be too late. Tsunamis can travel at speeds faster than you can run, so as soon as you are made aware of the risk you must move quickly.

- When a tsunami strikes, the initial wave can be devastating, but a tsunami can have more than just one wave. Repeated waves have struck coastal regions during a tsunami. You must stay away from the region until you are certain that the danger has passed.

- If you are at sea when a tsunami strikes you should move away from the coast and head for deep water. However if the tsunami is accompanied by bad weather and you have enough time, it may be wiser to go to the shore and quickly try to get to high ground.

- After the tsunami has passed, sea conditions near the shore may become unpredictable and erratic. If you are at sea and intend to return to shore, after the wave has passed you must wait until the after-effects have finished.

Flash Floods

If there is heavy and prolonged rainfall in one place, from, say, a slow-moving thunderstorm, hurricane or tropical storm, flash floods can result. They happen when the ground can't absorb any more water because it is already saturated, or baked hard by the sun. The sudden accumulation of water will flow swiftly downhill. Depending on the topography, flash flooding can occur quickly after rainfall or up to six hours later.

The floods can happen in built-up areas, such as flat land where housing impedes the absorption of rainfall, or round drainage systems that become overwhelmed by large volumes of rainwater. In recent years, flash floods have claimed the lives of many people in the Philippines, Indonesia and Italy.

The sheer power of a flash flood can devastate entire areas, destroying roads, bridges and precipitating landslides as walls of water, mud and debris rage down narrow valleys and gorges. Water levels can rise by up to tens of metres in seconds, turning serene, picturesque streams and brooks into raging torrents. At a depth of just half a foot or about 15 centimetres, fast-flowing water can exert enough force to knock you over. If it's a bit more than half a metre deep, it can sweep your car away. And in remote and mountainous terrain, these floods can strike with little or no warning.

If you suspect an area you're visiting is prone to flash flooding, or if it's a low-lying area near rivers, streams, gullies and drainage ditches, consider the following points.

- Make sure you're staying in a place on elevated ground, out of the flash flood danger area. Get to know flood risks in your area. It's useful to know where the nearest tower block is, and the routes to get there. Ensure that you and all those with you are familiar with these in case a flash flood hits at night. Remember that areas can become raging torrents within a few minutes, so ensure you always have an escape route.

- After a serious flash flood, during which the water floods low-lying areas, drainage systems become deluged and raw sewage is disgorged onto the streets. This can create major health problems, as the contaminated water can flood shops and ruin food supplies. Stockpile some tinned food and bottled water, and ensure you have water purification tablets to hand. Or you can sterilise your water by boiling for 10 minutes. When the flood waters begin to rise, make sure to turn off the water supply to your accommodation.

- If you are camping, do not choose an area close to rivers or streams, particularly if you are anywhere near a mountain range. In my experience, flash flooding in jungle-covered mountainous areas can rise so fast it is frightening.

- If you are travelling through an area prone to flash flooding, monitor the condition of rivers and streams. If the water begins to rise, this may be the first indication that flash flood conditions may be forming upstream.

- If you are caught out in an exposed area and you see a flash flood heading downstream towards you, you must not try to outrun the flood – the water will be travelling faster than you can run. You should try to evade it by climbing immediately to high ground or at least to a high, solid object.

- Never attempt to swim or wade through even shallow water if it is flowing fast. During a flood, the current on the surface of the stream or river may appear manageable for anyone attempting to swim. However, you will not see any undercurrent, which may be much faster and stronger than you would be able to swim against. There may also be debris from destroyed buildings and felled timber under the surface.

- During periods of bad weather and heavy rain, pay attention to the bulletins from local television and radio stations. If you receive a flash flood warning, this will mean that the flood is imminent or the conditions exist for one to happen. You should take action immediately and head to high ground or even the upper levels of a tower block. It is important that you make a quick decision, as otherwise your escape routes may be cut off.

- Tell your children to avoid playing around riverbanks or the banks of any water feature during periods of heavy rain.

- Do not dive in to rescue people who have fallen into a flooded river. You're in real danger of becoming a casualty yourself. Instead, stay on the banks and try to reach them and drag them to safety. If this fails, throw something to them and drag them out.

- If you are travelling by vehicle, never cross a flooded river or stream even if it looks shallow. In these conditions, water can sometimes turn roads into fast-flowing streams. Much of the road will be concealed and it will be impossible to determine the actual condition of the surface. Remember, fast-flowing water under a metre deep can sweep away your car.

- If you are approaching a bridge and the river it crosses is in flood, turn around and go back. You could look for another route upstream, but don't attempt to cross or hang around the edge. The water can rise quickly and swamp the ground around the stream. Leave and seek higher ground.

- If your vehicle stalls, or the water is rising so rapidly you can't drive out, leave the car immediately and go by foot to higher ground.

- In areas susceptible to flooding you should avoid driving at night and after periods of heavy rain. You should also park your vehicle out of reach of any predictable high water marks on a road which will not be affected by the flood. In this way at least you will have an escape route if you have to evacuate.

- There is a strong possibility that the electricity supply in your accommodation will short out when it is exposed to water. You should turn it off before you leave, and be aware of downed power cables, which may still be live.

- If a flash flood happens, you'll need three days' worth of supplies to tide you over until the authorities are able to sort the situation out. Buy enough tinned food, bottled water and purification tablets to last, as well as a basic medical pack for minor ailments. Be aware that clinics and hospitals will in all probability be inundated by the injured, and that you as a foreigner may not get attention as quickly as you would like.

- When you return to your accommodation after the flood has subsided, you must not switch on your electricity or gas supply. The electric mains may have shorted and the gas pipes fractured. Also avoid handling electrical equipment if it has been left in your house during the flood. You should not use a naked flame such as a candle when moving around your house.

Avalanches

The beauty of remote, snowclad mountain expanses is an alluring prospect, both for those who enjoy testing climatic conditions and rough terrain, and those who are simply drawn to wild landscapes. Magnificent though these mountain wildernesses are, avalanches are a part of the package, and each year they wreak havoc in remote areas and popular tourist attractions.

Many mountainous resort areas have invested in avalanche forecasting measures – specially trained staff who constantly monitor snow and weather conditions, and sensors warning of changing snow conditions. Measures such as snow cannons, which fire small projectiles, or small explosive charges, are used to deliberately start an avalanche before conditions reach a dangerous state, and thereby reduce the frequency of major avalanches. However, it is difficult to predict the exact state of the snow conditions over the entire area. Another preventive measure is to put barriers up to deflect the flow of snow away from popular areas. Yet avalanches continue to kill. In 2000, around a hundred tourists in Austria and France were killed in a series of devastating avalanches.

Avalanches are massive falls of suffocating snow rolling unstoppably down mountain sides. They can lay waste to huge areas, and anyone caught in their path has little chance of surviving. They form when fresh snow accumulates on previous snowfalls. The different strata of snow have different densities and strengths. When old snow below the surface is weak, it often cannot support the new snow on the surface and as a result it can sheer off, causing an avalanche. As it gathers momentum, entire hillsides can be engulfed. Blocks of snow can reach speeds of up to 130 kilometres per hour within seconds – much faster than you can run or even ski.

When you add in the freezing weather and difficult terrain, you can see just how dangerous avalanches are. Your main defence against getting caught up in one is to know how they develop, read the signs around you and avoid them. The majority of avalanches occur on gradients of between 35 and 45 degrees, which just happens to be the ideal gradient for a ski slope too. A great number of avalanches can occur within a day of the snow falling and the main areas of concern are steep open slopes where, if the snow becomes unstable, it can slide down unimpeded. Areas where the wind deposits fresh snow and makes snow deep and unstable are particularly dangerous.

If you're skiing or travelling among mountains in winter, check out the following points.

- The most effective way to avoid avalanches is to avoid the areas where they are likely to form. Pay attention to avalanche warnings, which will be broadcast by local weather centres. Obey warning signs informing you to keep off dangerous areas of snow. Stick to the main tracks and question local employees or people who live in the area; they will be aware of snow conditions and will inform you when the situation is dangerous. Ensure that you obtain the correct phone numbers or radio frequencies of the emergency rescue services.

- Stay clear of mountainous areas after heavy snowfall, particularly if there was already snow on the ground. Be cautious if there has been heavy snowfall combined with high winds – this is the ideal condition for the development of avalanches. If you are already on the mountains when these conditions develop, find the safest route down the hill and head for a safe location. You must not enter steep, narrow re-entrants or descend steep open mountainsides. It is safer to make your way along the top of ridgelines, staying away from the edges where cornices can form, usually on the windward side. If you are within striking distance of a wide, flat valley bottom, make your way there, staying clear of the avalanche path.

- If you have any concerns about the condition of the snow, don't go out trekking or skiing until the snow has settled for at least a day and perhaps two. Stay aware of weather conditions. If it has thawed or rained on previous snowfalls, this will increase the chances of avalanche.

- When you go out on the hills in winter, avoid going out on your own. It is safer to travel in a group or at least with a friend. There will be someone else to keep an eye out for changing snow conditions and if you are caught up in an incident you will have assistance.

- When you are out on a mountainside, listen for sounds that may indicate an avalanche has been triggered. If you hear a low rumbling or a stiff cracking noise, this may indicate that the snow has sheered off and an avalanche has begun. As soon as you hear any such noise, you must look in that direction and assess your position in relation to the avalanche. Move by the quickest route to an area out of the path of the cascading snow.

- Before you go onto a hill, ensure that you have all the necessary equipment: warm dry clothes and sleeping bag, a high-energy food supply, a hot drink (in a thermos) or the means to make a hot drink. A shovel for digging others out would be useful, and an emergency-locating beacon which transmits on a distress frequency is invaluable as it enables rescue teams to locate you if you're buried beneath several feet of snow. It has been suggested that around half of all people caught up in an avalanche fail to survive longer than 30 minutes, so the faster they can find you the better. Wear your beacon in a secure place where it won't get lost.

- If you are unfortunate enough to become caught up in an avalanche, first call out to those with you and let them know what is happening and get rid of any cumbersome equipment such as skis. When the snow hits you in all likelihood you will be engulfed in a wall of snow. You should attempt to stay near the surface of the snow by making swimming motions. This will not get you out of the avalanche, but may help keep you near the surface.

- When you have come to a standstill you may find yourself buried deep in the snow. Hard-packed snow can be suffocating, so you must attempt to create a breathing space in front of your face before the snow becomes so hard that you will not be able to move. Try to get your hand up to your mouth and create a gap which will allow you to breathe.

- To prevent hypothermia if you're in an avalanche, it is essential that you are properly dressed while you are on the mountains. Keep yourself dry and have a windproof and waterproof outer layer.

■ Try to raise your arm up through the snow. If you do still have access to a ski or perhaps a ski pole, try to raise this to the surface of the snow. People will then know where to dig to get you out. Switch your emergency locating beacon on.

■ Keep control of your emotions and fight off the urge to panic by consciously relaxing. If you panic, you will hyperventilate and use up the available oxygen more quickly. Stay as calm as you can.

■ If you observe any of your companions becoming caught up in an avalanche you must identify the last place that you saw them in the snow. Follow the track of the avalanche with your eyes, then search down slope from the last place you had a positive identification after the snow has stopped moving.

■ When you are digging someone out use whatever tools you can get your hands on, a ski or ski pole or any material that you can find – your hands if necessary. If there are any other people on the slope you should attract their attention so that they can assist you. The more people searching, the better. Time is limited and you need to work quickly. If you have access to a radio or a cell-phone you should call the local emergency services. Remember that you must recover the person buried within half an hour at the most.

■ Whenever you prepare to descend a snow-covered mountain either by ski or by foot, you must assess the condition of the snow. Test its solidity and select your route to ensure that the snow is safely stable along it. If you are skiing in a group you should ensure that you arrange a meeting point at a prearranged time, at a safe point at the bottom of the hill. If someone fails to make the meeting point on time, you will then be alerted to the fact that something has gone wrong and you can take the appropriate action.

■ If you see or hear of an avalanche in your area, make your way to a safe location. Tell all the people you see on the mountainside. If avalanche conditions exist in or near your location, there's a probability that the conditions for an avalanche exist where you are. Leave the area by the safest route.

- If you are travelling by vehicle in an area prone to avalanches you must stay aware of the weather and snow conditions. Tune in to the local radio station and monitor the weather reports. Ensure that your vehicle is prepared for driving in winter conditions, with a supply of warm clothing, food and water, a full fuel supply, snow chains and suitable tyres.

- In areas prone to avalanches there will be traffic-warning signs indicating the conditions of the road ahead. You must obey these warning signs and if the roads are closed you should not enter. You must monitor the conditions on either side of the road, especially if you are in a narrow, snow-filled valley. If you are driving in a mountainous area and the weather conditions change – it begins to get warmer or even starts to rain – you must take notice of this as these conditions may precipitate an avalanche. If the conditions are really bad, stop at a safe point until they improve.

- If you are driving in a mountainous area while it is snowy or snowing and are caught up in an avalanche, do not attempt to drive through it. You should stay in your vehicle, as a person on foot is more likely to be swept away than a vehicle. In addition, after the first avalanche wave has passed, there may be others.

- Remain inside your vehicle and put on warm clothes. You may decide to switch on your heater, but you must be aware of the dangers of carbon monoxide poisoning. If you are fairly deeply buried and your vehicle does not have sufficient ventilation there may be a build-up of this noxious gas. If you are running the heater, check to ensure that you have sufficient ventilation. If not, keep it on for around 20 minutes at a time in order to avoid a dangerous build-up of carbon monoxide.

- If you have access to a radio or cellphone, try to inform the emergency rescue services about the condition of the snow and the weather at your location. Tell them how many people you have in your party and most importantly follow their instructions.

Tornadoes

Every year, millions of tourists head off to that tornado hotspot, the US. The tornado season generally lasts from April to the end of July, and in some states it brings fear and trepidation. The largest tornado on record struck in the Midwest in 1925, killing 625 people and injuring thousands more. In April 1991, more than 50 tornadoes were reported across the Midwest, killing 24, injuring over 200 others and causing damage estimated to be more than 250 million dollars. Tornadoes cause devastation in many other countries, too.

Even with the advances made in tornado forecasting and the information available, there are similar tragedies every year. Tornadoes are one of nature's most powerful and unpredictable weather phenomena, and can lay waste to entire areas. They develop when warm air collides with cooler, drier air to form ferocious whirlwinds that travel over land in a very narrow path and are accompanied by dark, sinister, telltale clouds. They can be the most extreme winds on the planet, reaching speeds of over 480 kilometres per hour, and yet a kilometre or so away from the tornado the wind can be relatively light. Tornadoes are often accompanied by heavy bouts of rain or hail.

Tornadoes tend to pass through four stages. Initially the funnel of the tornado develops and touches the ground, then it grows to its full size. The funnel then diminishes in size and eventually breaks up. Even at the final stage it can still be destructive. Many people are killed or injured by these winds because they do not understand the signs of a tornado, nor what to do during one. In most developed countries, weather forecasting authorities issue warnings of severe weather.

Be on the lookout for these, and if you are visiting a tornado-prone area, read these points.

- Tornadoes can strike very suddenly, so you need to know what to do beforehand and develop a contingency plan. Discover when that country's tornado season hits.

- Choose well-built accommodation that will provide protection should a tornado strike. Identify a safe location you can return to quickly. Ideally this will be below ground, in a cellar or an underground basement. It's got to be close to where you are staying, as you will need to get to it very fast indeed. The maximum time you can expect to remain in this emergency shelter will be no more than a few hours.

■ If you are visiting a tornado area during the tornado season, monitor either the local TV or radio stations. If a storm develops with the characteristic signs of a tornado, the local authorities will issue a severe weather warning.

■ Because tornadoes develop so fast, it's not always possible for warnings to be issued. If the authorities issue a *tornado watch*, this means that the conditions exist for the formation of severe thunderstorms, which may precipitate a tornado. You should carry out your emergency contingency plan. It is essential that you listen for further bulletins and follow the advice and instructions issued.

■ If a *tornado warning* is received, this means that a tornado is imminent. You need to be aware of what they look like – the vortex-like funnel, with the narrow point on the earth. The actual track of the tornado, although somewhat predictable in some areas, can veer off in any direction. So if you are in an area where you can actually see the funnel, you must take emergency action as you could be in danger.

■ When a tornado strikes, the biggest threat is from the high wind speed and the projectiles that are being thrown around. In powerful tornadoes, even large objects can be thrown at high speed. It is essential that you are under cover, so you are neither hit by flying objects nor carried away by the wind.

■ If you are caught in the open and you see a tornado, seek shelter in an area below ground level. Look for low-lying ground, drainage ditches, road culverts, small re-entrants or even under small bridges. Get into one of these areas and lie down flat. If you have any equipment with you try to cover your head with it.

■ If there is a tornado warning and you are in accommodation with a basement or cellar, go there immediately. Otherwise, go to the bottom floor of the house and the end of the building furthest away from the tornado. If the tornado is strong enough, the walls may collapse. Walls usually fall inwards and in this case you should seek shelter beneath solid objects or heavy furniture. Improvise with the materials you can lay your hands on to make a shelter.

■ If you have the chance, switch off your power supply. Downed electric cables will be dangerous and may cause fires. Try to switch off your gas supply too, as this will also be a fire hazard.

■ If you are in a vehicle and there is a tornado warning or you can see one, pull over at the nearest opportunity and go to a suitably strong shelter. Do not attempt to outrun a tornado: they move faster than you can drive.

■ If you are in a built-up area or an area where there are large concentrations of people, be aware that people may panic and stampede. Stay calm and move away quickly into a secure building.

■ If you are in a built-up area or a hotel, find out where the emergency shelters are. To ensure that you can find them at night, walk the route during the day.

■ Be aware that when you are walking around outside after the tornado has passed, there may be danger from structurally damaged buildings, downed electricity pylons and fractured gas mains. Use caution when moving around and avoid using naked flames as a source of illumination.

Hurricanes

Hurricanes – known as typhoons in South East Asia – are produced by the actions of the tropical oceans and atmosphere. Heat from the sea generates the hurricane, which is driven by the prevailing winds and its own potent energy. The wind speed at the area immediately surrounding the centre, or eye, of the hurricane can be tremendous, and if you are at sea, conditions can be treacherous. Yet the eye itself can remain almost completely calm.

When a hurricane meets the land, the consequences can be catastrophic. Winds of 120 kilometres an hour or even greater, with gusts of up to 160, can drive in quite far from the coastline and destroy huge built-up areas. Torrential rain, resulting in dangerous flooding, can accompany the wind. Hurricanes can even generate tornadoes. Such tornadoes normally strike some distance away from the eye, but sometimes near it – and this is the major threat to areas well inland. But coastal areas are the most vulnerable. They can be deluged by the massive surges of sea crashing in, and severely flooded, particularly at high tide.

Each year many hurricanes develop over both the Pacific and Atlantic Oceans, but few make it to land. In the Western Pacific and other regions, hurricanes can occur at any time, but off the southern and Central American coast they develop around the middle of May and in the US during mid to late October. Because so many people live on and visit coastal areas, they are a significant threat.

Weather monitoring authorities receive early warning of hurricanes. In most developed countries, evacuating the area is the best way to escape the effects of a hurricane. If the area is heavily developed, however, this will be a far from straightforward process.

So, if you are heading to a hurricane area, you'll want to know the following points.

- Familiarise yourself with the seasonal weather conditions there. When does the hurricane season begin and end? Identify the local risks and learn how the authorities intend to deal with the situation. On the coast and islands offshore or in areas prone to flooding, the dangers will be greater. If you will be staying in a tower block or on high ground, the intense winds can increase the risk. In any case, choose solidly constructed accommodation.

- If you are told to evacuate the area, immediately head inland away from the coastal strip. Identify the quickest routes for doing so. Remember that everyone else will be trying to evacuate at the same time, so look for the least congested way.

- In areas frequently hit by hurricanes the authorities may have established a number of hurricane shelters. Find out where they are and how to get to them. Ensure that if you are travelling in a group, everyone travelling with you is also familiar with these details.

■ Hurricanes can zoom past coasts and travel inland great distances. You must have access to a TV or radio in order to monitor the emergency broadcasts from the authorities and find out whether one is heading your way.

■ If the authorities issue a *hurricane warning* for your area, a hurricane will strike within 24 hours. Get ready to leave immediately, and remember that the earlier you leave, the better the chance you have of avoiding the crowds.

■ Ensure that you take enough supplies to last you for at least three days. Take a battery-operated radio so that you can monitor the emergency services information on the progress of the storm. Ensure that you have enough tinned food and bottled or sterile water to last you. If you sterilise water by boiling it, remember to do so for 10 minutes. Have a basic medical kit to treat all minor ailments for at least three days – pharmacies and medical facilities will also have been evacuated. Keep the fuel tank of your vehicle full. You don't want to have to queue at a petrol station. Pack dry, clean clothing and a supply of batteries for your portable radio and torches.

■ If you decide to stay at home, ensure you have shutters or a similar cover on your windows and doors. Stay away from windows, doors and large objects made of glass, as glass can become a secondary projectile and cause serious injury. Seek shelter in a small room without glass on the first floor – this will provide protection against flooding and also from the wind. Ensure that you close and secure all exterior and interior doors.

■ If you are staying in a tent, caravan or mobile home, pack up and evacuate as soon as you hear a weather warning. Tents will be blown away even with you in them and caravans and mobile homes have too high a profile and are generally not heavy enough or secured tightly enough to be safe. If you are warned in good time, hook up your caravan or drive your mobile home inland.

- Use the material inside your house or hotel room to create a shelter under which you can seek refuge. Heavy tables or other items of furniture will provide protection against objects displaced by the wind.

- Be aware of going outside after the storm has passed. Many people have been caught out by assuming that the storm has blown itself out, only to find that they had entered the eye of the hurricane. After the eye of the storm has passed the wind will quickly return to its ferocious velocity, but it will be blowing from the other direction. Many years ago I was travelling with a group caught up in a tropical typhoon while on a mountainside in Hong Kong. The wind had caused a huge amount of damage and we had to seek shelter in a basement. Midway through the storm the generator that had been supplying our power switched off and we had to send someone out to fix it. We tied a rope around his waist and sent him out into the storm, which abruptly stopped. There was a clear blue sky and relatively no wind. He busied himself with the generator. Then the wind abruptly began howling again and our friend was almost blown off the mountainside: it took three of us to haul him back to safety.

- If you are in your vehicle and you either hear that there is a severe weather warning or you see the signs – unusually high winds, black rolling clouds and torrential rain – you should seek shelter immediately. It is dangerous driving around in these conditions. The velocity of the wind may knock trees over or at least displace branches, which can fall onto the roads. Flooding will also make driving conditions hazardous.

- After the storm has passed, wait until the authorities have declared an area safe before you try to re-enter. Some buildings may be structurally unstable after their battering by the ferocious winds; there may be downed electricity pylons and possibly fractured gas mains. If live electric cable lands in a pool of floodwater, it may turn the water into an electrified pool which can be fatal if touched.

- If roads have been blocked off or you see warning signs indicating that an area is out of bounds, do not enter. If you are living in the area which has been blocked off, contact the authorities before you re-enter it.

- As the hurricane develops and heads for land, the wind speed will increase, and bridges, flyovers and even roads may be closed. It is essential that when you receive the warning to evacuate, you do so quickly.

- If you are in a developing country where they do not have contingency plans in place you will have to have your own. Ensure everyone you're with knows it. If you are travelling with children, gather them together as soon as you receive the severe weather warning. You should have identified a safe location inland, which you can get to easily. This may be a hotel, a friend's home, and any area where you will be able to easily seek shelter from the storm. Remember that in most developing countries the buildings are not built as solidly as those at home. You must seek out a solidly built structure that can withstand ferocious winds.

- Before you evacuate your accommodation you must ensure that you switch off your electricity and gas supply, and that you drain your water tank. Remove any highly flammable material from the house and place it in a secure area outside. When you re-enter the building you must avoid using a naked flame for illumination. If there has been a gas leak you will be in danger of creating an explosion. Use a torch instead. In addition you must be alert to the signs of structural weakening of your house. If you identify any you should leave the house immediately.

- After a hurricane has struck, regular lines of communication will at least have been disrupted. Telegraph lines will have been blown over and possibly cellphone re-broadcast antenna may have been destroyed. Ensure that you have a mobile phone charged up as there may not be an electrical supply for some days. You can at least get to an area where the mobile phones are still working and communicate with your friends, relatives and the emergency services.

12

Terrorism

ON 11 SEPTEMBER 2001, TERRORISTS LAUNCHED the most destructive and well-coordinated terrorist attack yet witnessed, killing nearly 3000 innocent people at the World Trade Center in Manhattan, emotionally traumatising millions and triggering a war against terrorism. This was cutting-edge terrorism planned by ruthless, sophisticated fanatics intent on destroying the very fabric of our social order. The Al Qaida terrorist network have been responsible for other acts of terrorism: the World Trade Center bombing in 1993, bombings of the US embassies in Tanzania and Kenya, and the attack on the *USS Cole*. While all these have targeted the US, any other member of NATO is, in effect, involved. But the military action against the Al Qaida in Afghanistan highlights the difficulties in fighting this new and insidious strain of terrorism. This is an enemy without institutional structures, borders, governments – or, in fact, any scruples about killing innocent people to achieve their aims.

Terrorist groups tend to strike at soft targets – civilians, rather than states themselves. And although the action in Afghanistan is continuing, this risk will continue to be a significant international security problem. Terrorism is fuelled by tensions over nationalism, regionalism, religion, and by ethnic, political, social and economic inequalities, and these are not going to disappear any time soon. The shockwaves have hit many countries prized as holiday destinations. Spain, the Philippines, Indonesia, Mexico, India, Greece, France, Thailand, Kenya, Jordan and Egypt have all been subject to recent terrorist attacks.

In 1997 my family and I were holidaying in the southern Philippines island of Borocay. At the time there was Islamic insurgency in the area, but it had been poorly publicised. One day my daughter came in and asked why there were men on the beach with guns. A heavily armed Philippines military unit was patrolling outside our beach hotel; I later discovered they were protecting the resort from attack by terrorists from the infamous Abu Sayaff. Later, Manila was rocked by a series of bomb attacks.

In 2000 there were around 430 terrorist attacks worldwide – an increase of 8 per cent over the previous year. While the statistics for 2001 aren't in yet, the heightened tension and violence round the globe will inevitably show a dramatic increase in terror activity.

At any given time, national and international travel networks – be they aviation, rail, road or sea – provide the ruthless terrorist with a tempting target. But the capricious nature of terrorism and the choice of targets available mean that predicting when and where they strike is extremely difficult. Terrorist attacks are random and sporadic, making it almost impossible to protect yourself completely. Increasing numbers of terrorist groups are now motivated less by a desire for publicity than by a need to take revenge. Some terrorists, such as the Basque group ETA, have targeted popular holiday destinations in Spain in an attempt to destroy its lucrative tourist industry. Fortunately no tourists have been killed there yet.

Others have been less lucky. As I have mentioned elsewhere, extremist Egyptian terrorists attacked tourists visiting Luxor in 1995. The attack claimed the lives of 58 people in one of the most cold-blooded terrorist incidents of recent times. The Egyptian government lost an estimated $1.5 billion in desperately needed hard currency.

After every terrorist attack, security forces around the world coordinate and boost their security. They look at what went wrong, then invest in and intensify their security efforts to combat the threat. Terrorists anticipate this reaction and move on to select another of the endless list of targets. So at the moment, air travel has never been so safe. It would be very hard for terrorists to carry out a similar act: reinforced armoured doors now protect aircraft cockpits and many airline companies employ highly trained security professionals on flights.

You still need to be vigilant, however. Here are the essential points.

- The best strategy for avoiding terrorist attacks is to avoid areas where terrorists have been known to operate in the past. In your traveller's risk assessment (see Chapter 1, page 9), identify if there have been any recent terror attacks in the countries you are intending to visit. In countries with internal instability try to identify the regions within the country that are exposed to terrorist violence. If the country has had terrorist activity in the past, chances are that there will still be terrorist groups now. The most infamous terrorist organisations have been around in one guise or another for decades. Their initial objectives for taking up arms are lost over time and replaced by the lure of money to be made through perpetuating the conflict. If there has been a history of kidnapping or other terrorist-related activity, you have to ask yourself whether this trip is really essential.

- Ensure you book a nonstop flight to avoid stopping over in a dangerous location. While travelling in a high-risk country ensure that you check whether there have been terrorist attacks on rail or road routes you intend to use. If so, you may decide to reroute, travel by air or at least wait until there is a big enough convoy which you can go with to ensure your safety.

- When travelling in a high-risk area, raise your level of awareness to become familiar with changes in the local situation. Remember that terrorists, like criminals, prey on the weak and the defenceless. The majority are not religious fanatics who want to die for their cause, but cowardly types who want to minimise the danger to themselves. Terrorists will look for easy and accessible targets following predictable patterns of behaviour. If you have very regular habits, you will make it easy for those hostile to you to identify where you will be at any given time. Avoid travelling with large, prearranged tour groups. Small groups of tourists with unannounced schedules will reduce their chances of running into a spontaneous terrorist attack.

- Avoid discussing your travel details with strangers. If you are asked about them, be vague and evasive about giving accurate information. Don't even talk about travel details with your friends in public places; choose somewhere private.

- In high-risk countries, minimise your exposure by spending as little time as possible in airports and bus or rail stations. Terrorists attack travel hubs because they know they can make a big statement that way. Try to get out of them as soon as you arrive, and arrange connecting flights that depart shortly after you land to ensure that you do not need to hang around. Be aware that airport roads are another potential terrorist target. Keep your departure details secure by telling only those you can trust.

- When you arrive at your destination, quickly familiarise yourself with those areas you would consider safe – police stations, military establishments, main hotels where other foreigners are accommodated, or even the houses of friends and colleagues. If you feel threatened, you will at least know where to go. You should also know how to get to the nearest medical facility, what type of facility it is (does it have an accident and emergency service?) and opening hours.

- Spend as little time as possible in areas frequented by tourists or travellers, particularly Europeans or Americans, in times of tension. Terrorists may feel these are worthy targets. Avoid visiting tourist hotspots during anniversaries such as the commemoration of a battle, the arrest or execution of a prominent political or opposition figure, or simply a political announcement.

- In high-risk areas, cut out unnecessary visits to government establishments or foreign-owned multinationals. The recent trend in bomb attacks has indicated that terrorist groups want to do as much damage as possible to the infrastructure and economic base of the countries involved, as well as just create carnage. The bomb attack against the World Trade Center in 1993 contained just short of a tonne of high explosive. If this device had been placed in the right position it would have brought the building down.

- Be aware of vehicles illegally parked outside government buildings, tourist attractions or military establishments. If a vehicle is sitting low on its suspension this would indicate that it is carrying a heavy load in the boot. Many security forces all over the world are instructed to look out for such signs as this may indicate a terrorist bomb.

- In high-risk countries such as Israel or Sri Lanka avoid large public gatherings, bus queues or any other crowded places. Suicide bombers target such areas.

- When you are in a public place, be on the lookout for suspicious articles such as unattended luggage or packages. These have been used in the past to conceal improvised explosive devices and are another of the terrorist's favoured tools.

- In high-risk countries, avoid drawing attention to yourself. Dress, demeanor, language, even what you are carrying all give out signals about who you are. Try to blend in.

- It is safer to travel with someone else. Two heads are better than one when it comes to vigilance about security. The person alone is more vulnerable.

- Ensure that you have arranged a contingency plan for dealing with situations should they go wrong. Nominate who is to be contacted and in what order. Ensure that everyone in your group is familiar with how to behave in the event of a gun attack or a terrorist bomb, both out on the streets and while you are in your accommodation. In the event of a gun attack, for instance,, you should go to ground and never attempt to intervene by picking up a weapon which has been dropped.

- In a high-risk environment, check in at your country's embassy or consulate. If the situation deteriorates badly, the authorities may decide to launch an evacuation with military assistance. Plans will be drawn up for the evacuation of all Western nationals. If you check in with your embassy and keep them informed of your movements, they will be able to reach you.

- Avoid broadcasting your intentions by leaving personal information lying around in your hotel room. Passports, documents, flight tickets, even used – all these may inform people of your intentions. Never throw out any articles which may compromise the security of your friends, family or business connections.

- Most terrorist operations are planned with great care; the terrorist rarely exposes himself to unnecessary danger. Terrorists may place their targets under surveillance in order to identify their vulnerabilities. Be aware of people paying you too much attention or unfamiliar people hanging around your accommodation. In many countries children are given this job. It's best to trust no one in really dangerous areas.

- If someone knocks on your door unannounced, first confirm their identity. If you are not satisfied, inform them that you are unavailable and arrange for another date. This will give you time to check them out.

- Refuse an invitation to meet someone you do not know well in an isolated or remote location. If you do decide to meet them choose a well-lit area with lots of other people.

- Be cautious of accepting unexpected packages or letters delivered to your office or accommodation. A common terrorist tactic is to place a simple explosive device in an envelope or package that detonates when it is opened. If you think that you may be at risk and you receive a package wrapped in greaseproof paper or a package with grease stains on it, take it outdoors, leave it on the ground and call the authorities.

- One of the easiest methods of terrorist attack is the under-car booby trap. This enables the terrorist to strike at his intended target while removing himself from the danger. An under-car booby trap is a small amount of explosives packed into a plastic container containing a detonator and a power source. The container is painted black and attached to the underside of the car by means of a magnet. The device is activated when the vehicle moves off or when it goes up or downhill. Find out what the underside of your car looks like. Then, if you think you may be in danger from this type of attack, you can check the underside of your vehicle before you drive it to detect any foreign objects.

- If you have access to a garage, park your vehicle in it. Or park in a well-lit area. Whenever you approach your vehicle, inspect it first from a distance and then close to, to ensure it has not been tampered with.

Terrorist Weapons of Mass Destruction

Sophisticated weapons technology poses a new terrorist threat. While it was a concern before September 2001, now it is a major worry for the authorities. Terrorist groups have been trying to acquire weapons of mass destruction for some time, and some groups have actually managed to produce their own. The Japanese religious cult Aum Shinirikyo (meaning 'supreme truth') launched an attack on a Tokyo tube station in March 1995. Members of this bizarre cult released the deadly nerve gas sarin, killing 12 people and leaving nearly 1000 ill. Clearly, if other terrorist groups access or develop their own weapons of mass destruction and the knowledge of how to use them the consequences would perhaps be even more devastating.

The three principle areas of concern for the authorities are nuclear bombs, chemical weapons and biological weapons. But how feasible is their deployment by a terrorist group? For an analysis, see the following points.

- In reality, the ability of terrorists to deploy chemical weapons is dependent on factors other than the toxicity of the chemical agent. Because these chemicals are produced in the same way as insecticides, it's possible terrorists could make them. But dispersing them over a large area is a far more difficult task. The method of dissemination, weather conditions and the direction of the wind make accurate targeting of this type of weapon problematic.

■ A chemical weapons attack is thought to be the least effective weapon of mass destruction, but toxic chemicals are probably the most accessible. The Al Qaida terrorists in the US showed an unhealthy interest in crop-spraying aircraft, one of the most effective ways of disseminating chemical weapons. If you're abroad and there is a chemical weapons alert, or you notice a crop-spraying aircraft flying low over a built-up area, get indoors immediately. Ideally you should shelter in the upper levels of a high tower block. Most of the gases used are heavier than air and will eventually settle on the ground. You should avoid going into low-lying areas or basements, as the gas will settle in these areas and the concentrations will be greatest. Once inside, try to hermetically seal the room. Close all doors and windows and switch off any air conditioning system with air intakes from outside. Seal all the gaps between the doors and the floors, and then wait until the authorities react to the attack.

■ In the case of chemical attacks, the terrorists will have little opportunity for a test run, and they themselves will be in danger of contamination. In the Tokyo attack the terrorists left bags to release the gases on the subway, then made their getaway. If you are travelling by public transport, stay clear of unattended luggage. If you see anyone behaving suspiciously and wearing protective clothing or face masks, be alert. This threat may seem remote, but the success of the Tokyo attack could have inspired other groups.

■ Biological weapons are a major concern. Many millions of people were suddenly exposed to the threat of bioterrorism in October 2001, when anthrax began circulating in the US postal system. Anthrax is a naturally occurring, potentially lethal illness caused by a spore-forming bacterium, *Bacillus anthracis*. This disease is common in animals in some regions of the world. From a terrorist perspective, anthrax is a more effective option than other bacterial agents because it cannot be communicated between humans.

Other agents would cause large epidemics as disease spread across frontiers, and the terrorist would be unable to control the spread of the disease. With anthrax they are able to more accurately target their victims without having to fear that the disease will kill their own people.

- Anthrax can be transmitted either through touch, by inhalation or by ingestion. Pulmonary anthrax, from inhalation, is almost always lethal. The symptoms of anthrax manifest themselves within seven days and are different for each type of infection. If you have opened a suspect package or if you hear that someone else with whom you have had a close relationship is diagnosed as having any form of anthrax look out for the following symptoms. Cutaneous anthrax can occur when the bacterium enters the skin through cuts or grazes. A small lump resembling an insect bite forms, and within hours a painless ulcer with a central dark area develops. It is rare for people who contract cutaneous anthrax to die. The treatment is with antibiotics, and if caught early enough the victim will make a full recovery. Inhalation anthrax is usually fatal and the initial symptoms appear like a cold or flu. Within a period of days the victim will develop breathing difficulties and shock. Death can follow soon after. Intestinal anthrax is cause by ingestion of a contaminated material. The person will have abdominal pain, nausea, vomiting and loss of appetite and a fever. Victims can vomit blood or suffer severe bouts of diarrhoea. Between a quarter and a half of all those who contract ingestion anthrax die. If you think that you may have been exposed to anthrax and you begin to develop any of the symptoms, go immediately to the nearest medical facility where they should place you on a course of antibiotics.

- Nuclear bombs are a remote possibility, but terrorist groups – most notably the Al Qaida network – have been actively seeking nuclear devices. My feeling is that if they had had one they would have used it already. The former chief of Russian national security, General Alexander Lebed, stated that the Soviet Union had produced in the region of 130 'suitcase' nuclear bombs, capable of devastating everything round it within half a kilometre. The effects of a device like this are potentially much worse than the events of September 2001. It would be virtually impossible to stop a determined attack with such a weapon, and the radioactive fallout would contaminate areas well beyond the detonation zone. But the less lethal 'dirty bomb' is probably more likely. This is a core of explosives wrapped round with radioactive material, which would spread radioactive isotopes over a wide area. Major Western capitals and cities are the most likely targets. If you are travelling to a big city in the West and the unthinkable happens, you should if possible move upwind from the explosion to reduce your exposure to radioactive fallout.

Riots

In most of the West, people occasionally take to the streets in order to demonstrate about a particular issue, and on relatively rare occasions these can develop into violent confrontations. But in many regions with political, religious or socially charged environments, taking to the streets in protest is a way of life. Demonstrations all too easily turn to civil disorder, and an orderly crowd can take on a sinister and frightening dynamic when stimulated by agitators or security forces.

Travellers wandering accidentally into the path of such a mob may become the focal point of that anger, especially if they are unaware of what to do. In July 2001, I was in the Macedonian capital, Skopje, when a crowd of protestors demonstrating against Western intervention in their internal conflict surged up. We narrowly missed being torn to pieces by a rampaging crowd. Foreigners were attacked in the streets and beaten and all foreign-owned businesses in the city centre were smashed up. Luckily, a restaurant manager hid two of us behind a counter, and we came out unscathed. However, the danger was not entirely unexpected. There were signs that public disorder was only a spark away.

Demonstrations can and do happen in most countries for a variety of reasons. The big issues in particular – religion, nationalism, racial or socioeconomic inequality or antigovernment demonstrations – are very emotional and can ignite with the most innocuous of sparks. As a traveller new to the local environment you may have difficulty interpreting the local nuances, but you need to be aware of the signs. Inflammatory political or racial rhetoric broadcast on TV or radio stations is one of the most obvious signs: in many countries these transmissions are designed to whip up emotions and get people on the streets. There may be posters or graffitti pasted at strategic sites throughout the city informing of a coming demonstration, or you may hear something by word of mouth. Sports can ignite a riot, too: in many countries, big events such as the Euro 2000 football tournament saw drunken football thugs taking to the streets and causing riots.

If you are visiting a particularly volatile region, ask about the situation at your hotel or local colleges. Stay clear of areas such as government buildings, places of religious worship and police stations. If you know a demo is going on, avoid the area or stay inside.

If you are travelling in an area where violent demonstrations are common, consider the following points.

- Writing up a traveller's risk assessment before you go will give you an idea of the political and social climate at your destination (see Chapter 1, page 9). Local news sources will indicate the current issues. If these in any way relate to your visit – if you're there on business and it's a demo protesting about local industrial relations, say – you could end up exposed to violence.

- Pay attention to political anniversaries, which are often the focal point of demos. These could be religious, the date of a prominent individual's death, or the celebration of a political or national occasion.

- Before you venture out, ask about events in the area that may attract large crowds onto the streets. Identify where these gatherings will be so you can avoid them. Bring along a map or use a local guide so you know where you are at all times.

- Try to find out if there have been any recent violent demonstrations at your destination. Find out what the demonstration was about and how the authorities handled it. In some countries they will not tolerate dissent, and use excessive force.

- Identify those who are charged with maintaining authority on the streets. In many cases it's the army, and their response may be more robust than that of the police. Armies are trained to fight wars using maximum violence, and unless they have had comprehensive riot control training they can overreact.

- If you suddenly find yourself in or near a violent demo, just leave the area and find another route back to your accommodation. You don't want to be around when the security forces arrive, as there is usually a tense standoff that can quickly explode into violence.

- When the security forces decide to clear the streets, they will not differentiate between rioters and unfortunate tourists accidentally caught up in the incident. You will all be subjected to the same rough handling. In the May 2001 anticapitalist demonstrations in London many tourists were trapped by the police cordon at Oxford Circus. Fortunately this demonstration was not allowed to turn violent; had it done so, innocent people would have been caught up in a major disturbance and people would have been injured.

- Security forces generally have a number of ways to contain violent demonstrations and then arrest those involved. Blocking off the area of trouble is one way. If these incidents were happening near tourist areas, the security forces would try to prevent the demonstrators getting access to them. If you are caught on the wrong side of the cordon you may not be able to return to your hotel.

- If you are caught up in a demonstration, move to the periphery of the crowd, where it's safer. If you are in a commercial area, get into a shop, hotel or café and stay there until the demonstrators have passed.

- When the security forces decide to take action against a crowd of demonstrators, stay aware of the movements of the crowd. If they bolt in your direction you could find yourself in the security force's direct line of fire. If the crowd feels threatened, they may stampede, so ensure you keep your footing. If you have children protect them by placing them between you and a wall or similar object.

- When you are walking around in an area that sees a lot of street demonstrations, don't go alone. Find out if anyone else (preferably a local) is heading to that part of town and persuade them that it is safer to go together. In this case you can at least look out for each other. If you do go out in a team, stick together and maintain visual contact.

■ Be aware of what you are carrying with you. If you are carrying a camera around your neck you may be mistaken for a journalist or even a member of the security forces – or be an easy target for a thief.

■ If you get caught up in a big crowd and you witness people with weapons or wearing masks, move away and try to seek shelter in a building or escape down a side street.

■ If you notice civilians on the street with firearms, leave the area immediately. The security forces may open fire on the crowd if they even see a weapon. When firearms are used in a built-up area there will be ricochets that can kill or injure people more than 100 metres away.

■ If firearms are used, take cover as quickly as possible. Get behind some hard cover such as a wall or even better, a building, and get out of the back door and leave the area immediately if safe to do so.

■ If you are in an exposed area and shooting breaks out, take cover behind the nearest shelter, although never a place where there have been shootings. If you decide to take cover behind a vehicle, do so at the front behind the engine. Then you must look for a way out; the engine block will only offer limited protection.

■ If you think that the crowd is becoming angry, emotional, anxious or excitable you should be alert. In this state the group can act in ways that the individuals themselves would not normally act.

■ Many peaceful demonstrations attract radicals or agitators with the sole intention of causing trouble. If you are caught up in a demonstration look out for those who are trying to manipulate the crowd by spreading rumours of heavy-handed security force tactics. They may themselves try to attack the security forces or whip up emotions by shouting or chanting. If you are near someone who sticks out in the riot, move away as they will come under scrutiny from the security forces.

- If you notice people who have been drinking or taking drugs, give them a wide berth. Their behaviour will be erratic and the security forces will notice that.

- In some demonstrations the security forces show brutality to the crowd. Even a peaceful demonstration can attract the fury of the authorities. In a volatile country do not be tempted to go along with even a peaceful, law-abiding crowd.

- If you notice police at a demo putting on their gas masks, they are probably about to use teargas. Teargas is a nonpersistent irritant which will attack exposed areas of skin, causing a burning sensation, irritate mucous membranes and if inhaled will irritate your respiratory tract. Teargas will make your eyes stream, can make you vomit, and can cause a burning sensation on your skin. If you notice the security forces putting on their gas masks, immediately find out the direction the wind is blowing. Try to get upwind from the crowd. If this is not possible try to get into a building.

- If you are in the open and are exposed to teargas, cover your mouth and eyes and try to get away as soon as possible from the crowd. Teargas can be deployed in a variety of ways. A grenade will billow out a thick white cloud of gas. It can be fired from a grenade discharger with a range of up to 30 metres, or it can be sprayed from a handheld dispenser, which has a range of around a metre.

- If you are exposed to teargas you must leave the area as quickly as possible. You can reduce the effects of teargas by using a citrus fruit such as a lemon or lime, rubbing the juice onto the exposed areas. Rubbing onion juice onto exposed areas will also help reduce the effects of the gas. You should, however, seek medical attention if you have inhaled teargas, particularly if you suffer from an ailment such as asthma.

- If you will be near a demo where teargas might be used, avoid using sunscreen or perfume. The teargas molecules will stick onto both sunscreen and perfume. Similarly, if you wear contact lenses you must be careful not to rub your eyes. If you get the teargas behind your lens the effects will be more severe and you will have difficulty seeing.

- The tactics some security forces use to control riots can be frightening. In many regions the security forces will react with extreme violence in order to put down dissent. In some countries, the first response from the security forces is to use live bullets. Try to find out how the security forces reacted the last time there was a riot in the region you're visiting.

- The security forces can use plastic or rubber bullets to disperse a crowd. These are fired from riot guns and have a range of about 20 to 30 metres. The bullets themselves are around 15 centimetres in length, have a diameter of around 10 centimetres and have a very low velocity. You can see them tumbling through the air when fired. The intention is to hurt but not seriously injure protestors. However, people have been killed and many injured when these bullets have been fired too close or have hit people in the head. Other riot control bullets are made of plastic or metal and rubber. If any of these are being used you should get to the edge of the protest and leave the area immediately.

- Water cannons are light armoured vehicles which contain a large water tank. There is an adjustable water hose on top, which can direct a powerful jet of water with enough power to knock you off your feet. The water can also be directed in a fine spray, and chemical irritants and even ink can be added to it. Once more, if you see water cannon, get away from the crowd.

- The security forces will attempt to disperse a violent protest as quickly as possible. When they do this there is a possibility that instead of one large crowd you may now be faced by small angry mobs which have spread throughout the entire area. There may be running battles throughout the city. If this occurs you should try to get into a tall building which overlooks the area. From here you will be safer and be able to monitor where the trouble is. Remain in this position until you decide that it is safe to leave the area.

- In many regions a demonstration is inevitably followed by a spate of crime, robbery and looting. If you are living in an area where tensions are high and you expect disorder, conceal your valuables. Avoid overt displays of wealth when walking in sensitive areas.

- If you are travelling by car and see an unruly crowd up ahead you will have to consider your options. If you can find an escape route, drive out of the area. You may decide to make a U-turn and drive away from the crowd. If this is not an option, you may consider parking the car at the side of the road, locking up and getting out of the area on foot. If you remain in the vehicle and are caught up in a disturbance you may increase the risk.

- If you are confronted by the threat of violence, just try to keep out of striking distance. Avoid aggressive body language such as pointing and do not touch or push those confronting you. If possible, avoid speaking unless you can convincingly sound like a local. If the situation is deteriorating and becomes dangerous, push the aggressor out of the way and try to get out of the situation by running into the crowd or to the security forces.

Guns

A number of countries in the West have stringent gun laws, and Britain is one. Yet there are an estimated 250,000 illegal firearms in circulation there. The criminal use of weapons has shown a dramatic surge in use in recent years. In my recent travels to war-torn areas such as the Middle East, Somalia, and Pakistan, guns are simply part of the culture. It is rather alarming when you arrive at such destinations to be confronted not only by police and military who are 'trained' to handle firearms, but also by ordinary civilians, many with no training at all, legally wielding guns. Afghanistan is an extreme example, where to be a man you must possess an AK47. In my recent trip to this country, the number of young boys with weapons was positively frightening.

Many parts of Europe and further afield, including some popular tourist destinations, have been swamped with weapons after the wars in the former Yugoslavia and Soviet states. A by-product of these conflicts is an illegal trade in cheap and easy-to-use firearms. And of course, in the gun-ridden US there are an estimated 200,000,000 firearms in circulation – and around 8000 gun murders a year. In any region with easy availability to firearms, incidents which would normally result in nothing more than an argument can end in tragedy. On one visit to the US, a friend parked our car in someone else's parking space. The infuriated American saw this, pulled a handgun on him and told him to move the car.

In a gun culture, people simply have fewer inhibitions about using weapons, so you have to take the threat seriously. Consider the following points.

- In countries such as the US, handguns can be treated like a fashion accessory. The group most likely to use and be victims of firearms are young men between 15 and 24. The majority of gun crime occurs within cities, and weekends seem to be particularly dangerous. When travelling to notorious gun blackspots, be cautious about becoming involved in an altercation with young men, particularly on weekends in big cities where drinking has been going on.

- Handguns are the most common weapon, and are particularly dangerous because they can be concealed. Anyone carrying a rifle or other similarly long firearm will at least be obvious and you can stay away from them.

- Handguns are low-velocity firearms: the bullets are less powerful than others, but they will still kill. Handguns are only accurate to around 30 metres. They come in two main types, the revolver or the automatic pistol. A revolver can fire six shots before it needs reloading; the automatic, 12. Some automatics can fire up to 18 bullets before reloading.

- Someone using a handgun will pull the weapon when they are close to their victim, because of the weapon's short range. In this situation it will be difficult to escape, as at this close range the weapons are very effective. In a robbery it would be better to hand over your possessions; nothing is worth more than your life. It is usual for gunmen to escape after they have committed a robbery and the victims are generally left unharmed.

▪ High-velocity or assault rifles are the other type of weapon you may encounter. These include the ubiquitous AK47 (of which there are an estimated 60 million in circulation worldwide). These weapons are very dangerous because they have long barrels and so are more accurate up to a range of 300 metres. The bullets, however, can travel up to 4 kilometres if they do not hit their target and can still kill or injure at that distance.

▪ Inevitably, these weapons are more powerful than handguns and have more penetration power. They mostly come with 30 round clips and can fire on single shot or on automatic, which in effect turns them into machine guns. However, when fired on automatic they are relatively inaccurate.

▪ If you confront someone brandishing a weapon, you must make a calculated risk assessment about what you are going to do. If you run in blind panic you may actually run into trouble. You must fight the initial urge to run, make a decision and get away from the gunmen. If you cannot identify where the gunmen are you should keep low to the ground and get away from the noise.

▪ If you spot someone brandishing a handgun more than 20 metres away, you may decide to escape. If you do decide to run, head to the nearest shelter running as fast as you can; even expert marksmen will have a problem trying to hit a fast-moving target at this distance. If the gunman is to the front or the rear you may consider running in a zigzag. This will make it more difficult for them to aim. However, if the gunman is off to a flank you should run as fast as you can. By zigzagging in this scenario you would just prolong your exposure to danger.

▪ For firearms to be effective, they must be well maintained. If you look at the condition of a weapon you can assess how dangerous they are. If it's dirty or rusty or has parts missing, chances are it will not work as intended, and will be less accurate. However, it will still probably work. If someone pulls a gun on you, no matter how bad it looks you must treat the threat seriously.

■ If there are buildings nearby, seek shelter in the nearest one. As soon as you have entered it, look for a rear door or window and exit it as soon as possible. Then make your way out of the area.

■ When you take cover, choose a substantial and solid object that will provide adequate protection from bullets. Any solidly built wall, thick tree trunk, or engine block of a car will absorb much of the impact from low and high-velocity bullets. Lie down on the ground behind the object until the danger has passed. While you are sheltering behind it, look for an escape route, and move after the shooting has stopped. Be aware that even behind a solid object you will not be entirely safe; after repeated bullet strikes many solid objects will collapse.

■ Never be tempted to look over whatever it is you are hiding behind to get a better view. A bullet may actually go through whatever you are hiding behind. Stay close to the ground and look round the object you are hiding behind. By doing this you will minimise the amount of your body you are exposing to danger.

■ If someone is firing a weapon, even if you are not the intended target there is the possibility of a ricochet. In a building, for instance, bullets can ricochet off the walls. Ricochets can be as dangerous as aimed shots. Take cover as quickly as possible and leave the area as soon as you can.

■ Be aware that after a shooting incident, the police or security forces will arrive and they will be armed and ready for a confrontation. Depending on the country, there is a danger of becoming caught up in the incident. If you can get out of the area you should do so, but be aware of the dangers of running around after a shooting incident. In some countries, the police or army are just as likely to shoot anyone running around.

■ If you are caught up in an incident where people are firing at each other, go to ground and stay there. Seek shelter and crawl to the nearest cover. If you are travelling in a group, ensure everyone knows what action to take. The sound of gunfire can be very loud and make it difficult to communicate. If you are travelling with children, grab them and haul them to safety.

- In some gun cultures it is normal to fire weapons in the air during celebrations. During a trip to Kosovo, I saw the entire city erupt in gunfire while the population celebrated the anniversary of the declaration of independence. These bullets must come back down to earth and they can still kill or injure when they do. If you are in an area when the locals are firing in the air, seek shelter under hard cover. Head to the nearest building and take cover until the celebrations have ended.

- Machine guns are so-called 'area' weapons, intended to hit targets within an area and not to be pinpoint accurate. The aim is to put many more bullets in the area of the target in order to increase the chances of hitting it. Machine guns are generally used in war, so you will be unlikely to see them. But if you are caught up in an incident where machine guns are used, you should behave the same way that you would in any other shooting incident. Go to ground, make your way to a covered area and look for an escape route for when the firing stops.

- Shotguns are dangerous weapons at close range. They have a range of about 20 to 30 metres. They use a solid shot pellet that fires a single lead shot, but can also fire a buckshot cartridge that scatters small ball bearings in a wide arc. In some countries these weapons are used for riot control. However, they can kill. If someone points a shotgun at you, it could be lethal within the weapon's range. Outside of this the pellets will still be able to reach but will be less effective.

- Replica weapons are so realistic that it is generally not possible to identify whether or not the weapon is fake. Treat all firearms as real; it is just not worth the risk.

Crossing Borders

While travelling overland from country to country outside the European Union, one of the biggest difficulties is trying to negotiate international frontiers. In many countries this is a relatively simple procedure, you roll up to the border, flash your passport, get it stamped and you're in. However, in many volatile countries you can end up treated like a major international war criminal under the same circumstances. If there is tension or conflict in the region, there will be other serious problems. It is not unusual to travel to an area that has just recently come through a conflict, and find that the border posts are besieged by thousands of refugees wanting to return to their homes. Crossing the border between Pakistan and Afghanistan was one of the most tense experiences I have been through. There were refugees on both sides who were living in abject poverty, and on the Afghan side the former regime of the Taliban was very much in evidence and everyone had a weapon.

In other countries, the immigration officials are scrupulous about their work, and it can take a long time to get your passport stamped. Occasionally you will be required to throw money at the problem, but you must ensure that you read the signs correctly – if you try to bribe the wrong man you could find yourself in trouble. Border posts are often the scenes of fighting in areas that are in conflict. Before you depart, research your destination to ensure there has been no outbreak of fighting there. If you intend to make overland frontier crossings consider the following points.

- First ensure that you have all your documents. This will include your passport and visas, entry or work permits, vaccination certificates and anything else demanded by local authorities. It is worthwhile contacting the embassy in the country you are leaving and asking them about the protocol at the border and what documentation you will require.

- In many regions, people have close affiliation with ethnic kin just across the frontiers. In times of tension these frontiers and those who man them can become flashpoints. If you are visiting such a country you should avoid travel by land. If you must travel overland between states try to find a route outside the conflict area.

- In many regions, weekend scenes around border posts can be like a mass exodus. In Brunei on the island of Borneo the crossing point into the Malaysian state of Sarawak was always choked by thousands of people waiting to go there for the weekends. This was mainly due to that country's liberal attitude to alcohol and its cheap shopping. The result was anything up to six hours in the stifling tropical heat trying to cross a border only a kilometre away. Research the patterns of activity around the border area at your destination, find out when the border post opens and when it closes and, more importantly, the quiet time. Many border areas are jampacked during rush hours and lunch breaks. This is particularly important if there is an expatriate community with people who travel into neighboring states for leisure, and during public holidays.

- Come prepared: dress well, and remain unflappably polite. This will help if you are confronted by a particularly nasty or even hostile customs official. On no account antagonise them. Depending on where you are, women may have less of a problem negotiating grumpy border officials. Sometimes you simply have to put up with the capriciousness of these officials. Once when I was travelling to Kenya with a colleague, the immigration official looked at our passports. Both had the same visas and both of us were legally entitled to stay for up to a month. The official decided that he did not like me and told me I could stay only for a week.

- Pass through the passport control before you attempt to go through customs. In some countries it is difficult to tell one from the other. To avoid complications and accusations that you were up to no good, follow the instructions.

- Be wary of accepting offers of help to speed your way through the border controls. I once watched someone hand over his passport and ticket to someone he had met literally seconds before. Had it not been for our intervention, the dim-witted traveller would have been stranded, as his 'helper' was about to make off with the goods.

- Ensure that you have enough cross-border currency to get you to your next destination. Some border dwellers will accept both currencies but you must check before you attempt to cross and ensure that you are up to speed with the exchange rate. The last thing a weary traveller needs is to be stranded at a border post or worse, having to walk to the nearest town some distance away.

- If you are driving, ensure that you are carrying your international driving licence and your insurance documentation. Your documentation may be valid for one country but not for the bordering country; check this before you go on holiday. In addition if you are driving a hire car and you intend crossing over the border you should ensure that your insurance covers you for the trip. Otherwise you could end up picking up the tab for a stolen or damaged car.

Kidnapping

Terrorist groups have long used kidnapping to exert political leverage over authorities or perhaps demand the release of a member of their organisation from detention. However, there has been a rise in kidnapping as a purely criminal enterprise. This crime is endemic in some parts of the world, and has become a business in countries such as Colombia, Mexico, Brazil and the Philippines. Countries of the former Soviet Union have also seen a tremendous increase in kidnapping for ransom; there were over 100 cases in 2001.

Kidnapping can end brutally. In July 1995 six tourists were kidnapped on a hiking holiday to the Himalayan areas of Kashmir. One managed to escape, one was decapitated, and the rest have sunk into oblivion. Elsewhere in this book I tell of the horrifying kidnapping in Chechnya of British telecommunications workers. Recent evidence has revealed a connection with Osama bin Laden's Al Qaida terrorist network. Apparently Al Qaida contacted the Chechen terrorists and offered to pay up to 50 million dollars if the captives were killed instead of released. For the terrorists, it was a simple matter of arithmetic: they could make more by killing the hostages than by handing them over.

In many countries of the world, where officials are ill paid and

the system is corrupt, the security forces themselves have been implicated in kidnappings. Colombia is the kidnap capital of the world,
with more than 2000 people kidnapped for ransom every year. This
activity comes second only to the illegal narcotics trade as a money
earner. In such countries tourists from the West are viewed as an
attractive option because of the amount of money that can be
obtained from insurance companies if they're kidnapped. Compared
to the last decade, this kind of crime has increased by an estimated
70 per cent. In 2000 it was reported that the insurance industry had
doled out around 350 million dollars in ransom payments, and this
excluded political kidnappings. And there are other costs. Medical
fees, in-country legal representation, consultancy fees and running
costs can amount to almost as much as the ransom.

If you stay away from kidnapping hotspots, the chances of it
happening to you are not huge. And the vast majority of those taken
hostage are eventually released unharmed – more than 90 per cent.
But given all this, heightened tension round the world could lead to
more kidnappings. You need to conduct a risk assessment for your
destination. You also need to think about survival strategies, as
kidnapping is enormously stressful and potentially damaging, and
you'll need to control your fear and other emotions. Kidnappers will
often use violence to subdue the captives. They might direct this at
those who they think are aggressive or defiant and pose a threat to
the success of their enterprise, or to pressure the authorities into
acquiescing to their demands.

Kidnappings can happen in all sorts of ways – as a full-blown
assault on a house where you are staying, or a well-planned and quietly
executed operation in some isolated place. This part of the operation
is the most risky for the captors, which also makes it the best moment
for an escape bid. You might, for instance, be in an area you are familiar with, and know people in the vicinity. But it's far better to take
preventive action. They may have placed you under surveillance to
decide on how to abduct you, for instance. You can make this task
more difficult by being unpredictable in your habits and by blending into the local scene. Avoid drawing attention to yourself by loud
behaviour, overt displays of wealth or driving vehicles that don't fit
in with the local scene.

Here are the points you'll need to think about if you're planning on a trip to a country known for kidnapping – or simply if you want to be prepared.

- Avoid telegraphing your movements and broadcasting your intentions by loose talk. Tell this only to those who need to know. With anyone else be vague and evasive.

- When the kidnappers strike, they may be tense and nervous; this is the only moment when they are at risk. They may behave erratically and unpredictably. If they display firearms, you may have no choice and have to go with them. If they do not have weapons, you may decide to run or make a lot of noise to attract attention from passers-by. It has been suggested that the majority of kidnap attempts take place within 500 metres from either your home or your destination. Your movements are most predictable here, which leaves you most at risk.

- If you are abducted, try to stay as calm as possible and follow the instructions of the kidnappers. If you are kidnapped with others, ensure that everyone else remains calm. If the kidnappers are scared they are more likely to use violence. It has been stressed that those who do not cooperate with terrorists in this situation will be kept in detention for longer periods of time and they will be treated more harshly.

- After the abduction, the kidnappers will inform the authorities, your family or your colleagues that they have you, and they will make their demands. By contingency planning the authorities will be able to confirm that you are still alive and know which group you are with. In the past, gangs have traded their victims, selling them among different groups.

- Once you have been abducted, you must mentally switch on to the fact that you are now in captivity. You must accept that your life is now on hold until the time when the negotiations are complete and you are released. Initial emotions will be disbelief at what is happening, followed by fear – fear of the unknown, uncertainty about the future, fear that you are now under the control of armed and hostile men. It is essential that you quickly come to terms with this fear and begin to control your emotions: this is survival mode. At times of hostility when the terrorists are aggressive to their captors, your central survival strategy is to focus on the fact that you are of value, you have loved ones back home working to get you released. Never abandon hope, and try to combat the effects of depression.

▪ Normally, when terrorists have abducted their target, the security forces will swamp the area to intercept them. In this case, the terrorists may take their captive to a holding area where they will stay until the security forces activity has died down. Then the kidnappers may take their captive to a more permanent detention location. It is helpful if you can maintain an awareness of where you are going. Listen for signs that may help you figure out where you are going. Noises like the sound of traffic, aircraft, trains or large concentrations of people may help indicate where you are being held. Maintain an awareness of the details of where you're being held, your room and the layout of the building. Rural places will smell different from urban ones. This information may prove invaluable if you decide to try to escape.

▪ Remain polite when you are addressed by the terrorists. Do not antagonise them or show emotions. Try to retain your dignity and be cooperative with the instructions of the hostage takers, and try to remain focused and remember that most people are released unharmed. Terrorists use a number of techniques to subdue their captives. Their intention is to control the victims by fear in order to make them comply with their demands or to pressure the authorities into acquiescing to their demands. They could do this by depriving their captive of food, water and sleep, or by running a mock execution where they go through the entire procedure, then at the final moment return the captive to their room. Or they might inform the captive that they are about to be released, leaving the person devastated. Being prepared for such psychological manipulation should be part of your survival strategy.

▪ Try to build up a psychological profile of your captors. Watch their behaviour, and observe their mannerisms and how they react with each other. This should provide you with an idea of which of them are dangerous, and which less prone to violence. If you do identify those less likely to be aggressive, you may be able to build up a relationship that you can exploit later. If you can build up any kind of relationship with your captors, you will increase your chances of surviving the situation. Try to identify their movements, routines and predictable patterns of behaviour in case there is a chance that you are able to exploit their weaknesses.

■ If the terrorists have gone to the risk of taking you hostage it is in their interest to ensure that you remain in good health. You are no use to them if you are dead. If you suffer from any health condition that demands medication, tell them. They will try to ensure that you remain alive and well. Remember this if they withhold your food and water as a 'punishment'. They have to provide these to keep you alive.

■ In all probability, the food you are given will be what the hostage takers themselves eat. Eat everything that you are given, and show them that you are grateful for it – they may even provide some more. Remember that you are trying to maintain your strength for the day when you are released and can recommence your life.

■ For many it can be very demoralising to have normal sanitation arrangements taken away – another 'punishment'. You will have to come to terms with this quickly, and focus on staying healthy for the duration.

■ Ensure that when you are cooperating with the terrorists you do not divulge information that may cause problems for you. Try not to reveal personal information such as your address, which may compromise the security of both yourself and your family. If you are taken hostage as part of a group, try to fade into the background and do not become prominent in the group. Prominent individuals will be the focus of attention if the situation deteriorates. Avoid coming to attention by being the group spokesman, or wearing what may be considered antagonistic symbolism, such as religious or political symbols. If you possess any such articles, dump them at the first available opportunity.

- If you are taken hostage as a member of a group, one of your biggest assets will be the sense of unity in your group. There will be people in the group who may not like you and people who you may not like, but you need to put any differences aside in the task of getting out of the situation unscathed. The captors can exploit any fissures and play on group members' sensitivities, or may favour a particular individual or group, which will antagonise those left out. It is essential they you all work together for the same objective – survival of the group.

- Try to keep your mind and body active and focus on the fact that you do have something and someone to come home to. This is important to remember as the terrorists will be trying to break your spirit. You need to remind yourself that your life has value and it is the captors who are in the wrong. Try to keep track of time and organise routines. Remember that your life is on hold until you are released, and that when that happens you will want to quickly get back into your normal life. To do this it is helpful that you minimise the effects of your detention. Keep your mind active by thinking about all the things that you will do when you are released. Keep your body in shape with simple exercises such as calisthenics and stretching.

- If an escape attempt offers itself and you decide to take your chance, be fully committed. If you are caught you are likely to be treated with severe violence. So when you decide to escape, you must be sure that you have a very good chance of success.

- If you hear loud bangs or gunfire, you may find yourself in a hostage rescue attempt. In this scenario you must be aware of the dangers. The attacking security forces will be hyped up and, depending on who is conducting the rescue, may not be sufficiently trained for this type of operation. You should get on the floor and make yourself as small as possible. There is a danger of shots ricocheting off walls and floors. You should only get up and run if you feel that there is no other option. You should only attack the terrorists if there are no other options and all other avenues of escape have been blocked. If you are instructed by the rescuers to come out you must do so in a slow and deliberate manner with your hands in the air informing them that you were a captive.

■ Be aware that there is a great risk from fire during one of these operations. When the SAS stormed the Iranian embassy in London, the entire building was destroyed, as was the Japanese embassy in Lima. It is usual for security forces used in this type of operation to treat everyone in the building as a terrorist until the real identities have been ascertained. This prevents the terrorists from blending in with the hostages.

■ When hostages are released they may have been traumatised, and the effects of the ordeal may last much longer than the actual time spent in captivity. Many ex-hostages are so traumatised that they cannot let go of the incident and constantly question their decisions. Most people who come out of this type of traumatic ordeal will be offered counselling. It is wise to accept this offer, as many people can suffer from delayed stress, and symptoms won't show up until some time after the event.

Landmines

Landmines are a legacy of almost every conflict that has occurred over the last hundred years. In the 21st century, the majority of nation-states have signed the landmine ban treaty which prohibits the production and exportation of mines, but the United States, Russia and China have all refused – in effect making the treaty void. Afghanistan and Cambodia have long been riddled with landmines. And in late 2001 and early 2002, heightened tension between India and Pakistan has led the Indian government to mine the border with its neighbour. It's a problem that isn't about to go away yet.

Landmines have killed and maimed millions of people. Detecting them is still difficult, and the only effective technique is for people trained in mine recovery to get on their bellies and prod the ground with a long metal skewer. Once laid, they remain a threat for decades until they are recovered. It has been estimated that there are in the region of 100 million mines laid in over 65 countries. The UN estimate that there are some 9000 people killed and 20,000 seriously injured by them each year. Unless these mines were laid by military organisations with strict hierarchical structures that have the capacity to record where they have laid them, the chances of these devices ever being located are remote. The majority of landmines are unmarked and just waiting for some innocent and unfortunate civilian to trigger them.

On my recent trip to Afghanistan we ventured out to the airport area of Kandahar in search of the Al Qaida training camp. We found the area, which had been heavily mined during the conflict. A local driver had just stepped out of his car right onto a landmine and lost his leg – an all-too-common horror story. Cambodia, now emerging as a hot tourist destination, is also full of landmine victims and more tragic accidents waiting to happen, for decades to come.

As former conflict areas open up to tourist development, travellers may place themselves at risk when they venture off the beaten track in search of adventure. Most governments which have a landmine problem insist they are not a problem for travellers, but this is clearly untrue. If they knew where they were they would make the effort to recover them, but often they don't – and this presents a very real danger to travellers and locals alike. Again, this is something you will have to research. If the country has seen a recent conflict or even a conflict in the last two decades, you should identify the areas where fighting took place and avoid them. For instance, the Cambodian government forces heavily mined the ancient temples at Angkor Wat, which is now a major tourist attraction.

If you are travelling to a region which has seen conflict in the past, consider the following points:

▪ Landmines are explosive devices either concealed in the ground or hidden on the surface concealed in thick vegetation. They take two forms: blast mines, which rely on the blast and shock effect of the explosive detonation; and fragmentation mines, which are normally concealed on the surface and disperse fragments all around when detonated. Direct pressure, such as stepping on them, can detonate mines, or they can be blown up by remote control.

- It is very difficult to detect mines, so you need to know which areas to keep out of. Stay on roads frequently used by local civilians and the military. If you suspect that an area may have had military significance in the past, stay on the main routes and areas that you know are clear of mines.

- Only use official border crossing points. Governments which have had conflicts with neighbouring states may use mines to secure their frontiers.

- In counterinsurgency conflicts it is normal practice to lay mines on the main communications routes. Buses and trains have been targets of mine attacks in the past. Check to see if there have been similar attacks at your destination. If so, consider taking an alternative mode of transport.

- Stick to areas officially designated as mine-free and if you are in any doubt consider hiring a reputable local guide. Ensure that they really know the local area. If you identify any areas that have been cordoned off, heed the warnings and keep out.

- In areas which have recently seen conflict, mines may have been laid to terrorise the local civilian population. If you are travelling through an area which relies on agriculture for its economy, and there are fields left uncultivated, you must ask why. They could be mined.

- In many regions local people will send their domestic animals into suspected mined areas in order to clear mines. If you come across areas with dead domestic animals, leave immediately.

- If you notice areas that have recently been fought over you should avoid them. It is conventional military thinking to lay mines in order to protect your own position. Additionally it is common military practice to lay mines in areas which are out of sight from a main military position.

- If you're not completely satisfied by research you did before you left, ask the locals about mines. If there have been mine attacks in the past ask where they were laid and their intended target.

- If you hear any unexplained loud explosions when you are in an area that has seen recent conflict, backtrack to a secure area and then go back to your initial position.

- When you are in a group walking in areas that have seen conflict in the past, walk in single file with a large space between each individual. If there is an explosion caused by a mine at least only one person will be injured.

- If you are driving in an area which has recently seen conflict, stick to areas which are regularly used and avoid overgrown tracks. If the local people have not used them, there must be a good reason.

- If you must travel through an area which is currently undergoing conflict you should liaise with the authorities to ensure that your proposed route is safe to travel through. It may be wise to identify an alternative route.

- Never wander about in an area of conflict looking for souvenirs.

13

Dangerous Activities

F OR MANY OF US, TAKING ON the challenge of adventure activities almost feels like fulfilling a long-lost primeval instinct. Luckily, however, we now know how to minimise the risk: many of these challenges are controlled, trained instructors are at hand, and safety staff accompany us or are strategically placed to ensure that we get a relatively safe thrill. Essentially, we place our destiny in their hands. The vital thing is that they know what they are doing.

In many regions, they don't – not in the way we would hope for, anyway. They may only be one step ahead of us in terms of expertise. Add that to the fact that emergency services may not be available or easy to get to in some countries, and the situation begins to look dangerous. In many countries, adventure activities which can be safely conducted in, say, the UK are not regulated. Outfits that have emergency procedures may have never tested them, and they may be inadequate. A recent survey suggested that the casualty figures for tourists engaged in adventure activities may be almost as high as that for the number-one injury-causing activity, driving – but as there are far fewer people going on adventure holidays, they account for a higher proportion. This survey noted that just over a fifth of tourists who died on holiday from the late 1970s to the mid-1990s were engaged in adventure activities.

Dangerous activities include bungee jumping, rafting, parachuting, scuba diving, wilderness trekking, mountaineering, skiing, horse riding and cycling. For those with expertise, the risk is considerably lower than for the hordes of young travellers from Western countries who are tempted to try one of these activities for the first time during a trip abroad. Not surprisingly, it's testosterone-filled twenty-something men who are most at risk.

Research has shown that when these activities are conducted under proper supervision by a regulated authority you will in all probability get that buzz of excitement and still get home safe. However, in many popular tourist destinations adventure activity companies are small, locally run affairs. Once, on a trip to Bali I decided to go diving. I was already a qualified diver and had a good idea of what to look for. When I checked in at the dive office on the beach I was informed that all the equipment was on the boat, which was just about to leave. I should have noticed something was wrong, as I was the only diver to board. Later, as we got ready for the dive, the 'dive master' began stuffing rocks in his shirt. When I asked what he was doing he informed me that the hotel had had to sell off most of their equipment during the currency crisis in South East Asia. I refused to dive unless I was provided with the proper equipment, and eventually I was. It made me wonder how a less experienced diver would have reacted.

Trekking and Mountaineering

Mountaineering and trekking in remote areas are arguably the riskiest adventure activities for a number of reasons. The relative ease with which one can get to these areas and the sheer number of people pursuing this type of activity mean that there is a greater chance that people will be injured. The main reason, however, is almost always a lack of preparation.

People who are unused to conditions in mountainous or remote regions can underestimate the severity of the environment. The tragedy that befell a British schoolgirl in 2001 on Kina Balu mountain in Borneo is a sobering example to us all. The girl went climbing with her family and she and her brother became separated from them as well as the local guide. Her brother went off to find help, leaving the young girl alone on the mountain. Days later her body was found; she had died from exposure.

Two years before, my wife and I had climbed this mountain, using the same track. We found it a wonderful experience although it is a fairly demanding climb. We rose at 2 am to make the rather desolate trek to the summit in order to catch the sunrise. It was pitch-black and absolutely freezing – and this is in tropical South East Asia, where just a few kilometres away lush tropical jungle is growing. We were carrying spare winter clothing, hot drinks and spare food. When we reached the summit we were soon joined by other trekkers, mostly Europeans. I was surprised at how many people were totally unprepared for the conditions. Many people crowded round the small solid fuel cooker I had lit to boil some water, just to get warm.

Whenever you venture into the hills or go trekking in a remote area, prepare for it. Treat mountains and remote areas with the respect they deserve, even if you are only intending to go on a day trip into the hills. Whether you're going for 24 hours or two weeks, the equipment will be more or less the same; you'll just need more food and water for a longer trip.

- Prepare thoroughly for your trip. Check out the activity organisation before you go to see if they are legitimate. Remember to check your insurance policy to see whether you are covered for the activity you will be doing.

- Once at your destination, do not be tempted by locals offering exciting adventures who are touting their trade on the street or in a market. The chances are that they will be unqualified, with little or no back-up and no insurance cover. This would mean that in an emergency you will be on your own. You should use bona fide organisations with enough logistical support to get you out if you get into trouble.

- Buy a guidebook and learn as much as you can about the area where you will be trekking. Get an up-to-date map and study it. Try to identify the area where your tour group are expecting to go. If you have an idea of where they operate you can check up on the situation within the area before you go there. If there have been violent incidents in or near your area, give serious consideration to whether you should continue.

- In volatile regions, violence occasionally spills over into neighbouring countries. Ensure that you inform your contacts where you will be going, the routes you are expecting to take, how long you will be there for and when you expect to return. Try to inform your contacts if your plans change.

- Ensure that you are carrying the right equipment for the conditions. Be aware that at altitude, even tropical regions can be freezing and you will require winter clothing. In scorching-hot deserts you will require warm clothing for the night, when temperatures can plummet. When trekking you should pay more attention than normal to your footwear; you will need a boot that offers good ankle support with a good sole and solid grip. You may need sunscreen and sunglasses too.

- Bring your map of the area with you, as well as a compass, and ensure that you at least know the basics of how to use them. You will need to study the map before you embark on the trek, to work out a route. If you are using a GPS you should not rely on it entirely. It is an excellent navigation aid, but you must be able to transfer the information from your GPS to your map. (See Chapter 18.) If there is a local mountain rescue or park ranger station you can check for information about the current conditions before you depart. Ensure that you obtain their emergency telephone number or the radio frequency.

- If you are an independent traveller, ask whether you need permission or even a permit to trek in some areas. In addition, there are designated camping areas. You should use these, as they are known and people will know where to look in the event of an incident.

- You should also carry emergency equipment such as water purification tablets. Even in pristine wilderness the water may have been badly contaminated by a dead animal upstream. It's vital to drink enough water. The temperature, altitude, wind and in many regions the low humidity will further increase dehydration. Extra clothing, spare food and cooking materials, a torch and a whistle in case you need to attract attention, should all be packed. You will need a mobile phone or radio to communicate with your companions or people back home. You should at least have a small battery-operated radio, which will enable you to receive the local news and weather reports.

- You must have a contingency plan when you are trekking or climbing mountains in case you find yourself in an emergency situation. Your plan should cover how to deal with casualties, what to do if you become lost or separated, and what to do if you are late. It does not make sense to make several different plans for different scenarios. Have one generic plan, which can be altered to fit every scenario. Be aware that although you've worked out your route, you should never push on regardless; if you encounter a problem it may be better to turn back.

- When you are trekking, go at the pace of the slowest person and never leave anyone behind.

- If you find out that one of your group is missing, stop and determine the last location where the missing person was positively seen. You must then organise a search of the route to find the lost person. The terrain will dictate which search pattern you adopt. However if you keep control of your group, you will notice quickly if one is missing. If you are the one who loses touch with the group you should shout as soon as you become separated.

- When you find the missing person check them for injury. If they are injured and you are not able to treat them, leave someone with them, along with sufficient food, water and equipment, and go for assistance.

- Unless you are an experienced and capable mountaineer with the appropriate equipment, avoid glaciers, steep snow-covered mountains, and fast-flowing water features. If you intend to travel over such terrain and are unfamiliar with the area, you will need to hire a local guide.

▪ When you are in a remote area be cautious about lighting fires. In hot, dry regions there is a danger that it will get out of control and have devastating consequences. If you intend to light a fire, find out if they are allowed. In some countries the penalties for lighting illegal fires are severe. During 1998 to 1999, many parts of South East Asia were aflame as forest fires raged out of control for months. Huge areas were shrouded in thick smog for weeks on end, with untold health consequences.

▪ Be cautious about going near wild animals (see Chapter 14). Treat them with the respect they deserve and give them a wide berth. Wild animals will attack if they feel threatened. If you are travelling with children, they will need to understand how to behave around wild animals.

▪ If you are trekking in mountainous terrain, pay attention to the weather conditions. Visibility can shrink in seconds as weather fronts close in. Across the world there are in the region of 40,000 thunderstorms each day, accompanied by 8 million lightning strikes in any 24-hour period. Lightning can be very dangerous if you are caught on an exposed hillside; in the US alone there are around 100 fatalities and 250 serious injuries each year caused by lightning strikes. When a lightning storm strikes high up on a mountainside you should descend immediately and find cover. Stay away from tall structures such as radio antennae or even tall trees – they can act as lightning rods and attract the terrific surge of electrical energy. If you are caught out on a hillside in a lightning storm, you should insulate yourself from the ground by sitting on your rucksack and keeping as low to the ground as you can.

Altitude

At altitude, outdoor activities can take a heavy toll on your body.

Even people who are supremely fit are at risk from altitude-related illnesses. Those most at risk are people who are not acclimatised and try to make an ascent over around 2500 metres too fast, or those who are not yet fully acclimatised but make a quick dash up. Recent studies revealed that of those trekkers visiting Everest base camp at between 5500 and 6100 metres, something like 47 per cent suffer from the effects of altitude sickness. Altitude can also affect those suffering from medical conditions such as asthma, high blood pressure and heart conditions.

If you intend to climb to an altitude of 4500 metres or more (that's about 15,000 feet), you may consider a visit to your doctor to confirm that you are healthy enough. If you decide that it is safe for you to go you should conduct some hill training before you depart. If you are reasonably fit there is no reason why you should not be able to move freely up to 4500 metres and possibly beyond. So long as you move slowly you will move without any difficulty.

It is at this altitude that some people begin to experience an illness relating to altitude. Some people can feel the effects of acute mountain sickness or AMS at altitudes of 1800 metres above sea level. At about 3000 metres breathing can become laboured. Above 3600 metres (12,000 feet), oxygen can be scarce and a more serious form of altitude-related illness could hit, such as high altitude pulmonary edema or HAPE. Many inexperienced people climb to this height without knowing the risks from altitude-related illness. Those with medical problems such as asthma or heart problems should not go to this height.

At 4300 metres, your body will be exposed to physiological stresses as the available oxygen is depleted to around 40 per cent of what it is at sea level. Some people at this altitude are not only at risk from AMS and HAPE but are also at risk from high altitude cerebral edema or HACE. And no matter how fit you are, at an altitude of around 5500 metres (18,000 feet), the air pressure is very low and any symptoms of altitude-related illness may be constantly felt, leaving you debilitated. It is vital that those trekking or climbing to this height are monitored for any signs of HACE and HAPE.

There are a number of factors that influence the rate and effects of altitude sickness. The quicker the climb, for instance, the higher the risk. If you sleep, stay for a long time or work hard at altitude you will increase your risk. Meals high in fat and protein and a lack of fluids will heighten your risk. The ability to quickly identify the signs and symptoms of altitude-related illness are essential for those who intend trekking above 2500 metres (8000 feet). The signs and symptoms of altitude sickness can manifest themselves as quickly as 6 hours after ascending to altitude and can last between 2 and 6 days. The effects of altitude sickness are felt more when breathing rates decrease – during sleep, for instance – and hence the effects are normally worse during the night.

Acute Mountain Sickness

The symptoms of AMS include headache and a general feeling of apathy, accompanied by nausea and loss of appetite. Swelling of the face and hands is an obvious symptom. Sleep patterns are disturbed, as breathing becomes difficult and erratic. Lips, fingers, ear lobes and other extremities will become bluish (cyanosis) as a result of oxygen deficiency. AMS can be avoided by acclimatising yourself to altitude. Above 2500 metres you may require up to four days to acclimatise fully. Drink enough water and treat your headache with a mild analgesic such as aspirin. If the condition deteriorates and the symptoms worsen you can develop more severe altitude-related illness.

If someone with AMS begins to lose consciousness, get them back down to where the symptoms first began, normally a descent of about 600 metres or more. Ensure that they rest and are given plenty of water and in cold conditions, hot sweet drinks. If their condition deteriorates, get them down to an altitude where their condition improves.

High Altitude Pulmonary Edema

HAPE is a life-threatening illness caused by an abnormal build-up of fluid in the lungs. This condition rarely occurs below 2500 metres. Young men are more likely to suffer from HAPE than any other group. Symptoms of HAPE usually manifest themselves 1 to 4 days after you have climbed to altitude.They include all the signs of AMS, and short-ness of breath accompanied by a general feeling of fatigue. The person may develop a dry, rasping cough, which will develop into a produc-tive cough. They may cough up a bubbly, blood-coloured sputum. If you were to listen to their chest with a stethoscope, you would detect the rattling sound of fluid on the lungs.

The person's heart rate will be fast – as high as 110 beats a minute – and the respiration rate could be as high as 30 breaths a minute. At the first sign of these symptoms you must descend a minimum of 600 metres right away. If you have access to oxygen, give it to the casualty as soon as possible. If the person's condition deteriorates, keep descending until the symptoms disappear. Cold can intensify the effects of HAPE. If the attack of HAPE was mild, the casualty may be well enough to ascend after a few days' rest. But for those suffering from a more serious attack, they must be evacuated off the hill to a medical facility. Even those who have had mild attacks are susceptible to a relapse.

High Altitude Cerebral Edema

HACE is the most severe altitude-related illness, and is a swelling of the brain resulting from a lack of oxygen. This condition normally occurs higher than around 3600 metres, although in some people it can strike lower than this. The symptoms of HACE are weakness, disorientation, amnesia and unconsciousness. The person affected may display the other signs of AMS, as well as seizures, hallucina-tions, paralysis and disturbed vision. They may complain of a lack of feeling on one side of their body. The only real treatment for HACE is to descend as quickly as possible to an altitude where the person regains consciousness, and if you have access to oxygen you should administer it as soon as possible.

Acclimatisation

To reduce the chances of suffering from any of the altitude-related illnesses, you need to acclimatise before you climb to higher altitudes. You will need to climb slowly. Climbing too quickly will not allow your body to cope with the stresses placed on it by altitude. If above about 3000 metres (say, if trekking in Nepal), remain below that altitude for two or three days before ascending. For every additional 600 metres' height gain, spend at least one night at that altitude. Ensure that you have an adequate supply of fluids to prevent dehydration – and you will need to drink a lot of water. (The urine test will indicate if you are receiving enough fluids: it should be clear, and if it is has a yellow tinge you will need more fluids.) Avoid a high-protein diet, as this will dehydrate you; but eat a limited amount of protein to allow your body to repair tissue.

Scuba Diving

Almost every tourist resort with a coastline now offers foreign visitors, even those with little or no experience, the opportunity to explore that astounding environment which covers almost two-thirds of our planet. Scuba diving, which was once deemed to be the exclusive domain of the dedicated adventurer, is now available to those with enough money to hire the equipment. Most beach resorts employ trained staff to conduct this activity, but in some regions they are inexperienced.

This section is not intended for dedicated and qualified amateurs, but for those who are about to embark on a scuba diving course for the first time. It is one of the most thrilling adventure activities – and one of the most dangerous when things go wrong. Each year many thousands of Westerners are enticed into beach-side dive shacks with the promise of a quick course followed by an open-water dive. Most have little difficulty, but a few are injured and some killed. Even experienced divers are at serious risk from this sport: they account for just under a half of all diving accidents.

Humans do not belong in an underwater environment. To go there we need detailed instruction on what to do and what dangers to look out for, as well as sophisticated equipment and logistical support. If instructions are not followed, the equipment is faulty or the logistics are suspect, the consequences can be fatal. There are dive shops in many parts of the world which are unregulated and run by unqualified individuals who would not know what to do if trouble struck. You must consider the quality of your dive operator. That means checking the certification of those who are employed as instructors, ensuring that their equipment is safe and functional, and making sure they have contingency plans.

Before you embark on this most exciting of adventures, consider the following.

- Select a registered diving establishment. They should be British Sub Aqua Club (BSAC) or Professional Amateur Diving Institute (PADI) registered, and they should have sufficient insurance documentation. Your travel agent or tour operator should be able to put you in touch with a suitably qualified organisation.

- Have a proper medical examination before you go. You will be required to provide medical certification before you are allowed to dive. If you are not asked to provide medical proof that you are fit to dive, the organisation is flouting the rules and is probably not a properly registered company. Stay clear!

- Enquire about their procedures for dealing with decompression sickness. Where is the nearest decompression chamber and how would they propose to get you there?

- Ask your tour operator to put you in touch with someone who has dived with that organisation before. Call them up and enquire about their safety record. In addition, make sure that you are insured for this type of activity. Diving accidents can be very costly. Transport to a decompression chamber and the medical aftercare for decompression sickness can be very expensive.

- Check to ensure that they have the appropriate certification and that the instructors are qualified. You may want to check the dive instructor's log so that you feel comfortable that they are sufficiently experienced to be leading a team of novice divers. The dive leader should be a qualified dive master and in addition to that will also be trained in lifesaving emergency techniques and recognising the signs and symptoms of decompression sickness. If you do not feel happy with their documentation go to another more qualified dive club.

- Ensure that they have sufficient people to ensure the safety of those diving. Do not go diving from a boat if there is only one crew member. In addition to someone leading the dive, ideally you will require someone dedicated to handling the boat and a standby diver who is on the boat with a full set of gear ready to react if there is a problem down below. Any less than three crew members on a boat, and you will be taking a chance.

- An organised dive with a number of divers in the water at the same time is all about teamwork, and you the novice diver are looking to those in charge for guidance and safety. You should question those in charge about their intentions and safety procedures. If you are not happy with their answers or if they do not sound convincing, do not place your safety in their hands.

- If you are diving from a boat, ensure that the boat is seaworthy. If it looks a mess, this generally means that it is, and may well be unsafe. Give the engine a cursory check. If it takes too many pulls to start it or if the engine emits too much smoke it may indicate trouble. You do not want the engine to stall when you are in trouble. Check to ensure that the boat has suitable decking – a rough surface that will provide a good nonslip foothold. When a diver is putting his equipment on at sea, the last thing you need is to fall over and break something because you could not keep your footing. Additionally, a good dive boat will have strategically placed handholds that will provide support for divers standing with all that heavy equipment on.

- After you have completed your dive you may feel extremely tired. When you are hanging on the end of the boat in rough weather with heavy equipment on, you need to be able to get back onto the boat easily. Many divers have been injured trying to do this. You should ensure that the dive boat has provision for easy access, a platform at sea level, or steps that extend a metre or so beneath the water.

- Ensure that the boat is not overcrowded and there is enough room for you to manoeuvre, and that there is a life jacket for everyone in your party during the journey to the dive site. If you do not wear them during this trip, at least identify where they are and familiarise yourself with their operation.

- Ensure that the boat is carrying the appropriate equipment – a secondary propulsion unit, fire extinguishers, an emergency radio, a diver recall system (normally an underwater detonation charge which alerts divers in the area of danger), a medical first-aid pack, and an emergency supply of oxygen in order to treat decompression sickness. The boat should also have some means of assisting divers to approach the boat in a fast-flowing current. This is normally a line which can be thrown to a tired diver, or which they can grab. This line should be highly visible and attached to a float, and should stay on the surface and drift on the water from the stern of the boat.

- When you decide to go diving, stick to dives within your limits and do not be tempted to go deeper than you should. Novice divers should go no deeper than 30 metres. Decompression sickness is a real danger and everyone can be affected. You must ensure that you are physically capable of completing the dive. It can be a demanding activity and you should be in good physical condition. If during a dive you feel that you have had enough, inform the dive leader who should then escort you to the surface and attract the safety boat.

- Follow the instructions of the dive leader. He will inform you of the interval between dives and about decompression halts when you are diving. Your ascents must always be controlled and slow and even after shallow dives you should stop for a period of three to five minutes at a depth of around 5 metres. If for whatever reason your ascent goes out of control, you are in danger of having an embolism. You should try to regain control using your arms, and have your head back and your mouth open. When I went through dive training I was told that in an uncontrolled fast ascent I had to throw my head back and scream. This allows the expanding air to escape and will help prevent an embolism.

- When the dive leader is briefing his dive team he should include the route, the decompression halts if any, and the procedures for becoming lost or separated, recapping on the hand signals to be used. He should inform you of the duration of the dive and the signals for attracting the attention of crew when you surface.

- Before you set off you should check your equipment and ensure that everything is in good order and serviceable. Your instructor will go through this check with you. If you are uncertain about any article of equipment you must request that it be replaced.

- During the dive brief you will be paired off with another diver or a buddy. Essentially you look after each other during the dive. Before you get in the water, check each other's equipment and after entering the water check each other for leaks. During the dive you will continually monitor each other's equipment and health.

- Have a light meal two hours before you expect to get into the water. Don't eat right before. The last thing you want is that you throw up into your demand valve at 25 metres.

- Constantly monitor your gauges, your depth gauge and the rate at which you are using your supply of air and your time. You may on occasion find that you are using air quicker than you normally would, so it is essential that you constantly monitor your air supply. This is particularly important when using decompression stops. When I was diving once in the Philippines, one of the group ran out of air just when we started our decompression halt. He panicked and almost lost it; fortunately, the dive leader was a very experienced New Zealander who allowed him to breathe from her set. Do not be tempted to stay down longer than the time agreed during your dive brief.

- While you are diving and you feel yourself begin to labour and your respiration rate increases, it can seem a bit much. Some novice divers have panicked. Control yourself, alert your buddy, stop and take deep even breaths. If you still feel you have had enough, inform your buddy, make a controlled ascent and attract the attention of the safety boat.

- If you are concerned about the weather or the sea conditions, or if you feel that the dive is too deep, or even if you are feeling slightly unwell, cancel the dive until you feel more confident.

- You should never hire gear and go diving on your own. There are many shops that will allow you to hire equipment even without the proper documentation. If you do this you are taking a big risk, and with an organisation like this the chances are that the equipment will not have been well maintained.

- Check the local weather conditions before you set out. If the weather is rough you should abort your dive until it improves. Remember that thunderstorms are often accompanied by lightning strikes and water is a good conductor of electricity. You do not want to be bobbing around in the sea during a thunderstorm.

- Remember that when you are in the water, you may be exposed to extremes of temperature. Even in the tropics it can still be cold at 20 metres. Ensure that you are wearing the appropriate clothing while you are diving. In warm water, if you have to work hard there is a possibility that you could overheat. The salt water, combined with the warm temperature and your workload, can leave you dehydrated. Drink enough water to top up after your dive.

- Ensure that you do not intend to fly within 24 hours after finishing your dive. There will be a possibility that the changes in pressure can result in decompression sickness. The nitrogen in your body will not have had time to dissipate and you could increase your chances of decompression sickness.

Bungee Jumping

Bungee jumping has proliferated amazingly round the world. In almost every holiday hotspot drawing the young and adventurous there seems to be a bungee jumping organisation. The only qualification you need is the money to pay for it. For most you do not need to provide medical certification, have previous experience or even be sober. In many Western countries these organisations must comply with stringent safety regulations, but abroad it may be completely unregulated.

Obviously, this is a potentially fatal activity, and it is normally subject to detailed planning and tight regulations. But the spate of injuries and fatalities caused by it indicate that there is very little by way of an international code of practice. So where the issue of safety is high on the agenda, you will get what you pay for: a thrilling, death-defying dive off a dizzyingly high platform, followed by a series of ever-diminishing elasticated bounces. When you stop you will be lowered to the ground and released unharmed, probably greatly relieved that your quest for a near-death experience is satiated. But if this fairly simple activity is not regulated or is run by slack organisations, the consequences can be tragic.

Reputable bungee jumping clubs will try to minimise the exposure to danger. But it has been estimated that the vast majority of bungee jumping accidents have been caused by simple human error. In June 2001, a young woman was killed and her friend injured after plummeting to the ground during a bungee jump in France. The jump organiser was blamed for the tragedy as he reportedly had failed to select an elastic rope that could support the weight of both jumpers. The rope snapped and the woman was killed when she hit the ground. If you are longing to go on a bungee jump, consider the following points first.

- Ensure that the company you intend using is a registered, legitimate bungee-jumping operator. Ensure that the instructors – jumpmasters – are qualified, knowledgeable and experienced. There are many operators out to make quick buck who have little or no training or poor equipment. The first person ever to die while bungee jumping was killed when the operators failed to attach the rope properly at their end. The cord was in fact hooked over a nail and simply came off. In addition, as with any adventure activity, get insured.

- There are a number of ways you can be attached to the cord – by wearing a body harness, or by an ankle, leg or arm attachment. Whatever the type, your life depends on the fact that it is correctly attached. If the attachment looks worn or if it is does not fit you properly, refuse to jump.

- There have been reported incidents where people have fallen off the crane as it was being elevated to the jump station. You must ensure that you are attached to the crane before it leaves the ground. Do not allow yourself to be attached to the bungee cord before you leave the ground. There is a possibility that the cord could become tangled.

- In many companies the jump station or jump platform may have different lengths of rope for different jump heights. They should be differently coloured and marked to indicate which size they are. Be sure that you question the jumpmaster about the rope size. If you are not happy with his response, don't jump.

- There are bungee jumping operators who reportedly offer what is considered to be dangerous practices. Tandem jumping is where two people jump together at the same time. As there are two people bouncing uncontrollably on elastic ropes in a relatively small space, there is a danger that they will crash into each other or even become entangled in each other's ropes. Unless they are very experienced and there is sufficient space between jumpers, you should avoid this.

- Another practice is known as sandbagging, where the jumper holds a heavy weight while jumping. The idea is that you release the weight after you reach the bottom of the jump. Due to the fact that you were heavier on the way down, the amount of energy generated by the elastic cord is greater on the way up than if you had jumped holding nothing. This way you can go higher than the platform from which you jumped. The risk is that you may actually be catapulted into the platform.

- Ensure that the weather conditions are good before you decide to jump. If the wind is strong, it may affect your trajectory while you are jumping and it may be unsafe to jump. If it is raining or has recently rained and the cord has been exposed to moisture, this may affect the elasticity of the cord and once more this may become unsafe.

- You must ensure that any equipment used during the bungee jump is secured before you make the jump. Many bungee jumpers are secured to the cord by means of a carabiner or a similar spring-loaded device, which must be screwed shut in order to be locked into position. You must ensure that this is done. There have been accidents where people have been injured after falling because these devices have come undone after safety staff failed to close them properly.

■ Do not go on a bungee jump if you have been drinking alcohol. Not only will this impair your judgement; it may also make you more willing to take risks and less likely to question the safety procedures of the jump organisers.

■ It is a good idea to check that the ropes are laid out in such a way that they are allowed to run smoothly. If they become snagged or tangled in any way you could be injured.

■ Many bungee jumping organisations use a safety rope, an additional cord secured to the jumper in case the main one breaks. There have been incidents reported where the main cord has snapped and the safety cord was the wrong length.

■ If the rope looks worn or frayed, don't jump. The ropes have a shelf life which is measured in the maximum amount of jumps it is safe to do before it must be replaced. It has been suggested that some bungee jumping operators exceed the maximum number of jumps for their ropes.

■ Bungee jumping is most popular in hot and sunny holiday resorts. The ropes can be affected by exposure to direct sunlight. The shelf life of the ropes must also take into account the maximum amount of time that they should be exposed to ultraviolet rays. If you want to jump, it may be better to do so in the morning before the ropes have been exposed to an entire day of high temperatures and ultraviolet exposure.

Whitewater Rafting

It's some people's idea of fun: hurtling downstream through violent, foaming waves in a rocky gorge so narrow the water spews through the gaps as if fired from a high-pressure hose, and huge rocks loom left and right, only for the rush of water to divert your rubber dinghy away from oblivion at the last minute. And yes, it is exciting, and incredibly dangerous. You have little or no control in a rubber dinghy, and are trussed up in a life jacket careering helplessly downstream.

You may feel ecstatic when you've managed to 'negotiate' such a stretch of river and finally reach calmer waters. Others have not been so fortunate. There are fatalities every year, as untrained tour guides take inexperienced tourists on the ride of their life – or the last ride of their lives.

White-water courses are graded 1 to 6, and it is possible to descend 1 to 5 in an inflatable dinghy. The higher the number, the rougher the ride. Essentially, you do not have to have any experience in rafting, just a fistful of cash before you are allowed to take the plunge. After you are kitted out and take your place in the dinghy, you are at the mercy of the river. Even though you are equipped with a paddle, these are of little use in such fierce water.

Before you take the plunge, slash through fiercely surging waves, whizz around whirlpools and narrowly miss chunks of rock by a metre or so, you might want to consider the following points.

- Ensure those who are qualified to do so are conducting this activity. It's a dangerous sport and the risks are high if they get it wrong. Ask at your travel agent's, tour guide or hotel about the details of this outfit, and check them out. Also check before you leave that your insurance company are aware that you intend to conduct this activity. People have suffered broken limbs, concussion and other injuries that have required hospital attention.

- Do not just show up at a rafting station and jump into the first raft that shows up. Nor should you just accept offers being touted on the streets of the local resort. Go to an authorised outlet.

- Before you get into the raft, give it the once-over. If it looks too worn, and there are too many patches, you should consider another boat. You must ensure that a safety boat is available. This should be used to rescue those in trouble. It will be unable to negotiate the rapids, but will wait downstream in calm water waiting to catch those who have been ejected from the boat.

■ Speak to those who are conducting the rafting, and make sure you are comfortable that they know what they are doing. Ask some pointed questions, and listen to the instructions. This is particularly important for actions on what to do if the boat capsizes or if you are ejected from the boat.

■ You will be required to sign an indemnity certificate, which basically means that if anything happens to you the company are not responsible. Refuse to sign if you are not happy, and do not sign or hand over your cash until you are certain that they know what they are doing.

■ Ensure that when you try on your equipment, crash helmet and life jacket, that they fit you and will not fall off during the action. Ensure that the straps and fasteners are in good order and that the vests and helmets are not damaged. Damaged helmets will not perform as they should, and you need to be able to depend on them.

■ When you get into the craft, do not tie yourself or attach yourself in any way to it. If the dinghy were to capsize and you are attached to it you will be swept off with it, and there is a possibility that you will be trapped under it.

■ Listen out for the instructions of the tour guide. Assuming they know what they are doing, they should instruct who should paddle, when and how hard in order to steer the boat. This may be difficult with the noise, and the helmet covering your ears, but you must pay attention.

■ If you witness someone fall overboard while rafting, do not jump in after them. There is very little you will be able to do, all that will happen is that you will exert all your energy keeping yourself afloat, and there will be two people in the water instead of one.

■ If you find yourself in fast-flowing water, try to get away from rocks by staying in the main stream of the water. Even in very small waterfalls, the currents can take you under. What happens is that the force of the water dropping forms a swirling current at the bottom of the rocks. This action can form a current beneath the waves, which can be difficult to get out of, even with a life jacket.

- If you were to become trapped in such a position, you are in big trouble. The wave will toss you around in a circular motion. The suggested method for escaping from this is to keep composed. Wait until the wave takes you down, where you can use your legs to propel yourself upwards and break through the cyclical motion of the water.

14

Dangerous Animals

PERHAPS THE MOST FRIGHTENING ANIMAL ENCOUNTER you've ever had was with a snarling dog. Certainly in Britain and most parts of Europe, encountering a big, dangerous wild animal is the stuff of fairy tales. But in many countries, getting off the beaten track or out of cities means you could encounter some fairly unpredictable beasts.

As travel has become easier and more remote regions are opened up, more and more of us are entering the habitats of wild creatures. And it's not only the large, carnivorous animals – lions, for instance – that are dangerous. There are biting and stinging insects, biting spiders and scorpions, poisonous snakes, and vermin such as rats. (Then there are sharks, which I've discussed in Chapter 5, page 136.) People are killed or injured by wild animals every year, but it is usually because they do not know what to expect or how to behave. For the animals, an encounter with humans is a danger and a threat – we are encroaching on their domain, and they will do their best to avoid contact. Unfortunately, many tourists harbour mistaken ideas of 'befriending' wild creatures.

African safaris and wilderness treks, for instance, are largely about the animals, and tour company brochures and commercials promote the experience of living among them as the ultimate adventure. But it's not all back to Eden. Tourists have been killed and injured after unexpected encounters with bears. They have been bitten by dogs, eaten by lions and trampled to death by bull elephants. And many of these incidents have occurred when tour guides were actually present. If we're going into the wild, we must cultivate at least a basic understanding of and respect for the creatures we may encounter.

Dogs

In Britain there are strict quarantine regulations on dogs which minimise exposure to diseases like rabies and dog-transmitted tetanus. In many other countries, dogs run wild. In some they are kept for protection only, and in others dogs roam around in feral packs. In some regions these animals have lost their fear of man and attack people. In the US, there are an estimated 800,000 dog bites each year, most from pets attacking in the home. The animals assessed as most dangerous are pit bull terriers, Rottweilers, Alsatians, huskies and Dobermans.

When you are travelling abroad, you should consider the following points:

- If when you arrive at your destination and you see dogs running wild in the area, there are a number of indicators that will enable you to assess how these animals will behave. The breeds of dog mentioned above have a genetic predisposition towards aggressive behaviour. Observe how the local people treat their animals. If they are mistreated, they are more likely to be aggressive towards humans.

- In exceptionally hot weather, dogs will also be more aggressive towards people. If the animal seems ill and is, say, foaming at the mouth, avoid it as it may have rabies.

- If you are out walking and you see a dog or a pack of dogs, give them a wide berth. By invading the animal's territory you will have issued a challenge and are likely to be attacked.

- Avoid a female dog if it is accompanied by its pups. The dog will consider any approach to be a threat and will instinctively attack. If you see a pack of dogs and there are young pups with them, avoid them.

- Do not try to threaten a dog if it is in your way. If you charge at the animal or pick up a stick or rock to throw at it, it may attack you. This is especially important if there is a pack of dogs. They will act more aggressively than an individual animal on its own.

- Do not let your children approach stray dogs when you are travelling overseas. Do not allow them to approach a dog that is sleeping. The animal's reaction will be to lash out if it is caught unawares.

- Do not tease dogs as if they were family pets at home. You do not know what treatment the animal has been subject to, and you will not be able to tell if the animal is ill. If you are travelling with children, it's vital to educate them in how to react when they are confronted by a dog. Tell them never to approach a stray, particularly if you have a pet dog at home and they think of dogs in general as cuddly.

- Never go too close to an animal, especially in developing countries; and never put your face close to the dog. As well as danger from the animal biting, the area of your mouth is a prime route in for any infection that the dog may be carrying.

- Never get too close to an animal if it is eating. It will consider this a threat and may attack you. You should never approach a pack of wild dogs if they are eating or if they are fighting. The animals are already excited and it will take only a slight intrusion into their territory to trigger an attack.

- If you find yourself confronted by an aggressive dog, never challenge the animal by screaming at it or staring it in the eye. An aggressive animal will accept this as a challenge and react violently. If a dog approaches you snarling and baring its teeth, do not run off; the animal will become more confident and will chase you. You should stand your ground, avoid staring it in the eye, remain still and do not flinch.

- If you are intending to travel to an area where rabies is present, you might consider a rabies vaccination. This is available from your local doctor, but you will have to make arrangements weeks in advance to give your doctor enough time to get supplies of the vaccination.

- If you are bitten by a dog while abroad, seek medical attention immediately. Even if the animal only grazes you, go to a doctor. The saliva of a rabid dog can transmit the disease through even the smallest graze in your skin. Your children must inform you if they come into contact with a dog, even if it does not bite them.

African Animals

The 'big game' of Africa have been celebrated in literature and legend, and for many of us are the ultimate exotics. But while they are both beautiful and fascinating, many of them are also exceedingly dangerous. I discuss the real bruisers below.

Hippopotamus

Adult hippos are one of the most dangerous animals in Africa. A fully grown bull hippo can weigh up to three tonnes. These huge creatures spend much of their time wallowing in water, which must be around 2 metres deep for them to submerge. Hippos are also seen roaming up to 2 kilometres away from water to feed, and have even been known to wander up to 30 kilometres in search of grazing ground. When threatened, they can use their teeth as weapons and have been known to kill each other fighting.

If you're in a small boat on a body of water, remember that hippos can be almost totally submerged and difficult to see from a boat. They have attacked boats for getting too close and people have been killed. If you are on a hippo-spotting tour, consider the following.

- As with all activities, ensure you are using authorised and qualified organisations. Make sure the boat is seaworthy and the crew have adequate safety equipment. Everyone on the boat must have a life preserver and there should be radiocommunications between the boat and the lodge/ranger post. Guides should have a high-powered rifle with them.

■ Hippos will spend their days resting in or near the water. Particularly when the sun is hot, they seek refuge in water. If the water is shallow they can charge at boats that come too close. When they submerge they can stay beneath the surface for up to six minutes, although some have been known to stay under for almost half an hour. Be aware that when they submerge they can come up anywhere, so you must ensure that you never get too close.

■ Hippos become active during the night when they move ashore to feed. They normally graze within 2 kilometres of the water's edge. If you are on an overnight safari and camp near a lake, be aware that hippos are likely to make an appearance around the water-side. They normally make their way back to the water by daylight. During the rainy season, however, they will stay closer to the water's edge. They use paths to travel to their grazing areas and have been attacked by lions on the paths. Be aware that if you are in an area which hippos use to move to and from the water, there may be lions in the area.

■ When a hippo feels threatened it will yawn. This characteristic trait is a signal to back off. On seeing this behaviour, many tourists try to get closer for a better photograph or video. Be aware that the creature is telling you to back off, and that getting any closer may invite a charge. Remember, more yawning means that the animal is becoming more aggressive.

■ If you see a female hippo (normally smaller than the male) with young hippos, back off to a safe distance. Female hippos with young are extremely aggressive and will even charge a pride of lions – or a boat – to protect their young. Bull hippos will attack to protect the females.

■ If hippos are disturbed suddenly they are more inclined to charge, especially if their young accompany them. It is a good idea to make a noise as you approach an area where you expect to encounter hippos.

- If you come across one hippo you should be on your guard; there will inevitably be more in the vicinity. Hippos live in large groups of up to 50 animals and the entire group can become aggressive if approached.

- Contrary to popular belief, hippos are very mobile on land and can travel swiftly over open ground. If confronted by a hippo on shore, get into an area of thick vegetation. Hippos find it difficult to manoeuvre in thick vegetation, and so do not go there. If you are observing hippos from the bank of a river or a lake, position yourself on a steep bank, as they cannot climb steep ground.

Rhinoceros

One of the most spectacular animals of the African plains, the rhino is also one of the most dangerous if you get too close. White rhinos are bigger than black rhinos, and second only to elephants in size. They are extremely short-sighted and rely on an exceptionally acute sense of smell to get around. They spend much of their time grazing on grassland, although they will sleep during the hottest hours of the day and resume their never-ending quest for food in the cooler hours.

The rhino is normally a solitary animal, although they can be found in groups with one dominating bull rhino. Before you visit rhino country, consider the following points.

- Rhinos can attack without being provoked, and have been known to charge safari vehicles. They can run over short distances at speeds of up to 55 kilometres per hour.

- Rhinos – mainly white rhinos – live on the flat plains in open woodland, with easy access to grazing. A safari warden should accompany you if you walk in such areas.

- When you are observing rhinos during a safari, stay downwind of them so the wind carries your scent away from the animal. Avoid using strong-smelling toiletries; if the rhino picks up your scent it could charge, or bolt and disappear.

- If you are caught out in the open and a rhino gets wind of your scent, you will be unable to outrun the animal. If a rhino attacks from close in, hold your ground and wait until it is near, then jump out of its path. The momentum of the rhino's charge will carry it some way before it can turn round. You will at least have some time to get out of the way. If you are near a substantial tree, climb it. Be aware that a rhino can easily knock over small trees.

- As most of us know, poachers hunt rhino for their horn. As a result, armed response units patrol the game reserves. Do not go out on your own in unauthorised groups, or you might be mistaken for poachers.

- Avoid female rhinos with young – they are exceptionally aggressive. Stay in the safari vehicle.

Crocodiles

Crocodiles have been around since the time of the dinosaur and have remained essentially unchanged since then. These predatory reptiles live in rivers, lakes, swamps and estuaries and their banks. In Africa, they are regarded with great respect, and no wonder: they can weigh as much as 1000 kilograms, and measure more than 3.5 metres in length.

The creatures can't move quickly when out of the water, although they can move relatively quickly over short distances. They attack with amazing speed and with a sideways swipe of the head, inflicting grievous injuries. Crocodiles have been known to grab humans who venture too close, drag them into the water and do a 'death roll', spinning the victim underwater until they have drowned.

Before you venture into croc country, consider these points.

- Crocodiles often sun themselves during the day. When disturbed, they scamper into the water and submerge. In known crododile habitat, avoid getting near water, riverbanks or lakeshores alone. Go with a trained park ranger who knows the animal's behaviour and is armed with a high-velocity rifle. If you are on a boat safari, ensure the boat is seaworthy and that you are issued with a life preserver.

- If you see even a small crocodile, there will probably be others nearby. They are excellent swimmers and will easily outswim you if you fall in. If someone does fall in, don't jump in after them. Use a pole or a rope in order to assist them, and be quick: the vibrations of someone struggling in the water will attract crocodiles.

- Crocodiles tend to hide in heavy vegetation at the water's edge, waiting to ambush their victims. Use caution in such areas, and avoid patches of vegetation, staying to open spaces where you can see all around. If a crocodile surprises you, run away fast. Some people advise using a zigzag motion, as the animal's bulk and short legs mean it cannot change direction quickly.

- Crocodile nests are mounds of mud and vegetation, and the mother crocodile remains near it for the entire incubation period. If you stumble across one, get away as fast as possible. The mother will attack if she feels that the nest is being threatened.

Bears

Brown bears live in the wild in Canada and other areas of North America, Russia and a few spots in Europe. They're known as grizzlies in North America, where black bears also abound. Both black and brown bears have killed and maimed people. You need to understand their behaviour before you go into the wilderness.

In North America, grizzlies can be brown, yellowish, reddish, or almost black. Confusingly, black bears can also be brown. Grizzlies are identifiable by their much larger size, shorter muzzle and distinctive shoulder hump. Bears generally spend a lot of time hibernating, in some parts of the world two-thirds of the year. Out of hibernation, they are voracious. They are very inventive in their quest for food – and this is the main reason they react aggressively when they encounter humans. Their keen sense of smell and huge appetite mean they find our food irresistible, and easy pickings.

In North America, bears can be active from late February to December. If you are heading to an area where bears are common, ask locals or park rangers when the animals are active. The riskiest times are when the animals are feeding before winter hibernation, when the females are giving birth and when they are accompanied by their cubs.

If you are heading on a trekking or even driving holiday in bear country, consider the following.

■ Research your trip. Find out where the bears are and learn about their habits from guidebooks and tourist brochures, and park rangers once you get to the area. Plan your route and tell some-one all the details – departure and arrival, the route itself and so on. Check whether you need to register or hire a guide before entering the area. Ask about any recent bear attacks.

■ If you are warned to stay out of an area because of bear activity, do so, and mark the area on your map. Know what signs to look for – bear tracks, feeding areas and droppings. Ask locals about bear sightings. Likewise, if you see a bear tell everyone you meet.

■ Hike with a friend or group in bear country. Bears are more likely to attack someone on their own.

■ Take a rucksack. Then, if you meet a bear you can at least throw the pack with your food in it at the animal. This may give you enough time to get away.

■ Bears react aggressively if startled, so make a lot of noise as you walk, particularly in areas of dense vegetation, near loud rivers, or on windy days when your scent may not reach them. You want them to know you're there so they can leave. Avoid using perfumed products such as highly scented soaps, perfumes, deodorants, sunscreens and insect repellants. All these may smell like food to bears, and attract their attention.

■ Whether hiking or camping, store all your food in airtight plastic containers and plastic bags. Double-bag any strong-smelling foods such as cheese. Never leave any food lying around, even if you are only stopping for a break, and especially at night when you're in a tent or caravan. Also bag all your rubbish. If you need to leave your camp for a while, bag your food and suspend it from a high tree branch by a rope.

- Stay on designated trekking routes. If the bears associate an area with humans, they will be less likely to go there. If you have to get off the trail, be cautious, make a lot of noise and avoid areas of dense vegetation.

- When you go to the toilet, move off your trail about 100 metres. Ensure that the wind is at your back, dig a hole half a foot deep, and bury it. Double-bag used toilet paper or any other materials and take them with you.

- Ask park rangers for the latest advice on how to survive bear encounters. Advice tends to differ for different species. If you encounter a black bear, stand and make yourself look as large as possible – put your arms up in the air – and make a lot of noise to scare the bear off. With a grizzly, stand your ground. Do not make any sudden movements. If you are carrying food, leave it on the ground and gently back off. If the grizzly gets very close or charges, get down on your stomach, tuck in your knees and link your hands over the back of your neck. Play dead.

- If you encounter a cub, back off immediately in the direction that you have just come to avoid getting attacked by the mother.

- At night tightly close your tent door. Torches, whistles and even firecrackers are good for frightening prowling bears away at night. If you are living in a caravan or mobile home, secure the windows.

- If you see bears on the road while you're driving, never get out of the vehicle or roll down the window, and never feed them. Tell your children the same.

- Be cautious if you have an open wound or, for women, if it's your period. Bears can smell and be attracted to blood over great distances.

- Bear repellent spray is relatively effective. Buy an established brand. It comes as an aerosol with a range of about 5 to 7 metres, and will stop a bear from attacking if you spray at that range and make sure you don't spray into the wind. If you hear a loud noise you think may be a bear, spray that area and as you retreat, periodically spray to prevent the animal from following.

Snakes

Snakes are most common in warm climates – particularly warm, moist ones. They can be very numerous in remote regions. I have had many encounters with snakes and have never yet been bitten; I put this down to a healthy respect for the animal and a bit of luck. In Cyprus I was out running and I noticed a large black object. Just in time I realised what it was and jumped as high as I could. The snake struck out and just missed me.

Be prepared if you are going to a place known for its snakes. A poisonous snakebite in a remote area could spell disaster. The rule with a snake is that they generally just want to escape. So always try to allow the snake to get away before it feels cornered. If cornered, it will strike.

If you're venturing into snake country, check out these points.

- Before you set off on your trip, research which species of snakes inhabit the area. If you're about to make a wilderness trek, ask at the nearest medical facility whether there have been any recent cases of snakebite, where and when it happened, what type of snake it was and whether they have stocks of the right anti-venom. Buy a suction device for getting venom out of snakebites before you go.

- In snake country, don't just barrel along. Move cautiously and deliberately, looking where you put your feet. Remember that in forested areas snakes may be hanging from tree branches.

- As they're coldblooded, snakes bask in the sun during the day. Move cautiously over areas exposed to direct sunlight, particularly patches of sunlight in forests or jungle. Be wary of drainage ditches, piles of wood, wet and moist patches of earth, still pools, deep grass and abandoned buildings. They can be anywhere: at the age of two my son found one in his bedroom in Brunei.

- Snakes are superbly camouflaged and will not move until the very last moment, so they're hard to spot. As you walk, look left and right in a sweeping motion and do not forget to check above in forested areas. Make a noise as you walk and the snake will probably get out of your way before you even arrive.

- Snakes may be attracted to certain foods, particularly uncooked meats. If you are in a remote area, be sure any food is sealed in an airtight container and packed away.

- When you camp in forested areas where snakes are a threat, sleeping in a hammock is safer. By impregnating the ends of your hammock and shelter with a strong insect repellent, you can deter any inquisitive snakes from disturbing your sleep.

- If you are trekking through an area where snakes are a threat, wear long trousers and ankle-high leather boots. In the morning, check your shoes: snakes will seek out warm moist holes and shelter there. Try placing two stakes of wood in the ground, and put your boots upside down on each stake to keep snakes or crawling insects out.

- Snakes like small, dark, secluded niches. Never put your hands into holes in the ground or in walls. If you are climbing up a tree or over an obstacle make sure that your foot and handholds are clear.

- Some snakes live in water. In warm climates, you'll have to check the shores of any lakes or pools before you camp there or even sit down, and be very wary when swimming.

- If you encounter a snake, back off and leave.

- In some snake-ridden areas, hiring a local guide with the right knowledge may be the sensible option.

- If you or someone who is travelling with you is unlucky enough to be bitten by a snake, note carefully what type it is. You must be able to identify its markings, colour and size, and where and when the incident took place. You may have to kill the snake if you can avoid getting bitten; if you bring it in with you when you are transporting the casualty to medical help, the doctor can then know precisely which anti-venom to administer.

- Stay with the person and send someone else for help if you can. If you are just two or on your own you must deal with the injury and as quickly as possible get to an area where you can summon assistance.

- Ensure the snake has gone, then move the victim to a safe area; there is no use in your getting bitten too. Depending on the snake and the site of the bite the victim may be in a life-threatening situation. Stay calm and look in control to help both yourself and the casualty.

- First find the bite. Remove any restrictive clothing and even jewellery. Tie a bandage above the site of the injury and bandage down to the site of the wound. This is to stop the venom from moving via the bloodstream any further into the body.

- Do not attempt to suck out the venom with your mouth. It's a toxic substance and you will make yourself ill, or worse. If you do have access to a suction device, usually a small rubber cup, apply it to the bite as soon as you can and apply strong suction. If you don't have one of these you can improvise with a flexible plastic bottle. Try to expel all the air to make a vacuum and apply suction. Venom can act quickly and destroy tissue, so the quicker you act the better.

- Clean the site of the wound with an antiseptic or alcohol to remove any residual venom. If you can, apply an ice pack to the area of the injury without interfering with the suction process. Don't leave the ice pack on for too long, as this will increase the chances of a cold injury.

- Immobilise the limb in a splint, and keep it lower than the level of the heart.

- Monitor the person for signs of shock. Keep them warm and still. If they move around, their heart rate and blood flow will increase and the venom will spread faster.

- You need to get the person to medical assistance quickly. It's best to keep them lying down and immobile, but if you can't, it is more important to get them there in any way you can.

Stinging Insects, Spiders and Scorpions

In Europe, a mosquito bite may annoy, but elsewhere it could transmit malaria. Developing countries generally harbour more insects, as they don't control them as rigorously as in the West; but dangerous biting insects, spiders and scorpions exist throughout the world. Most bites are not medical emergencies, and you can treat them yourself. Others will be very serious and you'll need medical attention. In any case, prevention is all, and if you know what to look out for it will be half the battle.

In one of my jungle excursions we had made camp deep in the jungle. I put up my hammock and shelter and decided to get some sleep. A few hours later I woke and heard a very low, dull noise. I reached for my torch, clicked it on and found the area beneath my hammock, the entire jungle floor and many of the surrounding trees moving. These were red fire ants – small, but with a very painful bite. I had treated my hammock straps and the ties from my jungle shelter with a powerful insect repellent, and when I woke in the morning I wasn't bitten – and every ant was gone.

To avoid getting any disastrous bites, just be sensible and bring what you need. If you know you are allergic to wasp or bee stings or bites, for instance, bring an adrenaline pen to counter any reaction. You'll need adequate supplies and a letter from your doctor describing what it is and what it is for in case you need to get more. If you are going to a malarial area, do the research to find out which strain is prevalent there, then take the appropriate prophylaxis. A strong insect repellent will reduce overall risk.

Remember, some developing countries will be teeming with an amazing array of creepy-crawlies. Here's what you can do to make the experience safer.

- When buying insect repellent, stick with what you know. Take enough – it may not be available abroad.

- Wear long trousers and long sleeves before you go out. In malarial areas it's vital at dawn and dusk, as this is when female mosquitoes feed. Get advice from local people on the key times for covering up.

- Apply insect repellent on all exposed areas of skin. In areas with major insect problems, impregnate your clothing and shoes with repellent.

- If you are travelling in rainforest, consider tucking the bottom of your trousers into your boots, and applying a liberal amount of repellent over the area. This will prevent small ground-living insects and creatures like leeches from crawling up your boot and onto your legs. Reapply repellent daily.

- Leeches are a problem in moist rainforests, woods, and around rivers and streams. They are essentially harmless, and you may not even feel them bite. They will attach themselves anywhere but prefer areas where they will not be exposed. After they have finished feeding they will just drop off. However, the wound they leave can become infected. Apply insect repellent to keep them off. At the end of each day inspect your body for leeches. Apply a small amount of insect repellent and they will drop off. Wipe the wound with an alcohol wipe and keep it clean.

- When bitten some people get small bumps and others sore, itchy and infected areas. In either case apply a topical cream such as Eurax or a substance like topical Benadryl to stop the itching. Or try a recommended local solution. If something big like a large horsefly bit you, clean the area and cover it with a sterile dressing.

- Tick bites are irritating and can itch. Some ticks spread disease, and if you do not catch them early they can burrow into your skin and will be difficult to get out. If you are in an area where ticks are a problem, check yourself each day. Remove them with tweezers; pull slowly but firmly until the tick lets go. If you pull too fast the head may stay imbedded and infect the site. Swab the bite with antiseptic.

- Hornet and wasp stings can be very painful (or life-threatening). Many nest in the ground, so be careful about where you put your feet in a remote area. Or their nests can hang in trees or bushes. Sometimes they give their presence away with a gentle buzz. If you detect any hornets or wasps, take a different route.

- If someone is stung by hornets or wasps, give them an antihistamine tablet and monitor them for signs of deterioration. If they are stung repeatedly, consider taking them to a medical facility. Certain types of aggressive hornet can sting up to 10 times in quick succession.

- Hornets and wasps are really only a problem during the day, as generally people do not move around these areas at night. However, there are many creatures attracted by light at night, from torches, candles or fires. One of the fiercest is the night hornet, a solitary, large black hornet with a painful sting that is found all over South East Asia.

- When a bee stings it will leave a barbed sack containing the toxins behind. This painful sting can be removed by scraping the surface of the skin with your fingernail or a hard sharp-edged object. The sting will leave a characteristic red circular patch with a small puncture mark on the skin. The area of the wound must be cleaned, and if possible an ice pack should be applied to minimise the swelling. The person should be monitored to see if they suffer from anaphylactic shock.

- Bites from insects such as the horse fly are dangerous, as in parts of South America they are responsible for the spread of serious diseases such as leishmaniasis. They have a painful bite and the wound often becomes infected. Seek medical attention if you're bitten by a horse fly. Even in locations where the horse fly does not spread disease, you should clean up the wound even if it is just to prevent it from becoming infected.

- If someone with you is bitten many times by small insects such as ants or biting flies, monitor their condition for an adverse reaction. Repeated bites, each carrying a small load of toxins, may cause an adverse reaction.

- Spider and scorpion bites can be serious: there are species of both which can cause severe reactions. A black widow spider bite can make you ill but rarely kills. In Africa and Asia there are spiders and scorpions whose bites can be fatal if left untreated. Be aware of where you are putting your hands. Do not grab onto branches or put your hands down holes. Check your boots in the morning before putting them on, and check your equipment when you repack after spending time outdoors.

■ If someone is bitten by a spider and you do not know which species it is, treat the injury as if it were a snakebite (see page 328). This will ensure that if they were bitten by something serious at least you will have it covered. Some spiders, like the brown recluse, can cause serious tissue damage around the area of the wound. If a spider – especially a brown recluse, tarantula or black widow – has bitten someone, get them to a medical facility fast. First apply an ice pack over the bite and keep that area below the level of the heart.

■ If a scorpion stings someone and they are not suffering a major reaction, give them antihistamine and a painkiller. The person should be prevented from doing anything strenuous.

■ Sometimes scorpion bites swell up excessively, and cause moderate to high pain. If the person bitten is suffering a serious reaction, they may develop a fever and complain of feeling nauseated, vomit and develop difficulty in breathing. They need to get to a medical facility fast.

15

Dangerous Places

YOU CAN TRAVEL ANYWHERE ON EARTH, if you know what you are doing. Even the most high-risk country can be reached if you appreciate the dangers involved: the crime rate, drugs, civil unrest, war, endemic diseases, harsh or taxing climates, poverty, social and minority group inequalities – the list is endless. Of course, what one traveller considers dangerous may be totally acceptable to another. So with all these factors, it's very hard to identify which countries are the most dangerous; but in this chapter I've attempted to do just that.

For many of us, travelling to high-risk countries is a challenge that fulfils our sense of adventure. I wrote this chapter in what was, by anyone's standards, probably one of the most dangerous locations on this planet: Kandahar, Afghanistan. It is a devastated city where poverty has reached an almost biblical scale and everyone is armed to the teeth. I entered the city within days of its surrender to the alliance forces and stayed there for a month through Christmas and New Year 2001. The place teemed with menacing, battle-hardened men armed with the ubiquitous AK47s or RPG rocket launchers. Although there were many hostile faces in the crowds we attracted, there were no direct attacks other than throwing stones and shouting. One thing that was noticeable was the absence of the anarchy that almost always accompanies military defeat. We were able to move around more or less freely although we were always accompanied by armed guards (in some cases as many as 50). This almost orderly transition from war to relative stability was, I think, down to war weariness – and the fact that there is no alcohol. I firmly believe there would have been much more disruption and indiscriminate violence during that period after military collapse had the Afghan culture permitted the use of alcohol.

There are many other countries in the grip of violence. In Jamaica, 1100 people were murdered in 2001. The authorities have tried to shield the tourist industry from the raging drugs war but tourists have been caught up in the trouble. The US, of course, has had a tragic and ongoing affair with the gun. In the past 20 years there, an estimated 600,000 people have died in gun-related incidents, almost as many as have died in the Afghan wars over the same period. Since 11 September 2001, the stakes have been raised and terrorism is a part of the American scene.

These are dangerous countries. But it has to be said that absolute safety is a myth. After the violence of 2001, anyone who thinks that there is going to be a sudden outbreak of rationality and peace in the world is a hopeful idealist. Even apparently stable nations can suddenly go haywire. Security situations can and do change quickly: in the normally peaceful Argentina, political and economic meltdown provoked riots and violence in many cities, leaving scores dead and a precarious security situation over Christmas 2001. In the same period, the tension between India and Pakistan escalated almost to nuclear boiling point as both of these poor countries deployed weapons and troops to their shared border.

Travelling to dangerous and volatile areas can make us feel very afraid and full of uncertainty. Worrying simply leaves you feeling physically drained and unable to function, however. The cure is simply facing your fear, which over time will help you raise your fear threshold. You'll better understand your own body's reaction to danger – the rapidly increasing heart rate, tightening muscles and surging adrenaline. And then you can channel this energy into positive action, which will give you a better chance of surviving life-threatening situations. It's healthy to be afraid in the face of danger, and using that fear will help you minimise risk in a dangerous situation. In terms of travel, you'll have much more of the world to visit.

In the late 1990s an organisation called World Pulse conducted a survey of the most dangerous countries and cities in the world at that time. Using a rating scale from 1 to 10, with 10 being the most dangerous, the safest countries included Japan, Paraguay, and the UK; next were countries such as the US, Belize and Brazil; and the most dangerous place on earth was deemed to be – Afghanistan. By my own estimation, this last list should now include quite a number of others, among them Algeria, Somalia, Sierra Leone, Liberia, Burundi, Israel and Nigeria. I discuss these trouble hotspots below. Remember: this is not an exhaustive list. Situations change, and danger can be encountered anywhere. This chapter will help anyone contemplating visiting these countries, and may provide insights into other countries having similar problems.

Afghanistan

Afghanistan is one of the most impoverished countries of the world devastated by over 20 years of war. It has been estimated that around US$3 billion in weapons gushed into Afghanistan courtesy of the Western powers. The legacy is that boys are now taught that the use of the gun is the only real and meaningful occupation, many female children are not taught and the country is littered with landmines which will take decades to recover. Even after the Taliban had fallen in December 2001 women were scarce on the streets, and those who dared venture outdoors were covered by the now famous burqa.

Afghans have been in a perpetual cycle of conflict for the last quarter of a century. After the Soviets were booted out in 1991 and with no one left to fight, the warring factions turned on each other, resulting in a civil war which lasted until the mid 1990s. Large numbers of Afghans fled the country – many to northern Pakistan where, lacking any other opportunities, they were attracted to the *madrassahs* or Islamic religious schools and indoctrinated with fervent Islamic teaching. They returned to Afghanistan in order to halt the spiral of atrocities, crime and rapes. Enter the Taliban, who introduced a fervent strain of Islamic law into the country and established what they saw as a pure form of Islam, a literal interpretation of the Koran.

The West was outraged at scenes of public executions and the absolute oppression of women, who were forbidden from working, driving and even riding bicycles, and of course that most provocative of actions – showing their faces in public. However, the world tolerated the Taliban even if it meant the law enforcement people from the Ministry of Vice and Virtue were able to publicly beat women because they made too much noise while they were walking in the streets. All this changed on 11 September 2001. Osama bin Laden made a catastrophic error of judgement when he tried to launch a global challenge to the dominance of the democratic world. His Al Qaida movement was essentially destroyed and the Taliban were routed.

Afghanistan is now a country with no infrastructure. There are no road networks, only eroded remnants of what were once roads. Journeys of any distance are tortuous affairs over desolate countryside ravaged by multiple wars. Water supplies are intermittent and electricity is erratic, and only available in the major cities. There are no telephones, although you can see warlords driving around in Mitsubishi Shoguns and new pickup trucks using the latest satellite telephones. There is no medical system as such: hospitals are abysmal places which the locals do their best to avoid. During my trip to Afghanistan I treated people with gunshot wounds, shrapnel wounds and many other ailments.

Afghanistan is just awakening from the most unimaginable nightmare and the future for this country can only look up. The international community must make good its promises and disarm this fractious tribal society. They must give people an alternative to violence, and this is not going to be an easy task. Travel in Afghanistan is difficult, as the country is a patchwork of fiefdoms controlled by armed warlords. Different tribes have enormous hostility towards each other. While we were visiting a house in Kandahar one man we met exploded in anger because he had to share the same room with someone from another tribe. The situation became so volatile that we had to beat a hasty retreat.

The prognosis for this most tragic of countries is difficult to predict. For those wanting to travel to the majestic mountains of the Hindu Kush, my advice is wait and see how things pan out over the next few years. Afghanistan's problems are far from over.

Algeria

Algeria, a country of around 30 million people, has been in a state of violent conflict for many years. After the French pulled out in the early 1960s an estimated 100,000 people were killed.

The latest bout of bloodletting has been raging since the cancellation of the national elections of 1991. Islamic hardliners were set to win the election when President Abdelaziz Boutafeflika cancelled the elections. What has followed has been a brutal and indiscriminate terror campaign by the Armed Islamic Group (GIA) which has claimed the lives of around 20,000 people, and some 20,000 GIA rebels.

The GIA is composed of hardcore Muslim fundamentalists, many of whom have fought in the war in Afghanistan as mujahideen against the Russians during the 1980s. There are also links to the Al Qaida terrorist network. Most of the violence has taken place outside of the well-fortified capital Algiers, although major terrorist bomb attacks have taken place in the capital. The Algerian armed forces have not exactly covered themselves with glory during this time and have been accused of partaking in the country's bloodlust, either by committing atrocities themselves or by doing nothing while innocent people were being slaughtered by the rebels.

The mainstay of the Algerian economy is the oil industry, which has been targeted by the fundamentalists. This is such a vital national asset that the oil companies operating in this war-ravaged country spend many millions trying to secure their business.

There have been so many atrocities committed in Algeria that it is difficult to isolate one specific incident, but in late 1997 Muslim extremists attacked the town of Bentalha just south of Algiers. More than 300 villagers were literally butchered as the Algerian military allegedly waited outside the village. The GIA method of choice appears to be slitting the throats of their victims. No one has been spared in this desperate struggle – women, children and the old have all been victims. Western travellers have been told they are not welcome by the Islamic fundamentalists. There are routine illegal vehicle checkpoints outside the areas not controlled by the Algerian military and it is extremely dangerous for Westerners to travel on their own.

The prognosis for Algeria is not good. The legacy of the former French colony appears to be more violence as the Islamists try to topple the current regime. Those who wish to travel to Algeria do so at their peril.

Albania

Albania has assumed the title of the most lawless country in Europe, and perhaps one of the most lawless states in the world. Just around a two-hour flight from the UK, Albania has a reputation for violence, corruption and criminal gangs. So efficient are these that they have now spread their tentacles across Europe. Albanian criminals are alleged to control much of the prostitution and illicit drugs trade throughout Europe, including the UK.

One of the world's most impoverished countries, this former Communist dictatorship fell apart in the 1990s. In early 1997 the country erupted into violence when a pyramid pension scheme collapsed, leaving many Albanians devoid of their savings. In the aftermath of this financial disaster the society essentially ruptured, and riots and looting eventually led to full-scale anarchy. Military and police arms depots were looted and the weapons have been used to good effect. Many of these weapons subsequently found their way to both Kosovan and Macedonian Albanian fighters.

Albania continues to live with the legacy of this anarchism today, and it has permeated most levels of society including those who are supposed to uphold law and order. Into this quagmire entered Al Qaida as bin Laden tried to expand his multinational terror network by targeting American interests. Trafficking in refugees is a big earner and Albania has become a staging post for those seeking illegal entry into the European Union. Albanian society is very much a feudal society where blood feuds are common. The entire male membership of some families can be confined to their homes. The country is also split between many different communities. Albania is not at war, but don't let that fool you: there is no country on the European mainland which is better placed to trigger the next spate of Balkans bloodletting.

As with most very poor countries, petty crime is rife and the Western traveller may face corruption from officials, banditry, vehicle hijackings, armed robbery and even kidnapping which is a pastime in the north of the country. You'll need to prepare your journey thoroughly and if possible arrange to have a contact or an in-country fixer who knows the ropes. In short, the prospects for law and order are bleak.

Brazil

Brazil, with its shimmering white beaches and frenetic festivals, has an almost hypnotic effect on sun-seeking tourists. Nature-lovers venture into the riches of its vast tracts of unspoiled Amazonian rainforest (which is, however, being decimated at an alarming rate). However, there is a more sinister side to this country seemingly packed with travellers' delights. This is a country of corruption, petty crime, and a one-sided distribution of wealth where those who have, have plenty and those without have virtually nothing. It is estimated that around 50 per cent of the nation's riches are in the hands of less than 1 per cent of the population.

As with many such societies those who suffer most are the weakest, and in Brazil's case, the street children who are either abandoned or have lost their parents are at the bottom of the pile. There are an estimated 5 to 8 million street children living in the underground sewage systems of many of the major cities, treated literally like vermin and hunted by groups of off-duty armed police. Local businessmen who suffer at the hands of the thieving youngsters pay the police to murder them; it is suggested that many are murdered each week. Travellers must be aware of charitable handouts to street children; after you have given once you may find yourself surrounded by a ravenous crowd.

The police in Brazil have been described as corrupt and trigger-happy. Petty crime is rife in the main cities. Shantytowns surround many of Brazil's cities, and violence reigns in them. Many people end up destitute, drugs are a major problem and prostitution has fuelled the spread of HIV. Travellers will not have a problem getting around, as the country's infrastructure has developed apace. But you need to be aware of where you are going. Venture into a shantytown late at night and you will be at the very least relieved of your possessions.

There are adequate medical facilities if you have the money to pay, and most of the tourist areas are sheltered from the reality of the street. In the current economic climate Brazil is faring better than other South American economies. But unless the imbalance in the country's distribution of resources is rectified, Brazil will always have the potential to implode.

Burundi

Burundi is a small landlocked country just south of the great-lakes region of eastern Africa. Dominated by the Hutu, it has been wracked by the ethnic violence that has laid waste to the area for a decade and has claimed the lives of an estimated 250,000 people. To the north lies that other infamous genocidal African quagmire, Rwanda, where the systematic slaughter of an estimated 800,000 Hutu and moderate Tutsis over the period of a few weeks exposed a festering wound of deep-rooted enmity.

This madness has essentially continued since the country became independent after the Belgians pulled out in the early 1960s, but has assumed its genocidal dimension only over the last decade. Some have suggested the violence is not over yet. Moreover, this is a poverty-stricken area, which ironically possesses fertile farmland and abundant supplies of natural resources. The capital, Bujumbura, is frequently subjected to bouts of fighting and bomb attacks. There are estimates of many hundreds of thousands of displaced people living in environs of this small country. Anyone who ventures into this region must do so at his or her own peril. In December 2000, rebels stopped a bus full of passengers after leaving Bujumbura and everyone was ordered off. The rebels summarily executed most of them, including a British aid worker.

The Burundian economy is in tatters and there is no prospect that things will improve. Petty crime and corruption are rife and the traveller can expect to be targeted by the opportunist criminal and pay hefty bribes to get anything done, although there are moves to stamp out corruption. The country lacks infrastructure and in many areas there is no electricity, very little healthcare facilities and roving gangs of armed National Liberation Army rebels. It is unsafe to travel around, especially at night, and journeys outside the main towns and cities where there is no government troop presence are considered dangerous. The Burundian military try to enforce law and order over this war-ravaged region, but they are ill trained and poorly equipped.

The prognosis for Burundi is not good. Successive rounds of peace negotiations have come to nothing: there are still sporadic bouts of fighting and many thousands of displaced people. Until both communities realise they have to share this small, beautiful country and work around their differences rather than hacking each other to pieces, the violence is set to continue, Burundi will be visited only by unsuccessful UN peace negotiators and aid workers, and the people will languish in a festering inter-ethnic mess.

Chechnya

The South Caucusus region erupted in 1994, when the truculent Chechens rebelled against Russian rule, claiming an independent Islamic state. The Russians vilified the Chechens as gangsters, terrorists and brutes, and the Chechens did their best to live up to this image. Fuelled by years of what they viewed as Russian subjugation of their culture, the Chechens rose up and rebelled, and the Russians responded by sending in the tanks, literally.

The first Chechen war was a disaster for the Russians, who essentially used the same tactics the Germans used when they tried to capture Stalingrad 50 years earlier. The hardy and well-seasoned Chechens attracted volunteers from elsewhere in the Muslim world. The Chechen guerrillas then retreated to the hills and launched a successful campaign that eventually broke the spirit of the previously feared Russian military machine and resulted in a Russian withdrawal.

While the Russian military was left to brood over its humiliation at the hands of these rugged inherently clan-based Chechen rebels, the country was ruled by the gun. Kidnapping became a national sport (and still is) and many people were butchered in despicable acts of savagery, much of it recorded on homemade video. Aid workers were kidnapped, tortured and raped and the country descended into madness, lawlessness and anarchy. Money that was intended to rebuild the shattered country never arrived.

The brooding Russians had not forgotten and after a series of suspicious bomb attacks there that left hundreds dead, they returned to Chechnya. Their second venture was better planned and better organised than the first but was always doomed to fail: they may control the capital, Grozny, but much of the country remains the domain of the Chechen rebels. Essentially Chechnya is a no-go area, with no infrastructure to mention. The danger not only comes from the brutal Chechens, with their sadistic streak, but from the Russians themselves, implicated in uncountable atrocities.

Post September 2001, when the Russians joined the international coalition in the fight against terrorism, one can only expect more of the same as the West presumably turns a blind eye as the price for Russian acquiescence. For those intrepid adventurers intending to travel to this wartorn part of the earth, my advice is: don't. It is difficult to travel without an armed escort, you may stand the risk of kidnap, medical facilities are overwhelmed by war casualties, the country is littered with mines and of course the war continues as the Chechen guerrillas continue their campaign.

Colombia

Colombia is a country very much in the grip of violence. Some 20,000 people are murdered there each year, and 1400 are kidnapped. In the capital, Bogotá, it is estimated that there are 800 murders for every million people.

There are also a number of terrorist groups operating in Colombia, the main one being The Revolutionary Armed Forces of Colombia (FARC); the other principle group is the National Liberation Army (ELN). In an effort to pacify FARC, the government ceded a piece of territory larger than some European states to their control. This grand strategy has failed, and after tortuous rounds of jungle diplomacy conducted in the Colombian rainforest, the rebels have reneged on their deal and recommenced their insurgency. ELN has not been silent, and continues its campaign of terror and sabotage against government and international interests. A vital oil pipeline was attacked and blown up by this group over 200 times in one year. The ELN even imposed a million-dollar 'war tax' on foreign oil companies operating on its patch. Then there is the illegal narcotics trade which funds the majority of FARC's activities, its other main money earner being kidnapping. Several hundred hostages are currently languishing in the Colombian hinterland.

In 2000 the American government assigned more than 3 billion dollars in military hardware to the Colombian authorities to help fight drugs and terrorism. Most of the cocaine produced in Colombia is destined for the American market, and is Colombia's number one money earner.

Colombia has become a lawless society. Assassinations are commonplace, innocent *campesinos* are butchered by both sides for allegedly supporting the other side, corruption and violence have become endemic. Yet Colombia is a relatively developed country and the infrastructure, when not under attack by one of the terror groups, is usable. For the foreign traveller, however, the risks are evident. In particular, you'll have to insure against kidnapping – not a very cheap option these days.

The Democratic Republic of Congo

This vast and potentially wealthy African nation has been a tragedy from the start. First it was brutally exploited by its Belgian colonial masters, and since it has been essentially destroyed by a series of conflicts. The former dictator, Mobuto Sese Seko, used the nation's vast natural resources and wealth as his own personal bank account. He was to become one of the world's wealthiest men as his people descended into abject poverty and, eventually, savage wars that continue to this day.

The most recent of these conflicts grew out of the carnage to the east in Rwanda and Burundi in the mid-1990s. After the bloodletting in Rwanda, the Ugandan-backed Tutsi military began to settle old scores against their former Hutu opponents. An estimated million Hutu fled west into Zaire, where they teemed up with the remnants of the Rwandese Hutu military. They began to strike back at the now Tutsi-dominated Rwanda, and launched an extension of their genocidal campaign against the Tutsis living in Zaire. The Zairian authorities joined the fray and tried to kick out the Tutsis living in the east of the country. Ugandan and Rwandese forces invaded the northeast of the then Zaire in order to stop this and installed their own man, Lauren Kabila. Kabila led this new army on a surprisingly easy march across this vast country and ended up within striking distance of the capital, Kinshasa. The rebels then entered the capital and installed Kabila as president of the renamed Democratic Republic of Congo (DRC). Kabila soon fell out of favour with his Rwandese and Ugandan backers, who then invaded once more. Ultimately, a full-blown African war developed. Angola, Namibia, Zimbabwe, Uganda, Rwanda and Congo's own forces battled it out as this seemingly intractable conflict raged.

There have been several attempts at peace and the deployment of

UN peacekeepers, but at the time of writing this there is a long way to go before the conflict is resolved. What has all this done to the country? There was little infrastructure anyway, as Mobuto had squandered the nation's wealth. There is not much by the way of medical care and the hospitals are fearful places. To top all this, at Christmas 2001 the deadly Ebola virus broke out in Congo-Brazzaville just across the river – and there is no country better placed for a full epidemic of this fatal disease. Congo has one of the world's biggest Aids problems, and the vast majority of people subsist well below the internationally recognised definition of poverty. Crime is endemic too. Those who decide to travel to this region must expect that at some time someone will try to rob you and you will be expected to bribe almost every official you come across.

India

This country, home to over a billion people and a remarkable historic legacy, has an almost irresistible allure for many. But there's trouble in paradise, and some of it has ancient roots. The caste system is one problem. People have been murdered for developing relationships with those from other castes. The longstanding hostility against Pakistan, its neighbour, is another (see page 350). During each of three wars with Pakistan, India has claimed victory – and left Pakistan more furious than ever. The central worry here is that both countries are now nuclear powers, but are still developing. It could add up to a nightmare scenario. As I write, the biggest buildup of troops in the region for some years continues apace.

India faces other serious issues. The country faces rebellion in the east, and there is the equally protracted problem in the south with the Tamil Tigers, who assassinated the Indian Premier, Rajiv Ghandi, in a suicide bomb attack. The economy is faltering; there is a chronic lack of investment in the country's vast infrastructure. The medical service is inadequate to serve the needs of its people and, by Western standards, almost medieval. There is endemic petty crime and the emergence of organised criminal networks, drug trafficking and reported corruption.

However, even with all these problems India is still a welcoming place and the majority of people are glad to see visitors to their country. Violence is generally not targeted at Western travellers as long as you stay clear of the troublespots. Just remember that travel there can be exhausting: train journeys are long and hard, and the road networks gruelling.

Israel

The birthplace of Jesus and one of Islam's holiest places, for many Israel is the centre of all things spiritual. It is also, of course, a boiling cauldron of religious tension. The battle between Israelis and Palestinians seems now unlikely to finish in the foreseeable future. The current round of slaughter began in 2001, as the second intifada was sparked by a visit to the Temple Mount by the hardliner, and now Israeli president, Ariel Sharon. This intifada has claimed around 1000 lives so far and both sides seem entrenched in their positions. Even after the well-intended (but utterly futile, at the time of writing) rounds of shuttle diplomacy by the US, EU, UN and others, both sides seem further away from peace than they have ever been. The ongoing fight over land is a huge factor. Between American-backed Israeli military might and Palestinian suicide bombers, hundreds of people are being assassinated in endless, useless reprisals. Born from this mayhem are radical Islamic organisations such as Hamas and Hizbollah, who have stated their intentions at various times to push the Israelis into the sea. Israel also faces potential hostility on all four of its land borders, with Egypt, Jordan, Syria and Lebanon.

That said, Israel is a developed country with all the amenities – excellent medical facilities and good transportation systems. The problem is that the transportation system is a frequent target for Palestinian terrorists and the medical facilities are often overwhelmed with casualties from the intractable conflict. Foreign travellers are not normally selected as targets as both sides are too busy concentrating on each other, but the indiscriminate nature of the suicide bomber and the riot control measures used by the Israeli military ensure that many innocent people have been killed in this bloody war.

Iraq

The history of the Gulf War, when Iraq invaded its next-door neighbour and was then defeated, is well known: the 'mother of all battles' turned out to be the mother of all walkovers. Presiding over all was that increasingly rare phenomenon, the military dictator. The war was Saddam Hussein's second catastrophic miscalculation, his first being the invasion of Iran, a country twice as big and with huge resources. He only got out of that fix with an estimated million dead, two collapsed economies and assistance from the US, who viewed him as the lesser evil. Since then the US and its allies have failed to topple Saddam.

After the Gulf War, which killed 100,000 Iraqis, the country lay in ruins. Its infrastructure was torn apart and the Iraqi military machine had been destroyed. Saddam had spent a lot of time and money fashioning homegrown weapons of mass destruction and had acquired a network of research establishments and production sites for chemical and biological weapons plants and nuclear weapons research centres. And he persists in his quest for weapons of mass destruction.

The international community has been imposing sanctions against Iraq for over a decade now, yet the country has rebuilt much of what had been destroyed. It's hardly stable, however. There are strong links with international terrorist groups including Al Qaida. Saddam himself exhibits remarkable staying power, instigating frequent military purges to head off any possible takeover, and allowing only the most trusted confidants to hold positions of power. He is protected by the fiercely loyal Iraqi republican guard. But the fate of the Iraqi people hangs on Saddam's death, as only then will they be allowed back onto the world stage.

Ever since the conclusion of the Gulf War there has been continuous Western military activity in the skies over Iraq. The international community imposed a no-fly zone in both the north, to help protect the Iraqi Kurds from the dictator's grasp, and in the south to protect the Marsh Arabs. In October 2000, an aircraft carrying Westerners was hijacked and landed at Baghdad airport. Bizarrely, the hostages found themselves at the centre of an Iraqi tourist drive, and the reports suggest that the aircraft was hijacked deliberately to convince them what a nice destination Iraq was. They were put up at the best hotel and treated well for a few days, and appeared on TV enjoying the hospitality.

Even in a country with such potential wealth, most Iraqis languish in abject poverty, crushed by UN sanctions and spiralling inflation. A UN-sponsored accord permitted the Iraqis to export oil in return for cash with which they could buy badly needed food and medicine. However, the regime has manipulated this deal, and where the money ends up is anyone's guess. The prognosis for Iraq is not good while Saddam remains in power.

Liberia

Liberia has been in a state of chaos since its birth over a century ago. Coup after coup has ensured a perpetual state of instability and conflict. Even though a peacekeeping force was deployed during the early 1990s, successive deals collapsed and the fighting continued. The country saw some of Africa's worst atrocities during this time, and an estimated 200,000 people perished until the fighting was brought to a nominal end in 1997.

Liberia's economy faltered long ago and what infrastructure had existed was destroyed by neglect and this most recent war. When former rebel commander Charles Taylor came to power, a relatively calm period ensued. The fighting greatly diminished but Liberia was still bristling with weapons and there were, and still are, sporadic outbreaks of fighting. Then Taylor allegedly backed the Revolutionary United Front (RUF) in its even more brutal war in neighbouring Sierra Leone. Liberian military units have been engaged in bloody skirmishes on their border with Sierra Leone.

The Liberian people live in poverty, with little prospect of improvement. Petty crime is endemic and corruption is rife, allegedly right up to the highest officeholders in the land. The traveller who ventures here will be watched by security services, and fleeced by almost everyone you meet in the main towns and cities. The medical facilities are basic and not even sufficient to look after their own people, and the transportation is what you would expect after decades of instability and under investment. Western travellers have ended up in prison for even minor transgressions. Surprisingly, however, the prognosis for Liberia is good. They have an almost stable government which is democratically elected – a rarity in this region – and the war on their border has not affected the country too much.

Nigeria

Nigeria is Africa's most populous nation and could have been one of its wealthiest had it not been for the plundering of its national coffers by former rulers. After it gained its independence from the UK in 1960 and emerged from the devastating Biafran war, the trouble began. As a major African oil exporter the country should have been a success story. However, like many other potentially wealthy African states, the reality has been somewhat different. It has been fleeced by its own political leaders, many of whom were UK-trained senior military officers.

Nigeria is an ethnic and religious hotbed. There are tribal tensions among its divergent groups in the south of the country and religious tensions in the north. In addition there are tensions between the Muslim north and the Christian south, which have erupted into violence. My guess is that all this will fracture the country along its north-south divide.

When I recently visited Lagos, I found a poverty-stricken, rundown, decaying and neglected city. The crime rate is high and violence is everywhere. The police cannot be relied upon to settle disputes so inevitably there are flare-ups. In the days after I left, there was another outbreak of violence in the city which left hundreds dead. But if you travel to the capital, Abuja, you might almost think you were in a different world. Boasting one of the biggest and best hotels in the west of Africa, there are no street hawkers, no violence on the streets, no beggars. It is only after a closer inspection that you realise this is because most ordinary people are not allowed into Abuja: police and army checkpoints and cordons keep them out. Still, Nigerians are a resourceful people and even in Lagos there are many impressive survival stories.

Travellers to Nigeria need to know that the country has become a centre for all sorts of scams. Some of the people offering them are highly convincing, but you will be stitched up. Be warned.

Pakistan

Pakistan came into being after the British retreat from India, when that country was divided in two after a nasty civil war. Pakistan itself was divided, and what was East Pakistan later seceded and became Bangladesh. The legacy of this bloody history is a volatile country that regularly erupts into violence.

Pakistan was the first truly Islamic state. Its laws are based on the teachings of the Koran and its leader must by law be Muslim. The majority of Pakistanis are Sunni Muslim, and tensions between them and the Shias, who make up 20 per cent of the population, frequently break out into wholescale slaughter. The country's small Christian community also suffered in December 2001, when Islamic terrorists killed 20 of them as a response to the US-led bombings in Afghanistan. If you visit Pakistan, note where places of religious worship are located, and avoid them.

Most people in Pakistan are poor and few receive formal education. In Northern Pakistan, armed tribesmen rule without much interference from the government; in Islamabad guns are freely available and drugs are widely used. In fact, there are areas of the North West Frontier Province where men will knock up a very respectable home-made AK47 in a few hours for less than £50.

Then there is the ongoing dispute with India over Jammu and Kashmir. The two countries have already fought three wars over the province, with Pakistan losing each time to its richer neighbour. The danger here, of course, is that both Pakistan and India are nuclear powers, and the situation could escalate beyond threats to actual nuclear warfare. As I write, the international community is trying to defuse yet another round of fighting before things go too far.

Pakistan is a still a wild and beautiful country. Its majestic mountains, including the second highest peak on earth, K2, still attract many adventurous Westerners each year. Groups in certain areas of

Pakistan target foreigners, but this is fallout from the troubles in Afghanistan to the north. Karachi is one of the most violent cities, and in the current climate you'll have to use extreme caution when you visit it. The country's infrastructure is generally underdeveloped and healthcare is basic. But on the whole, I felt welcome in most of the places I visited in Pakistan. Islamabad is relatively safe and most people are very friendly. If you stay away from the areas bordering Afghanistan, you could – with care – have an unforgettable time.

Russia

Since the breakup of the Soviet empire, Russia has plummeted to earth with a bone-crushing crash. A superpower no longer, the country is plagued by wars on its borders, corruption at almost every level, a rampant AIDS epidemic, chronic economic problems and, of course, endemic crime. Russia claims to be a modern, developed democracy, but this is simply untrue. The actual standard of living was higher in the days of empire than it is today. In order to compete in a free market economy, the Russian people have had to undergo severe economic hardship. Real incomes have gone down and prices have gone up. The only people making money are a select few entrepreneurs and the organised criminal gangs.

Russia has also had to deal with its fiercely independent former sister soviets, such as the Chechens (see page 342). Impoverished as they are, the Russians have spent hundreds of millions on military hardware trying to keep hold of the Chechen province, which I presume will at some stage break away anyway. The reason for this futile war is the trans-Caspian oil pipeline: Russia does not want to be cut out of the lucrative oil riches which are sure to start flowing when this project finally begins.

Russia is a violent country. You can purchase guns, artillery pieces, tanks and reportedly even suitcase-sized nuclear devices there if you have the cash and the right contacts. As you might expect, the murder rate is one of the highest in the world, with an estimated 28,000 a year on average. The organised criminal networks who battle it out on city streets are responsible for much of this, as well as assassinations of the politicians and journalists who dare to work against their power base.

The country's infrastructure is suffering from chronic underinvestment and neglect, and its aviation industry has the dubious record of being one of the most inefficient in the world. Its health service cannot cope with the AIDS epidemic, and its population is beset with other serious diseases, TB among them. The prognosis for Russia? It appears to be more of the same, as no one is going to bail them out of their economic quagmire. They will have to steer dead ahead and suffer more economic austerity, stamp out corruption and tackle the growing menace from their homegrown mafia. If they bite the bullet, the chances are that this country may one day emerge as a truly modern democratic and economic powerhouse, but it will take time.

Somalia

It is hard to say this about any country, but Somalia seems very much a lost cause – a disease-ridden tragedy on the Horn of Africa. If the gun-toting warlords who control it do not change, its poverty, violence and lawlessness will simply persist.

Somalia has been subject to wars, famines and droughts since anyone can remember. The recent bout of violence commenced after the collapse of the communist regime of Said Barre. Two warlords – the notorious Mohammed Farah Aideed and the lesser-known Ali Mahdi Mohammed – then formed an alliance of sorts, but it proved to be shortlived. They were soon wrestling for control of the country. Civil war broke out as the clans in Somalia ignited a violent struggle which, with famine and drought, brought the country to its knees.

It is still prostrate more than a decade later. A small and costly US-led intervention by the UN managed to achieve nothing except the loss of many UN soldiers. Americans had to watch as the bodies of dead US servicemen were dragged through the streets. The UN and the US both pulled out and the country reverted to ritual clan warfare and slaughter. There have been sporadic flashes of hope, but no progress. Somalia may not survive as a nation; regions within it have formed their own governments, and are one step short of outright secession.

I have spent time in Puntland, like the rest of Somalia a hopeless, barren desert wilderness littered with destroyed towns. There's nothing there you could call an economy, infrastructure or healthcare – just poor people who deserve better. Refugees and displaced persons huddle round the borders hoping for salvation from the international aid agencies, who are frequently forced to withdraw after their staff are killed or kidnapped or their supplies taken off them at gunpoint. It was here that I contracted malaria and dysentery. Near the filthy town of Bossasso, the shores of the Indian Ocean are littered with thousands of animal carcasses: after the animals are butchered their bodies are chucked unceremoniously onto the beach in a pile. I began feeling rather ill and decided to pay a visit to the local medical facility – a dirty, badly lit mud hut. I noticed the price list for the various services. Malarial screening was relatively cheap. As the treatments descended in order of severity they increased in price and included tooth extractions, amputations and a frontal lobotomy, which I was assured by the cheerful medical receptionist was cheaper than you would find anywhere else in the region. With its mud huts, dusty roads, and hostile population, Puntland made Afghanistan seem like Ibiza.

The other parts of Somalia, including the wrecked capital in the south, Mogadishu, are in no better state – and probably worse because of frequent clashes between the warring clans. The northwest is probably the best hope for this entire region. Somalia is now going through yet another round of negotiations trying to find a way out of this morass, trying to find a way of making the warlords happy. This will be no easy task. Even when I was there in 1999 there was talk of oil discoveries on the border between Puntland and Somaliland, and this triggered border incursions from both sides and military clashes between them. The country cannot feed itself, there is persistent drought on the Horn of Africa, and the rule of law is the gun. Even offshore is unsafe: there are pirates round the coast. So the prognosis for Somalia is gloomy.

Sierra Leone

Since its independence from the UK in the early 1960s and more recently, Sierra Leone has become synonymous with rape, pillage, torture and mutilation. After a military takeover in the early 1990s, opposition groups rose up and the clashes began. Resentment grew among the poor, who had to scratch a meagre existence in the jungle, against those in Freetown who squandered the nation's riches, mainly diamonds. This potentially wealthy state is a disaster zone, and one of the poorest countries on earth. Petty crime is rife, there is little infrastructure, and no healthcare provision outside that offered by the aid agencies.

After the rebels – the Revolutionary United Front (RUF) – threatened to take control of the country, mercenaries were brought in. When the lucrative diamond mines were threatened, a second and better organised mercenary group from South Africa entered the fray and almost succeeded in putting down the revolt. Eventually the diamond mines fell back into the hands of the RUF. War resumed. Enter the Nigerians under the guise of ECOMOG, the UN peace-keeping force. The RUF relaunched their campaign of terror. Torture, rape and murder were the daily routine, and no one was spared; and when the rebels entered the capital, Freetown, at the end of 1998, the atrocities were horrific by anyone's standards. They simply amputated the limbs of anyone not on their side, and also killed perhaps 50,000 people. Members of the ECOMOG force were routinely attacked and many were killed, triggering some of them to commit atrocities, too.

The RUF continued to have the upper hand until a deployment of British Special Forces and tough, no-messing paratroopers were sent in and took up positions around the capital. The RUF were forced back into the jungles, where they remain today. They still control the diamond area of Sierra Leone. Meanwhile the British military train and equip the government forces for the day when the newly formed Sierra Leonian army takes control of the entire country.

The RUF are extremely dangerous and Westerners have been targeted and killed by them. If you have to travel in this country, research which areas are under their control and avoid them.

Sri Lanka

Until the events of September 2001, the terrorist attack that same year at Bandaranaike airport in Sri Lanka's capital, Colombo, was probably the most successful ever launched. The atrocity at the airport was planned to mark the anniversary of the massacre of thousands of Tamils by the Sinhalese majority. The civil war in Sri Lanka has been raging for the best part of the last 20 years and has been punctuated by Tamil suicide bomber attacks and major government offensives which have left around 50,000 people dead on both sides. The Tamils receive their support from the Indian state of Tamil Nadu, and are determined to secure a Tamil homeland in the northern Jaffna area of this small and once beautiful island.

The result is stalemate. The Tamil Tigers are brave and ruthless fighters who think nothing of committing to an assault against overwhelming odds, knowing that this means certain death. The Tigers have not limited their attacks to the north of the island and they periodically strike at prestige targets in the south, although tourist areas there have been left mainly unscathed. There have been bomb explosions and assassinations in Colombo, and suicide bomb attacks in the cities of Trincomalee and Baticaloa. Sri Lankan naval vessels have been attacked and sunk, and port and harbour facilities have been attacked so often that insurance companies placed huge premiums on those using the port facilities in order to do business.

And that's not all. The Tigers have launched major offensives against Sri Lanka's transport networks. Airports, trains, buses and roads have all been targeted in this intractable conflict. Numerous diplomatic missions have been dispatched to the area by the international community, with no success. And frequent conciliatory gestures from the north have failed; the Tigers continue to launch their attacks, and then the government retaliates.

While the government protects the island's infrastructure, it is impossible to guarantee 100 per cent protection against such a determined terrorist group. The prognosis for Sri Lanka is not clear. After shedding so much blood and uttering so much vitriolic rhetoric it will be difficult for the Tamils to settle for anything less than an independent state. The government stance of retaliatory strikes seems just as entrenched. So it's more of the same, I think, for the foreseeable future.

United States

America: land of the free, the world's most liberal democracy, the home of Disneyland, Coca Cola, Macdonald's, and a favourite holiday destination for a lot of people. But unfortunately, the US is also a mecca for gun owners. There are around 200 million guns in circulation, and 4 million are added every year.

Now, of course, terrorism has been added to the mix. The US now finds itself the target of Islamic fundamentalist terrorists, and the attack of 11 September 2001 struck a deep psychological blow to the once unassailable American psyche. The chances are that there will be another terrorist attack of some sort.

The US also has spiralling crime rates, immigration problems and a fascination with all things violent. Across the country every week, there are an estimated 340 murders, 10,000 robberies and 2000 rapes. There have been infamous incidents of children shooting children. Although not of Russian or Colombian dimensions, the casualty rates are high. That said, travelling in the US is generally a real pleasure. People tend to be friendly, much of the country is beautiful, and the infrastructure is obviously excellent. But you can't take it for granted. You need to exercise the usual caution in urban areas and keep a weather eye out for trouble.

16

Safety in Cities

Dangerous Cities

In Chapter 15, I mentioned a number of cities – Lagos, Kandahar, Bogotá among them – that are not perhaps the best place for a midnight stroll. But what features, precisely, actually make a city dangerous? After all, even in high-risk areas it's relatively rare for people to become victims of crime.

In looking at safety in cities, the most important factors for the traveller are the crime rate, security situation and stability, environmental factors such as the weather and terrain (covered elsewhere in this book), and perhaps safety standards and medical facilities. Regardless of the country, cities attract the best and worst of humanity, and all things in between. It is often said that crime rates in any major city outstrip rural crime rates, and this pretty much stacks up. Many people travel abroad assuming that as they are on holiday they can relax and let their guard down. And why not? The problem is that criminals and other devious types know this, and take advantage of it.

New cities, new customs, new problems: many tourists arrive in a city and suddenly realise they haven't prepared for the reality. They become easy victims. In the early 1990s, for example, there were a spate of attacks against British tourists in Florida, where an estimated 2 million Britons holiday each year. Seven tourists were murdered and many were robbed at gunpoint. Sexual assaults, robberies and further killings of foreign tourists followed. The crime wave was so serious that insurance companies ratcheted up the premiums for those travelling to the Sunshine State. Tourists were issued maps warning them off certain areas – not an ideal start to a long-planned family holiday.

So never take risks you wouldn't if you were at home. Be wary of people: you do not have to look very far in every major city to find the flotsam of humanity.

In 1996/1997 a survey was conducted to find the most dangerous cities in the world. The following cities were rated on a scale from 1 to 10, with 10 the most dangerous. From least to most dangerous, cities rating from 2 to 5 included Tokyo, Hong Kong, La Paz, London, Montevideo, Buenos Aires, Quito, Managua, Santiago, Belize City, Los Angeles and New York. Rated 6 were Caracas, Guatemala City, Lima, Manila, Mexico City, Moscow, Panama City, San Salvador and Tegucigalpa. Cities such as Bogotá were rated 7. São Paulo received an 8, and the most dangerous city in the world was Kabul in Afghanistan, with a rating of 9.

While these statistics are a little dated, they still provide a good rough guide. Highly dangerous cities such as Baghdad, Algiers, Kinshasa, Karachi, Jolo in the Southern Philippines and Jerusalem were not mentioned, as they are not much visited by tourists.

Wherever you go, prepare, be aware of the risks and take sensible precautions. Constant worry will ruin your trip. And regardless of whether you are travelling to a war-torn city or to a major tourist resort, consider the following points.

■ Get to know your way around, when things open and close and so on. In tropical countries towns shut down for a few hours during the heat of the day, when the streets are deserted. This information may be obtained from friends who have just returned from the city, from tour guides, fellow travellers or even hotel staff.

■ Get a city map and mark the areas that you should avoid. Mark the hotel address on the map too so you will be able to show taxi drivers where you want to go (assuming you don't speak the local language).

■ To orientate yourself with the city, go to a high point or a high building overlooking it and try to familiarise yourself with the layout. This will enable you to get a feel for city streets and major landmarks.

■ Also look at the skyline. Try to identify landmarks: in this way you will be able to locate areas of the city by referring to them. You can head to the nearest major landmark on the way to your destination.

■ Learn local landmarks – main roads, monuments, parks, rail and other transportation hubs, safe taxi areas, major hotels. You do not need to know exactly how to get to each of these locations, but this will provide a general overview of the city. If you more or less know where you're going you will look and act like a native of the city and reduce your chances of becoming a victim of crime.

■ Do not stop and pull out your map in city streets. There may be people who see that you are lost and take advantage. It is safer to go indoors to consult it; a shop, café or restaurant will conceal you from those on the street.

■ Locate the nearest medical facilities, security force base or police station. Find out the telephone contact numbers of each and record them on your mobile phone, if you've brought it, so that you can speed dial them in an emergency. If you have no mobile phone, write the numbers down on a card, buy a local telephone card and make sure you know how to use the public call phones.

■ Identify any points where you will need to stop or slow down – traffic lights, one-way streets, entrances to shopping precincts, industrial or economic centres. All these areas attract crowds of people, and are places where you have to stop or slow down, all of which makes you more vulnerable to criminals. If there are permanent police or military roadblocks on the streets, get to know where they are and if at all possible avoid them. They can become tempting targets for terrorists and insurgents and a source of tension, too, as you can be strong-armed into giving up your hard-earned cash.

- City parks are generally safe during the day (although you need to research this), but at night can become criminal hunting grounds. Avoid city parks after dark.

- In the event of an attack, some men and women are seized by 'behavioural inaction', freezing in response to shock. Carrying a small portable alarm in your pocket that emits a loud, high-pitched noise and can be activated with a switch will deter attackers and could give you the time you need to get moving and get away.

- In areas with a history of terrorism, research how and why it happened. Be aware of likely targets – rail networks, for instance. Avoid hotels next to government or opposition political buildings, security force locations or anything which may come in for terrorist attention.

- Try to identify the patterns of crime in the city. Ask at your consulate or embassy – they will provide you with an overview of security. There may be areas where the risk of a particular crime is greater. Thieves may congregate in an area with plenty of choice of victims and good avenues of escape. If you are told that a particular area is a high-crime area, do not go there; or if you must, take the minimum of valuables with you.

- Being a part of a large gathering of people – on the street, or at protests, carnivals, or sporting occasions – can be risky. There will be criminals looking for victims and you may stand out from the crowd. And the current international security threat is serious: you should be aware that sooner or later terrorists may attempt to have a go at a large public gathering somewhere. At the 2001 New Year's celebrations in Times Square in New York City there were an extra 7000 police on duty, equipped with radiation and chemical detectors.

- In some high-risk areas the authorities may impose a curfew. It is essential that you find out what time it begins and ends, and the consequences if you are caught out. In Kandahar during Christmas 2001 the newly appointed authorities were very quick to open fire on anyone out after curfew. In many high-risk environments you may be required to carry your identification documents, and may even be required to know a password, as was the case in Afghanistan.

- Alcohol and crime can go hand in hand. Be aware of closing time for pubs and clubs and make sure that you are not on the street when they come out. Most violent incidents in Britain, for instance, occur over Friday and Saturday nights. In some of the Spanish hotspots people behave in a similar way, but the party goes on all week, and so does the violence.

- Avoid shortcuts – you may become lost. Off-street areas are where drug deals are done, and stolen materials are bought and sold. Always ensure that you use routes that you know well and that are busy and well lit at night.

- Avoid walking around on your own at night. Arrange to travel with a friend, or to be collected and dropped off at your destination.

- Most city dwellers have low tolerance thresholds and the chances of becoming involved in an altercation can be high. In hot countries, you may see furious drivers or pedestrians having a go at each other when it's warmest at midday. Stay clear and do not become involved.

- Be aware of anyone approaching you in the street trying to sell you something. If you show the slightest interest you'll be hounded. Stare straight ahead and do not even acknowledge them. Never hire a guide on the street, but only at recognised agencies and on the recommendation of a trusted friend or colleague.

- Be aware of common tricks used by thieves. They often work in gangs, and while one 'accidentally' bumps into you, his cohort is busy relieving you of your wallet. Or someone will stop you in the street in order to ask directions, say you've dropped something or that there's something amiss with your clothes, and then have their colleague nab your goods while you're preoccupied. Be very wary of distractions and keep hold of your valuable items.

▪ Street crime is not only conducted by young males, but also by children and women. Children may be bolder and try anything, and can also vanish easily in a crowd.

▪ Before you go, compile a list of the valuable equipment that you are carrying with you, and if you lose anything you'll be able to authenticate your claim. Include a description of the item, the make, colour, model and serial number. Keep it separate from your equipment.

▪ Avoid carrying anything valuable in handbags, bags, single-strap shoulder bags, bum bags, or loose in your hands. Many street criminals are adept at slicing straps or snatching things from your hands. Use neck bags or shoulder holsters to carry your valuables, and ensure any straps or strings are out of sight. Keep both hands free as you walk, not in your pockets or under the straps of your rucksack. If attacked you would be an easy target this way.

▪ If you are carrying a bag, camera or video recorder in a crowded city street, put the item's shoulder strap across your chest. This will make it more difficult for the thief to snatch your bag. Carry the bag or camera itself on the side away from the road. Don't put all your possessions in one bag. If you feel the hotel security procedures are safe, leave your passport, flight tickets, and some of your cash at the hotel, but remember that even in major hotels your valuables may not be 100 per cent safe.

▪ Mobile phones are often targeted by thieves. Hide them away, and remove the SIM card when you are not using it. Then, if it is stolen you will not be hit with a huge telephone bill when you get home.

▪ Marking property can deter criminals and help identify your goods if stolen. You could use a serial number or your postcode as you do at home, or use high-resistant adhesives and a label, or invisible markers which can only be seen under ultraviolet light. Be aware that on smooth surfaces the writing may be visible if held up in good light conditions, and that the ink may wear off after a few months' travel.

- Don't walk around an unfamiliar city with a Walkman and earphones. You need to stay aware and alert to your surroundings.

- Be wary of vehicles parked at the side of the road with people sitting near the pavement side and the engine running. In areas with a history of kidnapping this is how abductors get their victims.

- If you are walking in a high-risk area and you witness a disturbance or a group of threatening people, try to make a detour and go to a safe place where there are a lot of people and lights. Pick shops, garages or hotels that are known safe areas.

- If you become lost, do not immediately stop someone and ask for directions. First walk around purposefully a bit and try to find out where you are, but do not walk past the same area over and over again – you will attract attention. If you are convinced that you are lost or if you must get somewhere quickly, go into the nearest big shop and try to ask directions. Make sure that the minimum amount of people hear you ask and after you have received an answer leave the area quickly. Or ask a local policeman or any other official-looking person.

- Ensure you understand the local laws and customs. In some states in the US you may be arrested and taken away in handcuffs for crossing the road on foot when the lights are red. The much larger concentration of police and security forces in cities also makes for a much greater danger of attracting attention for minor violations.

- In many cities the underprivileged head to the streets to beg for food and money. Unless you are really hard it is difficult not to be moved. But if the level of poverty is very extreme, think again. In Kandahar, Afghanistan, I bought a large bag of sweets to give to the hungry kids I saw on the streets. However, when I started to hand them out I was automatically rushed by every man, woman and child in the vicinity. The bag was ripped to shreds as people scrambled in the dirt for a few cheap sweets. Most of the kids got nothing and all I did was start a fight between hungry adults. My naïve good intentions only served to cause trouble in the street.

- When walking, trust your sixth sense; if you feel uneasy about a person or situation do not take the chance, leave before it develops into anything problematic. Be proactive rather than reactive.

- In unfamiliar cities, be cautious about drinking and going out and about. The alcohol will affect your judgement.

- If you become involved in an incident your best option is to talk your way out. In a physical tussle the chances are someone will get hurt. Retain control of the situation, fight the urge to panic and aim to get a sense of how to get out of the situation.

- Be aware that in some regions, you will be able to fight off an attacker but you are only allowed to use reasonable force. If you seriously injure an attacker, you may – strange as it may seem – find yourself on the wrong side of the law. In many regions foreign legal systems will look less favourably on foreigners than on wounded locals. If the attacker is intending to steal an item with little value, it may be better to let it go rather than start a major incident where someone is likely to become a casualty.

Shopping and Possessions

In many countries, shopping malls, markets or bargain outlets attract a regular supply of tourists – and criminals looking for easy pickings. Whether you are haggling over prices while buying a wooden artifact in an African market or trying to purchase the latest in computer technology in a major city, there may be someone on the periphery watching you. Or there can be street tricksters offering all sorts of cheap bargains and crooked shop workers who shortchange customers. Wherever money is being spent, criminals can congregate. The British Foreign Office reported that in 2000, an estimated 8000 holidaying Britons fell victim to pickpockets who relieved them of around one and a quarter million pounds. And this is only the petty thievery.

The way you behave and speak, and handle your money and possessions, all send out signals to criminals. If you are streetwise, confident, purposeful and keep a low and businesslike profile, they'll leave you alone.

You also have to be aware of other dangers while shopping. In many regions of the world, building and safety regulations are not up to the standard of those in the West. In Lima, Peru, over Christmas 2001, bargain hunters were confronted by a major fire in a shopping centre. More than 100 people were killed in the incident. China, the Philippines and a score of other countries have experienced similar accidents.

When you venture out on a shopping expedition in a foreign city, consider the following points.

- Do not walk around town wearing or carrying things that you would not or cannot afford to lose – expensive jewellery or equipment and the like. If you can't travel without them, make sure that you have insurance cover.

- Don't carry large amounts of cash around with you. Buy travellers' cheques before you go and only cash what you need. Ensure that you sign travellers' cheques only at authorised exchange outlets.

- If you must pay for an article or service, avoid taking out all of your money and flaunting your cash. You may attract attention. Keep about £20 in small denomination notes in your pockets. This way you will not have to take out your wallet unless you're making a big purchase.

- You should not be tempted by back-street deals of higher exchange rates. Unless you are changing tens of thousands of pounds you are not really going to notice the difference. You will, however, place yourself at risk by going along with these street sharks.

- Similarly, be cautious of deals which seem too good to be true. Cheap, rare or even illegal goods will be offered in many places. If you agree to buy you will place yourself not only at risk from the sharks trying to sell to you, but also the authorities.

- Many travellers have returned from abroad after having bought goods, only to find that they are faulty or are cheap imitations of original brands. Check that the labels or the brand-name markings have not been stuck onto locally produced imitations. Check that expensive items have still got serial numbers attached and that there has been no attempt to remove or alter the name tags or plates. Ensure that the user manual or the manufacturer's instructions are original, that the warranty or guarantee is included and covers you for your home country. Some of them are specific to the region where the articles are sold. In counterfeit materials the documentation sometimes looks shoddy and clearly homemade or a photocopy of originals. If you are offered such material, not only are you being duped; you will be breaking the law by importing such objects into your own country.

- If you are buying expensive articles abroad, ensure that you test them extensively before you leave the shop. If you find that there is a problem when you arrive home there will be little that you will be able to do about it.

- In some countries such as Turkey, it is illegal to trade in artifacts considered national treasures. Be wary of anyone who tries to tempt you. There have been crooked officials who have tried to sell artifacts, only to arrest the tourist trying to buy them. As you might expect, it would take a hefty bribe to get you off the hook. If you intend to buy an antique, ensure that you know what you are looking for, and get a letter of authenticity and documentation which will enable you to export the article. Do not be enticed to purchase items from secretive street dealers – they will be either fake or illegal.

- Before you go, take out everything that may cause offence and get you into trouble. Also take out all credit cards and cash cards that you will not be using.

- When using a cashpoint machine in a foreign city, choose one in a safe location. Ensure that there are no suspicious types hanging around before you use it. Identify the machine you want to use and wait until there is no queue, then approach the machine directly with your card in your hand and conduct your transaction quickly. Take your cash, quickly put it out of sight, and leave the area as soon as possible. Try to use them mostly in the mornings or during the day, as you're less likely to be targeted then.

- When using cashpoints, ensure that no one is looking over your shoulder trying to identify your PIN number. In addition there are some rather sophisticated fraudsters out there, so avoid using a cashpoint machine which is overlooked. Some have used video cameras with powerful zoom lenses to record the PINS of victims. The victim is then targeted by the gang and mugged for his or her card.

- Ensure that you also collect any cashpoint printouts. If they show your account balance, criminals finding them might target you. Some printouts have enough bank details on them to expose you to the risk of being electronically robbed.

- When you are trying to buy something, do not be bullied or pressured into making hasty decisions. There are many street touts and shop assistants who are expert in pressure tactics. Before you know it you have bought something which is no earthly use to you – you may not even be allowed to bring the article back home with you. Take someone with you when you go shopping, and when you feel pressured always have the courage to say no. Be aware, though, that in some regions all you have to do is get involved in negotiations about price to become committed to buying the object. If you then try to walk away you will become involved in an altercation. During a trip to Kenya I became involved in such a scene in Nairobi. After asking about the price of a wooden carving and bartering for a few minutes, I decided that the price was too high. I was then followed across the city by several angry street merchants shouting abuse at me.

- If you are paying for a good or service by credit card, ensure that the person receiving your card does not disappear with it. You should insist that the card stays where you can see it. Some tricksters may have access to card copying machines, which can copy the electronic information contained on the strip on your card.

- When paying by credit card in a foreign country I have always found it useful to engage the shop assistant in conversation. My aim is to make the assistant believe that I am a resident. Speak about what is going on in the city and try to sound familiar with it all. If they think you live there they will be less likely to rip you off, as you'll be around to deal with any mistakes on their part.

- Always recover your receipts after you've paid by credit card. If you scatter them around the street, a car or your hotel room, you will compromise your security: your card number, expiry date and personal details will be on the receipt. It is easy to pick up the slip and make an order over the phone.

- Another common fraud tactic is to write down your copy of a credit card receipt, then claim it has been done wrongly or for the wrong amount. The assistant then screws up the credit card receipt and it is tossed in the bin. After you have left they pick the receipt out of the bin and process it. You then lose whatever was written on the original receipt.

- Ensure you know how much credit you have on your card before you go. People have been arrested for trying to go over their credit limit, the logic being that if you were the card's rightful owner you would know how much your credit limit was. Take down the details of your credit card company so that you can call them up if you lose your card. You must do this as soon as you confirm your card as missing. Your company will then stop all transactions from that card.

- If you intend to shop at a local market take a trusted local with you. A local will almost certainly get a better price for the same object than a tourist. The local will also know the bartering procedure. You may end up saving a substantial amount.

- Try to identify in advance what you will be expected to pay for goods and services. Find out the price that the locals will be expected to pay and make an assessment of how much you will pay – tourists will be charged extra, so be prepared. In addition ensure that you receive the appropriate receipts and export documentation for any expensive items. You may not be able to export or even import the articles if you do not have this.

- Never agree to go with someone to pick up an article at an isolated location, and never agree to go outside with someone to discuss the price of an object. Never be tempted to go with someone you meet on the street to see a special object. The chances are that it will be a setup or stolen.

- In cities with a high crime rate, if you have made a purchase on the phone and the seller suggests that they bring the product to your hotel room or house, refuse. Pick it up yourself, or better still, arrange for it to be collected and delivered to you.

- Avoid walking around overloaded with packages. Snatching at your bags will leave you vulnerable; you will stand the chance of losing one or more of your packages and will be unable to protect yourself. Take someone with you to carry your bags, or better still arrange for a car to collect you.

- Some shopping centres are like elaborate mazes. In an emergency, many of them have inadequate safety procedures for evacuation in emergencies. You should study the layout when you enter and plan a route which you can access easily. Identify the emergency exits on each level, and routes out and away from the buildings. Be aware that many of the shop employees have had little or no training in managing situations in an emergency. Take this into account when listening to their advice.

- Terrorists often target shopping complexes and commercial areas because there are predictably large amounts of people and it's an easy way to disrupt economic activity. The terrorist group Aby Sayaff did this in Manila, as did Irish extremists in Britain. Stay clear of shopping centres if the tension within the city is too high or on politically sensitive anniversary dates.

Hotel Security

Hotels are a magnet to the local population. Workers, service or delivery staff, cooks and cleaners are all in and out of hotel grounds – as may less welcome types. In some areas, hotels will have their own security guards, and in countries like Nigeria or the Philippines these people can be armed with automatic assault rifles.

When we pay to stay at a hotel we expect to be comfortable and secure, unperturbed by any disturbances outside the hotel walls. In many areas hotels invariably attract local low-life intent on easy pickings from apparently wealthy tourists or travellers who have let their guard down in the relaxed environment most hotels promote. That's an obvious threat. There are also, however, hotel staff who are badly paid, and yet have access to your rooms – for some of them, a big temptation. Hotels in some regions are full of foreign travellers, and for terrorists with an obscure cause, what better platform for generating international recognition than an attack on a popular tourist hotel? This has happened in Thailand, the Philippines and Indonesia in 2001.

When you are planning to stay at a hotel consider the following points:

- Particularly in volatile areas, elect to stay in a safe location, not too isolated or poor. Book into a reputable hotel in a busy part of town with no graffitti and a well-kept look. All but the most determined of criminals will stay clear of efficient and well-managed hotels. If you stay in a lively part of town there will be a lot of activity on the streets, which may deter criminals from acting. Ensure that there are good lines of communication from the hotel to the local town, airport or other transport hubs, which do not take you through dangerous areas.

- Ask other travellers who have visited the area and get their impressions about how secure the hotel and the area around it are. Travel agents will link you up with others who have been there recently.

- In volatile or high-risk areas, request a room to the back of the hotel, not overlooking a car park. When terrorists target hotels with say, car bombs, they will normally leave the car at the front of the hotel or hidden among other cars.

- It's a good idea to book a hotel room for your first night from home. Do not travel to areas, especially volatile ones, and then try to arrange a room when you arrive. Chances are you will end up in a place where you would not normally choose to stay – that is, even if you get a room at all.

- Even in peaceful and low-crime areas it is better to stay in a hotel which has a visible security presence. If there are uniformed security guards at the door this will at least deter criminals coming in off the street. Ensure that when you arrive at your hotel room you count your luggage off the taxi or minibus, and make sure the bell-boy then has control of your baggage. Closed-circuit television and powerful lighting will also deter criminals. However, beware of hotels with an excessive amount of security measures: this may indicate that it has been a target of repeated criminal attack.

- If you have booked your room from home, ensure it is not on the ground floor. This will allow access to criminals through windows and doors. Rooms near the fire escape have stairwells leading from the ground floor and can also provide access to determined criminals.

- Take adjoining rooms only if the person in the other room is a friend or relative. Before you settle in, ensure that the window locks are serviceable, especially if you're in a ground-floor room. Check that the doors lock securely and have a peephole if at all possible, that you are happy with the room and with the toilets, shower room and other adjoining rooms. If you are unhappy with the room for whatever reason, immediately go to reception and demand another.

- Ask to see the hotel's emergency and evacuation plan. Make sure everyone you're with is familiar with the alarm system and knows what to do in an emergency. Count the number of doors to the fire exit and note which side of the corridor it is on. Walk the escape route, remembering you may have to do this at night, in darkness or when the corridors are filled with smoke. Make sure you know the procedures for raising the alarm. Your emergency evacuation plan may not only have to deal with conventional emergencies such as fire. In some high-risk areas there is just as much danger of your hotel being attacked by gunmen or bombers. Consider how these eventualities would affect your emergency planning.

▪ When you go out, take what you need with you and if you trust in hotel security, leave valuables such as your passport and return flight tickets, extra cash and other essential possessions in the safe. Anything you leave lying around your room may be in danger of being stolen, and anything with your personal details on it will compromise your home security. When you leave your room do not leave anything lying around and put your 'Do Not Disturb' sign on the door. This will let any passers-by know that your room is occupied, and will deter criminals.

▪ Intruder alarms, which are made to look like radios or clocks but emit a high-pitched noise as soon as someone moves in your room, are a good idea. Door wedges are a cheap and easy way to stop unwanted guests from entering your room.

▪ Other security devices will allow you to conceal your possessions. Safety boxes made to look like drink or food cans can hold valuables such as money or passports, but are only useful if concealed.

▪ When you are travelling with others, take note of their room numbers and telephone numbers. If you need help you will be able to phone them or at least run and knock on their door.

▪ Be cautious about opening your door when you don't know who is on the other side. If you have an unexpected visitor or stranger, tell them to wait in the reception area. You will then be able to confront them in an area where there are other people. Be aware of bogus officials trying to get you to open your door. Ask for identification and confirm with reception that they are genuine. Do not open your door to room service unless you have actually ordered something. This is a fairly common ploy: fake room service waiters arrive at your door, you invite them in and they walk out with more than they entered with.

- In some countries it is common practice for people to call up every hotel room with offers of goods or services which can be brought up. These conversations can be used to find out who is in the hotel room so that local criminals can then target tourists. If you are not expecting the call or do not recognise the person calling, just hang up.

- Even if you are only going to spend a very short time in your hotel room, lock the door. Intruders waiting in the corridor have followed people into their hotel rooms after they have been left open because the person had only popped into their room to collect something.

- If you are visiting a hotel in a high-risk environment on your own, and you decide to go out, ensure that you inform someone of your intentions. Other travellers or even hotel reception should be informed where you are going, when you expect to return and what to do if you fail to make it back on time.

- Criminal gangs have been known to use hotel elevators or lifts to target their victims. There's not much you can do against a criminal armed with a gun. If you feel uncertain about someone travelling with you in the elevator do not get in it. Wait and catch another.

- Be wary of accepting unexpected deliveries to your room. This could endanger you. Criminals and terrorists have also used this ploy to introduce improvised explosive devices into hotel rooms.

Home Security

When you travel overseas and opt to rent a house rather than live in a hotel, the security implications are rather different. You are living within the local community, without the benefit of hotel security measures, and are subject to the same degree of crime and threat of the local people. In some areas it may be very difficult to conceal the fact that you are a visitor to the area, and if the house you are living in is in a known tourist area, chances are that the local criminal fraternity will be aware of it.

When you are travelling overseas and intending to live in a private home, consider the following points:

▪ Ensure that the house is located in a safe area. If there have been repeated incidents of crime the chances are this will continue. If you are intending to travel to a high-risk area, where there is a conflict, ensure that you stay in an area protected and located near other foreigners. Ensure that it is not too isolated or exposed to danger by being situated near to high-risk buildings. Police stations, army camps and government buildings may all at one time come under the scrutiny of terrorists or criminals.

▪ Ensure the building you live in has access to the main communications routes, and to vital areas such as the airport, hospital and other foreigners' houses. Keep a map with all the relevant locations marked on it, and ensure that you know all the routes to them. If you are travelling with children, ensure that you know where they are at all times, identify the locations of playgroups and schools and the quickest route to get there. For long-term visitors to a high-risk country, compile a list of all of the essential telephone numbers in case of an emergency situation – embassy or consulate numbers, local fire, ambulance and police services, the numbers of friends and other members of the expatriate community. You may also want to include numbers of legal representatives, emergency home contacts, local and trusted service providers such as taxi numbers, couriers, home utility workers, and any other local contacts who might be able to help in an emergency situation.

▪ In high-risk situations ensure you have a contingency plan for emergency situations. Ensure that you and all of those who are travelling with you are familiar with the plan, and know what actions must be carried out. You should cover fire emergencies, security situations and any other situation that may cause you to evacuate your house. Remember, security measures are designed to prevent people from getting into your house, but your fire emergency plan is designed to allow people to get out. You must strike a balance. It may be that the risk of fire is greater than the risk from criminals and you should design you contingency plan accordingly.

■ If your home looks well protected, the criminal will look for an easier opportunity. Select a house with a medium-height wall or hedgerow with easy access to your garden. High walls can be counterproductive, as you can't see outside the periphery and thieves may be bolder once inside. If your property does have a high wall, ensure that there are no overhanging trees, telegraph poles next to the wall or streetlights.

■ You may decide to install closed-circuit television. However, most of the commercially available CCTV systems will require the monitor to be observed 24 hours a day, will have to be fitted by security professionals and will not be practical for the short-term visitor. Long-term visitors should select a property with CCTV already fitted. Ensure that the cameras cover all the vulnerable areas, that you change the tapes and that at least one camera is focused on your main entrance so that you can identify unexpected visitors before you open the door.

■ High-visibility illumination for your garden can also deter criminals. The illumination must have an adequate power source and an alternative power source so that in the event of a power failure it will keep running. It must be sited so that it will light up the vulnerable areas of your house or garden. It can be placed high up on your walls facing down to illuminate the area of your garden. In some gardens trees and garden furniture may cast shadows and provide black areas where criminals could lurk. If you are worried about this, illumination at ground level facing your home may be a better idea.

■ Consider an infrared alarm. They are light and easy to install and can be purchased in the UK and other Western countries and taken with you. In some regions they are unavailable or prohibitively expensive. If you are visiting an area and you have difficulty in obtaining an alarm, simply fit outside lights around the perimeter of your home. This will be less effective but may deter the local bad guys.

■ If possible select a property with an audio alarm fitted. This will emit a powerful high-pitched noise if anyone tries to force your windows or doors. If you are visiting a high-risk environment have a plan of action for dealing with an activated alarm. Be aware that weather, animals or wrong programming can accidentally trigger the alarm. The local police will quickly become irritated if they are called out to a false alarm, and eventually will not respond at all.

■ Do not leave out any garden equipment that might assist those intending to rob you. Ladders or similar objects will enable criminals to get access to vulnerable areas of your house. Lock them away.

■ Whether you are staying in a one-bedroom flat or a five-bedroom holiday villa on the beach, it is a good idea to quickly get into the routine of shutting down for the night. Ensure that an adult is responsible for locking all the windows (certainly at ground level) and securing all the doors. Ensure that the curtains are drawn and there are no valuable items on display near the windows. All your expensive equipment and essential documentation and cash should be secured in the room where you are sleeping. Keep it in a bag next to your bed, or hide it in an area where it will be difficult to find.

■ When we enter our homes we leave the world behind and desire a place of sanctity and security. And it's doors that make this possible. But a door is only as good as its components: even the most expensive and sophisticated locks will be of little value if the wood of the door and the door frame is weak. Ensure that you are happy with its condition. Check the doors to ensure that there are no weak areas – in many regions, the bottoms of doors can become weak after prolonged use. Ensure that the brickwork surrounding the doorframe is not crumbling, as this can weaken the entire structure. If you suspect that the door is weak, you can reinforce the door panels by attaching wooden panels to the weak areas. Ensure that all of the screw heads are on the inside of the door as criminals may be able to unscrew them and compromise the security of your entire house.

■ Make sure your door has a strong enough lock – a five-lever deadlock, obtainable from most DIY shops, is adequate. Put it in the centre of the door; a five-pin tumbler or other lock can be located beneath the mortise lock. Some doors are flexible at both the top and bottom corners of the door's locking edge. By placing a simple bolt at both the top and bottom corners of your door you will increase the protection factor dramatically.

■ If your house has internal doors, it is a good idea to lock the internal doors as well. This may stop criminals who have gained access to your home from ransacking the whole house. However, if your home is located in an area where no one will hear them, they may do more damage by breaking down internal doors as well. If you are in your house, locking internal doors may cause problems if you have to vacate the building in a hurry.

■ The other most obvious entry point for a criminal is the window. Check to ensure that the wood is not rotting and the window frames are strong enough to prevent them from being dislodged. Some windows have primitive locking mechanisms. You can revamp these easily. You should look for a window stable in its frame, with a locking mechanism where you can screw the lock into position or have a key where you can lock the device. By installing a very simple window lock you will increase the protection factor dramatically. The only alternative for the criminal is to smash the window, which increases their chances of being caught.

■ Many houses have doubleglazing. If you do, check to see that there is a locking mechanism on the window. There are many doubleglazed window styles that do not come with ready installed locking mechanisms. Many of this type rely only on the window handle for security, and these are not secure. If the window is very large you may actually require two window locks to prevent criminals getting access through the corners. If you have sliding windows and no window locks you can improvise by placing a strip of wood along the inside of the rails where the window slides.

■ In many sunny spots patio doors are an essential, but also provide the criminal with another avenue of approach. If your house has sliding patio doors, you can secure them by adding security bar locks or locks available from the local DIY store. If you think that you will need this stuff take it with you – it may not be available abroad.

■ Getting hold of your keys is the ideal criminal ploy. If you have a spare set of keys, leave them in a secure spot, with a trusted friend or neighbour. Avoid leaving your keys in on the inside of the door. It is a simple procedure to slide some paper under your door, knock the keys out of the lock onto the paper and then slide the paper under the door once more, with the keys on it. Keep your keys in a safe place, but not hanging on a peg near the door when you are not using them. Count the number of keys you have and make sure that only those you trust have a set of keys. If your house has been burgled you should change your lock the same day.

■ If you are hiring a holiday home for a few weeks in the summer, you are relying on the fact that no one else will have access to your home when you go out. However, the keys will have probably been in the hands of very many other people. The possibility exists that copies have been made and the house could be accessed when you are not there. Do not leave your valuables lying around in a house that you are hiring. The owners, cleaners and possibly other guests may still have keys.

■ A peephole is good door security. A security chain will enable the door to be opened but only enough to allow you to see and prevent the door from being forced open.

■ Many tourist houses come equipped with safety deposit boxes. If the safe is concealed you should be able to hide your valuables there. Most of the household safes available today rely on concealment for their security. If you are travelling with valuable items, check your insurance policy. Many policies insist that certain valuable items must be stored in safes of a certain standard. If your valuables are stolen from a safe below the standard stipulated in your insurance policy, you may not be covered.

- Be aware of those who call at your home offering services, or demanding to get access to the house. People posing as maintenance workers, gas workers, plumbers, electricians or a whole host of utility workers have in the past used this ruse to gain access to homes. Do not let them in unless you have called them. When you do call their office get the details of the individual who is being sent, and when they arrive you should question them to confirm their identities before you allow them in.

- Fraudsters have posed as workers, policemen, immigration officials or tour company officials. Many of these con artists are sophisticated and make a living out of tricking the unsuspecting into letting them into their homes. Ensure that you authenticate the identity of anyone who comes to your house, uniform or not. Demand to see their identity card, note the number and then contact their headquarters to check them out. If they are genuine they will wait and will understand your concerns.

17

Medical Safety

IT'S NOW POSSIBLE TO TRAVEL WITH ease to exotic locations which were once only the domains of the super-rich or the supremely adventurous. By the end of the last decade, around 5 million of us headed off to regions with a medium to high risk of contracting a potentially serious disease. Today, for those of us who can afford the ticket, we can virtually decide to turn up at the airport, get on an aircraft and jet off to the other side of the planet. Not too many years ago, people who were intending to take such a journey were subject to stringent medical examinations; today all we need is the cash. It's an attitude that could end up costing us our health.

For one thing, health services worldwide are varied, to say the least. Once in the US, when I had received a nasty gash on the head, I entered a hospital and was confronted by a receptionist who smiled at the sight of the blood and asked me for my credit card number. She reminded me of a supermarket checkout girl. In many countries, however, the medical facilities are no joke. Local people have to put up with the most appalling conditions, and going into hospital is deemed more risky than dealing with the problem yourself.

In a survey of British travellers, the three countries in which they were most likely to become ill were, starting with the worst, Peru, Kenya and India. There are endemic diseases in Asia, South America and Africa that we need to be very aware of. Yet an estimated half of all Britons travelling abroad to exotic locations fail to get their inoculations. Many travel unaware that they will be exposed to potentially dangerous or even life-threatening illnesses without the protection of vital vaccinations or prophylactic medication. Some who are aware choose to take the risk. Others who are immunised are unsure about whether their jabs are out of date. This is reflected by recent figures, which indicate that almost 1 in 8 of us who travel overseas will at some stage suffer from some kind of illness and that those at most risk are between 18 and 30.

Most of us will suffer no more than an upset stomach. But in 2001 more than 100 Britons contracted typhoid overseas, and more than 1100 came home suffering from malaria.

There's another risk factor: package tours. Apparently, you are more likely to become ill on them, probably because you eat food prepared for you, rather than pick and choose where you eat as an independent traveller.

When you are planning a trip, think about your health and consider the following.

Medical Preparation

When you are intending to travel outside Europe and North America, particularly to developing countries, you need to see your doctor between four and six weeks before your intended departure. Tell them where you are going and they can arrange the necessary inoculations. Be aware, however, that hardly any of the vaccinations will provide 100 per cent protection.

You need to get some vaccinations over a period of days or even weeks. For example, you will need two weeks for an inoculation against the food-borne illness hepatitis A, and a month for rabies. So you'll need to plan ahead.

- If you are heading off to a remote area, your local GP may not hold stocks of the right vaccinations. So before you go, call to see whether they have supplies.

- If you are travelling to a malarial area you must have the appropriate malarial prophylaxis. Your doctor should be able to find out what strain of this disease affects the area to which you are travelling, and more importantly whether or not the malarial strain has become desensitised to the normal prophylactic medication. This happened to me in Somalia; I was taking the wrong type of drug and it nearly cost me dearly. Ask your doctor about the side-effects of taking a specific drug. The malarial prophylactic Larium has caused serious problems in some of those who have used it.

- If you suffer from a specific condition, consult with your doctor about the impact of travelling on your health. If you take medication, ensure that it does not affect the drugs you have been prescribed to protect you when you are travelling. Ensure that you have at least one month's spare medication in case you are delayed. Carry your medication in its original packaging; you may even require authorisation from your doctor to enable you to carry the drugs. During your visit to the doctor, discuss how your proposed trip can affect your health, particularly if you have an allergy or are suffering from a condition such as asthma or diabetes.

- Keep a note of what immunisations you receive and how long you are protected for. In some countries you'll need to present your international vaccination certificate on entry. Failure to show this certificate may result in your being denied entry. In some states you will be required to pay a hefty bribe.

- When you are travelling to developed countries take supplies of medications with you rather than trying to buy local supplies. Locally purchased medications may well be out of date or in some other way inferior to those which you can obtain at home. This also applies to condoms.

- When you return from your trip, make an appointment to see your doctor if you feel ill. If you fall ill when overseas, keep a note of your symptoms and the dates and times when you suffered them so you can discuss them with your doctor. When you return from high-risk areas, even up to one month later, visit your doctor if you feel ill. Many of the infections travellers contract overseas have prolonged incubation periods, even up to a month or longer.

Amoebic Dysentery

Amoebic dysentery is caused by a bacterium that infects the intestine. You get it after eating food contaminated by human excrement. You may get it through contact with a person who is contaminated, as a result of poor hygiene conditions or via the use of human waste as fertiliser (known as night soil). It is widespread in Asia, Africa, South America and the Asian subcontinent and can be contracted almost anywhere. In many of these regions where there is little medical support, it can be fatal: around 50,000 people a year die of it.

The symptoms include abdominal cramps and pains and frequent diarrhoea. Victims may suffer pain when defecating and have a build-up of abdominal gas. They may have diarrhoea with blood or a mucus texture, and develop a fever and become listless and tired. If left untreated it can last up to two weeks and the victim can suffer recurrent bouts of diarrhoea and abdominal discomfort.

- The key to avoiding this infection is good hygiene, particularly when travelling in developing countries where food and drinks may be prepared in unsanitary conditions. Eat in establishments with adequate hygiene standards. Ask other travellers if they have eaten there. If anyone has become ill after eating there, go somewhere else.

- Avoid eating uncooked vegetables, particularly in areas where the use of night soil is common. Request that the vegetables be cooked. If the food is boiled or baked till very hot it should be safe to eat.

- Ensure that fruits are unpeeled and are never washed in unsterilised water. Peel fruits yourself, ensuring that you have cleaned your hands with bacterial moist wipes or clean water.

- Keep flies and crawling insects away from your food, cutlery, plates and table surface. When I was in Bossasso in Northern Somalia the cooking area was on one side of a wall, and on the other side was the neighbouring house's latrine. There were many flying insects. Not surprisingly, most of us became ill with dysentery.

- When you are living in a remote area ensure that the latrines are located far away from both the living and cooking areas. This will reduce the possibility of contamination. In short visits to remote areas you may consider taking your own secure food and water supplies with you.

- If you are a long-term visitor to a remote area or a developing country you may have to instruct those preparing the food in basic food hygiene. In my trip to Somalia we had to tell the cook about basic sanitation, and had fairly good results as fewer people became ill.

- It is essential that you have a secure, clean water supply. Bottled water is generally good, but be aware that people sometimes fill bottles from the local stream and reseal them to make quick money. The result for the traveller can be a debilitating illness. Check the seal on the bottle and if you are not happy about the state of it do not drink the water. Do not drink from a bottle or cup someone else has used.

- Carry water purification tablets or iodine with you to sterilise water. If you decide to boil the water, do so for 10 minutes.

- If you do contract this disease seek medical assistance. Depending on the severity of the infection, medical professionals will prescribe antibiotic treatment. It is also important to rehydrate, as diarrhoea can leave you severely dehydrated.

Cholera

Cholera is a potentially fatal disease that usually hits in regions with poor sanitation. The disease can reach epidemic proportions in the developing world, particularly where there is social deprivation, conflict and the migration of refugees.

Consuming contaminated water or food – including shellfish that have come from areas contaminated by raw sewage – can give you cholera. The disease can set in very quickly. First there will be sudden and severe bouts of watery diarrhoea. There is a very pungent fishy smell with a white or yellowish colour. Due to the frequent and very heavy bouts of diarrhoea, the person can become dehydrated and thirsty fast. They may have hot dry skin and a raised pulse rate and appear listless, with glazed eyes. Some people may suffer only mild symptoms, while in others the effects can be severe. In high-risk areas such as in unsanitised refugee camps, the disease can spread like wildfire.

Consider the following points if you are travelling somewhere with a history of cholera, or to an area where there is conflict or many displaced people.

- Talk to your doctor well before you go. Cholera vaccinations providing limited protection against the disease are available. Booster vaccinations to be given at six-month intervals can be obtained for those who are intending to remain in cholera-infected areas. Like most inoculations, the cholera vaccine does not provide 100 per cent protection against the illness.

- Travellers to high-risk areas must be extra vigilant about hygiene around food and drink (see 'Amoebic Dysentery', above). Even those travellers who have received the cholera vaccination must ensure that they protect themselves from contaminated food and water, and maintain high levels of sanitation and hygiene.

- If you're travelling to known infected areas, you must step up your vigilance even more round food and particularly water. It's very risky having any contact with people who have the disease, as they may transmit the bacteria.

- Most fatalities from those infected by cholera arise from dehydration. Anyone with the disease has to be given fluid replacement therapy. Medical facilities will have rehydration mixtures, or home-made versions can be made by mixing a half teaspoonful of salt and two tablespoons of sugar into 1 litre of sterile water. The patient can drink this or the fluid is administered intravenously. After rehydration, most people will make a complete recovery.

■ Severe cases will require antibiotics and it is essential that you seek medical treatment as soon as possible.

Diarrhoea

One of the most common health problems abroad is diarrhoea. Even though it is a minor complaint, it can be uncomfortable and disrupt travel plans; in more serious cases it can even ruin holidays. Travellers can pick up diarrhoea almost anywhere and at any time by consuming contaminated food or drinks. Those unused to travelling in exotic locations or who have particularly sensitive stomachs may also be affected.

Diarrhoea – frequent loose or watery stools – can last for a few days until your body becomes used to new conditions abroad. It may happen because you have an infection, or a reaction to unfamiliar food or even medication used to combat infections. Due to the sudden and uncontrollable nature of diarrhoea many travellers have to stay in their hotels so they have constant access to toilets.

In addition to loose stools, the person may complain of pain or cramps in the abdomen, bloating or nausea, and in severe cases blood in their stools. Dehydration can set in. Mild diarrhoea can sort itself out, but the condition can be symptomatic of many medical conditions, so it's important to seek medical advice for anything other than the mildest case. Definitely go to a doctor if there is severe pain accompanied by a high fever, or if it lasts for more than the usual two to three days. If the condition persists, oral rehydration or antidiarrhoea medication should be given, and in serious cases antibiotic treatment.

Consider the following points.

■ Practise strict hygiene round food and water. Drinks such as tea and coffee, fruit juices and dairy drinks may all present a risk if they have been contaminated. Ensure that you consume only bottled water; check to see whether the seals have been tampered with. Use bottled water to brush your teeth, and avoid having ice in your drinks. In many places ice is made from contaminated water and is stored in contaminated areas.

- If you are travelling in a remote region, ensure that you are carrying enough water sterilisation tablets or filters. Even in running water you might end up drinking contaminated water: upstream other humans or animals may use the river areas as a toilet. In one of my jungle adventures I was crossing a small river and decided to fill up my water bottles with the inviting, crystal-clear water. However, I then found the carcass of a dead pig 20 metres upstream. Had we actually drunk the water untreated, we would undoubtedly have become ill.

- Avoid eating fruits and vegetables which have been washed in unsterilised water. Ensure your cutlery and crockery are clean.

- Avoid drinking canned drinks straight from the can. Or clean the surface area of the can with an antibacterial wipe. Many canned drinks are stored in areas where rats and other animals have free access to them.

- Only use sterilised water to wash your face and hands. If no water is available ensure that you have access to antibacterial moist wipes. Pay particular attention to hygiene after leaving a toilet. Remember, even touching a contaminated door handle and then touching your mouth may be enough to pass on a debilitating infection.

- Make sure all your food has been sufficiently well cooked and is very hot when it arrives, to ensure all harmful bacteria have been killed off. On a recent visit to Hong Kong I ate a meal in one of the street food markets. The hygiene looked very basic, but the food was exceptionally hot. I had not even a minor stomach upset.

- You should avoid eating raw foods such as uncooked meats or fish, peeled fruits, vegetables and salads. In developing countries or in areas with poor sanitation, unpasteurised dairy products such as milk, yoghurts and unprocessed cheeses may also provide a route for infection.

- Simple diarrhoea can be controlled with over-the-counter medication. However, as I've indicated above, if the symptoms continue for more than a few days, include pain or cramps or if you there's blood in your stool, see a doctor.

- Replace fluids. Rehydration drinks are cheap and easily available and are an effective way of replacing fluids and minerals that are lost through diarrhoea. However sufferers must ensure that they drink enough clean and sterile water. Obviously, drinking contaminated water will prolong illness and in some cases cause more serious problems.

Malaria

Malaria affects up to 500 million people, and kills 1 million, each year. It is one of the world's biggest killers, and for Western travellers is one of the greatest medical hazards when visiting malarial areas.

The disease is caused by a parasite transmitted from person to person by the bite of Anopheles mosquitoes. The riskiest times are dusk to dawn, as this is when the insect feeds. The mosquito injects an anti-coagulant into its victim, which enables it to feed, and by this action transmits the parasite.

Normally a problem in the tropical regions of the world, malaria can be transmitted in temperate zones, but not during the colder winter months. There are different types of malaria affecting different regions of the world. The parasite has also developed resistance to many of the drugs used to prevent or treat the disease. When you are planning your trip, it's essential that you speak with your doctor or a travel advisory authority to identify which strain of the disease is prevalent at your destination. Medical authorities will provide information on the geographical distribution of the disease and the time of year when you will be in most danger from the infection, and more importantly, the appropriate prophylaxis for that region.

If you go to a known malarial area unprepared, you are taking a risk. If you contract the disease, the symptoms will manifest themselves within 10 to 30 days. However, in some people symptoms have arisen much earlier, and for some others much later – up to a year. The symptoms are cyclical and occur at intervals of between two to three days. They can include fever, accompanied by chills and profuse sweating. The victim may complain of feeling sick and may vomit and have a headache. They may also feel muscular aches and pains. If left untreated, the victim may develop diarrhoea with traces of blood, and develop a yellow, jaundiced appearance. In the later stages they will go into convulsions and lapse into a coma. Never forget that malaria is a life-threatening disease and must be treated as such.

I was unfortunate enough to pick up falciparum malaria, a particularly nasty and life-threatening strain, while on a trip to Somalia in 1999. I had been informed that one particular prophylactic drug was sufficient to cover me for my trip, only to find out that the strain of malaria in northern Somalia had built up a resistance to it. I managed to acquire the appropriate medication, but was left exposed for about five days. During this time I contracted the disease, and even though I had the drugs I needed to cut short my trip and return home.

If you will be travelling to a malarial area, consider the following points.

- Many of the local inhabitants of malarial areas may have developed immunity. As you obviously haven't, you'll need the right prophylaxis.

- Antimalarial prophylaxis is available from doctors and even from some high-street chemists. Because the malarial strain may have become desensitised to commonly used antimalarial medications, you have to be sure to get the appropriate one. You need to provide your doctor with a list of the countries you'll be visiting. With some malarial medications you need to begin taking them up to two weeks before and as long as four weeks after you have returned from your trip. Be sure you have sufficient supplies to last your trip. Pack more than you need and put them in different pieces of luggage in case some of it goes missing. Take enough supplies in your hand luggage in case you lose your other bags.

- As with other medical preparations, malarial prophylactics will not provide 100 per cent protection.

- You'll also need to guard against the mosquitoes that carry the disease. Apply mosquito repellent to exposed areas of skin. The repellent of choice should contain a mixture of between 20 to 35 per cent DEET.

- Wear protective, long-sleeved shirts and long trousers, especially during the night when the mosquitoes are most active. Apply mosquito repellent to your clothing, too, to avoid getting bitten through your shirt or trousers.

- Bring your own new mosquito net, which you need to check for holes. Impregnate your net with permethrin. It is also a good idea to sleep with the windows shut at night if there are no mosquito screens over the windows. Spray insecticides or light a mosquito coil before you turn in for the night.

- Even if you take the appropriate medication, you may still be exposed to the disease. Before you go, ask your doctor what the recognised treatment is if you were to contract the illness. In some regions you will have to buy the medication yourself and you will need to know the generic and brand names.

The most dangerous strain of this disease is falciparum malaria, and this must be treated as a life-threatening illness.

Rabies

Rabies is rare in Britain and some other countries due to stringent control measures. But in many other regions of the world there is little rabies prevention. It is a very serious illness, and if you have no protection and contract it, you have to act fast.

Rabies is passed on from the bite of an infected animal, or their saliva transmitting the disease through an open wound or scratch. It has even been known to be transmitted through the air in a cave inhabited by infected bats. Infected animals may be shivering, restless and excitable, and may become very aggressive and attack anything moving within striking distance, without warning. In later stages they can develop the classic foaming mouth and paralysis.

In humans, the symptoms can come on weeks or even months after exposure to an infected animal. The site of the bite or wound may itch and the person may feel depressed or agitated, develop a fever, headache and sore throat, be unwilling to eat and complain of muscle stiffness. The victim may also show an unusual oversensitivity to temperature changes, noise and bright lights. Sporadic cycles of excitability followed by rationality give way to seizures and painful spasms of the throat when the victim tries to swallow. If left untreated the person can die as soon as a week after the appearance of symptoms.

If you are intending to travel to an area where rabies is prevalent, consider the following points.

- Rabies vaccination is available to those travelling to high-risk areas. Your doctor will probably have to order it, so get in touch with them well ahead of time. The vaccination is administered by three injections over around 28 days. You may also consider this preventative measure if you are travelling to a country where treatment for the disease itself will not be available.

- If you have come into contact with an infected animal or if you are bitten by any animal in an infected area it is absolutely essential that you take action immediately, before the onset of any symptoms. If the symptoms are allowed to develop you will have little chance of recovery.

- The first thing you need to do if you have been licked, bitten or scratched by an animal in a high-risk area is immediately clean the site of the wound with soap and water. If you have antibacterial wipes, use them. Ensure that you wash away from the site of the wound, using gravity to drain off any infected saliva. If possible you should allow the wound to bleed, as this will reduce the chances of infected saliva getting into your bloodstream.

- Leave the area immediately and seek medical attention. In areas without adequate medical support, get the victim evacuated to an area with acceptable medical facilities as soon as possible. They will need to start the course of injections immediately – there are five of them over the course of a month.

- Avoid any contact with wild animals while you are in infected areas. Unless there are strict rabies prevention methods you should also avoid getting near any domestic animals. Ensure that if you are travelling with a pet you keep it under control, as contact with contaminated animals will invariably mean your pet will also become contaminated and may infect you. If you are travelling with children, educate them about the dangers of touching wild or stray dogs.

- Avoid the bodies of dead animals. If you come across an animal carcass, instruct the local authorities to come and dispose of it. In high-risk areas, ensure that your doors and windows are secured to prevent animals from entering your house.

Typhoid

Typhoid is common in many developing countries and areas with poor sanitation. An estimated 10 million people are infected with this serious and potentially life-threatening disease every year. The bacteria responsible for this infection is transmitted by consuming food or drink contaminated by faecal material.

Symptoms include a high fever, headache and a persistent feeling of fatigue. The casualty may develop a red, spotty rash, show an unwillingness to eat and complain of discomfort and pains in the stomach. If you have travelled to a high-risk area and you think that you may have been exposed to this disease, it's essential to seek medical attention as soon as possible for a diagnosis. Otherwise it can become a prolonged and possibly terminal illness. It is treated with antibiotics and if you start immediately you have an excellent chance of making a full recovery.

If you are intending to travel to a known typhoid area, consider the following points.

- You can be vaccinated against typhoid, either orally or by injection. The vaccine must be given at least two weeks before departure for you to receive maximum protection. So at least five weeks or so before you go you need to get in touch with your doctor to ensure that they have adequate supplies of the vaccine.

- For those who have already had typhoid vaccinations, check with your doctor to see whether you are still up to date. The protection offered by the vaccination diminishes after around two years and you may require a booster.

- If you travel to a typhoid area and have not been vaccinated, even prophylactic antibiotic medication will not prevent you from contracting the disease. So get vaccinated before you go.

- It is essential that you adopt the same vigilance with regard to food and water hygiene that you would with any other potentially serious illness.

- Do not wash in or brush your teeth with water from an unknown source.

- There is a possibility that the disease may still be passed on by people who have typhoid but no apparent symptoms. It is essential that those who have recovered from the disease avoid handling food. If someone you know has recently suffered from this disease, avoid contact with them.

- If you have had typhoid, even after your symptoms have disappeared you must maintain a high level of personal hygiene and continue to take the course of medication prescribed by your doctor. If you fail to complete the course the disease may return, or you may develop complications. It is essential that you receive follow-up treatment, which may include analysis of stool samples in order to confirm that the disease has gone.

Yellow Fever

Yellow fever is common in many parts of the developing world in both rural and urban areas. The symptoms appear around four to six days after a bite from the Aedes mosquito. First there are flu-like symptoms, headache and fever, often accompanied by vomiting and aches and pains – particularly backache. As the infection develops, the victim may experience bleeding gums and there may also be traces of blood in their urine. Their pulse rate may be slow and weak and they may take on a yellowish tint (jaundice).

It is important to be vaccinated before you travel to areas where the disease is prevalent. The vaccination will last for around 10 years, but if you are unsure as to when you were vaccinated you should consult your doctor. You will not be allowed into many countries unless you have your international certificate proving that you have been vaccinated against yellow fever. To arrange a vaccination, contact your doctor well in advance of travelling so they have time to order the vaccine. You'll also need to take the same precautions against mosquito bites as you would for malaria (see above). If, when you return, you develop any of the symptoms associated with this disease you should immediately consult your doctor whether you've been vaccinated or not.

Diseases by region

	Malaria	Typhus	Yellow fever	Rabies	Dysentery	Cholera	Typhoid	Polio
North Africa	✓	✓		✓	✓	✓	✓	
Sub-Saharan Africa	✓	✓	✓	✓	✓	✓	✓	
Central America	✓			✓	✓	✓	✓	
Caribean	✓			✓	✓			
South America	✓	✓	✓		✓		✓	
East Asia	✓			✓	✓			✓
South East Asia	✓	✓		✓	✓	✓	✓	✓
Asian Sub-Continent	✓	✓		✓		✓	✓	
Middle East	✓	✓					✓	
Pacific Region	✓	✓			✓		✓	✓

18

Basic Navigation Techniques

WHEN YOU VENTURE INTO THE UNFAMILIAR, whether it's a big city or a remote jungle, map reading is essential. If you are heading off to a remote area or a high-risk environment, taking a wrong turning or going too far in the wrong direction could have tragic consequences. Even travellers in the more remote areas of Britain have found themselves in trouble after becoming lost – each year we read tragic stories of those lost on lonely hillsides in Scotland. And there has been a spate of incidents in which young people on adventure holidays have become separated from their groups and lost. So basic navigation skills can be a life-or-death matter.

Not only do many of us jet off on adventure holidays with no navigation skills; many of the people leading the expeditions are only one step ahead of their clients. If you are paying for an expensive holiday, it is reasonable to expect that the leaders know what they are doing. But you need to be able to find your own way back if you're separated from the group.

You can read a lot of books on navigation techniques, but there's no substitute for practical training. Therefore this chapter will provide only basic information on map reading and some useful tips I have found to be beneficial over the years. However, if you will be required to navigate on your trip, you might need to take a brief course on map reading or get out and practise.

I hope the following helps you gain a real, if basic, understanding of the subject, and will give you the confidence to pick up your map and compass and get busy navigating.

Maps

When you will be travelling in an unfamiliar area, you'll need to buy maps before you go. It's easy to find good maps in Europe and North America, but maps you buy abroad may not be up to the same standard. On my recent trip to Afghanistan I found that the local maps were not particularly good.

You can find maps in high-street suppliers, or by shopping on the Internet. You must decide what level of detail you need in your maps. Maps of entire countries are not all that useful for trekking or driving: their scale (see below) is so large that local navigation will be difficult. Large-scale maps will normally be limited to the main towns, cities and road networks, and show most major topographical features such as mountain ranges and rivers. If you need more detailed information on a specific region within a country, look for a map of that region. Depending on the scale of the map, it will provide you with enough information to navigate accurately over even relatively small distances.

A map is basically just a two-dimensional representation of our three-dimensional world using relatively common symbols, colours and lines to provide you with a view of the region. There are different types of maps; but for the traveller, the topographical map detailing the lie of the land is essential. Most maps use basic, common features and symbols, and your ability to navigate accurately depends on your learning this 'language' and being able to use it. Most mapping is relatively modern and accurate; cartographers use high-tech satellite images for the information on them.

Scales

The scale of the map will be displayed on or near the title strip. If the scale is 1:50,000, this means that one unit on the map is the equivalent of 50,000 units on the ground. If you require a road map which will show the main road routes between the main towns and cities in the UK, for instance, you will be looking for a map with a scale of around 1:250,000. To cover the entire UK you would need nine maps of this scale. This scale will provide very little topographical information other than the main road routes and built-up areas.

If you intend to go hiking or into a mountainous region, or simply navigate while on foot, you will require a 1:50,000 scaled map. This scaled map will provide you with local information over a fairly large area and will show relatively detailed surface features – hills, rivers and small streams, and in some areas even single buildings. More detailed maps with a scale of 1:25,000 provide information over a smaller area than a 1:50,000 scaled map, but the detail is much greater. So the smaller the scale of the map, the more detail will be shown and the easier it will be to obtain an accurate reference. However, if you are covering a great distance it may be impractical to carry enough maps. If you were touring a country it would not be practical to carry 1:25,000 scale maps of the entire country – you would need perhaps hundreds. It is better to carry a large-scale map of the country and perhaps one or two detailed maps of areas which you are going to be travelling through or staying in.

Relief

A relief map shows the three-dimensional contours of the ground using contour lines. A contour line is a line that joins points of equal height. The contour lines are all separated by the same height difference, and together show the shape of topographical features. You are able to see how steep a hill is, for instance: if the contours are packed tightly together it's a steep slope, and if the contours are spaced widely apart it's a gentle slope. The contour height or contour interval will be marked on your map. In the UK, most maps have a 10-metre interval, but when you are overseas you must check the interval, as some countries use different systems.

There are two types of contour line: the normal line, which will not show any height value, and the index contour, which is thicker than the other lines and will have the height value written on it. The index contour will appear on your map every fifth line. You'll need to practise visualising the shape of the land using the contour lines. Looking at the mass of contour lines and trying to identify the height and shape of the ground can be difficult to do if you are not used to it. However, there are a few simple tricks to help you sort out high from low ground.

Obviously, water (coloured blue on maps) flows from higher to lower elevations, so following the course of any stream on the map will allow you to trace its course from hills to valleys. Lower ground is indicated by widely spaced contours. If on lower ground you find contour lines forming a thin finger that points to higher ground, this shows a valley, re-entrant or gully. If the contours are on high ground and form a finger pointing to lower ground, this indicates a spur or ridgeline.

Really tightly packed contours show a slope that is so steep it may be difficult or impossible to walk down. If the contours are open and widely spaced, the slope will be gentle and easy to walk on. A valley, as I've said, is shown by contours forming a finger or V-shape, and the contour interval will increase in numerical value as the V-shape climbs up the slopes of the valley. A valley will usually have rivers or streams running along the bottom, where the contour lines on both sides of the valley meet. A ridgeline will be indicated by contour lines forming a V-shape that descends in numerical value as the contours descend to lower elevations. The ridgeline is where the contour lines meet at the top of a feature. The summit of a high feature will be the inmost of a series of more or less circular contour lines ascending in numerical value. Craters or other depressions in the ground are also shown by circular contour lines, but these will descend in numerical value towards the centre.

Relief on a map is also indicated by colour. On larger maps, the colours used to indicate height levels will be shown on the map's legend. Areas of woodland will be coloured green. (Woodlands, it should be said, can change: they can be cut down or planted since a map was produced. If you're in an area with a lot of woods, try to get the most up-to-date map you can.)

Legends

The legend, which appears either on the margin or back of the map, is a key identifying the symbols and other information shown on the map. The map title will indicate the area of the map. You will also find the year the map was produced, the contour interval and, along the bottom margin, a scale. Every symbol or colour shown on your map will have an explanation in the legend.

Grids

The map's grid system lets us find positions on it. The grid system is a series of vertical and horizontal lines superimposed over the map picture. The vertical lines of the grid increase in numerical value from left (west) to right (east). As they move east on the map they are known as eastings. The lateral lines of the grid increase in numerical order from the bottom to the top of the sheet. These lines are called northings. Grid lines form 1-kilometre squares and enable us to identify with relative accuracy positions on the map. In order to identify a grid square on the map, all you do is identify the vertical line to the left of the grid square and follow it either up or down, whichever is easiest, to the vertical line number at the base or top of the map. Once you have this number, go back to your square and identify the horizontal line below the square. Follow the horizontal line either to the left or right, whichever is easiest, to the horizontal line number. You now have a four-figured grid reference. It can be difficult for those unused to map reading to remember which number comes first, but eastings (vertical lines) are first, followed by northings (horizontal lines).

The four-figure grid reference will give you the location of the 1-kilometre square, a reference with an accuracy of within 1000 metres. This is a large area, and generally a greater degree of accuracy will be required. To achieve this greater accuracy we use six-figure grid references. Identify the point on the map that you are looking for, then take the vertical line to the right and follow up or down to identify its number. You will have the first two numbers of your grid. If you can envisage the grid squares being further divided by 10 lateral lines and 10 vertical lines, estimate the number of lines from your position back to the vertical line. This will give you a third figure. For the second part of your grid, identify the horizontal line, and find its number, then estimate the number of lines from your position down to the horizontal line below. You will now have a six-figure grid reference and this will place you within an accuracy of 100 metres.

Using a Compass

The compass remains one of the principal navigation tools, even in the age of the Global Positioning System (GPS). There are areas of the world where the GPS may not work, such as deep in the rain-forest where the jungle canopy obscures the satellite signals. And of course if the GPS is in any way out of commission, people will have to resort to the tried and tested method of the compass.

If you will be navigating across country or in mountainous areas, a basic understanding of compass work is necessary. The compass is a basic navigational instrument and consists of a magnetised needle or north pointer (see opposite, above) that floats in fluid (alcohol) on a pivotal point, which allows the needle to freely move. If the needle is allowed to freely move, the north pointer (the red point) will continually point to the magnetic north, which is around 6 degrees west of true north (the North Pole). There are other features on the compass but essentially a compass consists of the following features:

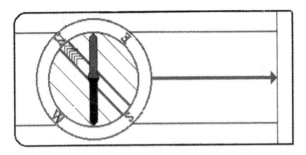

My aim here is not to delve too deeply into the intricacies of grid magnetic angles or magnetic deviation: these subjects are covered in much more detail in most outdoor books. I will cover the basic operation of the compass here, although without detailed knowledge of how the magnetic angle affects your compass bearings you may find that you will not be accurate.

There are basically three types of north - magnetic, true north and grid north, which is the north at the top of your map and is almost indistinguishable from true north.

Using compass and map together

The compass is used primarily to provide you with a direction, but for accurate navigation you must have an understanding of how to use you compass with your map. One of the first things you need to do when navigating is orient your map with north. That is to say, you must ensure that north on your map is pointing in the same direction as magnetic north, so when you look at the map the information will relate to the landscape.

To do this you must first identify where magnetic north is – remember, about 6 degrees west of true north. To orient your map, set your compass to magnetic north by rotating the compass dial so that the orientation arrow corresponds to the north pointer (needle). Place your compass onto your map with the orientation lines corresponding to the northings (vertical lines). You can then rotate the map with the compass on top, while maintaining the orientation of your compass to magnetic north, until both your compass and map relate to magnetic north.

Your map is now orientated and you will be able to relate the features on it to features in the landscape. Once you've done this, any bearings that you take from your map to your compass or from your compass to your map will be almost the same. (Of course, if you change your position you'll need to reorient the map.) Now, identify the prominent features on the ground and check them off on your map. Look for mountains, valleys and perhaps woods (which may have changed since the map was published), rivers and built-up areas, main roads, railways and electricity pylon lines. These are all fairly obvious features and should be easy enough to pick out. It is wise to note the lay of the land and remember the geographical features that you will be close to during your travels. If you can remember which features you should be seeing you will generally have a good idea of roughly where you are.

Your compass is principally used to provide direction, and this is done through bearings. A bearing is the horizontal angle measured clockwise from either magnetic or true north from one position either on your map or on the ground to another position. By following a bearing you will be able to accurately navigate from your position to another location, even at night. There are two types of compass bearing, a map or grid bearing if you are working from a map, or a magnetic bearing if you are taking it to an actual point on the ground. The compass has 360 degrees or 6400 mills, depending on the unit of measure used on your compass, and beginning at north the numbers increase incrementally clockwise. North is 000, or 360 degrees, at the 12 o'clock position, east is 90 degrees at 3 o'clock, south is 180 degrees at 6 o'clock, and west is 270 degrees at 9 o'clock.

Navigate using map and compass together. Identify a start point and a destination point on your map. Place your compass on the map so that the direction of travel line points towards your destination. The lateral edge should pass through both the centre of the start point and the centre of the destination point. You must then rotate the compass dial until the orientation arrow corresponds with grid north. The orientation lines on your compass should be aligned with the vertical lines (eastings) on the map. Remove the compass from the map and read the number on the compass dial (on our diagram above this is where the dial meets the direction of travel line). This is your grid bearing. If your map is within a few years old or less, you need not alter the bearing for magnetic deviation and as long as you are not travelling great distances you should have little problem. However, if your map is older and you are travelling over great distances, you will have to consider magnetic deviation.

Magnetic deviation depends on where in the world you are, and the magnetic information in the legend on your map. Once you've discovered the magnetic information for your location, there is a simple way to remember what you should do with it. 'Mag to Grid, get rid' will help you remember that if you have taken a bearing from the land and you want to use this information on your map, you take the sum away from your bearing. 'Grid to Mag, add' means that if you have taken a bearing from your map and intend on using it on your compass, you need to add the sum to your bearing.

After you have taken your grid bearing, hold the compass in front of you, ensuring that the direction of travel line is pointing at your destination. Keeping the direction of travel line pointing to the destination, move your body until the magnetic needle (red end) corresponds directly with the orientation arrow. If you are taking your bearing to or from a feature on the ground, you must ensure that the compass is held flat, so that the needle is allowed to move freely. Keeping the compass pointing to the target, rotate the compass dial until the orientation arrow corresponds with the north indicator (needle). The orientation arrow must be pointing in the same direction as the red part of the compass needle or north pointer. Read the number from the compass dial (from the same place indicated above) and this will give you a magnetic bearing. These procedures may appear difficult at first, but with some practice they are relatively easy to do.

Estimating Distance

When walking or trekking, especially over rough terrain, you need to keep track of the distance you have travelled. There are some basic techniques that can help you estimate how far you have travelled. The first is known as time and distance. Simply identify how fast you are travelling and keep track of the time you have been moving, and this will give you a relatively accurate idea of how far you have travelled. The speed at which you travel will be dictated by a number of factors – the terrain, your level of fitness and the load you are carrying. An unburdened adult will be able to move across flat ground at a speed of around 5 kilometres per hour or just over 1 kilometre every 10 minutes. However, the same person travelling over mountainous terrain or carrying a heavy pack will cover much less distance during the same time, and of course as you travel you will become tired and be less able to travel at this speed.

Consider the following:

Load (kilograms)	Terrain	Distance (kilometres)	Estimated time (hours)
No load	Easy terrain	5–6	1
16	Flat cross-country	4	1
18	Rough terrain	3	1
18	Mountainous terrain	1	Up to 3

Depending on the severity of the incline and the load you are carrying, you should consider adding 1 hour for every 300 metres climbed. It is also possible to calculate the distance travelled by using a piece of paper to measure the distance on your map, then calculating the distance you have to travel. Follow the route of your map and identify prominent features, record the distance to these features and as you pass them on the ground you will have a good idea of the distance you have travelled.

There are also technical devices that can assist in calculating how far you have travelled. Pedometers count how many paces you have taken and convert the distance into metres, but you must calibrate the pedometer to the length of your stride. GPS, if you're in an environment where it functions, is extremely accurate.

On my jungle excursions I knew that I took eight paces for every 10 metres on flat terrain. Going up steep hills I took 11 or 12, and going downhill around the same. Using this technique (called pacing) I would record every 10 metres by using a pacer, which is a small device with a numerical display that advances numerically every click. Others have used a knotted piece of cord, tying or releasing a knot after every 100 metres. Or you can carry some small stones in a pocket. After every 100 metres take a stone from one pocket and place it in another pocket. Then count the number of stones in the second pocket.

Planning Your Route

When you are navigating, it is a good idea to plan your route. Conduct a map study to identify the type of terrain you intend to travel over. After you have selected the route you want to cover, it is a good idea to produce a route card. The route card is a record of all the information you need for navigating. If you are travelling over a long distance, break the route into easily navigable legs. Recording the information for each leg will make the whole journey easier (see route card, below). Before you move off, spend a few minutes checking to see whether your calculations are correct. Check your bearings, distance (see below), the features you expect to encounter and what type of ground you expect to travel over. Time spent doing this is seldom time wasted. Consider the location of linear features, such as roads, rivers (including the direction of flow) and wood lines. Consider the elevation you will be travelling over. Will you be walking uphill, downhill or on the flat? This will help you calculate the time you will take. Identify any man-made features you can use as navigation aids – built-up areas, individual buildings or bridges. Record all this information on your route card.

Route Card

Leg	Bearing From	Bearing To	Distance	Terrain Description	Height	Check -point	Time
1	025 Deg Mag	057 Deg Mag	400 metres	Steep climb through wood	300-metre gain	Rockface	1 hour
2	057 Deg Mag	133 Deg Mag	750 metres	Traverse open rocky plateau	Flat	Corner of wood	15 mins
3	133 Deg Mag	010 Deg Mag	1.5 kilo- metres	Descend through wood, cross open field	300 metre descent	Bridge over river	30 mins
4	010 Deg Mag	220 Deg Mag	1 kilo-	Cross river, follow track to pick-up point	Flat	Pick up car park	20 mins

Lost Procedure

Whether you're navigating through Brazilian rainforest or trying to find your embassy in a big city, becoming lost is an occupational hazard. In fact, most people do not become totally lost. They become misplaced: they have a good idea of where they are, but do not know the exact location. In some situations where you are at risk, either through natural dangers such as the weather or through man-made dangers such as drifting into a particularly hostile area, the last thing you really need is to be lost and have no idea of what to do.

Most of us have experienced this. You're using a map or your memory, and you know generally where you should be going. However, you should have reached your destination by now. You become alert that things do not appear to be familiar. What do you do? Most of us push on a little bit further, and then a little bit further again – until we're lost. The trick is that you must identify what it was that alerted you in the first place. Perhaps it was a distant and long-unused sense that helps some people to navigate. The idea is to recognise that instant when things don't fit, then stop.

■ As soon as you have halted, use your map and compass and assess the information you have. Check the route that you have just covered, check off the major features you have seen. Look on your map for routes that look similar to the one you should be on. On one occasion I was with a party walking through a thick jungle-covered valley in South East Asia. We had been walking for days and had not found the location where we were supposed to be met. However, after a map study we noticed a valley of the same dimensions going in the same direction just over the hill from where we were. We were in the wrong valley.

■ Relate where you think your current position is to where the last identifiable location was. Consider the direction you have been travelling in. Check your bearings and ensure that your compass has not been moved from your original bearing.

■ Another good idea is to stop as soon as you believe that you have gone wrong, and walk 100 or 200 metres from your position in open ground, looking for an obvious feature. In heavily wooded areas this may be reduced to around 50 metres. If you fail to see an obvious feature go back to your original position. Then make another probe out and then back. You should continue these short probes until you have covered the whole area in the direction on your bearing.

■ Look around to see if you can identify a feature on the ground that you can relate to a feature on the map. You should be easily able to find your position if you can identify a major landmark in the area. You may have to climb to high ground so that you can have a good view.

■ Check the distance you have covered so far. Chances are, if your bearing is good you will either have gone too far or be short of your destination. Consider the calculations and bearing that you made at the beginning and mentally go through the process you used.

■ Consider where you are in relation to your start point. If you have not travelled far you may consider returning to your start point to begin again.

■ If you are completely lost and have exhausted all of the above ideas without finding where you are, look at your map and try to identify a linear feature, a river, road or perhaps the line of a large wood. Set your bearing to this prominent position and head off.

■ If you are in a really remote area and find yourself lost you may consider following a river. Water flows downhill, and by following the course of the water you will eventually find a main river that will eventually lead you to human habitation. The higher your elevation the less likely you will be to encounter areas of habitation. It is common in remote areas to use waterways as means of communication.

Navigation Tips

■ During the planning phase of your trip, buy the relevant maps. Be aware, however, that in today's security-charged world, carrying a detailed map in a sensitive area can raise suspicions. If you are caught with detailed maps that contain information on military establishments, training areas, police or areas which some authorities might think sensitive, you may find yourself under scrutiny. In some politically unstable countries, it may be wise to use the maps provided in travel guidebooks rather than walking around with detailed maps. Many maps commercially produced today look very much like their military counterparts.

■ If you are navigating in a high-risk environment, avoid putting marks on your map. Avoid indicating routes you propose to take or marking locations on your map. In areas where the security forces are on high alert, these marks may be interpreted as something sinister.

■ When you are navigating with your compass, don't walk with your compass held out in front of you. Take your bearing and identify a prominent object in the direction in which you are travelling, such as a distant mountain. You will be able to walk in the correct direction by relating to this prominent object rather than having to constantly check your compass.

- A common error is to use the wrong end of the compass needle when taking bearings. The red north indicator must always point in the same direction you are travelling in; if you use the wrong end you will go in the opposite direction.

- Another common mistake when taking a bearing from the map is to rotate the compass dial so that the orientation arrow is pointing to the bottom of the map instead of aligning with the eastings and pointing north on your map.

- You must also be careful to take a bearing from your map from the right direction. For example, if you are leaving location A and travelling to destination B, you must ensure that the direction of travel line points from A to B and not the other way around. This is a very common mistake.

- Your compass is essentially a magnetised needle, and being a magnet it will be attracted to certain metal objects – large metal divers' watches or even cars – or to electrical currents. There are rock formations with a high ferrous metal content and they can also attract the needle in your compass. Ensure that before you use your compass you are far enough away from metal objects for them not to interfere with your bearing. Also make sure that when you buy your compass, there are no bubbles, as this will prevent the free flow of your compass needle and may lead to an inaccurate reading. You should also check your compass after flying, as the change in pressure at high altitude may affect it and result in the formation of a bubble.

- While you are navigating, keep your map and compass to hand so that you are able to check your position regularly. You'll have to do this more often at night or in bad visibility. Ensure that when you take your compass out of your pocket you check the bearing. Many compasses have free-moving compass dials, which may move and give you a wrong reading.

- When you are planning your route and filling in your route card, ensure that you take account of stops. If you plan to stop for a rest or a meal, calculate the time in your overall estimations. Failure to do so may result in your failing to make your target, and this may mean an extra night out.

■ Use checkpoints – easily identifiable, prominent points along your route. You should be able to identify them and keep track of where you are and how far you have to go to reach your next stop. If you fail to identify your checkpoints you may have taken a wrong turn and be on the wrong route. Whenever you reach a prominent point it is a good idea to stop and confirm your position and relate where you are currently to where you are going.

■ If you are walking in close country, such as a wooded area where visibility is limited, or if you are travelling at night, it is easy to lose your sense of direction. Stop more often than you would in open country to check your map and compass. If you feel that you are confused as to which direction you should be going in, trust your compass. Unless there is something wrong with it or it is being affected by a magnetic attraction, your compass will always be right.

■ It is a good idea to maintain an idea of what the ground you should be covering looks like. If you begin to climb or descend a slope, you should remember this. Ensure that you check off the gradient on your map, it is pointless getting to the top or bottom of a hill and then finding out that it is the wrong one. Before you start to climb or descend, check your map.

■ Be cautious of using water features as navigation aids. While water always flows downhill, the course of a river can meander and in some regions of the world this can be extremely confusing. In many tropical regions the map information is collected by satellite, but due to the jungle canopy the actual course of the river may be hidden. There may be hairpin bends in the river which are not actually shown on your map. The map may indicate a straight river, but it may twist and turn. In a situation like this, you can hit the river expecting the flow of water to go one way, only to find the river flowing in the other direction. I have spent many days in jungle regions of South East Asia utterly confused – only to find out that I was at the right spot, but the map had not shown a twist in the river.

- When navigating in remote areas, ensure that you identify from your map any sources of water. It will be difficult to carry enough water with you, so make sure your route takes you near to a water source. Remember that water flows downhill and if you are about to start climbing, water will become scarcer as you reach the top. It is a good idea to fill up your water bottles at the base of the hill before you start to climb.

- When navigating in mountainous terrain, you can expend much energy in climbing up the steep slopes. You can also waste a lot of energy losing height too easily. By following a strict compass bearing in mountainous terrain, you will continually have to climb and descend and will become exhausted. It is much better to use the compass as a guide to indicate the general direction of your destination and maintain your altitude. This procedure, known as contouring, ensures that when you have gained height you follow contour lines around features and do not have to descend or ascend. If you remain at the same elevation, your hike will be less exhausting.

- When you are navigating with your map and compass, it is very difficult to be 100 per cent accurate. You will walk to the left and right of your original bearing. Most people will have a lateral drift of around 4 degrees. This is a critical error if you are navigating to a precise spot on, say, a river or any other linear feature. For example, you have been aiming to hit a bridge over a fast-flowing river in darkness or in poor visibility and have been travelling on a compass bearing. Knowing that most people will make a lateral error of around 4 degrees, the chances are that you will fail to hit the bridge and end up on the river, but which way do you turn to get to the bridge? The answer is that you would not know and may spend a long time searching the river in both directions before you picked up the bridge. The idea here is to use the procedure called aiming off. You should aim off to ensure that your bearing is to one side of the bridge; build in an error so that when you reach the river you know which way to turn.

- Overshoot points are linear features such as roads, rivers or wood edges, which lie beyond your destination and across your line of march. If you miss your target and go beyond it, you will end up hitting this instead, and can backtrack.

- When you are navigating in a remote area and come across an impassable obstacle, it is important that you maintain your course. After having passed the obstacle it can be tricky to get back on your exact line of march. By circumnavigating the obstacle in a rectangular shape, you should find getting back onto your original line of march easier. When you come across the obstacle, take a bearing to an object 90 degrees on from your line of march (on your right or left side). Walk out on this bearing until you have cleared the obstacle, keeping track of exactly how far you have travelled. Then turn back on your original bearing and walk until you have passed the obstacle. Take a further 90-degree bearing back to your original line of march, remembering how far you walked out on your first 90-degree bearing. Once you have reached this point, turn back on your original line of march and you should be back on your bearing.

Re-section

Re-section is a simple navigational technique that can assist in helping you to find out, with a relative degree of accuracy, where you are if you have become lost. For example, if you know that you are in an area but not with any precision, this procedure will provide a relatively accurate grid.

You must be able to see two prominent and distinctive features and must also be able to determine where they are on the map. Then you orient your map with your compass to ensure that it relates to the features on the ground. Place your map on a flat area, then take a bearing from your position to one of the distant prominent objects. However, what we really need is the bearing from the prominent object to you. To do this all you have to do is convert the bearing that you took to a back bearing. When we use a compass to give a bearing, we are reading a number from a circle. With a compass, this number range is from 0 to 360 degrees. A back bearing is simply the number at the opposite side of the circle. To calculate the back bearing if your original bearing is less than 180 degrees (a half circle), you must add 180 degrees. If your original bearing is more than 180 degrees, you must subtract 180 degrees. For example, if you take a bearing to an object of 045 degrees, by adding 180 degrees (a half circle) the back bearing would be 225 degrees. This would result in a bearing from the object back to your position. Then take a bearing to a further object of, say, 310 degrees. Because this number is greater than 180 we must take away 180, which will result in a back bearing of 130 degrees.

Once you have this information, you must plot it on your map. Draw a line from the two objects. Both lines will cross over and where they cross is your position. You can try three objects for an even more accurate fix. If you are on a linear feature such as a road, you can try this procedure with only one object. As you are already on a straight line, one bearing/back bearing should provide you with a relatively accurate grid.

References

Useful Journals and Websites

Rough Guides http://www.roughguides.com
Travel and music guide publishers include a complete online guide to destinations throughout the world, as well as a guide to various genres of music

Travel Holiday Online http://www.travelholiday.com
Comprehensive source for globetrotters. Get advice on how to get there, where to stay, and what to do. Travel the world on a budget and in style

Big World magazine http://www.bigworld.com/
Travel magazine for budget/independent world travellers

Travel and Leisure magazine http://www.travelandleisure.com/
Delivers travel reporting, access to destination facts, searchable archives

Travelmag http://www.travelmag.co.uk/
Monthly online magazine aimed at the independent or adventurous traveller

Wanderlust http://www.wanderlust.co.uk
UK-based magazine covering travel throughout the globe. Publishes every two months

Geographical   http://www.geographical.co.uk/
Magazine with illustrated articles on people, places, adventure, travel, history, technology, science and environmental issues

Web SurferTravel Journal   http://edge.net/~dphillip/wstj.html
Includes latest travel information, travelogues, new travel sites, all with a personal touch

Condé Nast Traveller   http://www.cntraveller.com/
Magazine offering travel ideas, competitions, and guides

TravelTerrific   http://www.travelterrific.com
An online travel magazine specialising in stories and photographs

TravelAsia Magazine   http://www.travel-asia.com/
Daily travel news and weekly articles on travel matters in South East Asia

Greatest Escapes Travel Webzine   http://www.greatestescapes.com
Travel magazine of travel articles by Victoria Brooks from various places around the globe

Power Trips   http://www.cedarcottage.com/powertrips/
Travel magazine devoted to the sacred places of Mother Earth. Information about Stonehenge, Machu Picchu, Glastonbury, Sedona, Mount Shasta, and Uluru (Ayers Rock)

Business Traveler   http://www.btonline.com
The latest business travel news for the frequent international traveller with a special European report, plus passenger complaints heard on Capitol Hill

National Geographic Traveler Magazine
http://www.nationalgeographic.com/media/traveler/
Publication offers articles and information on travel to destinations worldwide

Tourist Information Centres in the UK

Brazilian Tourist Information Office
32 Green St, London w1k 7at   Tel. 0207 629 6909

British Virgin Islands Tourist Board
55 Newman St, London w1t 3eb   Tel. 0207 947 8200

Canadian Tourist Office
Visit Canada PO Box 5396, Northampton nn1 2fa   Tel. 0906 871 5000

Cayman Islands
3rd Floor, 6 Arlington St, London sw1a 1re   Tel. 0207 491 7771

China
4 Glentworth St, London nw1 5pg   Tel. 0207 935 9787

Croatian National Tourism Office
2 The Lanchesters, 162/164 Fulham Palace Rd, London w6 9er
Tel. 0208 563 7979

Cuba Tourist Board
154 Shaftesbury Avenue, London wc2h 8jt   Tel. 09001 600 295

Cyprus Tourism Organisation
17 Hanover St, London w1s 1yp   Tel. 0207 569 8800

Czech Tourist Authority
95 Great Portland St, London w1w 7ny   Tel. 09063 640 641

Denmark
55 Sloane St, London sw1x 9sy   Tel. 0207 259 5958

Dominica
1 Collingham Gdns, London sw5 0hw   Tel. 0207 244 1166

Egypt
170 Piccadilly, London w1v 9dd   Tel. 0207 493 5283

Eritrea
96 White Line St, London n1 9pf   Tel. 0207 713 0096

Falkland Islands
14 Broadway, London sw1h 0bh   Tel. 0207 222 2542

Finnish Tourist Board
P.O. Box 33213, London w6 8jx   Tel. 0207 365 2512

France
178 Piccadilly, London w1j 9al   Tel. 0207 399 3520

Gambia
57 Kensington Court, London w8 5dg   Tel. 0207 376 0093

GERMAN NATIONAL TOURIST OFFICE
P.O. Box 2695, London W1A 3TN Tel. 0207 317 0900
GHANA TOURIST BOARD
c/o Ghana High Commission Trade Section, 104 Highgate Hill,
London N6 5HE Tel. 0208 342 7515/7520
GIBRALTAR
Arundel Great Court, 179 Strand, London WC2R 1EL Tel. 0207 836 0777
GREECE
4 Conduit St, London W1R 0DJ Tel. 0207 743 5997
GRENADA BOARD OF TOURISM
1 Battersea Church Rd, London SW11 3LY Tel. 0207 771 7016
HONG KONG TOURISM BOARD
6 Grafton St, London W1S 4EQ Tel. 09068 661188
HUNGARIAN NATIONAL TOURIST OFFICE
46 Eaton Place, London SW1X 8AL Tel. 0207 823 1055
ICELAND
172 Tottenham Court Rd, London W1P 0LY Tel. 0208 255 7373
INDIA
7 Cork St, London W1X 2LN Tel. 0207 437 3677
INDONESIAN EMBASSY
38 Grosvenor Sq, London W1X 9AD Tel. 0207 499 7661
IRELAND
150 New Bond St, London W1S 2AQ Tel. 0207 518 0800
ISRAEL GOVERNMENT TOURIST OFFICE
UK House, 180 Oxford St, London W1N 9DJ Tel. 0207 299 1111
ITALY
1 Princess St, London W1B 2AY Tel. 0207 408 1254
JAMAICA
1–2 Prince Consort Rd, London SW7 2BZ Tel. 0207 224 0505
JAPAN NATIONAL TOURIST ORGANISATION
5th Floor, Heathcoat House, 20 Savile Row, London W1S 3PR
Tel. 0207 734 9638
JERSEY TOURISM
Liberation Sq, St Helier, Jersey JE1 1BB Tel. 01534 500 777
KENYA NATIONAL TOURIST OFFICE
25 Brook's Mews, London W1K 4DD Tel. 0207 355 3145
KIRIBATI TOURISM COUNCIL OF THE SOUTH PACIFIC
203 Sheen Lane, East Sheen, London SW14 8LE Tel. 0208 876 1938

Korea National Tourism Organisation
3rd Floor, New Zealand House, Haymarket, London sw1y 4te
Tel. 0207 321 2535

Lebanese Embassy Consulate
15 Palace Garden Mews, London w8 4ra   Tel. 0207 727 6696

Luxembourg
122 Regent St, London w1r 5fe   Tel. 0207 434 2800

Macau Government Tourist Office
1 Battersea Church Rd, London sw11 3ly   Tel. 0207 771 7006

Malawi
33 Grosvenor St, London w1x 0de   Tel. 0207 491 4172

Malaysia
57 Trafalgar Sq, London wc2n 5du   Tel. 0207 930 7932

Maldives High Commission of Maldives – Tourism
22 Nottingham Palace, London w1u 5nj   Tel. 0207 224 2135

Malta Tourist Office
Malta House, 36/38 Piccadilly, London w1j 0ld
Tel. 0207 292 4900

Mauritius Tourism Promotion Authority
32 Elvaston Place, London sw7 5nw   Tel. 0207 584 3666

Mexican Ministry of Tourism
Wakefield House, 41 Trinity Sq, London ec3n 4dj
Tel. 0207 488 9392

Monaco Government Tourist and Convention Office
The Chambers, Chelsea Harbour, London sw10 0xe
Tel. 0207 352 9962

Morocco
205 Regent St, London w1r 7de   Tel. 0207 437 0073

Namibia
6 Chandos St, London w1m 0lq   Tel. 0207 636 2924

Netherlands Board of Tourism
P.O. Box 30783, London wc2b 6dh   Tel. 0207 828 7900

New Zealand
New Zealand House, 80 Haymarket, London sw1y 4tq
Tel. 0207 930 1662

Northern Ireland Tourist Board
St Annes Court, 59 North Street, Belfast bt1 1nb
Tel. 028 9024 6609

Norwegian Tourist Board
Charles House, 5 Lower Regent St, London SW1Y 4LR
Tel. 0207 839 6255

Pakistan High Commission for Pakistan
Consular Section, 36 Lowndes Sq, London SW1X 9JN
Tel. 0207 664 9200

Peru
52 Sloane St, London SW1X 9SP   Tel. 0207 235 1917

Philippines
17 Albemarle St, London W1X 4LX   Tel. 0207 499 5443

Polish National Tourist Office
310/312 Regent St, London W1B 3AX   Tel. 0207 580 8811

Portugal
22–25a Sackville St, London W1X 1DE   Tel. 0207 494 1441

Romanian National Tourist Office
22 New Cavendish St, London W1M 7LH   Tel. 0207 224 3692

Russia
Embassy of the Russian Federation, 5 Kensington Palace Gardens,
London W8 4QS   Tel. 0207 229 8027

Sierra Leone High Commission
245 Oxford St, Oxford Circus House, London W1R 1LS
Tel. 0207 287 9884

Singapore Tourism Board
1st Floor, Carrington House, 126/130 Regent St, London W1B 5JX
Tel. 0207 437 0033

Czech & Slovak Tourist Centre
16 Frognal Parade, Finchley Rd, London NW3 5HG
Tel. 0207 794 3263/4

Slovenian Tourist Office
49 Conduit St, London W1R 9FB   Tel. 0207 287 7133

South Africa
5–6 Altgrove, Wimbledon, London SW19 4DZ   Tel. 0208 071 9350

Spanish Tourist Office
22/23 Manchester Sq, London W1M 5AP   Tel. 0207 467 5506

Sri Lanka (Ceylon) Tourist Board
26/27 Clareville House, Oxendon St, London SW1Y 4EL
Tel. 0207 930 2627

SWEDISH TRAVEL & TOURISM COUNCIL
11 Montagu Place, London W1H 2AL   Tel. 00800 3080 3080
SWITZERLAND TOURISM
Swiss Centre, Swiss Court, London W1V 8EE   Tel. 00800 100 200 30
TANZANIA
80 Borough High St, London SE1 1LL   Tel. 0207 407 0566
THAILAND
49 Albemarle St, London W1S 4JR   Tel. 0207 499 7679
TRINIDAD & TOBAGO TOURISM OFFICE
Mitre House, 66 Abbey Rd, Bush Hill Park, Enfield EN1 2RQ
Tel. 0208 350 1015
TURKISH TOURIST OFFICE
1st Floor, 170/173 Piccadilly, London W1V 9DD   Tel. 0207 629 7771
TUNISIAN NATIONAL TOURIST OFFICE
77a Wigmore St, London W1U 1QF   Tel. 0207 224 5561
TURKS & CAICOS TOURIST INFORMATION OFFICE
Mitre House, 66 Abbey Rd, Enfield EN1 2QE   Tel. 0208 350 1017
UKRAINE
78 Kensington Park Rd, London W11 2PL   Tel. 0207 243 8923
UNITED STATES OF AMERICA
American Embassy, Visa Unit, 5 Upper Grosvenor St, London
W1A 2LB   Tel. 09068 200290
URUGUAY
140 Brompton Rd, London SW3 1HY   Tel. 0207 589 8735
ZAMBIA NATIONAL TOURIST BOARD
2 Palace Gate, Kensington, London W8 5NG   Tel. 0207 589 6655

Visa Information

In most countries outside the European Union, and certain other countries such as the US, Canada, Australia and New Zealand, visas are a strict requirement for entry. In many countries, if you intend to conduct business activities you will require a business visa. If visiting a country as a tourist, you may require a tourist visa. It is advisable to obtain a business visa if you are conducting business, as the penalties in some countries for using the wrong visa can be harsh. In addition, when you plan your journey, it is worthwhile ringing the embassy or consulate of your destination country and ask to know exactly what you need. In many countries you will not be allowed entry if you do not have at least six months left on your passport.

When I was trying to get a visa for Afghanistan I almost ended up not going. My passport had been stamped on each page. Even though there was plenty of room, the Afghan authorities in London refused to stamp my visa on a page with previous stamps. After a 24-hour delay and a new passport, I was rewarded with a rather nondescript visa. However I would have saved myself and everyone else if I had known what to expect. If you are a citizen of the UK and travelling to a destination where you think you may need a visa, the following information might be of use. These visa shops will inform you of what you need and will arrange for you to have the appropriate travel documentation.

Benmar Passport Services, 12 Henrietta Street, London wc2
Tel. 0207 379 6418

Rapid Visa Service, Adventure Travel Centre, 135 Earls Court Road, London sw5   Tel. 0207 373 3026

Thames Consular Services, 548 Chiswick High Road, London w4 5rg
Tel. 0208 995 2492

Visa Shop, 44 Chandos Place, London wc2   Tel. 0207 379 0376/0419

Visa Service, 2 Northdown Street, King's Cross, London n1
Tel. 0207 833 2709

West Tech Visa Services, West Tech House, 3 Woodstock St, London w1   Tel. 0207 408 1088

For British citizens who hold current passports with more than six months to run, the following countries will demand that you have an entry visa.

Country	Visa requirement	Time taken to issue
Algeria	Yes	1 week
Australia	Yes	1 day
Bolivia	No	–
Cambodia	Yes	on arrival
China	Yes	4 days
Democratic Republic of Congo	Yes	2 days
Ecuador	No	–
Egypt	Yes	1 day
Ethiopia	Yes	4 days
Guatemala	Yes	2 days
India	Yes	1.5 days
Jordan	Yes	2 days
Laos	Yes	15 days
Madagascar	Yes	1 day
Mali	Yes	10 days
Mongolia	Yes	1 week
Myanmar	Yes	4 days
Nepal	Yes	1 day
Pakistan	Yes	2 days
Paraguay	No	–
Peru	No	–
Romania	Yes	1 week
Russia	Yes	2 weeks
Syria	Yes	1 week
Tanzania	Yes	1 week
Thailand	Yes	2 days
Turkey	Yes	on arrival
Uganda	Yes	2 days
US	No	–
Uzbekistan	Yes	2 weeks
Vietnam	Yes	2 weeks
Yemen	Yes	2 days